MONEY

THE LIFE AND FAST TIMES OF
FLOYD MAYWEATHER

TRIS DIXON

This edition first published in Great Britain in 2017 by

ARENA SPORT
An imprint of Birlinn Limited
West Newington House
10 Newington Road
Edinburgh
EH9 1QS

www.arenasportbooks.co.uk

ISBN: 9781909715578
eBook ISBN: 9780857908438

British Library Cataloguing-in-Publication Data
A catalogue record for this book is available on request from the British Library.

Designed and typeset by Polaris Publishing, Edinburgh
www.polarispublishing.com

Printed in Great Britain by Clays, St Ives

CONTENTS

Tris Dixon is the former editor of *Boxing News* and has covered the sport for two decades. He was the ghostwriter for Ricky Hatton's bestselling autobiography, *War and Peace*, and went on to write the cult boxing classic *The Road to Nowhere*. He then worked as part of the Sky Sports Boxing team, appearing on their flagship *Ringside* and *Big Fight Special* shows. As a boxing expert, he's been a guest on CNN, TalkSport, BT Sport, Sky News and other mainstream outlets and he has been ringside at major fights on both sides of the Atlantic since 2000, covering the sport on four continents and in more than a dozen countries. He now freelances for boxing magazines and is a lead columnist for *Boxing Scene*.

ACKNOWLEDGEMENTS

YOU'D LIKE TO think that after spending a year researching Floyd Mayweather thoroughly, and having attended more than a dozen of his fights since he boxed Emanuel Augustus in Detroit, I would know who the real Floyd Mayweather is.

I don't.

My own dealings with him, generally at press conferences and media roundtables, have been exclusively positive. I know many others would not share those sentiments.

I do recall, moments before the grand arrival at the MGM Grand for the Miguel Cotto fight week, a young fan held a boxing glove in the hope of getting one of the stars to sign it.

When Mayweather walked in, and thousands crammed to see him in the hotel's expansive lobby, he spotted the boy and went to autograph the glove. The boy pulled it back. The son of a keen signature hunter, they already had countless Mayweather signatures from visits to his gym.

'No, I don't need yours,' said the boy, yanking it away. 'I already have it.'

Floyd gestured as if to say, 'Don't be silly,' grabbed the glove, signed it, picked the boy up and gave him a hug so his father could take a picture. The three laughed together as if no one else mattered. That would have stayed with father and son for a lifetime. Mayweather continued slowly down the line of those wanting an autograph or selfie, making their days, too.

One swallow doesn't make a summer; I know that.

And it is clear from the contents of *this book* there are different sides to the man who makes 'Money'.

Some of the people who have assisted me, and there have been many, have seen negative aspects of his life, others have seen positive. There is an awful lot of both.

But I would like to thank those who have shared their memories, including former opponents Reggie Sanders, Louie Leija, Sam Girard, Angel Manfredy, Tony Pep, Justin Juuko, Kino Rodriguez, Jesús Chávez, DeMarcus Corley, Robert Guerrero and Ricky Hatton.

Thanks to Rudy Hernández, Ray Woods, Pat Lynch and Micky Ward for sharing their memories of the late Genaro Hernández, Diego Corrales and Arturo Gatti, and helping to tell the tale of those rivalries with Mayweather.

I greatly appreciate the insight from the likes of Thomas Hauser, Nigel Collins, ESPN's Dan Rafael, Steve Kim, Eoin Mundow, Claude Abrams, Billy Graham, Freddie Roach, Sky's Adam Smith, HBO's Larry Merchant and Showtime's Al Bernstein who have covered Floyd's career over the years.

Others who have assisted include Lee Samuels, Bruce Trampler, James Slater, Bob Trieger, Al Mitchell, Antonio Tarver, Vonzell Johnson, Nate Jones, John Scully, Augie Sanchez, Mario Serrano, Fred Sternberg and Lou DiBella.

The quotes from Oscar De La Hoya about the end of his career come from an interview he gave me in 2010. Some of the Jeff Mayweather quotes come from an interview we did in that same year, too.

It would have been brilliant to have had the chance to speak to David Mayo, who has thoroughly chronicled the life and times of the Mayweathers for the *Grand Rapids Press* and *The Ring*, doing an excellent job, too, but while he wished me well with the project he did not want to be a part of it. James Prince was not happy to talk without Floyd's own involvement in the book, so his voice appears via clippings, and one of Prince's aids, Antonio Leonard, did not want to speak as his wife was working on a Mayweather book of her own.

Talking of clippings, the work in *Boxing News*, *The Ring*, *Boxing Monthly*, *KO*, *Boxing Digest* and several other publications has been an enormous help. Some of the writers I am proud to call friends and acquaintances, and their take on Floyd's life and times have been colourful reference points throughout. The likes of Nigel Collins, Eric Raskin, William Dettloff, Claude Abrams, Graham Houston, Bob Mee, Jim Brady, Greg Juckett, Sean Sullivan and others provided light from a time when there was darkness and little boxing online.

There has been plenty of help along the way.

Peter Burns, my editor at Arena, has shared the vision for this project from the start and I'm grateful to him and the team for their patience, support and trust in me. My agent, David Riding, has been through multiple highs and lows with me over the years but still picks up the phone with the same enthusiasm a few years on, not knowing what the next bombshell is going to be.

I'm fortunate to have some friends in the industry who, though very busy themselves, always make time to share advice. Huge thanks to *Boxing News* editor and former colleague Matt Christie, the wonderful Donald McRae and the gifted Elliot Worsell for their always unflinching encouragement.

Particular thanks to Don, one of my writing inspirations, for the quote used on the cover.

Another friend, Scott Healey, has provided incredible support throughout this project, providing the kind of dedicated and logistical assistance you need in life. The team at Sky Sports Boxing continue to support everything I do and I greatly appreciate that.

My mother and late father equipped me with the necessary drive, determination and work ethic to complete projects of this size.

Of course, taking on a book is a job in itself and the reason we work hard is to give those we love a better life. I'm sure Floyd Mayweather would agree.

To that end, I dedicate this to Ben and Lois, who inspire me to be a better writer, father and man every day.

PROLOGUE

THE MONEY MAN

BEING THE RICHEST man in sport does not just provide Floyd Mayweather with a decorative tagline about success and fame, it hints at a lifestyle that can be matched only by the world's wealthiest people.

For instance, Mayweather's house – the Big Boy Mansion, as it's known – is home to so much cash there's apparently even a money closet. The building itself, a $9 million, 22,000 square-foot, five-bedroom, seven-bathroom, custom-built pile sits on a golf course. There are luxuries aplenty. Some of those luxuries come with more luxuries.

As far as *MTV Cribs* goes, it would top most with its opulence and gaudy splendour. It reeks of extreme wealth. The place even has its own Instagram account.

Sometimes it seems like boxing's version of the Playboy Mansion. Its owner is often surrounded by, rubbed down by and massaged by scantily clad women.

Some of the vaulted ceilings, more than twenty-four feet high, house million-dollar crystal chandeliers. The vast walls are covered in varying materials, such as suede, bright red silk and textured glass. One of the enormous en suite showers has alligator skins on the wall.

There is designer furniture in each room. There's a home cinema that is two stories in height and touchscreen video-game consoles around a huge island in the kitchen.

Elsewhere there's a walk-in dressing room, 600 square feet

itself, where you can find Mayweather's array of fur coats. Most of the clothing still has the original off-the-shelf labels attached, as he has more than he will ever need.

Ziploc bags carrying more than a million dollars apiece are walked in and escorted out, often on their way to the sportsbook where they might double or treble in size, or vanish altogether, only to be won back via another football kick or slam dunk. There was speculation, later dismissed as just that, that Mayweather had bet $5.9 million on the Miami Heat winning in the play-offs, when they lost. Still, seven-figure fortunes have been won and lost on an almost routine basis.

The pristine garage in Las Vegas hosts a fleet of impeccably presented black vehicles. They have white counterparts at his Miami mansion.

There is a Ferrari 599 GTB worth $350,000, a classic $250,000 Porsche Turbo S, the $500,000 Lamborghini Aventador and a Ferrari 458 Spider that would have cost $350,000. Don't forget the half-a-million-dollar Rolls-Royce Phantom. Then you get to the expensive stuff.

The Bugatti Grand Sport Chassis 088 Matte White, the only one in the USA, is a $3-million-dollar car, while his pair of Bugatti Veyrons are $1.6 million apiece.

There are rumours of further extravagances – that he only wears each pair of shoes once and leaves them in hotel rooms for staff when he's finished with them. Does he really spend $6,500 a year on boxer shorts? The watch collection has to be valued at more than $10 million now. His $30-million Gulfstream private jet is made to feel even more spacious because he doesn't allow his entourage to ride on it. His bodyguards fly on a separate jet because their paymaster is afraid of having too much weight in the cabin. So legend has it.

Floyd Mayweather is the highest-paid athlete in the world. Ever. He made more than $200 million in one night. His record-breaking six-fight, thirty-month deal with Showtime guaranteed him a basic $200 million. All of this was without endorsements.

Some speculate that Mayweather could, one day, lose it all. They think his lavish spending and gambling will bring him down to earth with an almighty thud. Others reckon he now has more money than he could ever dream of spending, or losing.

His father, whom he has infamously not always got on with, said he could amazingly see his son wind up on skid row, due to his extravagancies.

'Another hundred million, two hundred million on top of what you already have looks like a tall thing. But you can do all kind of things with money,' he said.

'If Floyd does the right thing with his he will be alright for the rest of his life. But you can get through any amount in two years spending on possessions, trips, cars, women . . .

'Most fighters go down that hole. And when they do the friends go the same way as the money. It's the way of life, man.'

Surely, though, Mayweather and his $800 million fortune are secure and the chances of bankruptcy are negligible. They certainly should be.

To think of what he has is amazing, really, when you consider that when he was just a year old this ghetto kid from a broken home in Grand Rapids, Michigan was used as a human shield by his father when a loaded shotgun was aimed at him. The trigger was pulled, time stood still and boxing history was rewritten.

ONE

HUMAN SHIELD

'IF YOU'RE GOING to kill me, you're going to kill the baby, too.'

Floyd Mayweather Sr hoisted the infant-cum-shield, Floyd Mayweather Jr, between him and the man carrying a shotgun.

Floyd Jr was a year old, not quite two, when an uncle on his mother's side came calling to the family abode.

The gun was loaded and he had revenge on his mind. The older Mayweather, a handy professional fighter, had pinned him by his throat at a roller rink a few weeks earlier.

The man was called 'Baboon'. Others knew him more formally as Tony Sinclair, brother to the child's mother, Deborah Sinclair.

In dire trouble, as Floyd Sr stared down the barrel, he raised his boy into the firing line.

'Give me the baby,' Deborah screeched.

'She was pulling the baby out of my arms so her brother could shoot me,' Floyd Sr recalled. 'I wasn't going to put that baby down. I didn't want to die. It wasn't about putting my son in the line of fire. I knew he wouldn't shoot the baby. So he took the gun off my face, lowered it to my leg and *bam*.'

Much of Mayweather Sr's left leg was ripped off in the blast.

His life was not threatened but his movement was impinged and it permanently changed him as a boxer. He went from fringe contender to journeyman more rapidly than he otherwise would have.

So when Floyd Mayweather Jr says, 'I knew boxing before I

knew anything else,' that is probably the case, because that kind of violence came before he could remember anything.

There were drugs. There were guns. There were probably tears, prostitutes and all kinds of carnage, too, that one might expect in a Grand Rapids, Michigan ghetto.

Theartha Mayweather Sr and Bernice had nine children – four boys and five girls. Three of those boys would become professional prizefighters.

Floyd Mayweather Sr was eight years older than Roger. Roger was three years Jeff's senior. Two sisters had died by the time the youngest boy was born, one from cancer and the other in a fire.

Theartha was the family's patriarch and he died on 15 August 2009, aged eighty-one. Floyd Mayweather Sr reckons he was just fifteen when his dad left town, heading to Toledo, in Ohio, where he spent the final forty years of his life. Floyd Sr said they saw each other only a handful of times, maybe four or five, after the move.

'Not to be disrespectful but my father wasn't that different from a lot of other fathers, he didn't do anything for his kids,' he said. 'Kids, they feel it. And age fifteen, that's a devastating time to leave. But at the end of the day, he was still my father. He wasn't the best father in the world and he wasn't the worst father in the world. It was my mother who was there all of the time, no ifs, no ands and no buts. It wasn't me who didn't want to be close with my father. I didn't make that decision. I was just fifteen. The thing is, he was my daddy, man. That's the only thing I can say. He was my daddy.'

Around ten years before he died, a car hit Theartha. He had also suffered with brain cancer and had partial deafness.

One of the daughters, Anna, cared for Theartha in his old age.

'She's the queen,' Floyd Sr said. 'She definitely took care of her daddy, all the way. I can't say I did that. I gave him money. She couldn't give him money but she gave him much more than that.'

Jeff remembered only a couple of his father's all-too-fleeting appearances.

'My mum and dad were separated most of my life,' he said. 'I didn't really know my father other than he would come over from time to time. I remember once, when I was abut four or five, he gave me $100 and my mother was angry because I thought he was the greatest man on the planet. I thought it was so much money it would last me forever. He was more like a friend, but I didn't become rebellious and I didn't hold a grudge.'

In the end, though, it was down to Floyd Jr to pay for his grandfather's funeral. All of it.

'My son didn't know his grandfather like that but he still gave that money,' Floyd Sr said. 'He was getting his hands wrapped [before a fight], and I went over to him and kissed him, and hugged him, and I told him I appreciate what he did for my father.'

Of course, from the day he was born, on 24 February 1977, boxing was there for young Floyd. It was ever present with his uncles constantly in and out of the ring.

Roger was a fierce puncher, a two-weight world champion, although neither he nor Floyd Sr were wired with a great deal of sensibility. Roger was also susceptible to getting knocked cold. Jeff, the quiet one, was a decent contender.

They lived between fights and pay cheques.

Floyd Jr's mother, Deborah, was a hopeless crack addict.

Roger, who held the ring moniker of the 'Black Mamba' was the best fighter of the bunch. He'd had one hundred and forty-three fights as an amateur and professional, seventy-two in his paid-for career spanning eighteen years. He'd fought more than five hundred rounds and was a hard-hitting but vulnerable and exciting champion.

He was twenty-one years old when he won his first world title. Unbeaten in fourteen fights, and a year and a half after turning pro, he challenged excellent Puerto Rican Samuel Serrano in San Juan for the WBA super-featherweight championship in 1983. Serrano had made thirteen defences of his crown over seven years but was stopped by Roger and his career was all but over.

Four years later, and now up at light-welterweight, Roger defeated Mexico's René Arredondo for the WBC title. Mayweather, though, was what they call in the trade a 'chinny-banger'. Of his six losses, four saw him starched by a single punch. A huge Rocky Lockridge right hand caused him to fold like a deckchair in one round in 1984.

A dynamite Freddie Pendleton right hook catapulted him across the ring and into a devastating defeat in six rounds in 1986.

Rafael Pineda had worryingly levelled him with an almighty ninth-round left hook in 1991 for the vacant IBF light-welterweight belt.

A long-range Ray Lovato right dropped him heavily in two sessions in 1994.

Still, he was often the one causing the explosions and more often than not he boxed in top company, meeting future Hall of Famers such as Pernell Whitaker, whom he lost to on points, Julio César Chávez, who stopped him twice, and latterly Kostya Tszyu, who outscored him to defend the IBF light-welterweight title. Roger defeated world champion Livingstone Bramble, lost narrowly to Darryl Tyson and beat Harold Brazier on the scorecards.

The Brazier fight developed into a war and Roger refused to go to hospital afterwards. That typical Mayweather stubbornness reared its head. The next day he blacked out as he drove out of the parking lot at the Hilton where he'd been staying. He went back to his hotel room where he was treated for numerous minor injuries from the ensuing crash.

Make no mistake, Roger was good – although he was blighted by the perennial fighter's curse of carrying on too long.

He'd won fifty-nine contests and lost thirteen when he called it a day in 1999.

'People ask me all the time, "Man, do you miss boxing?" Hell yeah, I miss boxing,' he said. 'I liked boxing. But do I have injuries from boxing? I really don't know. To be honest, I don't know. If you've had that many fights, something happens. Somewhere along the line, something happens. But I just don't know what the fuck it was. But that's the risk of doing it, and I love boxing. I took my chances.'

'Roger had by far the best career of the Mayweather family and he was always my favourite to watch,' remembered Nigel Collins, the International Boxing Hall of Fame former editor of *The Ring*. 'He made good fights and was not afraid to take on the toughest opponents. He had a great punch, a mediocre chin and a mediocre work ethic. I think that probably contributed to how fun his fights were. At one time he was a predecessor of Manny Pacquiao in that he was considered a "Mexican Assassin". He fought quite a few Mexican opponents, some of them out of the Inglewood Forum [in Los Angeles] and he sort of became the bad guy as far as the Mexicans were concerned.

'My favourite memory of Roger was when he fought Vinny Pazienza. I was at the fight and Roger won easily, there was no real controversy about him winning, and manager Lou Duva charged him when the fight was over. Lou Duva used to do quite a bit of that, but it was one of those Muhammad Ali "Hold me back, hold me back" deals. This time nobody held him back and he went rushing over and Roger dropped him with a right hand – and he deserved what he got. That's the one thing about Roger that stands out from my personal experiences.'

'Roger was a hell-raiser,' agreed Jeff, whom Roger always felt protective over and affectionately called 'Jeffrey'. 'Because of the age difference between me and Floyd, I didn't really hang around with him. But Roger? Oh my god. He was a bad, bad kid. Bad, bad, bad. He was never in gangs or anything like that. He was a one-man gang. I'm serious. But even at a young age Roger was very, very intelligent and because I was younger I looked up to him. One time we were playing rocket football and Roger was too old to be on our team – the age difference was only two, three years, but I was like ten or eleven and he was like Joe Namath. He was calling his own plays and everyone was scared of him. And he was calling street plays, not stuff like the coach would give you.'

Roger was a troublemaker in his youth. He was repeatedly kicked out of major tournaments 'in a variety of creative ways' wrote David Mayo, who has covered the Mayweathers extensively for years.

'He once assaulted the late Max Harnish, a beloved referee, during a Golden Gloves bout. He got booted from the programme another time for backing up a van to a gym door and taking as much equipment as he could load.'

Jeff recalled, 'Then there was another time a group of around half a dozen of us were leaving football practice and went into this sporting goods shop. This is the kind of hell-raiser Roger was. He said, "Go and get that bat." So I went and got the bat. He said, "Hold it on that guy who's sitting down." So I'm right here with the bat holding it on this guy and all of the kids are taking whatever they wanted. Basically we robbed the guy, I didn't know what we were doing – but that's Roger. Don't get me wrong, it seemed Roger was older than he was. He used to do shows like Don King in our boxing gym. He would provide entertainment. You would have a main event, then you would have girls modelling and things like that. He was very innovative.'

In 1981, Roger fled to Las Vegas and Floyd Sr and Jeff were not far behind.

The fourth brother, Theartha Mayweather Jr, who died in 2010 at the age of fifty-two, had a few fights while in the US Army but did not pursue a career in the game. He ended up working in a factory.

'When we were youngsters, we all joked around, but we were all different,' Theartha once said. 'As a kid, I was more a street person. Roger, he had the mean streak. Floyd, he didn't go looking for trouble, but when it came, he dealt with it. Jeff, he never had a mean bone in his body.'

When he was only eight, Jeff had promised his mother he would graduate from college, an unlikely and improbable boast.

'She never thought nothing of it as nobody else went in the family,' said Jeff. 'Well, one of my sisters went but she never finished. I was in third grade, a long way from college, but that promise stuck with me. I suppose in the beginning it was more me fulfilling that promise to her than me going for myself. But when I got to college I guess I was just one of those people who was gifted. College was very easy. Once I got there I thought it was going to be something really big. But it was a breeze, a walk in the park – no different from high school or anything like that.'

He graduated from Western Michigan University with a degree in graphic design but he had also matured. It gave him a very un-Mayweather grounding.

'I think college moulded me in a different way because they interacted with people through boxing and that's a different type of circle,' he continued. 'They were not dealing with people who maybe one day would be president, or own Fortune 500 companies. Those were the kind of people I was dealing with. If my mindset was like that of my nephew or my two brothers I probably would have won a major world title and been champion for a long time, but I was totally different. I walked into boxing just by following them. Boxing was never my first choice. I loved basketball and the most important thing was finishing college.'

Still, 'Jazzy' Jeff was fighting as an amateur, even through his senior year, and eventually competing in the nationals – but while boxing was in his blood it was never in his heart.

He went sixteen fights unbeaten as a super-featherweight and lightweight in the pros, without climbing too far up the ladder, and he soon found a ceiling, losing to top contenders, champions and prospects. He was served up to Oscar De La Hoya, in the Golden Boy's fifth professional bout, and stopped in four rounds.

It was a calculated gamble on Team De La Hoya's part.

'I was very much like Floyd Jr,' remembered Jeff. 'I didn't get hit very much but they knew I couldn't punch so I wasn't a threat to hurt or knock him out. That's why I got the fight – and because I had a name.'

There were defeats to Joey Gamache and Jesse James Leija before he called it a day in 1997 with thirty-two wins – ten by stoppage – against ten defeats and five draws. He'd briefly held the lightly regarded IBO super-featherweight championship.

'It was easy to walk away because there were fights I was taking that I shouldn't have, against guys in their own towns or county, where I felt I was prostituting myself,' he lamented. 'But I could negotiate with them. If it was another fighter they would not have got any more money but because of my last name they gave it to me. I thought, "Hang on, if they want me to fight here they're going to have to pay me because I already know they have a "L" on my record. It was then I told myself, "No, I can't do this no more."'

Vonzell Johnson, a two-time light-heavyweight world title challenger who fought out of Columbus, Ohio, was a training partner of Floyd Sr – who fought out of Cleveland, Ohio – and Vonzell became Floyd Jr's godfather.

'We were like brothers back then,' said Vonzell of his relationship with Floyd Sr.

'I knew Roger and Jeff but I didn't really get close to those guys. I was only close to Floyd because we were stablemates, we had the same management. The manager was Henry Grooms, they called him Hank Grooms. Our camp was in Kalamazoo, Michigan. That was like forty-five minutes from Grand Rapids and that's where we trained.'

In the late 1970s Floyd Sr and Vonzell Johnson were part of a boxing scandal, however small their alleged roles, when *Ring* magazine was accused of falsifying fighters' records to shoehorn them into a televised Don King event. King had been working with ABC Sports on a tournament, the United States Boxing Championships, and intended to see United States champions crowned in eight divisions. Then editor John Ort was under attack. The publication had taken $70,000 to work on ratings for the event and he was said to have taken $5,000 in cash to alter records and inflate rankings so fighters could get involved. Johnson, Mayweather, Richard Rozelle and Greg Coverson were awarded eleven fake wins between them in 1975 and 1976. Plenty of other fighters were caught up in it, too.

Eventually, ABC associate producer Alex Wallau uncovered it with boxing crusader and newsletter writer Malcolm 'Flash' Gordon and the tournament was promptly cancelled.

'All the things that you see Little Floyd Mayweather do, Big Floyd did them better,' said Johnson, perhaps with some bias attached. 'They were comparing him in the late '70s to Sugar Ray Robinson. I remember reading an article once in Baltimore, Maryland, that this guy was the next Ray Robinson. He was a good fighter, with the shoulder roll and all that. And the apple don't fall far from the tree. Floyd [Sr] was arrogant. He was very arrogant, he was a helluva fighter, a helluva welterweight but he was very arrogant, like his son.'

Floyd Sr had already gone as far as he was going to as a marginal welterweight, following losses to future great Sugar Ray Leonard and a pair of defeats to world welterweight champion Marlon Starling. Leonard had dropped him twice in round eight before stopping him in the tenth. Floyd Sr complained he'd damaged his hand early in the fight but regardless, the Associated Press said he'd been well beaten.

'Aside from the first round, which Mayweather clearly won with a good flurry of punches,' read a report, 'the only round in which he held his own was the fifth. However, his punches had lost most of their zing by then.'

Sugar Ray Leonard once said, 'Floyd Jr fights just like his dad. It is just that Junior hits harder.'

Vonzell Johnson felt the injury had been crucial in Sr's defeat to Leonard, even though that is unlikely. 'His hand was hurt when he fought Sugar Ray Leonard. If his hand hadn't been hurting he'd have beaten Sugar Ray Leonard, I'm telling you. But his hand was hurting and that would have been the fight to launch his career, had he won that fight. It would have launched his career big time.'

As it was, his career faltered and he eventually quit in 1990 having lost his last three. Floyd Sr retired with a record that included twenty-eight wins, six losses and a draw. He scored seventeen knockouts.

'As far as Floyd Sr was concerned, he was a good fighter but a notch or two below the best – and he was at one point making quite a lot of money selling cocaine and that meant he didn't really need boxing as much as you might have thought,' Collins added. 'Jeff, he was nothing much more than a club fighter. That he was one of Oscar De La Hoya's early opponents was probably his claim to fame. I would say Roger was head and shoulders above his brothers, obviously he won several titles and he beat a lot of good fighters. The others were highly forgettable. Really, you didn't hear much about the other two when Roger was on top. People were aware of Floyd Sr if you were a hardcore boxing fan. I saw him fight in Atlantic City, he was a decent fighter but there really wasn't much publicity or interest in him and all of the focus was on Roger – until Floyd Jr started to fight.'

Floyd Sr maintained that he did what he did – on both sides of the ropes – to give his children a better life.

'All the times I was fighting I still had to hustle to get money because I had kids to feed,' he'd say. 'I wanted to make sure that little Floyd didn't have to do that when he was coming up.'

As a consequence he spent more time with his son, planting some early boxing seeds, and Floyd Jr's grandmother Bernice recalled the youngster wearing gloves before he could walk.

By the time he was two, he was being proclaimed – by his father no less – as a future world champion

While the boy's sisters did their homework, Sr had his son practising his autograph. Or so legend has it.

Other dads took their children to football or baseball, to barbecues and parties or on days out. Sr took Jr to the gym.

'He was training to be a fighter in the crib,' his father once said. 'No kidding. He was throwing jabs even then. And when he got a little older he'd be beating the doorknobs. I picked him up and told him, "You're going to be a boxer and your daddy's going to make you the champ of the world." It's his daddy who's made him who he is today.'

For a relationship that had some horrific origins, it is of little surprise that it would carry on in a rollercoaster-like fashion. Sr maintains he always did what was best for his prodigy; Floyd says he skipped childhood and adolescence and went straight to being a man. They both recalled going on an eleven-mile run when Jr was just eleven years old.

'I don't remember him ever taking me anywhere or doing anything that a father would do with a son, going to the park or to the movies or to get ice cream,' Floyd Jr countered. 'I always thought that he liked his daughter [Floyd's older stepsister]

14

better than he liked me because she never got whippings and I got whippings all the time.'

Apparently Sr would get frustrated if his son couldn't repeat what he'd told him in training.

'My father would beat me for anything I did, even if I hadn't done anything. I used to pray for the day I could become an adult and get away from it. I got tired of getting beat.'

He wanted approval, however, and he searched it out in the Tawsi and Pride gyms in Grand Rapids. They would run there in the summer and trudge through up to four feet of snow to get there in the winter.

The boy worked tirelessly. Fighters would scoop him up and put him on an old apple box so he could reach the speedbag.

At the age of eleven, in 1989, the youngster legally adopted the Mayweather surname, expelling Sinclair. It was another sign that he wanted to please his dad.

'Every day as a kid, I went to the boxing gym. I've had boxing gloves on since before I could walk and been in gyms all my life,' he said.

And that was the difference. The guns, the drugs, the violence . . . He didn't know what it was, even if he had become familiar with it. He had learned boxing, though, and knew its intricacies.

The shared passion of gym life appeased them both for a while, father and son. There was still no stability, though. One of the boy's aunts died of AIDS and eventually Floyd was packed off to New Brunswick in New Jersey.

They were, quite possibly, the worst of times.

'When I was about eight or nine, I lived in New Jersey with my mother and we were seven deep in one bedroom and sometimes we didn't have electricity,' he said. 'No heat, no water. Nothing. I basically raised myself.

'When people see what I have now, they have no idea of where I came from and how I didn't have anything growing up.

You know, as a young child I lay in my bedroom and I swore to myself then: "I'm not going to smoke and I'm not going to drink." And I said I'm not going to just say that when I'm a kid. I'm going to stick to that as an adult. I kept that in mind my whole life.

'At Christmas we never had a Christmas. My mother would go out and steal presents for me. She tried but it was hard and that's why I look after her now.'

Nigel Collins felt Floyd's difficulties ratified a sentiment that the majority of fighters come up the hard way.

'I believe most boxers come to the sport damaged emotionally,' he said. 'Floyd had been pretty much left to his own devices in many ways. It's not unusual for boxers to have emotional difficulties, obviously concussions can bring that on, but I'm talking about coming to the sport as wounded individuals. And if you think about all the fighters we've covered over the years there is a common thread and it can be something as obvious as poverty. Poverty is terribly damaging to a child. There are other things, broken families, traumatic experiences, living in a gang-infested area etc. etc. But you don't find many fighters who had idyllic childhoods and it's always been a strong theory of mine that most fighters are emotionally wounded individuals even before they step into the ring. That theory, and it is just a theory, would apply to Floyd.'

'It was like anywhere else in America,' Vonzell Johnson said of his own experiences in Grand Rapids. 'You seen the different cities. They had their bad areas. It wasn't that big a city. It wasn't a Chicago or a New York or a Philadelphia. It wasn't nothing like that. All cities have their bad areas.'

'I would lie in my bed, and I was nine years old, and say to myself, "I want to be the richest man in the world",' Floyd explained years later. 'I've come a long way from there. It was a pipe dream because outside the streets were alive, the body counts rising. My friends were hustling on the block, shootings, hearing guns was normal. If you didn't hear a gun during the week you'd wonder what was going on. My friend got killed, my friend got stabbed. There was all kinds of crazy stuff.

'I had a father who was a hustler and a mother who was on drugs. I was the man in the house from sixteen. That's just the way it was. I had to quit school so my family could be in a better position.'

He developed rapidly as a fighter, too, employing classy defensive techniques. His father educated him and most notably taught him the famed Mayweather shoulder roll.

That was in the orthodox stance that family members utilised, an old-school method where the right hand was often held slightly higher than normal while the left hand was draped close to the midsection. Meanwhile, the lead shoulder was raised to barricade the cheek, providing the chin with shelter and to block incoming shots.

The right hand was free to defend or parry, shielding the head from left hooks and all the while the fighter could slip, slide and deflect punches, twisting left and right in the opposite sync to the blows coming his way.

'He taught him all of that,' Johnson said of what was passed down from father to son. 'It was a Michigan thing, it's definitely a Michigan thing, but the trainers that we had, they utilised it. The old trainers when we were fighting then were the guys who had been around when there was Sugar Ray Robinson, Joe Louis and all them guys. They taught that. Our trainer was Delmar Williams and he gave us that. He trained Floyd [Sr] and I. It was Delmar Williams and Robert Mitchell. Those were our trainers.

'Over the years it's been taken out of context and a lot of people don't understand the way that it works. A lot of people try to do it and they don't understand the philosophy behind it.

'The shoulder roll – and I'm telling you, I learned it in a fight that I had – is if someone's got a quick right hand it's hard to catch it. But with the shoulder roll you roll away from the punch, you don't take the brunt of the punch. You're supposed to turn your shoulder away from the punch and then counterpunch. You roll away and you throw the right hand, almost simultaneously. And that's what it's supposed to be for. It's supposed to make a guy fall short or hit you on the shoulder and you hit him flush. Most people just put their hands below their stomach and just turn their shoulders. It's ridiculous. They imitate but they don't know the reasons or the philosophy behind it. You're supposed to roll and counter, you're not supposed to just put your shoulder up and make guys hit your shoulder. You're supposed to punch back.

'You would see Little Floyd do that at the beginning of his career but most of the time he has his shoulder up and he's not doing nothing.'

Hank Grooms later contended that Mayweather Sr pretty much came up with the style by himself, although he credited Bob Tucker, father of future heavyweight champion Tony Tucker, with passing on the knowledge.

Roger Mayweather said it was started by some of the trainers in Kalamazoo, even though evidence of it can be traced back long into boxing history, through videos showing the sophisticated talents of Joe Louis, Archie Moore, Sugar Ray Robinson and Jersey Joe Walcott.

Mayweather Jr once said, 'To be honest, I think it was a style that came from all the great gyms in Detroit.'

Some would call it a Philadelphia shell, claiming it originated on the East Coast, but Mayweather Sr had it down to such a tee that it simply became known as 'the Mayweather style'.

There were other specific elements to his teachings, though – and his son was a willing student. There were three types of jab: a regular one, an up jab delivered from a low position and a spear jab, the more meaningful of the three.

'You will see a lot of fighters move to their left and jab, but I do something no one else does – I walk out to my right and jab,' Mayweather Jr said. 'The left hook is the punch that can knock you out because you don't see it coming. I keep my right hand by my cheek to catch the hook. But I don't try to catch the jab.'

A Fort Knox-style defence was cultivated but by then the future pound-for-pound king of the sport had to contend with plenty of other things.

'Boxing is real easy,' he once said, speaking from the position of someone who's worked hard and been blessed with natural fighting gifts. 'Life is much harder.'

TWO

DREAMS AND
NIGHTMARE DECISIONS

YOU MIGHT NOT recognise the name Chris Holden. He would go on to become a service technician for the internet and phone provider Comcast but he fought Floyd Mayweather when the future boxing legend was just ten years old and weighed a mere 64lbs.

He was then known as Floyd Joy Sinclair, having not yet taking his father's Mayweather name and embracing the subsequent burden of expectation that would come with it.

It was 21 November 1987 when Mayweather and Holden briefly collided in a basketball gym at Baker College in Owosso, Michigan.

'I remember thinking to myself, "Wow, this kid's really good – it doesn't really make sense." It makes sense to me now,' Holden recalled, some two decades after Mayweather stopped him inside one round.

'He was so good back then. When I found out that it was him [later on], I was like, "Okay, that makes sense now." It was a quick fight. I know he came out there, threw a bunch of jabs, my nose started bleeding and they called the fight. But even back then I remember thinking to myself, "Wow, this kid's really good."'

He wasn't the only one.

The then long-time Michigan Golden Gloves director, Dave Packer, saw something special. So much so that he nabbed the ten year old's hand wraps as a keepsake.

'I didn't care who it was,' Mayweather later reflected of that night. 'I just wanted to fight. I remember afterwards we stayed at the Red Roof Inn. I slept with my trophy. I held my trophy all the way home.'

Holden's memories are unsurprisingly less fond. 'I mean, it wasn't much of a fight,' he conceded. 'But I got in the ring.'

Young Floyd would go from strength to strength, dominating state and national Golden Gloves championships.

The night before super-middleweight stars Roy Jones and James Toney fought in Las Vegas, on 17 November 1994, Mayweather lost a decision to future world bantamweight champion Martín Castillo. It was a USA v Mexico show and Castillo, despite winning narrowly 3-2, as he recalls, says he 'played with Mayweather.'

'The best way I can explain to you what I did is that I fought like Mayweather,' Castillo remembered. 'I tried to do everything he did, because at that time it was easy for me to fight in that kind of boxing. Hit and move, hit and move. Then I'd put my hands down and throw a jab and then move. I just played with him.

'I tried to make him feel mad because he couldn't hit me. Playing dirty, kind of like that.'

The names of fighters to beat Floyd Jr are few and far between. Arnulfo Bravo, Carlos Navarro and Noureddine Medjihoud . . . They do not mean a great deal in boxing circles. But they have all had their slice of fame. There is even an old amateur photo of Floyd Jr pictured with future pro rival Diego Corrales, Augie Sanchez, who was another amateur to defeat him, and Bravo, which has, of course, become more poignant over time given that he would face all three and lose to two of them. Bravo had beaten him in the semis of the National Youth Championships. Following a 'medical walkover', Greek Olympian Tigran Ouzlian is also credited with a win over Mayweather dating back to a 1995 tournament in Moscow, Russia.

But Floyd won both Michigan and National Golden Gloves tournaments in 1993, weighing 106lbs, and he earned the same titles in 1994 at 114lbs. Up to 125lbs in 1996, the year of the Atlanta Olympics, he took both crowns once more. There were other accolades along the way, too. In 1994 at the Nationals he won the Outstanding Boxer Award, a mantle he also collected en route to the 1995 National PAL (Police Athletic League) Championships. He enjoyed fighting. He loved the glory. He liked representing the Mayweather name in the family business.

'I felt bad when I won the Nationals because I was beating guys much older than I was,' he once recalled. 'I rode home in the van with this big trophy almost touching the roof. They said, "Floyd, you want to go in the store?" I said, "No, I don't want nobody bothering my trophy."

'When I was sixteen, you know what made me fight hard? I looked over and saw that big trophy and was like, "Wow, we getting that? Oh man, I'm gonna fight hard." And that was it. It wasn't about the money.'

Yet in 1992, when the prodigy was sixteen, his father – almost inevitably given what had gone before – was sentenced to five years in a federal prison in Milan, Michigan, on drug-trafficking charges.

Godfather Vonzell Johnson contended that despite the previous shooting incident, Mayweather Sr had not always been involved in crime.

'Actually, when he was fighting he was a real good guy,' Johnson reckoned. 'This all happened after his career, after he got shot in the leg for that domestic stuff, and after his career was over. He got caught up with some bad guys, some drug dealers in Michigan and that's how that happened. But all the time, before his career was over, he was a good guy. He never got involved in any kind of trouble.'

Around that time, Don Hale – who owned a multi-million-dollar hormone replacement company – became Floyd's unofficial guardian. Hale would become known years later as Floyd's 'white daddy'.

It was early in the 1990s and Hale was in Vegas. His brother was working with Frankie Randall and met Floyd's uncle Roger. Hale, who was also from Grand Rapids, instantly had some common ground. 'Roger said he couldn't handle Floyd, so he sent him back home,' Hale said. 'Roger told me, he's running the streets and needs somebody to watch after him. Would you be interested?'

Hale asked him to get Floyd to ring, and a few days after he made the call he was living with Hale, his wife and three children.

'His dad had just gone away and he missed his dad pushing him in the gym,' Hale recalled in a 2015 interview with *USA Today*. 'From there, I started taking him to the gym. I wasn't there every day because I had a business to run, but I always found a way to getting him there.'

Hale helped young Floyd in and out of the gym, even finding him work at a banquet centre where Mayweather once fell asleep on the job in the morning and co-workers were unable to rouse him because he had been training so hard.

'He said, "Don, I don't want to do anything but box. I'm going to make my living boxing." So I never tried to get him another job after that.'

Life was boxing. Boxing was life. Winning at boxing was winning at life. Hale remembered consoling Mayweather after two defeats in the amateur ranks. 'Floyd just put his head on my shoulder and cried like a baby,' Don said.

'I don't know if Floyd would want people to know this, but setting out, he wanted to be the bad guy. I remember when he was an amateur talking about how he could be a Sugar Ray Leonard. He said, "I don't want to be a Sugar Ray Leonard, I want to be the bad guy. People pay to see the bad guy." He wasn't that concerned what people thought because he thought that they would pay [to watch his fights].'

Uncle Roger, then still an active fighter, held the training reins and Floyd Jr kept on shining as a prospect. By that time Floyd was the biggest fish in the Michigan pond. 'I was running the gym,' he said.

Away from boxing, however, life was just as varied as ever.

'I was on my own at sixteen,' he once recalled. 'My grandmother [a cleaner] would go to work, she'd be home at midnight, I never had a curfew, even on school nights, I'd be coming in at one or two and I'd go to school but the day centred around going to the gym. Going to the boxing gym was the best thing in the world.'

He travelled with boxing. He'd been to Europe, around the USA and he'd fought pros and amateurs. He pretty much went where he wanted, stayed where he wanted and did what he wanted. He excelled, of course, taking on everyone to prove he deserved the Mayweather name, that he belonged and that he was going places.

'They were much bigger than me,' he remembered of several sparring partners. 'I would think, "I'm going to box so good, I'm going to make no mistakes." And when I went out there, outboxed them and made no mistakes I would be so happy. I would sleep good that night.'

Antonio Tarver would become an amateur teammate, friend and was a future world champion. He saw talent the first moment he set eyes on Mayweather.

'We were in Dallas, at the PAL national tournament and I think he got the most outstanding boxing in that tournament,' said Tarver. 'This was a guy that had incredible hand speed, he had the name and he was a brash, confident young guy and you always knew he was special.'

He was good. But one night in Colorado Springs, Augustine Sanchez – later a professional world champion known as Augie

– was better than an eighteen-year-old Mayweather. He was the last American to beat Floyd Mayweather Jr.

Sanchez was respected, but the buzz surrounded the multi-skilled Michigan teen.

'He's always been a gifted fighter,' Sanchez said. 'He always stood out. Everyone wanted to see this guy, they wanted to see him fight and see what he could do. Throughout the tournaments it was always, "Mayweather's here. Mayweather's here." And I was like, "So what? Bring him on." Especially when he came into my division. I really didn't care who was in my division. My goal was to be on the Olympic team and whoever was in front of me, that's who I was going to beat.

'What's funny about this is me and Floyd, we have known each other since 1994 and at that time he was boxing at about 108 or 112lbs and we were roommates at the Olympic Festival so we got something of a bond,' Sanchez recalled in 2014. 'And the next year he jumped two or three weight classes to fight at featherweight, my weight class, 125lbs. We ended up fighting at the end of '94 in the USA Nationals in the semi-finals, we fought in that one and no one really knows about that fight. That was the first one we fought and we fought four times in total.

'The first time he won, and I thought I beat him, man, but they gave it to him. It was a really good fight, really good, with the type of fighter I was, a pressure fighter. We went back and forth, I was pressuring him and he was boxing me. It was all-out war from the first round to the third round. It was a close decision. I thought I won and we really didn't end up talking much after that.

'When we saw each other he didn't want to have any kind of friendship, which was fine. We were going to end up fighting each other again so he didn't want any relationship like that.'

Sanchez understood and a one-time bond evaporated as they strived for the top spot and a place in the 1996 Olympic team, one that would see its stars competing on home soil in Atlanta.

'We ended up fighting again in the Olympic trials and that's where I beat him,' Sanchez continued. 'It was in the Olympic trials and we fought in the winners' bracket, because there was a winners' bracket and a losers' bracket. The loser gets to fight twice, like a second chance. So all the winners keep going and the losers end up fighting each other so they fought one extra day, they fought four days, the winners only fought three. Anyway, we ended up fighting in the final and again it was a good fight, it was back and forth. I was pressuring him, wanting to fight, wanting him to stay there and it wasn't happening. I forced the issue, I forced the fight from cornerpost to cornerpost and I ended up getting the decision. Actually, it was a draw. The judges then had to push the button to decide who they thought won the fight and I ended up winning. So Floyd went over to the losers' bracket and fought Carlos Navarro and he ends up winning and a few months later we ended up fighting in the box-offs, which coincidentally in 1996 was the only year they did that, so those guys had another chance and we fought in the box-offs twice.'

Floyd was confident he held the upper hand and won another tight decision to take their third encounter.

'I feel I'm the better man,' he said, nonchalantly. 'Tomorrow will probably be a shutout.'

It was not the whitewash he prophesised the next day when they met in the final match of the box-offs in Augusta, Georgia, in April 1996, though his victory was more comfortable.

'This time, more than any other, it was a war,' Sanchez continued. 'It was toe to toe. It was a good fight. He knew what he had to do in order to win and it suited my style. I thought I won. Of course, any fighter's going to say that. He fought better in that second fight. He fought a lot smarter and I felt the improvement in him.'

Using his stinging right hand in their 'do-or-die' match, Mayweather ran out a 20-10 winner, booking his Olympic spot.

Amateur correspondents observing noted his 'nice legs' and 'how he has more of a flighty pro style'.

Sanchez was just eighteen and a high school student from Las Vegas but lost out in what was recorded as an untidy affair. Regardless of the type of fight it was, *Boxing News* certainly was not sold on Mayweather's prospects.

'After the match, the winners got beautiful championship belts,' it reported. 'However, either these Olympians aren't nearly as good as in previous years or "computer styles" have muted their natural abilities – you just can't tell. Off this, neither is close to Sugar Ray Leonard, who brilliantly garnered gold in Montreal in 1976.'

It was a matter of job done for Mayweather who, aged nineteen, said, 'I've been dreaming of going to the Olympics since I was eleven.'

However, his Olympic coach, Al Mitchell, a veteran Philadelphian, was reserved about Floyd's prospects.

'It was close,' he said of the fight Sanchez won. 'Augie I think did just enough to get the decision but Floyd came back and beat Augie. He adjusted. He was only a young kid but he adjusted and Augie was a good, good fighter.'

It was not long, though, before Mitchell had to steer the Mayweather ship when he joined up with the Olympic squad, a talented but initially disorganised bunch of ghetto kids from across North America.

'When Floyd was first on the team we were together for four or five months and I was travelling all over with them – and I was made head coach a little ahead of time than they ordinarily do – and I know we had a very young team,' Mitchell said. 'Besides Tarver and Lawrence Clay-Bey, everybody else on the team were pretty much young kids, sixteen, seventeen, eighteen. Especially Floyd. I had Floyd up at the gym that I run in Marquette [Michigan] and we were also in two other different states and I watched him and really, he didn't impress me that much. They all looked good but he didn't impress me that much. He didn't stand out. The stand out was probably Tarver because that same year Tarver won everything, he won the World Amateur Championships, he won the Pan-Americans and he won the Nationals. That was the first time we had a boxer that won all three of them in the same year. The problem with that was Tarver thought he was walking on water and instead of trying to get better and better each camp, he was just relying on that. He thought he could just go through. He was the one people thought would get the gold medal.'

As Floyd Mayweather Jr readied himself to steal the show in Atlanta, he boxed on an American team against Russia at the Coconut Grove Convention Center in Miami, Florida on 17 June.

'The savvy quick-fisted teenager slammed Viacheslav Smirnov for a standing eight just thirty-one seconds in before battering him so thoroughly, mostly with lead rights, that it had to be halted after two minutes twenty-five seconds of the third round,' read a report. Mayweather sparkled, showing real promise. One old hack even commented, 'He already looks like a world class pro.'

Momentum was his heading into the Games and his teammates, including Nate Jones, Tarver, Alberto Guardado, Zahir Raheem, Fernando Vargas, Terrance Cauthen, David Díaz, David Reid, Rhoshii Wells and Eric Morel, began to call Floyd 'Pretty Boy' because of his unmarked face and the defensive techniques he could employ to preserve his fresh features.

Nate Jones was Mayweather's roommate in Atlanta.

'I met Floyd at the 1994 National Golden Gloves,' Jones said. 'I didn't like him because he talked too much. I'd just got out of prison, I wasn't ranked. My last fight was at 147lbs, I got out at 240 and I got down to 200 and I had to beat the top guy from Chicago to get to the nationals, Fres Oquendo – who I train now.

'I'd done armed robbery . . . Not gone to court . . . I'd done a couple of things. I was supposed to do two and a half years but I did my GD [General Diploma] and got out on good behaviour.

'Floyd was bragging every day so I didn't like him, but when I saw him fight I could see what he was talking about because he was the best thing I'd seen.

'I saw nearly all his fights as an amateur. Going to the Olympic trials he was on the blue team and I was on the red team, which was the number one team. He was really hurt by that. He was bothered to the core to go on the blue team. He didn't even want to wear the uniform. It really, really bothered him. I said, "Man, it's okay. Don't worry about it, we're going to win. We will be on the number one team," and he wouldn't speak to me because we were on separate teams and I was like, "Dude, it's okay." He ended up making the team and we both became Olympians and we had a lot of fun. And I love him, he's a great guy.'

There were squabbles within the squad. They initially pulled in different directions. They all wanted to rule the roost, even though that was only Mitchell's job.

'Everyone wanted to be the man,' Jones said. 'There was a lot of egos, you had Vargas, you had Floyd, you had Tarver, you had David Reid, there were egos. I was just blessed to be there but coach Al Mitchell got us together. We started to have each other's backs and we started supporting one another and when we fought at the Olympics the coach had us all show up at the fights, unlike in '92 when some of the guys didn't do that. We had to support them but more than that we wanted to support them, we wanted to have their backs.'

Mitchell was confident in his abilities as a trainer, but he had to learn how to become a counsellor, too.

'That was probably the hardest thing for me,' he admitted. 'Getting them to gel as a team and respect each other. I was born in North Philadelphia and each territory had their own gang, that's the way I came up and I had to set them down and break up fights and everything a couple of times. And I got to a point where I took the phones out of their rooms and I took their TV sets and I said, "This is the way it's going to be." Mayweather and Nate Jones, I still see them, and they said nobody liked me. Nobody liked me. But that's how I got them together to be as a team and we wouldn't have got six medals if I hadn't done that.

'Floyd was outgoing. Him, Nate Jones and Tarver were real tight. Everyone had a little crew that they'd walk around with. Jones, who works with Mayweather now, they was buddies. Tarver, too.

'It's funny, when you get everyone in from different cities in the United States, everyone is from a different territory and everyone thinks they're the boss of their territory. So you've got all that manpower going against each other and sometimes I had to break up arguments, but that last month before we went into the Olympic Games, everybody was a team, and that took me about two months to get them together to work like that.'

'I was pretty much tight with everybody,' Tarver reckoned, 'but we were close-knit because we were from the city, me and Nate were two of the older guys and Mayweather was a spirited cat anyway and we kind of clicked. All of the guys clicked, the guys from Philadelphia like Zahir, Terrance Cauthen, Rhoshii Wells – God rest his soul – all of those guys were cool. We didn't have no animosity or anything like that on our team. Guys got into it, like brothers do, but all that shit was nothing. We were a close-knit team, man. When I look back at it I see it as, shit, it was young guys competing and everybody ain't always going to be best friends, but when we made that Olympic team there was solidarity, we were the chosen ones so of course we came together. There were things that happened along the way when people may have had their feelings hurt but a lot of these guys were young men, very young men, and if things happen like that it's because there were misunderstandings and people got their feelings involved and they held grudges sometimes. But I loved every brother on my team, man. I didn't have a problem with nobody. I'm not saying my personality was favourable to everyone, no, but when you look back on it, everybody had a mutual respect and love for each other. That's how I view it.'

Mitchell recalls things differently. 'Floyd, like the other ones, was a young kid. They'd never been at that kind of level before so they pushed the envelope. As a coach it was my job to find a way to deal with them. You know, I took some psychology classes to deal with one or two of them and I think that helped me in the Games.

'They came late to training a couple of times and I got on them. Then, when they did, I took their TVs and phones out of their rooms. Sometimes I caught them arguing with each other. One time I caught them gambling and I took all the money, bought flowers with the money and put all the flowers in their dorms.

'My main thing was to get them to work together and finally, a month before the Games, they did. It was different; coaching is not hard to me. What's hard is when you have different people from different parts of the United States, especially if they come from poor neighbourhoods, because everybody has to fight for what they can get.'

Tarver said Mayweather might have been brash, but fundamentally he was decent.

'Floyd was always a good guy, man,' he explained. 'How can you label someone a bad guy? Who's the judge of that? Floyd was no bad guy, he was a young, hip cat that had his own identity and knew exactly where he was going. You can't fault anyone for that. You've got to appreciate that. I was the same cat, of the same mind. Basically, when you see into the future we both knew where we were going. There was no doubt.'

Mayweather's quest for an Olympic medal opened inside the Alexander Memorial Coliseum. Contests were three rounds, each three minutes in length.

He stopped Kazakhstan's Bakhtiyar Tyleganov in his first-round match. Ahead 10-1 on points, the fight was halted fifty-seven seconds into round two with the Kazakh bleeding excessively from his nostrils.

'I was so pumped up and ready to go,' said Mayweather. 'I wanted to tear the guy's head off.'

Then, reflecting on his circumstances away from the ring for a moment, he added, 'I appreciate the help the coaches have been giving me since my dad has been gone. But my dad is still giving me pointers while he's locked up. I have to thank my dad, because without him I wouldn't be here. I think he probably watched the fight.'

Five days later, on 22 July, Armenia's Artur Grigorian – a future professional world champion who reigned for eight years as WBO lightweight king – was dispatched, a 16-3 loser, in the second round with Mayweather again dominant. One writer said Mayweather boxed with 'real passion and urgency.'

Although it was something he would later become accustomed to, Mayweather made history in his third contest of the Games. He won a thrilling all-action battle with the excellent Cuban Lorenzo Aragón. It was 12-11 in the end, and it meant Floyd had become the first American to defeat a Cuban in an Olympic fight for twenty years, since Leon Spinks had whipped Sixto Soria in Montreal in 1976. Boycotts meant the countries had not met in 1980, 1984 or 1988.

Aragon, tall and gangly, threw more punches in the opening round while Mayweather was happy to counterpunch, as was his custom.

Trailing 5-4 by the second, the American stepped things up, became more aggressive and finished that session in the lead 10-

7, even though the judges – utilising a much-maligned computer scoring system – failed to count almost any of his successful body shots.

Things became untidy in the third and final round and although the Cuban started to close the gap it was ultimately not enough.

'Where he impressed me was in the beginning of the medal rounds when he fought the Cuban and he beat him by one point, that was a great bout,' Mitchell beamed. 'The thing about it was Mayweather was a defence fighter then, but to win that fight he couldn't box defence, he had to fight, he had to be more about the offence. He had to pressure the Cuban and fight him back. If you look at Floyd's other fights he would box and move. This time he had to go forward and he surprised me. The Cuban was a very good boxer. It was a helluva fight but that's where Floyd impressed me and I thought, "Woah, this kid's better than I thought he was."'

Mayweather progressed to the semi-final where he faced Bulgaria's fancied Serafim Todorov, a three-time World Amateur Champion and a three-time Olympian, though he'd never made it that far before. As a flyweight in 1988 he'd lost 4-1 to the eventual gold-medal winner in the quarters. Kim Kwang-sun was a South Korean who struck gold in those Seoul Games. Four years later, Todorov lost in Barcelona to North Korean Li Gwang-sik, 16-15.

The moustachioed European had won all three of his bouts in Atlanta via decision, outscoring Ukrainian Yevvheniy Shestakov, Australia's future professional world IBF super-featherweight champion Robbie Peden and quality German Falk Huste in his quarter-final.

On 2 August, in his featherweight semi-final, Floyd looked faster from the opening bell but Todorov – with height and reach advantages – was sturdy, experienced and patient.

There was plenty of action. Young Mayweather was trying to get in close, fire off clusters of blows and then return to safety. The pro-US crowd applauded his work when he countered with a left but it failed to register a score on the judges' computers.

Replays showed Mayweather landing several shots in the round but only one had scored and he trailed 2-1 at the end of the session.

'You're hitting him with the jab but you're moving back too fast,' Mayweather was told when he returned to the corner. 'You can't do that. You've gotta stay on the inside when you do that. You're down; you've gotta put pressure on him.'

Sure enough, he glided into the lead in the next round. Todorov was moving well but Floyd connected with a brace of single straight rights. He flurried to the body at one stage, and although the judges were again unmoved he had done enough to go in 7-6 up with just three minutes separating him from a final berth. It all hinged on the last round.

'Make him move, make him move,' Floyd was advised between sessions. 'Now the right hand is the key. The right hand. Straight. One other thing, when you're in close, every once in a while a hard body shot, but make it hard. Then right back upstairs with the right hand.'

Mayweather looked unlucky not to score as the opening seconds of the decisive round ticked on and moments later he was 8-7 down, a big Todorov left hook landed.

Mayweather fought with more immediacy and the partisan crowd sounded their approval. Two rights seemed to find the target so the audience clapped and cheered but the score remained the same. Floyd had a nosebleed but levelled matters when a long left caught Todorov pulling backwards in a straight line, although the Bulgarian edged ahead and a thudding right hook put him two points clear with thirty seconds to go. With ten seconds remaining, Floyd poured it on. He clipped his foe to make it 10-9 and desperately tried to equalise as the clock ran down and then out. Todorov's team congratulated him in his corner.

As the two waited for the verdict in the centre of the ring, a confident Mayweather, in the blue corner and wearing a blue vest, shorts and headgear, held his index finger up and then raised his hand hopefully, seemingly sure of progress into the gold medal match.

Those watching on TV were aware of the score but it was a different matter in the auditorium.

The verdict of the five judges, Stanislav Kirsanon of Russia, Argentina's Osvaldo Bisbal, Najah Moussa of Martinique, Dharmasiri Weerakoon of Sri Lanka and Allan Walker of New Zealand, revealed that the winner was actually in the red corner. Egyptian referee Hamad Hafaz Shouman hoisted Mayweather's arm aloft in error.

Looking uncertain as to whether he had actually got it, Todorov was sheepish as boos rained in.

The decision caused a furore among Team USA. The crowd whistled and jeered and history remembers it as one of the Games' many dubious decisions over the years in boxing.

Mayweather's old enemy Augie Sanchez caught the highlights later but he had been pulling for his rival.

'Of course,' said Sanchez, who only took eleven losses in his one hundred and eighty-six amateur fights, three of them against Mayweather. 'He was representing the US. I couldn't do anything but root for him. He did great. I thought he got a bad decision but he did great. I couldn't understand how they gave it to the other guy. Floyd was just picking him off but when you go to that international level, it's a different ball game with what these judges are looking for. It's politics, too. There's politics all over boxing. I thought that he won that fight.'

America filed a protest. They alleged that judges feared recriminations from Emil Jetchev who was the head of officials at the Games, and Bulgarian. Three of his countrymen finished in gold medal matches in the boxing.

US team manager Gerald Smith argued that Floyd had landed punches that were not recorded, contending that Todorov was awarded points even when punches had not scored.

US boxing judge Bill Waeckerle felt so strongly about the decision he quit the Games, resigning as a federation judge, too.

In a letter to federation president Anwar Chowdhry, he fumed, 'I refuse to be part of an organisation that continues to conduct its officiating in this manner.

'The judging was totally incompetent,' he added.

Some remained more stoic in their assessment. One reporter noted how Mayweather had come 'tantalisingly close' to defeating the world number one, concluding that he had lost by the 'agonisingly narrow' margin of a single point. There was no mention, on this occasion, of controversy, even if it was being cried elsewhere.

Todorov went on to claim silver; the US protest was unsuccessful.

The man who ended Todorov's gold medal run was Thailand's Somluck Kamsing, who had earned his final berth with a 20-8 semi-final victory over Argentina's Julio Pablo Chacón. He defeated the Russian 8-5 in the final.

Mayweather tried to sound nonplussed afterwards, as though he was taking the heartbreak in his stride.

'You know and I know I wasn't getting hit,' he argued. 'They say he's the world champion. Now you all know who the real world champion is.'

His teammates, and Mitchell, stood behind him.

'I thought it was one of the worst robberies I'd seen,' said Jones, who won bronze and watched Floyd's loss from ringside. 'I almost started crying when they read out the decision. I really felt bad for him. It made me feel bad. I thought Floyd was going to join Reid in the finals and we'd have two in the finals but then he got robbed. It really crushed me, but he brushed it off and bounced back – and look at him now. I've seen some bad decisions but Floyd's really hurt me the most. I had lost already, we were both in the semis, I fought earlier, he fought several fights after me. I thought he won and it affected him. He didn't break down until we got home. When we got home it really touched him. It really bothered him. He felt he'd let down his country by not winning gold. I had to tell him, "You got a bronze, you did good. Number three in the world, how can you complain?" He didn't want the bronze. He wanted to be a gold medallist. It's all he trained for, it's all he talked about, going to the Olympics and winning gold.'

'Mayweather, I thought did enough to win, he didn't get the decision,' Mitchell remembered. 'But I've been in a lot of internationals where, when you've got an athlete that is there year after year after year, people remember that and they respect that and they see and watch them a little bit more than they watch the other one. I thought Mayweather won, no question about it. But he didn't get the decision. You can't dwell on that. When you look at the fight, take your time, you'll see what I mean. When you get five different judges, some score body punches, some score head punches, and if you don't win real big you're in trouble. That's in any tournament. I thought he did enough to win it. I thought it was a bad decision. Not an outrageous decision but a bad decision. It wasn't like the Roy Jones decision in 1988 but I had him winning and I'm not saying it because I was his coach, he should have been in the gold-medal round.'

Did Mitchell not expect his fighters to get a verdict if it was close, given they were the home nation?

'Not necessarily,' he contended. 'I look at the scores, I look at the people and different people come from different countries. Even though it's our own country here, you've got to remember the judges are not from here, and they try to be fair but sometimes you see judges that favour certain guys and the kid he lost to had been around a long time. So everybody knew him. With the young US team, they come in and they go. That's what hurts us. Our kids, as soon as the Olympics or World Championships are over, they go pro. Those other kids from Europe and elsewhere go to Olympics after Olympics and World Championships after World Championships. Americans, because they're poor and they don't have the money outlet, they go professional.

'Floyd, like most people, he was a little hyped at first with the decision then I told him, "Listen, the pro people are going to like you, so don't worry about it. I had you winning it and everyone else had you winning it, so I know it hurts but you'll get over it." He did, and look where he's at now.'

Tarver felt he had been hard done by, too. While David Reid won gold, Tarver was one of five bronze medallists on the US boxing team; Wells, Jones, Mayweather and Cauthen were the others. 'I was the favourite to do well because leading in I had done very well,' Tarver admitted. 'So I feel like I did well in the Olympics. I think my fight had just as much controversy as anybody's fight but that's water under the bridge. If I didn't get the gold in the amateurs I can say that when you look at my career and the body of work that I've done I can truly say that I was rewarded in the pros. I don't have no ill feeling about my Olympic experience. It made me a better man, a better fighter and I got everything out of it that I was supposed to. I learned from my experiences, took them with me and it's always going to be a great feeling to know that I represented my country and made my country, my loved ones and my supporters very proud. Really, no fight got a lot of publicity that stated it was a blatant robbery, not like the way Roy Jones got robbed in the Olympics. It wasn't anything like that. Things didn't always go to plan. Things didn't always go right. But it was all experience.'

Nate Jones agreed with that. 'A lot of us came back with medals but I think we should have got more. Vargas got robbed, Tarver got robbed, Clay-Bey got robbed – well, he fought Klitschko on the first night and whoever won that was going to win the gold medal. So he lost the first fight. David Díaz lost a close decision. We had a really good team, probably one of the best of all time, but the best thing was how we came together.'

'Man, we travelled all over the world fighting,' Tarver reminisced. 'When you look back on it, it's obvious we should have had more gold medals, but hindsight is always 20/20 and it doesn't always take a gold medal for you to have success in the pros. If you have it you have it and the cream will always rise to the top. That's the truth.

'We had a great Olympic team, man, and even when you look at the whole Olympic boxing programme at that time it was healthy. You had guys like the Klitschko brothers in those Olympics, Vassiliy Jirov, the Cubans, that was a real superstar class and there was a whole lot of talent.'

'Remember, that might have been America's youngest team ever,' Mitchell said. 'We mostly had a bunch of kids, and they had to deal with that computer scoring. There wasn't no boycotts either. All the big boxing countries were there.

'When people look back, they're gonna say it was one of our better teams, no matter what the medal count was. Mayweather wasn't the only one of our guys to get a bad decision. He just got the worst one. And you know what? They still did alright. What they did was unbelievable.

'We were only projected to get two medals, I think it was Zahir and Tarver, and Tarver was projected to get the gold, but everyone said we wouldn't get any more because we were a young team. We did way better than anybody thought. I thought we would get four or five medals. Mayweather should have at least got into the gold medal round, so at least a silver, only my guy

David [Reid] got the gold. If Nate Jones had studied the tapes like I'd asked him to the day before – against Canada's David Defiagbon – he would have been further up. And if Fernando [Vargas] would have kept his hands up . . . he lost a close fight. We lost some fights by one or two points so we were right there. It was just a little more seasoning and discipline that was needed.'

Cuba's Aragon, Mayweather's victim, would be back at the 2004 Athens Games to win silver. Years later, Todorov's claim to fame was still that he was the last man to hang a loss on Floyd Mayweather Jr, even though only one of them was cashing in long after Atlanta.

'My wealth in this life is my clean mind and my pure soul,' Todorov said. 'Those were my millions. I'm the rich man Serafim, because everyone in Bulgaria knows that I am a man of honour, a hero, a big patriot and those are my millions. But I was never a real millionaire.'

He regretted turning down substantial offers from America for the rest of his life but said his biggest disappointment was not winning the Olympic gold medal. He claimed it didn't happen because of 'one very powerful leader in the boxing federation.'

Of the Mayweather fight, he simply recalled, 'I defeated him and it wasn't that hard. For those Olympic Games I trained no more than twenty-five days and he probably trained that whole year. And I really beat him, but I can't say that I was much better, he was an excellent fighter, a persistent fighter that gave me a hard time.'

He said that amateur politics were such that any victory that was not by seven or eight points might have gone either way and joked, only mildly, that if he was given three months to train for a rematch he would give Mayweather trouble today.

'I might not win, but he will experience some hard times,' he smiled.

He went on to have a brief pro career, finally going 5-1,

retiring in 2003 and later setting up a Facebook page on which he was called 'Floyd's conqueror: Serafim Todorov.'

A statement on the page reads, 'The last man to beat in the ring boxing superstar Floyd Mayweather is Serafim Todorov. They met in the semi-final of the Atlanta '96 Olympics.'

Despite the allegations against the Bulgarian team, the Val Barker award for best boxer at the Atlanta Games went to Kazakh light-heavyweight Jirov, Tarver's conqueror.

Disillusioned with the unpaid code, and with an amateur record of eighty-four wins against six defeats – with twenty-one stoppage victories – Mayweather opted to follow in the footsteps of his father and two uncles. He went pro.

It caused acrimony with his 'white daddy' Don Hale, who believed he would be hired to manage the prospect. He thought Floyd's desire to be the best, have the best and make big money caused him to move away from the Hale fold.

'It was never enough, he always wanted more,' said Hale. 'He was the best-dressed amateur boxer in the world, I guess because he wanted all the best clothes. He wanted name-brand stuff. He was the first to get the [Nike Air] Jordans and that sort of thing.'

By the time Hale realised any grip he might have had on Floyd was slipping it had disappeared altogether. 'Floyd had a bunch of new clothes and a wad of cash in his pocket. He told me that [another promoter] gave it to him.'

Mayweather agreed terms and signed a professional contract – including a $100,000 signing bonus – with promotional powerhouse Top Rank. Headed by Bob Arum, a man who'd graduated in law from Harvard, the company had promoted the likes of Muhammad Ali, Roberto Durán, Marvin Hagler and Tommy Hearns.

'When we went to Atlanta,' Arum recalled of scouting the Olympic team, 'we thought Floyd had the potential to be the best professional of all our Olympians. Floyd showed me a professional style, very quick hand speed, a lot of power. We thought he could be a great one.'

Instead of Mayweather receiving the fanfare, however, Philadelphia's golden boy David Reid was the biggest winner from the US boxing team. It was predicted, after his thrilling come-from-behind gold-medal knockout of favoured Cuban Alfredo Duvergel, that he would go on to make $50 million or more in his career. 'This young man is a superstar waiting to happen,' said promoter Dan Goossen.

That 1996 US Olympic team had five fighters who would end up as professional world champions. Mayweather, Reid, Antonio Tarver, Fernando Vargas and David Díaz all wore gold at some point in their careers, while Eric Morel, Zahir Raheem and Rhoshii Wells all challenged for world crowns.

No, they were not as successful as the historic 1976 and 1984 teams but the squad was packed with talent.

Ironically Reid, the superstar who rightly turned over sporting the moniker of 'The American Dream', won the WBA world light-middleweight title and had seemed destined to enjoy a brilliant and lucrative career. He felt Mayweather would, as well. 'He has great talent,' said Reid, who also picked out Fernando Vargas for world title success, 'A whole lot of talent.'

But when Reid was paired with vicious Puerto Rican Félix Trinidad in the pros he was ferociously beaten and never the same again. He retired with seventeen wins and two losses after a career that lasted just four short years. By then, a droopy left eyelid that could not be corrected by surgery – something he became cripplingly insecure about – and the physical and psychological wounds from Trinidad seemed too deep to overcome. He wound up toiling at a much lower level before retiring in 2001. During Mayweather's extravagant pay-per-view years, Reid endured depression and suffered from severe mood swings.

'Here's the thing,' said Mitchell, who ended up working with him in the pros and looked out for him in retirement. 'Dave Reid, I told him I turned down the Trinidad fight. Dave went over my head and took it and I said, "You've got to listen, son. He's had about forty-five fights and you've only had thirteen." And we won the title in twelve fights – almost a record. And the thing is that eye came down and I said to him to have it seen to even before the Olympics, but he never went to the doctor so he just let it get worse and worse and worse. Then, on top of that, he knocked Trinidad down and after seven rounds he came back to the corner and said, "I can knock him out." I said, "Woah, that ain't the game plan, just keep boxing." He went out there and he went toe to toe and from that he never recovered. He went the distance but he never recovered and after the fight I said, "It's time for you to retire." He had money saved and put away but he went back to Philly, listened to people and just took the money out that was in a retirement plan for him. People don't understand, but the doctors told me, the reason he got depressed was he couldn't fight no more. And the doctors have seen it in a lot of athletes, athletes that have reached the top of the mountain and when it's time for them to quit they don't want to quit and they get depressed.'

Reid later lived alone in a two-bedroom apartment in Michigan, moving from Philadelphia to be near Mitchell. The majority of his money had gone.

'He eats alone. He works out alone. He attends church alone,' reported *Ring* magazine when they caught up with him in 2012.

'I like to be by myself,' he stuttered.

His American dream was over.

His cocky teammate Floyd Mayweather's was yet to truly start.

Floyd reconciled with Hale several years later, flying him to Vegas for big fights. Floyd once told him, 'I think of what you and Dixie [Hale's wife] did for me every day and I want you to know that I haven't forgotten about you and what you've done to me.'

Floyd's real Daddy, however, was languishing behind the high prison walls in Milan, Michigan, and his son, the Olympic bronze medallist, was asked why he wanted to fight in the pros.

'When I was in the ring at the Olympics, it was my father's words that I was hearing, not the coaches,' Mayweather said. 'I never listened to what the coaches said. I would call my father and he would give me advice from prison.'

Floyd Sr's actions had cost Mayweather five and a half years of having a full-time dad and, seemingly more importantly, a full-time coach.

'I wanted to cry seeing him like that,' he once said of his prison visits. 'But I was supposed to be a man so I didn't. I talked to him on the phone a lot. Almost every day. He told me that the streets is not good for you. He's my only friend. We had a talk last night. He said everybody wants to be your friend when you're on top, but when you lose nobody wants to be around. If you get locked up, let's see who's gonna send you cards or send you money. When I used to go and see him I didn't like it, seeing him locked up. But the time went fast because I was always travelling and fighting.'

Fortunately for his boxing, another two Mayweathers were free men and able to help. Uncle Roger, the 'Black Mamba' had more than one screw loose but he knew the sport and could continue to teach Floyd its subtleties, even if Floyd would miss his father. Uncle Jeff was on hand, too.

But Floyd Jr remembered his dad holding him up so he could use the speedbag. He remembered their trips to the gym. He said he wanted to succeed as a professional so Floyd Sr would not be eating baloney sandwiches in jail his whole life. He wanted him to have steak.

THREE

INVESTING STOCK

ROBERTO APODACA FOUGHT just four professional contests. When he retired in 1998 he disappeared home to El Centro, California, into obscurity and was not heard from again.

'I don't know where he came from, where we got him, he was just an opponent,' said matchmaker Bruce Trampler when asked in 2015 if he recalled how he found the man to stand in the opposite corner for Floyd Mayweather's professional debut. 'I have no idea.'

Of Apodaca's four fights, he went the distance once, losing on points to little-known journeyman Ramón Acuña in a six-rounder in Mexico. He was then defeated by a prospect named Hiram Bueno inside five rounds and exited stage left with a three-session loss to Héctor Velázquez, who would go on to beat some top contenders and challenge for a world title.

The shortest straw he would scoop, however, was when he made his prize-fighting bow. Facing him was a brash American with a point to prove, a name to live up to and perhaps a little anger to unleash given what had happened in Atlanta a couple of months earlier.

Floyd Mayweather was nineteen years old and he was born to do this. He wore dazzling black shorts and a glittery matching jacket while the temperature fell in the car park of the Texas Station Hotel and Casino about ten miles north of the Strip. Across the back of that jacket was the branding of Bullenbeiser

Boxing Gear, a company owned by future Ultimate Fighting Championship boss Dana White.

'Floyd wore my stuff for his first four fights,' White, who also came from Las Vegas, worked with amateur fighters and had trained alongside Roger Mayweather at the United Champions Gym, would later reminisce. 'I still have the stuff somewhere, though I don't know where it is.'

Slender eight-ounce gloves encased Floyd's fists. There was no headgear. The amateur vest had been shed. Floyd Mayweather was no longer in the fight game, he was in the fight business.

As far as a professional debut goes, his was innocuous. Almost understandably, Apodaca was a proverbial deer in the headlights while his teenage opponent looked as though he was gearing up for nothing more strenuous than a massage.

Composure rather than pressure bubbled to the surface and weighing in just a pound over the super-featherweight limit, at 131lbs, he scored a routine win.

With uncle Roger in his corner, Floyd bounced up and down calmly while chewing gum as he was announced to a compact crowd. The fighters came head to head for the instructions of referee Kenny Bayless; Apodaca looked as though he had strapped himself into a rollercoaster and was nervously awaiting its launch.

This ride, for him, would not last long.

'Floyd Mayweather is a power puncher,' announced ESPN2 commentator Al Bernstein, as the former Olympian started sharply. 'He's a guy who can hurt you and knock you out with one punch.'

Mayweather was too fast and too powerful. He landed a succession of left hooks and finally one to the body that dropped his opponent onto his haunches after sixty-four seconds.

'Do you want some more?' asked referee Bayless when the Californian rose forlornly at eight.

Apodaca nodded warily.

Floyd went to complete the job. His foe caught him once but otherwise was trapped in a blizzard of red leather.

Early in round two, another left to the gut folded Apodaca like a mousetrap. He rolled on the canvas, clutching at his side, trying to encourage some air back into his body. Sickened, he spat his mouthpiece out into the referee's hands and Mayweather nonchalantly posed for the cameras before returning to his corner where he was greeted by Jeff and Roger. Just thirty-seven seconds of the session had elapsed.

Afterwards, Floyd thanked his uncles – along with God – and said of his brief evening's work, 'I know he could take a good headshot so we went to the body tonight. I took my time and did what I had to do. I'm proud of my performance.'

Uncle Roger was satisfied, too. 'He performed very well for a kid just coming into the pro game and not using his headgear and using smaller gloves. There are a few more little things he can do but I think, fighting more often, it's going to come to him naturally.'

There were also stoppage wins on the bill for Mayweather's old amateur rival Augie Sanchez, himself a novice pro looking to make a name for himself on his way to going 4-0, and a tall puncher named Diego Corrales who would become a Mayweather co-star in later years.

The developing skills that had earned Floyd that tainted bronze in Atlanta were too much – far too much – for the Hispanic fodder brought in to face him and boost confidence he was hardly short of.

Perhaps Floyd didn't look a million dollars, but he did not need to. These early stages were about familiarity with another side of the sport he had been born into.

'I did his first pro fight and a few after that and I did the Olympics,' recalled Al Bernstein, now Showtime's lead boxing announcer. 'I worked for NBC when he was there competing, when he beat the Cuban and he ended up with the bronze medal.'

'The funny thing is, early in his career it really looked like he was going to be a volume puncher and when you're fighting fighters of that level maybe you are but it looked like he was going to be more of an action fighter, really. I remember saying in the first fight, and even as an amateur, that his volume was pretty good.

'That's so funny and I look back at that now and think, good god, what was I thinking? But he was really throwing power punches then. He changed the way he did things and I think that impacted him a little bit but when I hear those tapes I cringe and think, "Well I guess I was wrong about that."'

It was still only Floyd's first class in his first semester.

Mayweather had endured harder sessions in the gym. That, though, is not an insult to Apodaca given that the American had already shared a sparring ring with two 1990s boxing stars in all-time great lightweight Pernell Whitaker and world champion Frankie 'The Surgeon' Randall.

He was only seventeen when he fell under Randall's influence, inside and outside the ring. 'When I boxed him I didn't box him hard, I boxed him light, because we hung out and I wanted to keep our friendship, but I knew I could outbox him at the age of seventeen,' Mayweather later said. 'I didn't want to, I was just keeping the work kind of even because I wanted to remain friends with him. He was a cool guy.'

Randall, he added, was the first person to buy him a pair of Versace shades. Floyd was driving his fast cars, they trained together, spent time together and Mayweather had a crash course in what life was like atop the sport. Randall used to get drunk and Frankie's wife would get the teenage Mayweather to go and look for him.

Then there was Pernell Whitaker. The famous Duva

promotional family invited Floyd to spar with their southpaw star, one of the great pure boxers of all time. Lore has it that Floyd had the better of their sessions, something he would neither confirm nor deny with a smirk later on in his career.

'I got respect for champions,' he explained. 'It was good work for both of us. I don't ever bad-mouth old champions because they paved the way for me to be where I'm at. He was a small guy like myself who moved up in weight and beat big guys. Naturally. He had skills and I've got skills.'

Floyd was a perfectionist. His father had insisted upon it, even though his dad's own career path and lifestyle choices were far from perfect.

Mayweather chose to be promoted by Top Rank. There were other suitors but he decided the tried and tested methods of Harvard law school graduate Bob Arum – with four decades of experience promoting – would stand him in good stead.

'I came to Las Vegas,' Floyd remembered. 'I was nineteen years old, I had no money in my pocket, basically, I got on a first class flight, they [Top Rank] had a cheque for me for $100,000 then they said they were gonna give me another $25,000. I thought about my mother and her predicament, my grandmother and her predicament, I thought about my family . . .'

He'd had enough of travelling from Michigan to New Jersey and back so he upped sticks altogether and headed to Mayweather town, Sin City, where the uncles had been living.

He would never leave, not properly, although his next fight was in Albuquerque, New Mexico.

Mayweather might not have struck gold in Atlanta, but he wore it for his second bout. Resplendent in a gold blazer and matching trunks, he was being showcased on an ESPN afternoon show inside the boiling Tingley Coliseum. Hometown hero Johnny Tapia, defending his WBO super-flyweight title against Adonis Cruz, headlined the bill.

Left-handed Reggie 'The Assassin' Sanders, from Fort Wayne, Indiana and with a win and a loss on his two-fight ledger, stared across the ring from Floyd. Roger stood by his nephew's side, headphones plugged in and a tracksuit on as if he'd just finished a run, while the commentators reminded viewers that Floyd Sr was languishing behind bars. They paraphrased Floyd Jr while referencing how his father used to lift him onto his shoulders so he could punch the speedbag when he was a child saying, 'When my dad comes out of jail I will be there for him. I will put him on my shoulders and make him a better life.'

It was scheduled for four rounds and Floyd started off with his hands down, paying southpaw Sanders little respect. The challenger tried to whip in rapid lead right hooks and shots to the body.

Commentating for ESPN, Al Bernstein again talked about Mayweather's power. 'He's capable of boxing, make no mistake about that,' noted the veteran observer. 'But he is, in many respects, a pure puncher.'

Emboldened by a steady opener, Sanders flew at Floyd to start the second, catching Mayweather off balance with a jab. Mayweather momentarily stumbled but the Grand Rapids prospect began to find a home for straight rights and left hooks to the body and then head.

However, when the action slowed halfway through round three, the crowd began to boo and jeer.

To make matters worse, Mayweather was cut over the right eye from either a punch or a headclash as the action became untidy and tactical.

He began to potshot. There were further boos in the fourth and final round as Floyd let single punches go and stayed out of trouble. Bizarrely, but tellingly with no objection from those watching, the bell sounded with fourteen seconds left in the round and the fight was over.

The final scores, 40-36, 39-37 and 40-36, indicated the

contest had been close at times but that the better work had come from the favourite. *Boxing News* said Mayweather was 'a disappointment' and that he posed far too much. Damningly, his punches were 'too wide, tentative and slow.' He claimed his hands had been 'killing him.'

Sanders thought he had done enough to earn a draw, though conceded he could have worked a little more.

'He was only young, and like I tell everyone today, I didn't fight the Floyd Mayweather everybody is seeing now,' said Reggie Sanders in 2015. 'Yes, I fought Floyd Mayweather, but not this guy. He wasn't that flashy back then. He was a normal young guy. That was it.'

Why did Mayweather not sparkle against him?

'I guess being a southpaw, I moved a lot and that gave him a problem,' Sanders added. 'If you see his fights before my fight and the fights after that he knocked everybody out, so I thought if I moved and made him come to me I would do a good job, but I didn't throw enough punches I don't think.

'I thought it was a draw, but hey,' he continued. 'I knew he would go on to become something good because I'd followed him as an amateur and I knew his amateur background. So I knew he was going to be something good but I didn't know he was going to be *this* good, how good he is now.'

Sanders went on to become a journeyman, winning only eleven more fights from the next sixty and getting stopped or knocked out on six occasions. 'He was the best I ever fought,' concluded Sanders, who now works on an assembly line for General Motors at home in Fort Wayne, Indiana. He never saw Floyd again. 'Like I said, before that fight, I knew of him, I saw him in the amateurs but I never spoke to him. I'm proud I fought him but I think I fought him at the wrong time. I think I should have fought him fifteen or sixteen fights into his career so I could have made a little money!'

Jerry Cooper was nicknamed 'Thumper' but connected with just thin air on the brief occasions he did venture on the offensive against Mayweather on 18 January, three months after the Sanders tussle.

Cooper's mullet was snapped back early by left jabs and one such shot made its way through to his body, sticking him on his rump in the opening exchanges. Just thirty seconds had gone and HBO commentator Jim Lampley noted moments later that it was 'an obvious mismatch' while hard-hitting colleague Larry Merchant added that the prospect had faced tougher foes in the amateurs.

Mayweather softened up his man with further shots to the body and Cooper soon found himself back on the deck, perched between the bottom two ropes. He stood and made his way back to a neutral corner but there he was withdrawn from battle by sympathetic referee Mitch Halpern. Cooper protested, pointlessly.

In the ring, promoter Bob Arum proudly gave Mayweather a high five; Lampley and co-commentator George Foreman praised Floyd's work to the torso. It had lasted just ninety-nine seconds and Mayweather pocketed a reported $7,500 for the outing. Oscar De La Hoya, with a 1992 gold medal rather than 1996 bronze to his name, was earning around $50,000 at the same stage of his career and made the first defence of his WBC light-welterweight title with a decision over Miguel Ángel González in the main attraction that night. Mayweather didn't even make the fight poster to advertise the show, but Kostya Tszyu, Michael Carbajal and Johnny Tapia all did – and were substantially bigger names then.

Cooper, who going into the fight had won six and lost three, finished his career with sixteen wins, sixteen losses and a draw. He was stopped or knocked out twelve times. Mayweather was canned for taking the fight in some quarters. 'He calls himself

Pretty Boy Floyd and he's in no danger of having his features damaged by the likes of Cooper,' said one report.

'I just wanted to do something to get the crowd going and make them like me,' Floyd said. 'I went out there first to win and second to impress people.'

That was clearly the goal a month later, in February 1997, when he took his first fight in California. Edgar Ayala was making his professional debut at the Swiss Park Hall in Chula Vista and seconds after the opening bell he was on his backside for the first time in his career courtesy of a short counter-left. He bled profusely from the nose as the round progressed and desperately tried to circumnavigate the ring to prevent further damage. After a couple of minutes, Floyd beckoned him to stop running and fight. Ayala had a fragile look about him. He couldn't land his rangy attempts and would not get in close enough to engage.

That pattern continued for much of the second round until Ayala threw a desperate long right hand which Mayweather saw coming, slipped and then countered with a pulverising left hook that promptly separated Ayala from his senses and sent him flat on his back, his head ricocheting off the mat. The referee did not even need to count and the 'Pretty Boy', who winked at the camera in celebration, was now unbeaten in four.

Ayala had lasted a minute and thirty-nine seconds of round two. He would fight three more times, losing the rest of his bouts against less remarkable opponents.

Mayweather was again on the receiving end of some criticism in the boxing media, with *Boxing News* observing that he 'continued to feast on an amazing collection of cream puffs,' going on to say that poor Ayala 'had no business being in with someone this good.'

Al Bernstein thought Floyd was being moved at the right pace, not that he was being held back.

'No, I really didn't because it was so early in his career and you knew he was going to move up and Top Rank wanted to make sure the Olympians they had were moving ahead,' he assessed. 'It was standard operational procedure.

'He looked very good, and you could tell in the amateurs when he got a bronze medal that he was going to be good as a professional. You know, [he had] hand speed, combination punching, great boxing pedigree in terms of a family that had been full of very good boxers and he knew the sport. You could tell he was a student of the sport. That boded well for him to be a very good fighter. He had a genuine chance to be terrific. And you got the impression that he was going to be very, very good. His overall knowledge of what was going on in the ring was very good and he took more chances then.

'It may have been the competition, I don't know, but you still get the sense he was calculated about the way he did it. You can't tell how someone would progress and you wouldn't have guessed he'd get to this point, but also you might not have guessed that he would become this master boxer.'

Bruce Trampler, who made the matches, said there was no difference moving Floyd to how he would move any other top prospect.

'In those days it was different than it is now, it wasn't difficult at all,' explained Trampler. 'It was really kind of strategic matchmaking. For example, when he fought Genaro Hernández we tried to get him a couple of tall guys before because Genaro was a taller fighter. But with Floyd we knew from the outset he had the chance to be a special fighter, even though I'd seen him get beaten in the amateurs by Martín Castillo you just knew he had ability and he wasn't tough to match.'

In March, Floyd also made short work of Arkansas-born Kino Rodriguez. It wasn't really a headline story that Rodriguez lasted just 1-44 of round one, what the newspaper boys liked was that the Mayweather family, Roger, Jeff and Floyd, were all fighting in front of their home crowd in Grand Rapids, Michigan, at the Stadium Arena. Jeff saw off Eric Jakubowski over eight rounds, Roger won the IBA's little-known bauble with a twelfth-round stoppage of Carlos Miranda at welterweight but Floyd arguably made the biggest impression.

Rodriguez was game and bombed forwards for what it was worth, but he paid for his reckless ambition when Floyd poked him to the body with a left hook. Winded and paralysed, Rodriguez reluctantly rose. Referee Frank Garza waved it off and Floyd got in Kino's face to make a point of victory.

Eventually, after listening to Floyd's animated words, Rodriguez found a safe haven in his corner. He sat on his stool where his team tended to him. Floyd's display of arrogance, when he implored Ayala to stand and fight and the flashy display of showmanship against outgunned Jerry Cooper, when he dropped his hands and smiled, indicated a more confident character might lie beneath the surface of a fighter who was now just 5-0. As Rodriguez recovered, Floyd bounded onto the ropes calling on the crowd to support him.

Kino fought five more times, losing to future world champions including Paul Spadafora, István Kovács and Clarence 'Bones' Adams. He retired to Tijuana in May 1998 to work as a carpenter.

'Floyd is a very good, fast fighter and hits hard,' Rodriguez remembered from Mexico. 'Yeah, I'm glad I got in the ring with him. In a way I'm proud of that.'

It turned out Roger only had a couple of fights left in him. His stellar career was winding down and he'd had seventy contests, many of them hard. He'd also been on the wrong end of some damaging knockouts. Jeff retired, but would occasionally spar Floyd to help him.

Both of the uncles had a fresh focus, and it was their promising nephew.

It was only April when Floyd had his fourth fight of the year, meeting Louisiana southpaw Bobby Giepert.

Floyd's father had been released from prison just days before and was in a halfway house in Michigan. He was set to join the posse in Vegas providing he could keep his nose clean for six weeks.

Meanwhile, Floyd Jr accelerated to 6-0 with five stoppages, breezing by the Gretna man – an electrician by day – in ninety seconds. Giepert – who was having only his second fight in twenty-nine months – was dropped twice, bloodied and in no state to continue when referee Joe Cortez called it off. The second occasion he went down hard on his side, where he remained for some time.

Giepert, who'd had twenty-eight fights and who'd gone the eight-round distance against Australia's former IBF world lightweight champion Philip Holiday before nearly retiring, had now been convinced to hang them up for good this time with a $3,000 pay cheque to cash.

There was far more money in the main event. Hispanic prodigy Oscar De La Hoya, making $10 million, outpointed Pernell Whitaker ($6 million) on a huge night in the Thomas & Mack Center in Las Vegas.

Fight number seven saw more of the same for Floyd. One member of the American commentary team had been speaking with legendary Detroit trainer Emanuel Steward, who had opined that Mayweather could go on to win two or three world titles and become one of 'the best ever.'

'Well tonight,' the commentator said, 'you have the chance to get a glimpse of perhaps one of the best ever.'

It was still early days, and there was no way one would know that was how Floyd would commonly refer to himself in future years, as 'TBE' – The Best Ever.

He wouldn't get the chance to prove that against Tony Duran

either, whose previous bout was an eight-round decision loss to Jeff Mayweather some three months earlier.

Reports said Floyd looked good in the short time it took to dispatch Denver's Duran, but seventy-two seconds was not long enough to showcase many of his talents.

Some reckoned his chin looked on the high side while others observed the familiar Mayweather movements, the shoulder roll and the sharp right-hand counters.

After softening Duran with a left hook to the body, he forced the Colorado man to the ropes and nailed him with a spiteful right. Duran landed flat on his back. He staggered to his feet, although it did not look like he knew what had hit him. Referee Tony Gibson stepped in, despite Duran's half-hearted protests. It would be the quickest win of Floyd's career and his fourth and last first-round finish.

'He can certainly dig,' stated one onlooker, as Floyd bagged his sixth stoppage in seven wins. Duran, who had gone unbeaten in nine to begin his career, had lost nine and drawn one of his previous ten before facing Floyd.

Larry O'Shields, with twelve wins, three losses and a draw on his record –unbeaten in his last six – was not quite a proverbial bug on the windshield as he lasted six rounds with Mayweather when they boxed in San Antonio, Texas, a month later. Again Mayweather was on an Oscar De La Hoya pay-per-view undercard, with the gifted Los Angeles idol taking just two rounds to defeat Kenya's overmatched David Kamau.

It was Mayweather's first scheduled six-rounder and Houston's O'Shields was mostly missing his elusive target while Floyd helped himself to clusters of shots as and when he wanted. O'Shields was more experienced but limited and one-paced. Mayweather swaggered through the gears, boxing within himself safe in the knowledge that he'd been in with better fighters than O'Shields, in both the amateurs and the gym.

The commentators said Floyd, as he stuck his tongue out, needed to learn the difference between showmanship and showboating as a methodical beatdown continued.

O'Shields spent the majority of the remainder of his career in the 'L' column, used as a stepping stone until calling it a day in 2000 with a record of seventeen wins, twelve losses and three draws.

On a smaller bill in Biloxi, Mississippi, left-handed Mexican Jesús Chávez lasted into round five before his game resistance was curtailed. He cut Floyd early on, over the left eye, and the wound reopened later in the fight but Mayweather was the boss.

Chávez began the fourth with a flurry but Jesus was down from a left hook moments later. Although it was said Mayweather had a 'surprisingly tough time' with Chávez, the result was never in doubt. In the fifth he lumped Chávez with a right hand and sweeping left hook. Chávez dropped, took a knee, contemplated his future, rose at eight but turned away when the referee, Paul Sita, checked if he wanted to continue. Sita terminated the fight.

Chávez became a serial loser. He won just three of twenty-six fights and was knocked out in nineteen of his twenty-two losses. There was also a draw. He retired in 2011, drifting in and out over the ensuing years, fighting sporadically.

The 1996 Olympic Team were all making their moves in the pro ranks. David Reid, the only gold medallist from the '96 US boxing squad, was publicly tipping Mayweather to go to the top. 'Floyd Mayweather; he has great talent, a whole lot of talent,' he said. 'Fernando Vargas; he has talent. Those guys believe in themselves. They hit hard, and they believe they're gonna be champions. I think those two will be real good pros.'

Mayweather, of course, agreed. 'What I'm looking forward to in boxing is winning as many titles as I can win, stay undefeated as long as I can possibly stay undefeated,' he told Daniel Herbert of *Boxing News*. 'I just love boxing. I'm real happy. I couldn't ask for a better life. I enjoy my job. I'd like to bring more and more people to the fights if I could. I'd like to be a very exciting fighter. I plan on being a fighter of the future, a fighter to watch. I don't feel nobody can beat me. Anybody can lose. I'm not saying I can't lose, but I just feel any fight I'm in, I'm going to win.'

Promoter Arum was certainly confident in his charge. While his significant cash cow at the time was Oscar De La Hoya, he told *Boxing Digest* magazine that Floyd was 'a kid he was developing' who 'will be a future superstar' and elsewhere called him a cross between Sugar Ray Leonard and De La Hoya.

Meanwhile, Mayweather kept busy with a second-round win over fringe contender Louie Leija in El Paso, Texas, in September. The fight was supposed to mark Mayweather's step up in class and was his first scheduled for ten rounds. *KO* magazine, however, reported that it merely turned out to be 'target practice.'

The main event that night saw the all-Mexican duel between Daniel Zaragoza and Érik Morales, with the latter having his hand raised while, down the bill, Leija was blitzed, dropped four times and nearly knocked out of the ring altogether after twenty-three seconds of round two. He was over once in the first and whipped the rest of the way until another right hand put him out of his misery.

Larry Merchant, calling the fight for HBO, told his audience that they would only find out whether Floyd had what it took to be a champion when someone who could punch hard hit him on the chin.

Leija, cousin of a much better Texas fighter with the same surname, Jesse James Leija – who held the WBC super-featherweight title – was decked by a right over the top in less than two minutes and given a sympathetic eight count, even though he had not gone down, as Mayweather followed up with a sustained assault.

Huge chants for Leija opened the second session but after a couple of minutes another right hand sent him sprawling. As Floyd followed in one more time, Leija took cover on the ropes and was shipping punishment. He was sent through the strands and referee Jerry McKenzie finally called it off. Two minutes and thirty-three seconds of the round had elapsed.

Louie won just two of his next fourteen bouts before calling it a day in 2010. When Floyd Mayweather was on a press tour to announce his 2014 mega-fight with Saúl Álvarez, one of the media stops was in San Antonio. Leija stood amazed, quietly at the back of the pressroom, witnessing how big a star his old foe had become first hand.

'Floyd was a very fast and skilful fighter,' said Leija, who still lives in Texas and now works as an electrician. 'He was just way too fast. I thought he was going to be as good as he's turned out to be. It was his speed with power that made him so good. I was doing good against my sparring partners but they're not Floyd. He's a lot faster. I was surprised by his speed. My strategy was to work the body and try to rough him up. He caught me with a sneaky right and I went down. After that first knockdown I was frustrated. I was just concentrating on surviving.'

Leija reckoned Floyd was up there with Jesús Chávez and Derrick Gainer as the best he fought, certainly no better, though admits if he boxed Mayweather again he would have employed different tactics.

'I would have used more head movement,' he lamented, also regretting that he left it late to shed the last 6lbs before the fight. 'I probably would have used more pressure because he was way too fast for me. I'm proud to say I fought Floyd, he will be in the Hall of Fame one day and so my name will be in there as well.'

According to *The Ring*, the performance 'certified Mayweather's status as a future superstar.'

'Afterward,' wrote Matthew Aguilar, 'Mayweather fired up a

pro-Hispanic crowd that had been pro-Leija, taunted the packed El Paso County Coliseum by standing on the ropes and flexing his muscles.'

Again, Roger Mayweather was bullish. 'By the time he's had fifteen or sixteen fights, he'll be ready to fight for a championship.'

Steve Kim, an internet boxing writer, was cutting his teeth at some of the smaller shows but had begun to take note of Mayweather's rapid rise. 'When he fought Leija, in his ninth pro fight, he blew out a pretty solid, tough veteran. He just dismantled him and you got the sense that he would be very good. I was at some of his preliminary fights in the Olympic Auditorium back in the late '90s and I actually enjoyed those Floyd fights more than the more recent ones.'

Boxing News editor Claude Abrams noted Floyd's star potential. 'I saw a lot of Mayweather on the way up in Vegas and even once went to Grand Rapids to cover him,' he said. 'When I saw a fighter like him come along – much like Roy Jones – I wanted to be on his trail. He struck me early on as someone who was going to be truly great.'

Others, however, remained more sceptical. One was HBO commentator Larry Merchant.

'The early impression was he had a launching pad into the professional ranks like very few fighters before him,' he considered. 'If you go back, Joe Louis was a great amateur and Sugar Ray Leonard had the launching pad of the Olympics and Leonard's first professional fight was on television in America – which I think was unique. But he had the family name. His uncle Roger was a terrific fighter, I thought, and I had seen his father against Sugar Ray Leonard so the family name, plus the Olympic connection, meant he came out of the chute with everything going for him. Plus he had talent, so he was one of those young fighters you wanted to follow. I've seen a few fighters where I've said, "I'd like to have stock in him." I don't think I thought that of Mayweather at the time. I didn't foresee that he would become a star or megastar and huge attraction, and nor did I foresee that he was coming into professional boxing when, for the next couple of decades, there would be no serious [American] heavyweights, and how that might affect fighters in the lower divisions and give them an opportunity to shine the way some of them did.

'Mayweather was ambitious. That was clear. He was arrogant and narcissistic, like a lot of young fighters who have the world out there to conquer.'

'It's so easy,' Floyd said after taking out Leija. 'I mean, this sport ain't hard. You've just got to stay focused and do what you gotta do and that's to win. I feel I'm winning because of my skills, my will, my determination and I can punch with either hand.'

Before defeating little-known 'Ferocious' Felipe Garcia, a thirty-seven-fight veteran, in Boise, Idaho, next Mayweather boasted that he would beat the world champions of the time, WBC ruler Genaro Hernández and IBF king Arturo Gatti.

'I don't just have talent inside the ring,' he said, 'I have talent outside the ring. I have charisma. I have character. People like me. I'm just a showman.'

He was also becoming a businessman. In the build-up to the fight, while the boxers worked with TV production crews, Mayweather coaxed a more camera-shy Garcia to stand in the right positions, directing him through their *Tuesday Night Fights* shoot. The grizzled thirty-nine-year-old Garcia nonchalantly followed the young kid's instructions.

Still, whether anyone took Floyd too seriously after a six-round pounding of the fleshy club fighter was another matter. It certainly proved little. Body shots paved the way for the finishing blows in the sixth, a sharp left hook and two right hands that had Garcia, who'd enjoyed only moments of scrappy success, looking up at the lights above the ring. There were four seconds of the round remaining. He had only been stopped once in ten years and had been known for taking young prospects the distance.

However, *Boxing News* was not impressed by Floyd, who still utilised the combination of his manager and uncle Jeff and trainer and uncle Roger in his corner. It was understood that Jeff would be in this role until Floyd Sr could take it on.

'As good as he is,' wrote *Boxing News*, 'he ran out of ideas before finding the old-timer's chin. Garcia, old enough to be his father, drops to 19-18-1 (10).'

That October fight had come a year and three days after Mayweather's pro debut. He was now 11-0 with nine wins by stoppage.

A bloodied Angelo Nunez did not last three rounds in November of 1997 in the Olympic Auditorium in Los Angeles. Mayweather, who was booed by the crowd before the first bell, was beginning to really look the part. Those boos might also have been for Roger, back in the auditorium in front of a largely Hispanic crowd where he made his 'Mexican Assassin' name taking out Mexican fighters. Perhaps the jeers were also because Floyd had been actively calling out their hero, Genaro Hernández, who they were there to see.

Regardless, Floyd was fast, sharp and threw hurtful punches to the head and body. He waffled Nunez with some straight rights that had the crowd gasping. One interested ringside observer was boxing star Oscar De La Hoya, the world champion who had stopped Nunez in four on a cut four years earlier.

Nunez had said before facing Floyd that he would never fight again. He never did. By the second round his face started to bust up, his left eye was swelling while the right eye was cut.

In the third round, perhaps sensing the end could be near, Nunez pinned Mayweather on the ropes but with virtuosity the prodigy slipped, slid and countered with hard punches. Nunez was paying a price for his pressure and ended up having to retreat. As he did so, referee Lou Moret deemed the fight should be stopped. More boos fell on the ring but there was only one fighter in the contest. And it was not Nunez. It was stopped, officially, because of the cut.

Nunez was proud of his performance though Mayweather was less satisfied. He thanked God, thanked his sponsors and then said he wanted a world title shot. 'I believe I'm ready. My uncles believe I'm ready. I probably need to polish up with a couple of ten or twelve-rounders to sharpen up and then I will probably be ready for the winner of this [Genaro Hernández-Carlos Hernández] championship fight tonight.'

Uncle Jeff was in agreement. 'I think he will be ready in April, May, as long as they keep bringing him these tough guys, the ones who give him rounds,' he said. 'I think he will be ready for these guys. Skill-wise, he's ready to compete on any level right now, but it's just a matter of getting that seasoning and experience by going in with tough guys.'

In the main event that evening, Genaro Hernández and Carlos Hernández met in a battle for the WBC super-featherweight title. They were firmly on Floyd's radar. After all, he had finally made the fight poster alongside them and other undercard attractions including Lucia Rijker and Alfonso Sanchez. *Boxing News* at last thought he was ready. 'Don't be surprised if he beats, or even stops Genaro Hernández, who looks ready to be taken,' they reckoned.

Floyd had a way to go before reaching that level, but to do so he needed to step up. His talent and potential, though, was being well recognised. As *The Ring* analysed the progress of the Olympic team, they felt Mayweather was the standout graduate and 'steamrolling toward a title shot . . . Although he only won a bronze medal in Atlanta, few people can argue that the twenty-year-old Mayweather, a native of Grand Rapids, Michigan, has emerged as the superstar of the Games.'

As with the astute Larry Merchant, they were waiting to see what happened in a fight when Mayweather finally did not have things all his own way. 'While he seems destined to win a world title,' *The Ring* commented, 'it will be interesting to see how he handles adversity – assuming he faces some.'

There was speculation that he might tangle with former amateur rival Augie Sanchez in a bout that would propel one and cause the other to have to rebuild at an early stage of their careers.

It was a commercially natural fight, although Floyd was filling out and seemed destined to move up through the weights. It was a ready-made feud dating back to their early teens and Sanchez, too, had turned professional with Top Rank.

As 1998 opened, *The Ring* stirred the pot, hearing from both sides about the other. 'I wish him all the best but there's a competitive thing between us,' said Sanchez, who had by then sparred the likes of Wayne McCullough, Johnny Tapia, Azumah Nelson and Tim Austin and still felt the wrong man had gone to the 1996 Olympics to represent Team USA. 'He has been saying some negative stuff. I wish him all the best until he fights me. Then I'll wish him all the best after I beat him. To beat him I just have to pressure him. He can't run forever.'

Mayweather responded, saying, 'I don't need him; he needs me. What am I gonna get out of fighting Augie? He's not on the same level as me. I'm a ten-round fighter, he's still fighting six-rounders against guys with losing records. He's a kid, I'm a grown man. We fought amateurs, but he never got hit by me when he had no protective gear on and I was wearing eight-ounce gloves. I'm on another level now and he's too slow to do anything with me. I can go ten rounds or fifteen rounds or twenty rounds if I have to. I run in the mountains every morning and box at least eleven rounds a day. Boxing is the sole focus of my life. I'm twenty years old and all I think about is boxing.'

Roger Mayweather was also becoming increasingly outspoken about his nephew's prospects, adding, 'This fight could happen only because both guys live in Las Vegas and the Olympic controversy,' he said. 'I watched Augie grow up [in Las Vegas gyms] just like I watched my nephew grow up. There is no comparison between the two right now. I know Augie like a book. I even used to train both his brothers for a while. I watched them grow up, too. I know everything about them, and Augie couldn't beat my nephew on his best day. I like Augie, I just can't understand why he wants this fight so bad. I mean, doesn't he know what he's getting himself into?'

As far as business was concerned, Top Rank far from ruled it out. 'Both of these guys are fine prospects with unlimited potential,' said the promotional outfit's publicist Lee Samuels. 'Augie is extremely anxious to fight Floyd and is really convinced he will beat him.'

'In the beginning, when he first turned pro, that's what I wanted,' recalled Sanchez many years later. 'I wanted that fight with him. But, you know, in reality of course it didn't happen. It would have made sense because I was up and coming and he just turned pro and was up and coming, we both had the same promotional company, which was Top Rank. They never wanted to put us together to fight and I called him out a few times as a pro early in his career but looking at the situation now years later, it made sense that it didn't happen. We were both growing, undefeated fighters and he won the title – and I was on the undercard of that fight.'

There were plenty of tests out there for them both to move up the ladder, with scalps to claim from veterans like Tom Johnson, Tracy Patterson, Julien Lorcy and Gabriel Ruelas while a hard batch of contenders including Angel Manfredy and Jesús Chávez – though not the same Jesús Chávez Floyd had already beaten – and Robert Garcia waited in the wings.

South Korea's Yong-soo Choi held the WBA belt while Jersey City warrior Arturo Gatti and Los Angeles star Genaro Hernández owned the IBF and WBC titles respectively. Mayweather was looking up, not sideways or down towards Sanchez.

To be fair, he was not the only one. *KO* magazine speculated what might happen if the young upstart faced veteran Genaro Hernández for the WBC title, polling analysts and fighters about the mooted fight. Veteran *Boston Globe* boxing scribe Ron Borges reckoned Hernández would win a decision but that Mayweather would learn plenty from the fight. Fellow super-featherweight contender Ruelas felt experience would see Hernández stop Mayweather. 'In fact, I think Genaro would win decisively,' he said. ESPN analyst Al Bernstein tipped Floyd, as did ex-pro Sean O'Grady. All agreed it would be a good fight. There were some, though, who noted that at the age of thirty-one the champ was showing signs of decline.

Boxing News, however, headlined that Floyd was not the finished product following a five-round victory over Puerto Rico's Hector Arroyo in Biloxi, Mississippi, in early '98. Mayweather, the trade magazine insisted, 'failed to impress as he churned, slashed and flailed.'

Arroyo had once been rated at the top of the pile by the WBA but he lasted only until 1-21 of the fifth session. Again a Mayweather fight was marred by boos, though by the end they were aimed at referee Fred Steinwinder III who intervened after what appeared a succession of glancing shots landed on Arroyo. The crowd had been spiteful towards Mayweather when he was introduced and it was a bad-tempered, prickly affair. Steinwinder warned both for using their heads early on. On one occasion, as Arroyo attacked, Mayweather pulled back, lowered his guard and blew kisses. Cue more jeers.

It never looked like ending early. Experienced Arroyo was 15-5-2 (9) but had seen better days, going 3-4-1 in his previous eight. The thirty-one-year-old was too slow. Floyd made the breakthrough in the fourth and Arroyo went down hard from a left hook at the bell, coming back out somewhat wearily in round five. Mayweather began to go through his repertoire. Yes, more missed than landed and as Arroyo seemed destined for the mat he helplessly tried to grab and actually collapsed to the deck in desperation. He was given a count until he made it back to his feet and as Mayweather bombed forwards to finish the job, Arroyo swayed this way and that, ducking and weaving to stay out of trouble. Floyd mounted yet another assault and finally Steinwinder withdrew Arroyo. A decisive ending seemed inevitable but Floyd was denied it, Arroyo saved from it. It seemed fair, though there were some who classed it as premature, including a large section of the crowd who jeered. Floyd revelled in their displeasure.

Now 13-0 (11), his already insatiable confidence was spiralling. 'I don't want to rush it, but I feel I'm ready to face a world champion or a top contender,' Mayweather said. 'It's obvious that I'm getting close. I want to be a world champion as quickly as possible. The WBC is the biggest belt out there. I want to fight for their title. It would mean a lot to be a WBC champion. Me and Genaro have the same promoter in Top Rank's Bob Arum. He's old and will be out of the sport soon. I'm a young, up-and-coming fighter. I need to get a shot at him and that title.'

'He is not as exciting as predecessors Howard Davis or Meldrick Taylor,' charged *Boxing News*. 'To compare him with Sugar Ray Leonard is a sacrilege.' They said he still had 'amateurish habits' against Arroyo. The accusation that his chin was too high resurfaced, then there was the view that he swiped and slapped instead of punched. There was also criticism for his 'short' jab.

Mayweather was nonplussed by the boos. 'Some love ya, some hate ya. Look at Héctor Camacho. He sells tickets. I sell tickets. I'm a performer. I don't need nobody to sell me. I sell myself. Let them boo, it's no problem. That's part of boxing. Some love you, some hate you. I love myself.'

While the promoting was still the job of Top Rank, Mayweather tinkered with a winning team as he brought his father into the fold for his next fight, employing him as the cornerman for the first time since his release from prison.

Hall of Fame *The Ring* editor Nigel Collins was there in Atlantic City that night. 'I remember early in his career how friendly and accessible he was,' he recalled of the young fighter. 'You see that with a lot of fighters. As they climb the ladder they kind of forget the writers who did the first story on them, but Floyd was a very exaggerated case of that. I remember him coming to our office in Ambler, Pennsylvania, after a dozen or fifteen fights and he couldn't be more accommodating. He was very boyish still, in his attitude and of course he looked like he was about fifteen at the time and you wouldn't have predicted at that point that he would turn out to be the sort of guy he is today. Maybe it was in him. The first fight, after Floyd Sr got out of jail, was in Atlantic City and I remember someone coming to tell me Floyd Sr was in the dressing room and I didn't even know he was out and Floyd was just over the moon to have his dad there, and, of course, that [relationship] underwent a lot of changes over the years.'

That night, in Bally's Casino, Floyd Mayweather Jr was rocked to his boots. His legs betrayed him. He was in the second round and fearless Rhode Islander Sam Girard had given up showing him respect. He'd landed a big right hand and Mayweather was in trouble. Unfortunately for Girard – who had been dropped at the end of round one – his success only seemed to aggravate Floyd who, after a spell of clinching and circling out of danger, suddenly broke through with his own right hand. Girard was down once again for four seconds, given a count for eight but Mayweather applied the coup de grâce with another right, and

Girard was counted out at 2-47 of round two. The storm was in a teacup but there had finally been a mild one. Floyd had been rattled for the first time and responded in dominant fashion.

'I trained hard for the fight. He was a human being like I was,' recounted Girard in 2015. 'He had two arms and two legs just like I did. I wasn't scared of him, that's why I went in there and I rocked him. You can see it on YouTube. I shook him up real good. I remember feeling it in my hand when I hit him, but I regretted not going for his chin after that, I was just going for the temple and eye area but I should have gone for the chin. That shot I hit him with bounced him off the ropes – he would have at least gone down for an eight count. That was a solid shot. I had him going but I couldn't finish him.'

Girard, who knocked out nine of the seventeen guys he beat in his career (against seven losses and a draw) added that he would have opted to box rather than brawl had he been able to live the fight one more time.

'Back then, I didn't think much of what he accomplished. Now, I say I always wanted to fight the best and I did. I haven't seen Floyd [since] but my friends once got a chance to chat with him and, yes, he remembered me – and that shot.'

Girard fought twice more and then worked in an autobody repair shop, although he was still sparring, training and working with young kids in the gym by the time Floyd was topping iconic rich lists.

'I'm very proud to have faced him,' Girard said. 'Not many can say that – and I rocked him!'

Floyd Sr was out of prison, in the corner and now training Floyd Jr full-time. Yet as grateful as the son appeared to be, discord already seemed to be surfacing even if it was only playful.

As they shot a joint interview ahead of Mayweather Jr's next fight, against Miguel Melo in the Foxwoods Casino in Mashantucket, Connecticut, less than a month after the Girard bout, the younger man wanted it to be known that he was making his own name.

'He's little Floyd, that's my son, I'm big Floyd,' said Sr. 'He don't like me to call him Lil Floyd. He can't be anything but Lil Floyd however you want to look at it. I'm big Floyd, [this is] Lil Floyd,' he said turning to his son with a smile.

'Don't call me that,' grinned Jr.

He still preferred the 'Pretty Boy' moniker. 'I know a lot of people want to see me and my father break up. They want to see the break up,' the young fighter continued, but it ain't going to happen because I know he's the best thing for me, and I know I got this far from his teaching. I'm glad he's back in my life and when he rides me that's what makes me a winner.'

Melo had taken the fight at two weeks notice and had not boxed for ten months. Even then he had lost to the unspectacular Richard Kiley but he had previously defeated Sam Girard on a split decision for the USA New England lightweight belt. Floyd himself was only a bit part player on the fight poster. The show was billed as 'Oscar's Night at the Fights' as it went head-to-head with the Oscars. No, De La Hoya was not fighting that evening, but his starpower was enough for him to 'host' the event and become the official headline act without resorting to wearing gloves. He commentated from ringside.

Melo bled from the nose early on and was dropped by a flush right hand and a pair of rights to the side in the second. He landed shots too, though, and crimson also flowed from Floyd's nostrils. Mayweather even lashed in a late right hand as the bell sounded, prompting a caution from referee Steve Smoger.

While Melo had some success, he was down again in round three, this time from a flashy left hook as he bundled forwards.

Back on his feet, Melo shook his head, looking as though he did not want any more. It turned out he did not. He never fought again.

Despite his impressive, burgeoning record, cynics lined up to knock Mayweather, who no longer had uncle Roger as part of the team. Trainer and cutman Miguel Díaz was draughted in while Jeff retained his spot alongside Floyd Sr.

Boxing News's acidic Jim Brady was still far from convinced. He wrote that Floyd 'hardly looks the next great American Olympian'. He expanded, saying, 'Maybe he needs a better trainer? Maybe he is being rushed, or maybe he just doesn't have it?'

Mayweather, however, believed otherwise. He was seven months away from his first world title fight but with his father by his side there was time for two more contests and the chance to convince Brady and the doubters that he belonged at the next level.

He was back in the Los Angeles Olympic Auditorium less than a month after clobbering Melo and he went the full ten rounds with Argentine Gustavo Fabian Cuello. By then, it seemed the fight with Genaro Hernández, who was on hand to commentate on the fight, was imminent.

One observer had underestimated the Buenos Aires man and called him 'surprisingly clever'. Finally, there was some grudging praise from *Boxing News's* Brady, who said Mayweather seemed to be 'smoothing out' and 'kept shooting his blindingly quick jab.'

It was a good learning fight. Cuello, who entered the ring with seven defeats against twenty wins, was cagey and gave Floyd plenty to think about. Floyd even had a point deducted for hitting on the break – which caused Cuello to drop face first from a right uppercut – to close the third session but certainly his victory was never in doubt. He proved hard to hit cleanly, countered happily while under any remote pressure on the ropes and helped himself to numerous sharp shots before running out a 99-90 winner across all three cards. The only point he lost was the one for the foul. On the bill, a blazing Sacramento-born Las Vegas-based puncher called Diego Corrales stormed to a one-round win over Juan Carlos Salazar while Augie Sanchez saw that once-anticipated Mayweather fight go up in smoke with a shock loss to Edgar Garcia inside a couple of action-packed minutes when, having had Garcia down and hurt, he went to apply the finisher but walked onto a big punch and was stopped.

There was talk at the time that at some of Mayweather's fights he would have three or four girlfriends sitting in different parts of the arena. When asked about that he laughed. 'It's true,' he said. 'Girls might want to get serious, but I don't, not right now. My career's more important. Way more important.'

Floyd had not fought big names but he was racking up some experience. Sanders had nicked a round or two off him and was a southpaw, he'd been cut by Chávez, he'd gone the ten-round distance with Cuello, he'd fought on big bills underneath the hottest name in the sport – Oscar De La Hoya – and he'd recovered after being rocked by Girard. He'd quietly ticked a lot of boxes while looking dominant in the process.

In June, the step up in class for Floyd finally arrived in the shape of lanky Canadian Tony Pep. Mayweather was 16-0 with thirteen stoppage wins and the fifty days or so of inactivity was the longest he had been out of the ring since turning over.

Pep was full of the usual sound bites. He thought Mayweather was overlooking him, that Top Rank had overmatched their young stud. The brainstrust, however, felt the taller Pep was an ideal prep fight for Hernández.

'He ain't never fought anybody like Floyd Mayweather,' said the cocksure contender. 'So it's going to be something different for him.'

Pep remembered feeling confident. 'The thing was, at the time I was trying to get a [title] shot,' he said. 'You know how it is, we're all trying to get a shot at the title and an opportunity and they offered me to fight him and I said, 'Well, isn't he fighting Genaro Hernández?' I already knew they were going to fight him. They said they wanted to use me as a tune-up and that the money wasn't great but the opportunity was great. If I beat him, I got a shot at Hernández. It wasn't the money necessarily, it was getting a shot at Hernández. That's what I wanted.'

Pep had twenty-nine more fights under his belt and more than two hundred and fifty rounds of experience behind him. It proved virtually worthless.

Mayweather danced lucidly as he entered the ring in front of a sparse crowd at the Trump Taj Mahal in Atlantic City.

Floyd was in a different league, really. He was in control from the get-go and began working over Pep's body in the second. He landed more hooks in round three and burst through with a hurtful right which jolted Pep's head back on his spindly shoulders while the ESPN2 commentary team wondered whether the twenty-one year old Mayweather might become one of boxing's biggest characters over the next five years.

A downcast Pep went back to his corner after round seven and disconsolately shook his head. 'I can't hit the fucking guy,' he forlornly exclaimed. In several rounds he had thrown plenty of shots but landed in only single figures while being made to pay for his rare moments of success. In the tenth round, as Floyd motored around the ring's peripheries, Pep tried to hack his way forwards but the Canadian ended up throwing his arms up in dismay. He could do nothing.

The final punch statistics revealed that Mayweather had landed an incredible fifty-one per cent of the four hundred and ninety shots he threw while Pep scored with sixty-six of four hundred and seventy-four, or fourteen per cent.

Simply put, Mayweather had never looked better. He won 99-91 and twice by 100-90. The main question was how judge George Hill gave Pep a round. It was a controlled dissection. 'I wanted to take his jab away and establish my combinations,' Floyd said, thanking Jeff and his father. 'I proved I could box.'

He had done more than that. He had proved he was ready for the world.

'I had a hard time hitting him,' Pep admitted in 2015. 'I couldn't hit him. I couldn't hit him the way I wanted to. I hadn't fought in eight months, I was waiting to fight someone else but it fell through so I took that fight. I just felt afterwards that he was sharp because his fights are all arranged well ahead of time. He knows his next four fights so he was busy, he was active – not to mention fourteen years younger than me. I could have done better than that if I'd been fighting regularly, but that wasn't the case.

'And the guys that were in my corner, I didn't even know them. The guy who trained me for that fight was a guy named Dick Woods, who knew Floyd Mayweather. He trained fighters in Colorado Springs in the mountains and he knew Floyd because he used to work with the US amateur boxing teams [who trained in Colorado]. I was training for six weeks with this guy and the day before we were due to fly out he had a neck brace on and said, "I can't fly, Tony." I said, "What?" But you know what I think it was, seriously? I think it's because I started looking good and I don't think he wanted to be involved if anything were to happen in that fight [if Floyd lost] because he was an American, right. All of a sudden he got a strange injury and he didn't come to the fight so I had two guys in my corner I didn't even know. I'd never even worked with these guys.'

Pep, though, is not bitter. He still lives in Vancouver and works as a personal trainer. His clients get to say they work the mitts with a guy who went the distance with Floyd Mayweather.

'It was good,' Pep said of the young star's speed and power. 'He hit good. At the time he had a ninety per cent knockout ratio. I fought him at super-featherweight. Manny Pacquiao had it easy. He fought him at thirty-eight; I fought him at twenty-one. As time went on I'm glad Floyd did what he did because to a degree it reflects well on me, so I'm grateful for the things he did. He kept me [his name] alive, basically, even when I'm not fighting. All of the things he has done, it's helped me.'

FOUR

ANGELS AND DEMONS

'PEOPLE SAY I'M moving him up too fast, but I say we ain't moving fast enough,' charged Floyd Mayweather Sr, when asked whether he was rushing his son into a world title fight. His boy had fought just sixty-four rounds as a professional, but he was adamant that was enough even though plenty questioned whether he would be able to cope with the South Central Los Angeles star and WBC champion Genaro Hernández.

'If he wasn't ready for him, I'd be the first one to jump and say we don't need that fight right now,' said the older Mayweather. 'I'm the one that chose this fight. I call the shots. And I told my son to whup his ass. People talk about Genaro Hernández, the legend. Hernández is a fucking bum.'

Simple yet insulting instructions, sure, but Floyd had not yet had twenty fights while Hernández, nicknamed Chicanito 'little Mexican', was regarded as the finest super-featherweight in the world.

Eric Raskin, previewing the fight for *The Ring* magazine, was concerned about the psychological damage a defeat might cause Mayweather and how he could bounce back from a loss. 'There's no question that Floyd Jr has all the tools necessary to be one of the great ones; dazzling handspeed, sensational movement, knockout power in both fists, and so much confidence you wonder where he finds room for it in his 130-pound frame.'

Raskin spoke to Mayweather, who was living in Las Vegas with his father, at the time for the preview and said he was 'less salty, though undeniably arrogant' in comparison to his father.

'I want to be world champion,' he said. 'I want to be the best. I'm just in this sport to be known as a legend. I don't care about being nice, I'm going to treat Hernández like a preliminary fighter. A lot of guys out there say I don't deserve it but I'm not ducking or diving no one at the 130 lb weight class. I'm willing to fight everybody and all comers.'

Mayweather Jr was more concerned about what he brought to the table than his opponent, saying he was younger and stronger. That was a fair comment. Floyd Sr, however, wheeled out more trash-talk. 'Hernández ain't got no power, no legs, no head movement.'

Floyd Jr told *Boxing Monthly*, 'Hernández is just an average fighter. I don't see nothing spectacular about him. He's had a lot of wars. I've got speed, youth, head movement, good defence and the best coach in the world. I want to be in the sport a long time, so I don't want to get hit. The less you get hit, the longer you last. I don't plan on getting in no long, gruelling fights. You'll see. October 3rd, I'm going to frustrate him. I'm going to take my time, slowly, and break him down, slowly.'

He was also interviewed by Graham Houston ahead of the fight, who asked him whether boos in his previous fights had affected him. 'It don't matter,' he retorted. 'I'm used to it. It's nothing. It don't matter if they boo, even if they throw stuff in the ring, because guess what – they paid their money to come and see Floyd Mayweather.'

Hernández, however, did have the respect of the fans and the boxing world and he did not hesitate trying to put Sr in his place as he responded to the pre-fight barbs. 'He barely came out of the pen and now he's piling on a lot of crap,' he responded. 'Floyd and his dad are talking a lot, but I will be more motivated than ever to prove what they got in front of them is no bum.'

'I'm not predicting how I'll do it but I'm going to get the

victory,' said the challenger, who had hired former foe Tony Pep as a sparring partner for the Hernández fight, taking his camp to Big Bear in California to focus on the job at hand.

Pep said it was while in camp he finally got to see Mayweather as a person, and as a future great despite having already lost to him.

'I did get to know him,' Pep recalled. 'I beat him at bowling! I think I'm the only sparring partner to have boxed him and bowled with him. I beat all the Mayweathers [at bowling]. I got to know him though. He was a good guy. He was a hard worker, he worked hard in the gym. He was on a mission, he didn't want no-one to stop him and he was focused. I knew he was going to be something. I knew he was going to be great. I talked to him when we were in training camp and he said, "Tony, people mistake my confidence for cockiness. It's not even about that." He looked me in the eye and said, "I really believe I just can't be beaten right now and when people say I can I'm just going to stick up for myself. I'm going to say this guy can't beat me or that guy can't beat me because I really believe I can't be beaten."'

It was not just Mayweather's words that stayed with Pep, the sparring kept him up at night, too. He admits he'd even gone to the camp hoping for a slice of revenge having lost their fight. 'I thought I was going to get him then because I would get everybody after a couple of days and I would start using my reach on them,' he remembered. 'But I would be in my bed in training camp just laying there wondering what I was going to do with him the next day. And the next day he'd have an answer. Slowly, as the days went by, I knew he was something special.'

Meanwhile, Mayweather credited Top Rank, Bob Arum and Todd duBoef for getting him the title shot. The young contender was the bookies' favourite, though plenty were tipping the experienced champion and Las Vegas sportsbooks had a hard time recalling a fight with such two-way wagering.

Hernández had lost only once and that was when Oscar De La Hoya shattered his nose, causing a grand total of seven breaks and forcing his retirement from a weight division above super-feather, where Genaro was at his best. In fact, he was a two-time champion who had held the WBA belt between 1991 and 1994 following a victory over Daniel Londas in France. He moved up to lightweight for a shot at boxing's golden boy, De La Hoya. After that one-sided loss, he dropped back down to super-featherweight and regained a slice of the title, the WBC version. He was a genuine super-featherweight.

He was also a fighter's fighter. He rose from an after-the-bell knockdown against Ghana's great Azumah Nelson and opted to fight his way to the win rather than capture victory by disqualification. Unfortunately for him, though, *KO* magazine reckoned he was now there for the taking. 'He struggled mightily to solve awkward Russian Anatoly Alexandrov, barely escaping with his title belt around his waist. He then engaged Carlos Hernández in a war before falling back on his true talent to fence his way to a decision . . . Hernández relies on subtle moves that require full use of his cat-like reflexes. Should those gifts abandon him, his time at the top will end.'

Boxing News's Jim Brady was finally nearly sold on Mayweather the man as well as the fighter, saying, 'Floyd is wisely toning down his strutting, loudmouth, know-it-all act.' He also prophesied that Hernández was ripe for the picking. 'Mayweather belted him [Pep] back and seems almost certain to do the same to Hernández in October.'

Mayweather had also made a fan of former WBC bantamweight champion Wayne McCullough, the Las Vegas-based Irishman who sparred Floyd for the Hernández fight.

'He was quick and hard to hit,' recollected the granite-chinned former champ. 'His speed was unreal. He was here, then there, and could hit and move like no other fighter I've been in the ring with.'

TV analyst Dave Bontempo, favouring Hernández, said the bout was what the sport needed. 'As a fight fan I applaud the guy [Floyd] stepping up. If I were his manager I might want to wait a while, but the problem would be that you never know if the fight will still be there a year from now. If it is premature, it's just a tad premature . . . It didn't bother Mayweather to lose at the Olympics, so I think he could bounce back. The sport of boxing is in absolute dire need of a matchup in which someone fights someone with a pulse. Anything negative about pushing Mayweather too fast is cancelled out by what this does for the greater good of the sport.'

It was not that good for Hernández. Blood leaked from his mouth in the first round as Mayweather's blurring hands put distance between him and the thirty-two-year-old champion. Wearing bright red shorts with white trim and matching boots, Floyd's jab was delivered with speed and spite, his right hand was laced with malice and fired with frightening rapidity.

In a fairly messy opening two rounds, both boxers visited the canvas, but more from pushes and tangled feet than knockdown punches. As the second opened, George Foreman, the former heavyweight king turned HBO commentator, said Floyd was 'one of the most natural fighters around.'

'You're looking good, baby,' said Floyd Sr in the corner before round three.

'So far, young Mayweather is simply beating Hernández to the punch,' assessed Merchant as Floyd adopted the aggressor role in the third.

Hernández had expressed concern beforehand that if the rounds were close in Las Vegas, they would be awarded to Las Vegas resident Mayweather. The rounds were not close.

Floyd even began walking him down in round four, leading with sharp left hooks while Hernández was either finding thin air or the challenger's guard with his punches. 'Hernández grew as tentative as a pre-teen boy at his first dance,' jibed *Boxing News*.

If Mayweather was the future of the sport, then after five rounds against Genaro Hernández the future was very bright. He started to go through the gears, pinning Hernández on the ropes and letting his hands go. When Hernández punched, he was countered and stung. Miguel Díaz, trainer of Mexican great Érik Morales but working as Floyd's cutman for the night, told Mayweather to be patient when Hernández backed up.

Jim Lampley observed how, in forty fights, no one had done to the old champion what Mayweather was in the process of doing. The right hand, either as a lead or uppercut, was starting to bust the veteran up. 'You've lost all five rounds,' Hernández was told in the corner. 'Yes I have,' he acknowledged.

It seemed the writing was on the wall, certainly after six rounds when Merchant dryly noted who the top super-featherweights were. Robert Garcia and Angel Manfredy appeared on the HBO infographics, as did Hernández. 'Gernaro Hernández is in the process of being replaced by Floyd Mayweather as a new force,' he said.

'He ain't got no more fight in him, he's just trying to survive,' said Floyd Sr.

Hernández looked sadly out from his corner before round seven. It appeared resignation had kicked in.

The fighter's heart caused him to chug forward in the next but the crowd oohed and aahed Floyd's fizzy punching. Lampley praised Hernández's tenacity, saying he was 'willing to stick his head into the middle of the meat grinder and try to find something doing.'

Hernández surged forwards but it appeared to be in desperation and only served to cause a head-on collision as neither backed down from a mid-round firefight. Mayweather was happy to outbox him, or outfight him. Hernández could not compete on either playing field and Floyd got the better of a furious exchange.

There was talk in the weary champion's corner about stopping the fight before the eighth session began. The gap in class was that great. Hernández, now little more than a thin, trudging heavybag, had been cut by the right eye, was massively behind on the scorecards and there was no sign of him finding a foothold in the fight.

Floyd commanded the centre of the ring. the champion's right eye had an ugly swelling beneath it and Genaro's brother and trainer, Rudy, said, 'That's it,' when his sibling returned to his corner.

'You want to quit?' referee Jay Nady asked the fighter.

'Whatever my brother says,' replied Genaro.

Rudy looked at Nady and crossed his arms signalling his decision to withdraw his beaten sibling from battle.

An emotional Floyd Mayweather wept.

'I done it, I done it,' he cried, as he dropped to his knees and sobbed. He was consoled by his mother, congratulated by Top Rank's Todd duBoef and embraced his uncle Jeff, who was also in tears. He had earned $150,000, his biggest purse to date.

The fighters were reunited in the centre of the ring and this time they hugged.

'He's quick, smart and experienced,' lamented the loser, who made a career high $600,000, more than he made in defeat to De La Hoya. 'I did my best but my reflexes aren't what they were. He defeated me the way he said he would. He was quicker than me and he was smart. Experience has nothing to do with it. He was too quick, I knew I was defeated, and he's going to be a great champion.'

Soberly, he added, 'I was defeated in a real bad way. I never thought I'd lose a fight the way I did tonight.'

'Mayweather is an exceptional talent, who could be on the way to becoming the game's next great fighter,' said *Boxing News*.

'What was a young upstart with only seventeen pro bouts to his name going to do against such an accomplished performer? Answer: Damned near anything he wanted,' wrote Nigel Collins in *The Ring*.

'We believe in our heart of hearts that Floyd Mayweather is the successor in a line that starts with Ray Robinson, goes to Muhammad Ali, then Sugar Ray Leonard . . . We believe that he epitomises that style of fighting,' said promoter Bob Arum.

Mayweather marked himself an eight of ten, but graciously gave Hernández the lion's share of the dais at the post-fight press conference. Hernández said Floyd was selling himself short with an eight. 'He's lying,' stated the deposed champion. 'I don't care how many fighters are out there, ain't nobody could beat me the way he did tonight. I'm a two-time world champion. I don't miss much [with punches] but I missed a lot today with Floyd. So I rate him as a ten.'

Plenty of others were impressed.

'I remember how fast he was,' said Steve Kim. 'He was a brilliant young talent. Incredible quickness and speed. Hernández had no defence for that quickness. He looked like one of the best young fighters we were going to see in that generation.'

Perhaps Hernández had been able to see that. He was a warrior, no question, but according to one journalist even he was not confident ahead of the bout. 'I will be lucky if I win,' he supposedly told one writer.

Brother and trainer Rudy also knew the older man was in for a hard night. 'When that fight was offered to us I thought that Top Rank was trying to take the belt away from my brother because I didn't see how my brother could beat Floyd,' he conceded. 'You know how that saying goes that styles make fights? I thought that Floyd's style would be too difficult for my brother to handle because my brother's more of a counterpuncher and so was Floyd, but seeing as my brother didn't want to make adjustments leading into the fight it was going to be even harder to win. It was a big step up for Floyd but there are some people who have something special about them, when you know they're better than average and I for one could imagine him being as good as he's been. It's a different era but Floyd Mayweather would have been competitive in any era. My brother says that had he been in his prime it would have been a tougher fight for Floyd. My brother said he would have beaten him, but that's why they're champions, right? That's why they get where they get, because they believe.'

And what of the trash-talk that manifested itself before Hernández-Mayweather? Well, Rudy blamed Floyd Sr, not the young fighter. 'Once a knucklehead always a knucklehead,' he snapped, before defending the younger Mayweather. 'No, listen, one thing about Floyd Jr is he's never talking smack, he's just talking normally. When he's saying he's great and he's better than everybody else and he will show his talent come fight night he does. I don't think there was ever a time where I felt he was being disrespectful or that he disrespected anyone. I honestly don't recall him doing that. His dad, on the other hand, was a knucklehead. There was no hard feelings between them [Genaro and Floyd Jr]. I kind of didn't like him because he beat us, but my brother once told me that Floyd Jr was a really nice guy and every time they would run in to each other he would say, "Hey, Hernández, what's up?" He would greet him with grace and he was a very humble person when they talked.'

Mayweather always remained grateful to Hernández for what amounted to his breakout win. 'That's where it started for me,' he said. 'Genaro Hernández didn't have to give me my opportunity. He didn't. I was number eight or number ten at super-featherweight. He didn't have to give me my opportunity.'

Proud Hernández never fought again. 'After the fight, a week later,' Rudy recalled, 'he felt like something was wrong so he went to the doctor. I get the phone call from the doctor because my brother was not answering his phone and the doctor was trying to get hold of him. They had found traces of blood on the brain, so I went with my brother to the doctor and it turned out he had a tiny spot of blood on the brain, kind of like when a pen hits the paper but only barely, like a blot of ink, and that was what was making my brother feel a little bit different. It affected his vision. So from that moment on my brother was pretty much ready to retire anyway. He thought about coming back but he didn't have it any more.'

More battles lay ahead for the Hernández family. In 2008, the two-time super-featherweight world champion was diagnosed with fourth-stage cancer of the head and neck. It was a rare strain, rhabdomyosarcoma, which attacks muscle fibres. He was treated and went into remission in 2009 but the cancer returned.

'I feel like an old man that somebody needs to take care of,' he said, a little more than ten years after facing Mayweather. 'I lost fifty pounds. I limp. I've got tumors on both shoulders, one on each thigh, one on my neck and three on my back. I haven't been able to produce any saliva for the last two years. I'm hanging in there.'

He fought on bravely. A few days before his death he stopped chemotherapy as his family tried to make him more comfortable. He passed away on 7 June 2011, aged just forty-five and was survived by Lilliana, his wife of twenty-one years, his son, Steven and daughter, Amanda.

Promoter Bob Arum had paid for his medical bills. Old foe Mayweather stepped in and paid for all of the funeral costs.

'He didn't help pay for it, he paid for it,' said Rudy. 'He paid for the whole thing. I got a call from his advisor Leonard Ellerbe who told me Floyd wanted to pay for the funeral and he said that after everything boxing had done for him it was the least he could do and we accepted the help. He didn't want no one to know and me being the nice guy that I am, I told everybody! I put it out there, told a few people from the media . . . Everybody always talks about the negative things about Floyd but rarely does anyone know about the positive things about him.

'I believe that Bob Arum and Floyd Mayweather have one thing in common. They know how to handle people coming at them with negative comments. You take them out of their comfort zone when they're being praised for doing something nice. That does not sit too well. They don't know how to react. When people talk bad about them they can defend themselves and even get a kick out of it. But if you tell them they're nice guys, it doesn't sit well with them because they don't know how to handle it too well. He didn't come to the funeral but he took care of the funeral and I think the most important part was he respected my brother and my brother respected him and when he did run into my brother he showed a lot of kindness that no one really knew. When my brother was going through cancer he saw my brother at one of the fights and he told him, "Here's my phone number. If there's anything I can do for you, just call. Money, doctors, whatever it is I will be there to help you." I think he had more than just respect, I think he had a lot of love for my brother.'

It was an undoubtedly classy move, and after defeating Hernández in 1998 Floyd became one of boxing's hot properties. Not only had he cleanly taken out the best fighter in his division, he was looking to face the best opponents. Fight fans were becoming excited about a seemingly special talent who wanted to showcase that ability against the top opponents. Even before the Hernández win there was talk that the victor would face off with Angel 'El Diablo' Manfredy, the 130lbs tearaway who'd built his reputation with a big eighth-round cuts win over the thunderous Arturo Gatti, whom he'd floored in round three.

In a letter to *World Boxing* under the headline 'Floyd doesn't avoid' one supporter wrote, 'Floyd Mayweather is the next superstar in boxing . . . Mayweather, regardless of whether he beats 'El Diablo,' said something interesting when he announced his fight with Manfredy, "To be the best you have to beat the best." That in itself tells me this kid is a winner. I hope he remains a champion for a long time, so other world champions could take a tip from him and go after the best.'

The mood around Mayweather was high and the Manfredy fight was announced for December. Yes, supremacy at 130lbs weighed on the outcome but so did 1998's Fighter of the Year honours. Mayweather had scored six wins, including the dissection of Hernández, while Manfredy had topped Gatti when the underdog and he had gone on to defeat John 'The Beast' Brown in a rough bout in the theatre of New York's historic Madison Square Garden as he chalked up three wins in the calendar year.

It was Mayweather's dismantling of Hernández that made him the pre-fight favourite. Looking ahead for *Boxing News*, then editor Claude Abrams wrote, 'Floyd proved in the seventh against the taller Hernández that he had the ability, when required, to stand toe to toe and blast back with accurate, stinging combinations. His edge in hand and foot speed, I believe, will prove decisive.'

Manfredy felt otherwise and even claimed he was going to become boxing's biggest attraction since Muhammad Ali, bold when you consider that his amateur background was minimal and he lost two and drew one of his first five bouts as a professional. He was stopped in two sessions by Charles McClellan on his pro debut in June 1993, but the tattoo-laden warrior from Gary, Indiana, who wore a devil's mask into the ring before his fights, had turned things around. He outscored McClellan over eight rounds a year later and, a couple of months before Floyd won his Olympic bronze, Manfredy travelled to South Africa where he defeated Mthobeli Mhlophe in five to win the lightly regarded

WBU title at super-feather. Bigger wins followed over Wilson Rodríguez – outpointed over twelve – and Jorge Páez, stopped in eight, before the massive win over hotshot Gatti.

'Mayweather fought a good fight against Hernández,' conceded the former street thug called Angel. 'I can't take nothing away from him. But let's face it: Genaro Hernández didn't come to fight. He gave the belt to Mayweather. It was almost like he was saying, "Here. Take it. I don't want it no more. It's your turn now." It's easy to look good against somebody who ain't fighting back. This is a fight where I can get the respect I've been wanting. I feel that Mayweather is not ready for this fight. It's not his time. His time is two years from now – that's when he will be peaking and becoming a star. Right now it's my time.'

Some questioned whether Mayweather had taken the contest too soon after the Hernández fight, just two months later. But he wasn't dragged through the trenches on that night and emerged unmarked.

The abrasive Mayweather Sr opined that the Manfredy bout would be 'a walk in the park.'

'He'd have a better chance of running through hell with gasoline in his drawers,' he said of Manfredy's hopes. 'There's no doubt in my mind he will get stopped, but he will get stopped quicker if he brings the fight on.'

While Floyd Sr talked the talk, some noted how his appearance back in the camp had a soothing affect on his son. 'He made him cut out all that showboating crap,' said Top Rank matchmaker Ron Katz.

'I'm trying to prove myself in the boxing world by not dodging nobody,' Manfredy said. 'They are calling out Gatti and saying he was all that. "Okay, put him against me and we will see how good he really is." And I proved to the world what I can do. Now everyone is saying, "Mayweather, Mayweather." Hey, put him in front of me and let's see what he can do.'

Both were contracted to HBO, but the loser supposedly had his contract on the line.

'I was at HBO at the time and I didn't really feel that way,' said Lou DiBella, a network chief there. 'I always thought Mayweather was the superior talent and that Manfredy had a lot of pizazz and he fitted in with that Arturo Gatti, Micky Ward, Ivan Robinson crew of fighters that were very evenly matched but, frankly, Mayweather was a notch above all of those guys in terms of talent. It was just a different level of talent.'

Floyd seemed certain he was the future.

'I'm smart,' he said. 'Years from now people will look down the line and say, Floyd Mayweather, he was an exciting fighter, a great champion who fought the best and he was willing to fight anybody.'

Manfredy was escorted to the ring by his friend, Kid Rock, the hip-hop/rock artist who rapped, shouted and sang through a mic on their arrival, rallying the crowd. Manfredy carried his devil's mask this time, choosing not to wear it. Whether that meant things were not right in his mind before is open to interpretation. He would later claim they were not, but then fighters who lose nearly all do. He also said that his hell-raiser days were behind him and when he strode into the ring he hurled the mask into the crowd, apparently signifying the elimination of the demons that had encircled his life. He'd earlier told reporters he had dreamed that God awarded him the championship belt and on the night wore a glittering silver jacket with 'Angel' written across the shoulders and a halo above the letters, with golden wings on the back.

Mayweather's entourage was growing and most wore shiny red and blue garments. His was a more old-school entrance, less fuss.

The crowd at Miccosukee Resort & Gaming, Miami, simmered as the fighters met in the centre of the ring for their final instructions. Moments later the disparity in speed of foot and fist was alarmingly clear. Manfredy kept coming. He exerted his will and some pressure. Into the second he had spots of success but Floyd turned southpaw and still boxed at his own pace. With thirty seconds left in the round, Mayweather caused Angel's legs to dip from a straight right. Sensing his moment, Mayweather leapt in and let his hands fly.

A left uppercut snapped Manfredy's head back and Mayweather piled in behind left hooks and right hands. Floyd pounded away, landing with some, missing with plenty while showing Angel no mercy. Manfredy could not get off the ropes. With thirteen seconds left in the round, referee Frank Santore called it off, pulling Mayweather from his prey.

Some wondered whether Manfredy should have taken a knee to activate an eight count and earn some respite. He didn't. He was in trouble and not fighting back. He was protecting himself but he was under an avalanche of pressure. 'I was throwing combinations and he wasn't throwing back,' Floyd said. 'It was a good stoppage.'

As Mayweather was held aloft to quiet cheers in front of the deflated crowd, Manfredy cried, 'Bullshit.' He sounded off, calling the end premature and then gave Santore a piece of his mind. The official spoke to HBO's Larry Merchant afterwards. He said he had stopped it because when he asked Manfredy to fight back he did not. 'I said, "Angel, you've got to fight back," and he didn't respond.'

'The fight shouldn't have been stopped,' raged an emotional Manfredy. 'That's bullshit. Hell, I wasn't hurt. That wasn't a championship fight. That's not boxing. That was politics. They knew what they wanted to do.'

'Some will contend the stoppage was premature,' read the *Boxing News* analysis. 'But this was a fight, not a beheading, and it seemed correct.'

Of course, Floyd was beginning to prove the sceptics wrong, while others were being shown to be right. Former *The Ring* magazine editor Nigel Collins was one of the latter.

'I think it was realised right from the get-go that he was a special talent,' he said. 'And he was nowhere near as defensively oriented in those days. I went to Miami to see his fight with Angel Manfredy and one of the reasons I went is they were both candidates for Fighter of the Year. They both had very good years. We used to give a belt for Fighter of the Year and the decision was made to give it to the winner and then write the story about who was the Fighter of the Year. I have vivid memories of that fight and maybe it was stopped prematurely but there was no doubt that even though Manfredy was a good fighter and he was on a hot streak, he wasn't in Floyd's league. Floyd came out, threw a lot of combinations and stopped him early.'

'Floyd's so good it's scary,' said then HBO Sports vice president Lou DiBella. 'There's plenty of guys at 130lbs, but after what I saw tonight, it's going to be hard to find competitive fights for Floyd. Manfredy was the roughest guy and he blew him away. I think that down the line you're looking at Mayweather and Shane Mosley in a matchup between two of the best pound-for-pound fighters in the world.'

Manfredy took home $750,000. He boxed on until 2004, scalping some good fighters – including Philadelphia's Ivan Robinson and lightweight prospect Julio Díaz, but nothing came close to topping the Gatti win. He called it a day with forty-three wins against eight losses and a draw and remained deluded about the Mayweather fight. Premature or not, he couldn't let it go.

'He didn't want nothing to do with me,' said Manfredy, hopeful of a rematch nearly two decades on. 'He was scared of me the whole time. He's still scared of me. He won't even talk to me. I'm calling him out. He was very fast. What impressed me is he was very fast but it was a premature stoppage. The fight wasn't over. It still bothers me today that the referee stepped in. I wouldn't have done anything differently. I never saw him again after that night. He's scared of me. He's scared of me. He's not going to achieve nothing else if he don't fight me [again]. He's waiting for me. He thinks it's going to be an easy fight for him. I should have fought the De La Hoyas, the Fernando Vargases, the Chávezs. It should have been me the whole time. Mayweather knows that. I put it on Facebook that he had a payday with me but he needs to pay me $15 million to fight him. $15 million dollars. I won't fight unless he pays me $15 million. He's a punk. I don't curse, but he's a punk. I got unfinished business with him.'

Floyd was now looking at some serious money. Within a year he'd gone from young prospect to a feature of many pound-for-pound lists, mythical rankings that signify the top ten fighters in the sport in any weight class.

'He made very, very good fighters, high-pressure fighters, very strong fighters look average,' said Lou DiBella. 'It was that period of time that I first began sensing how good he would be. He began making people look silly.'

Floyd Sr was confident his boy was ready to move up to lightweight to fight IBF champion Shane Mosley in a mouth-watering clash of skills and personalities. 'Little Floyd will whip Shane Mosley, I'll tell you that,' he said. 'The only thing is, there's no point for Little Floyd to move [up in weight], he makes weight too easily. If he was struggling to make weight, I'd be the first one to say we'd fight Shane Mosley. He's got too many skills for Shane Mosley. Little Floyd ate breakfast [before the Manfredy weigh-in] and still made weight easily. I'm not going to be stupid, just because my son has the skills he has, and is as good as he is, to push him [into the lightweight division] when he's not ready. Little Floyd is the best fighter out there without a doubt. In two years as a pro, how many kids do you know who have done what he's done? He's done whipped the top two guys in the division already. He won't bar [dodge] nobody at the weight, and whenever my son decides to move up, Shane Mosley and whoever had better start finding another division.'

After sizzling against Manfredy and Hernández, though, the bar had been set high and when Mayweather faced Carlos Rios on TNT in the second defence of his WBC title it ended with Rios being dragged through twelve rounds that failed to deliver excitement. 'Unexceptional, though totally superior,' wrote Claude Abrams for *Boxing News*. Beforehand, Mayweather said he was aiming to break the record of former heavyweight champion Joe Louis of twenty-five title defences.

Rios had challenged and lost in a bid for the WBC crown a division below at featherweight fourteen months earlier, stopped in six by the very good Luisito Espinosa, and in two fights before taking on Mayweather he was defeated by César Soto, a solid Mexican who would dethrone Espinosa later in 1999. Soto lost in his first defence to fast-rising English star Prince Naseem Hamed.

Mayweather was enjoying a homecoming of sorts, boxing in front of a crowd of 12,696 at the Van Andel Arena in Grand Rapids. Veteran trainer Gil Clancy, commentating, reckoned Floyd might have put pressure on himself trying to impress his hometown fans. Rios was far from starstruck. He tried to rough Mayweather up a couple of times in the early rounds but the man who for a living delivered ice in Argentina and held a dream of owning a farm back home was a step behind when it came to skill and speed. As Mayweather went to the ropes near the end of the second he stuck his tongue out at potential rival Shane Mosley, who was part of the TNT team of analysts. With fifteen seconds to go, Floyd landed some body shots which sparked a ferocious exchange to the bell. Rios obliged him every step of the way.

The third was quieter, Rios attacked more in the fourth but Floyd was doing enough to take each round. 'Floyd, Floyd!' chants sounded as he stung Rios in a corner during the sixth, but the challenger survived. He'd earned Floyd's respect as Mayweather's punch output dropped.

He was choosing to box smart rather than fight on Rios's terms. He rocked Rios with a right near the end of the eighth and tried to finish the job but could not. Mosley commented that the referee might consider stopping it given the cumulative punishment he was taking. He was hurt again in the ninth – to the head and he was being leathered to the body – although the Argentine was still firing back on occasion. There was a moment's respite for him in the tenth, when he was struck low and given time to regroup. He took more and more punishment through the eleventh, gulping down numerous right hands to the delight of Mayweather's electric crowd. Before the start of the final session, TNT interviewed Floyd's grandmother, Bernice. She slated Rios for excessive holding, which seemed unfair, and said that's why her grandson couldn't get off his punches the way he wanted to. 'He's still winning,' she said, stoically.

'He's playing with him now,' said Clancy as Mayweather switched southpaw in the final round, during which he spent most of the time on his toes.

At the bell, Mayweather circled the ring, saluting the crowd and then hugged Rios. Scores of 119-108, 120-110 and 120-109 confirmed his absolute superiority.

'Floyd's tough and he has heavy hands,' said Rios. 'Especially the left, and I think he'll be champion for a long time.'

'You can't knock everybody out, but I'm just happy with the win tonight,' said Floyd, who thanked his team, mother and the hometown fans. 'I'm glad it went twelve rounds so I could show people all over the world that Floyd Mayweather can go the distance,' the WBC champion continued. 'Carlos Rios was a very tough opponent. He came to fight and that's what I wanted tonight. I want to get twenty-six title defences, this was my second one so I've got twenty-four to go.'

Floyd Sr joked that his son allowed Rios to go the distance. The crowd laughed, then he gave the Argentine his props, saying how tough he was. 'We take our hat off to Rios,' he added. 'He's strong and gave his best.'

Promoter Arum was unperturbed by his man's failure to continue the dazzling streak that had accounted for Hernández and Manfredy. 'He's up there with Oscar, Érik Morales, Roy Jones and Shane Mosley as the best five fighters in the sport today,' he claimed.

Rios remained busy in the ring until 2004, mostly boxing in Argentina and often on the losing side. After ten years out, he returned to fight in 2014 and beat an unknown on a small show in Santa Fe.

Mayweather, on the other hand, felt he was on the fast track to greatness. 'I ran five miles a day with combat boots and I chopped trees,' he said of his training camp, 'I'll be around for another ten years.'

As 1999 progressed, *KO* magazine, sister publication to *The Ring*, pondered whether Mayweather or Shane Mosley was the future of boxing. 'Both are young. Both are undefeated. Both seem to have it all,' wrote the *Boston Herald*'s Ted Bodenrader, adding that Mayweather was 'boxing's Evel Knievel, a dare devil who throws caution to the wind in favour of performing jaw dropping stunts and crowd-pleasing spectacles.'

Floyd was 20-0 (15); Mosley was 32-0 (30). 'It took two years as a pro for Mayweather to establish what Mosley has yet to in six,' the author continued.

'It's not just the way this kid fights,' said Sugar Ray Leonard, who was interviewed for the piece and felt Mayweather was going to be the bigger star. 'He's got something else. What I see in Floyd is a natural charm that you just can't teach. He has a natural cockiness from the environment he's come up in. I'd call it confidence, but it's so reassuring it becomes cockiness. That's what I had.'

Bodenrader said Mayweather shared some of Leonard's attributes, saying, 'Millions loved him. Millions hated him. But everybody tuned in to him.' Then he summarised of the Mosley-Mayweather debate, 'One of them is sugar, the other one spice. One of them you love, the other you could hate. One of them can flash, the other can smash. And yes, one of them is the sport's future matinee idol, the sure-fire hit who's plotting to smash through all boundaries of boxing. The other one is named Shane Mosley.'

Oscar De La Hoya topped the bill at the Mandalay Bay in Las Vegas, the first boxing show in their new arena and in front of 11,528 fans, and once again Mayweather was summoned to fill a slot on the undercard. It was May 1999 and Mayweather was due to meet Goyo Vargas but he withdrew from the fight, citing flu. That was a story in itself. His promoter, America Presents, said Vargas had medical issues, while HBO's Lou DiBella had heard Vargas had skipped camp a fortnight earlier to get married and that even his trainers did not know where he was.

Whatever, at seventy-two hours' notice in stepped Uganda's Las Vegas-based Justin Juuko, who had been due to fight the following week against James Crayton but took the opportunity to feature on a big card against one of the sport's hottest names, for more money. Juuko was ranked number fourteen by the WBC, and his top fifteen rating made him eligible to box for the title.

'I had been ranked in the top ten for a couple of years and no one would fight me,' Juuko, who had sparred Floyd's uncles as a budding pro, reminisced in 2015. 'Genaro Hernández was due to fight me, I was supposed to be the WBC number one contender but he didn't want to take a chance fighting me. So Top Rank called me. Floyd was ranked number eight or nine and I was higher but HBO wanted Floyd to fight Hernández, he was American and he'd been on the [Olympic] team. It [Floyd fighting Hernández] was political. I was told I would maybe fight Floyd in two or three fights' time.'

Juuko was a pupil of Los Angeles trainer Freddie Roach, who was on assignment in Mexico with Johnny Tapia ahead of his bout with Paulie Ayala. However, Roach missed his morning flight to Vegas so Ruben Gomez, Juuko's cutman, became chief cornerman for the night. It is fair to say the odds were never in the underdog's favour.

He'd lost to the experienced Mexican Antonio Hernández inside eleven rounds in his previous fight but was well travelled and experienced. He'd boxed in Africa, the UK and in America. He'd outscored Tony Pep, too, though it was hard to make a case for him to beat Mayweather, no matter how much notice he had.

'They called me on the Wednesday, we fought on the Saturday,' Juuko went on. 'I had been waiting for a big fight so I had to take a chance.'

So it was that Mayweather's speed and variety kept Juuko guessing for several rounds. His accuracy kept the challenger honest and cautious, too. Boxing historian Bob Mee said it was a joy to watch. 'The champion would feint, turn a shoulder and deflect shots with his arms and gloves like an old-time pro.'

Some fans booed the meticulous nature of Mayweather's dominance and he did not endear himself to them when he stuck his chin out for Juuko to hit by way of a reaction to them.

After eight rounds of rather one-sided action, HBO's Jim Lampley said, 'Justin Juuko isn't gone yet.'

Eighty seconds of boxing later he was. Just when it seemed Juuko might see out the fight he came apart. Mayweather staggered him with a pair of looping rights and sent him crashing with a follow-up third, almost lifting him off his feet. Referee Mitch Halpern counted out Juuko as he attempted to rise.

'This guy's a star now, I'm telling you,' said George Foreman, working behind the mic with Lampley for HBO. 'Sign him up now, pay him now, pay for it later.'

An over-excited Bernice Mayweather gave her grandson a huge kiss on the lips as he celebrated. It was all too much for her, though. She promptly fainted and had to be given oxygen and helped from the ring.

Juuko congratulated Mayweather and then told an interviewer, 'I was okay. I was just a little tired. I didn't have any stamina. I only had two days' notice. I couldn't turn down the fight. Really, I needed to train for about six weeks. I've trained for two.'

'He's very tough,' said Mayweather. 'I took my time and listened to my corner. The right hand was landing all night.'

'Floyd was good,' Juuko said, in his Ugandan lilt. 'The thing is with him is he's very technical. He's a very technical fighter. His experience came from his amateur background and they taught him how to win. You know, how to score points, so that was a big plus for him. He doesn't throw many punches, he throws less punches but connects more. His opponents throw more punches but connect less. If he throws three punches, he's going to land two. He's an old-school fighter, he's one of the old school who can control the pace of a fight. Most fighters don't know the little things. They know punching, they know conditioning, but the little things make the difference. Floyd knows the little things. I was from the old school of boxing, too. I was trying to control the pace of the fight so my lack of conditioning [from the short notice] would not be revealed later [in the fight].

'I knew he was very technical and very fast but I knew he didn't have the punching power to hurt me. That's why I took the fight at short notice. I'm old school too, so I knew how to handle him but I wasn't [physically] prepared to fight at that level. I thought at least I would go the distance with him and put up a good fight, and I did that [the latter]. I believe I gave him one of his toughest fights. He was very good, he had very quick hands and he was a very fast thinker.

'If they had given me months to prepare, can you imagine what would have happened? Can you imagine if I had beaten Floyd? But I'm proud to say I fought him. Definitely, because me, I'm so proud. I came from a different place and different background and when they look at Justin Juuko they say, "Who did he fight?" I fought Floyd. I fought Diego Corrales. I fought Miguel Cotto. I fought the top fighters. They don't say, "Who did you win against?" They say, "Who did you fight?" And to fight those people you had to be at that level. You can't fight them if you're not at that level. To get in the ring with them you have to be at that level. Floyd started boxing when he was three or four years old. That's his life. That's all he knows. His father, his uncles, maybe even his mother, they were all fighters. One hundred per cent of his life has been boxing. I learned boxing when I was fourteen to get girls in school. When they thought I was tough, that was it! There's a saying, you can't know where you're going if you don't know where you have come from. That's Floyd's life; boxing. Look at it. Look at where he's come from.'

The Ring magazine raved about Mayweather's standing, saying he was an 'awesomely talented kid who was still getting better.' However, they claimed Mayweather, who made $400,000 for the Juuko bout, had a clear case of 'Oscar envy.' That was less than ten per cent of what De La Hoya made for stopping Oba Carr on the same bill.

'Although he believes his sizzling talent ought to entitle him to millions each time out,' wrote *The Ring*, 'Mayweather has yet to learn that the fans don't pay to see talent. They pay to see action.' He was now 21-0 (16).

Mosley was heading to light-welterweight so a seemingly

logical 1999 or 2000 blockbuster between the two now seemed highly unlikely. In fact, Mayweather had cleaned out a division and if he was to improve his high standing in the sport he would have to look elsewhere for the bigger challenges and the bigger money.

Certainly if he wanted to separate himself from De La Hoya undercards and De La Hoya's undercard money, the way forward was to headline his own show, but he would need a dance partner and the pickings at super-featherweight were now super slim. Azumah Nelson and Gabriel Ruelas had left the scene. Mosley was moving up. Naseem Hamed was only a featherweight and Arturo Gatti had begun his own climb in weight. The Americans felt Hamed would steer clear of Mayweather, who had said he was prepared to travel to the UK to face the Sheffield showman. There was still IBF champion Robert Garcia, and the WBA belt holder Takanori Hatakeyama in possible unification bouts, but they were not mega-money fights. Mayweather had said he was only interested in seven-figure paydays, he also threatened to take a year or two out after disposing of Juuko.

'All over the world fighters are working out every day, looking for championships,' wrote Ivan Goldman in *The Ring*. 'At least some of them ought to be suitable opponents for Mayweather, who, now all of twenty-two years old, must find new worlds to conquer.'

Juuko found new places to lose. Two fights later he was shelled in ten by that lanky puncher Diego Corrales, then he lost three of his next five, returned to Uganda for three possibly confidence-building wins before being brought in as the 'opponent' to lose to Manchester's Michael Gomez and California-based Mexican José Armando Santa Cruz. There were more wins, a few more losses but he ended his career with a 2013 defeat to Mayweather's 1996 Olympic teammate Zahir Raheem on a small show in Tacoma, Washington.

As far as Mayweather was concerned, while he was now demanding big money, the numerical consistency came from his punchstats. According to CompuBox, who recorded many of his fights, he was often throwing a similar number of punches to his opponents but frequently landing double, meaning he was accurate and efficient and defensively extremely difficult to catch.

Puerto Rico's Carlos Gerena allowed CompuBox to illustrate an increasingly samey set of statistics. By the time Richard Steele stepped in to save him from Mayweather's flashing fists Floyd had landed 220 of 346 punches while Gerena had scored with just ninety-nine of 308. Floyd's strike rate was sixty-four per cent, exactly double Gerena's thirty-two per cent.

It was 11 September 1999, and Gerena had been asked to fill the void when Gregorio Vargas withdrew against Mayweather earlier in the year. Juuko had stepped in and Vargas was now ringside for the Gerena fight to see what he would be up against if he and Mayweather were to ever tangle. Gerena had been training for a ten-rounder and so said he had been underprepared to face Floyd earlier in the year. He could have had a lifetime to get ready, it would never have been enough.

Gerena, who had lost on points to Genaro Hernández in a previous world title bid and who held a win over tough future lightweight champion Jesús Chávez, was down twice in round one.

It was the week before the Oscar De La Hoya-Félix Trinidad megafight. Roy Jones, Mike Tyson and other luminaries were ringside, as Floyd set about trying to get the fight week media talking about him rather than De La Hoya and the others.

First, Gerena was staggered by a right uppercut into his side before a roundhouse right clubbed him to the deck. With only seconds left in the round Mayweather, brilliantly flashy and incredibly poised, this time broke through with a left and Gerena, legs still not properly beneath him, was promptly on all fours. Referee Richard Steele picked up the count again and as the beleaguered Bayamon boxer walked in to seemingly accept his fate the bell sounded.

He struggled in round two as well, though he tightened his defence in the third as Mayweather continued to land eye-catching blows.

'Listen to what I'm telling you,' shouted Mayweather Sr after round three. 'If you do what I'm telling you it will be over.'

That was not up for debate and Larry Merchant, on comms for HBO, wondered how much pressure that was putting on Floyd.

'With his high estimations of his son, he makes Richard Williams, the father of the brilliant [Venus and Serena] Williams sisters seem like a wimp,' joked Merchant.

Mayweather banged away at Gerena in the next session, the gutsy Puerto Rican even imploring him to up his efforts by waving him in. Floyd picked his shots, scored and then moved off. His speed, once again, was simply too great for the man opposite him. Mayweather hacked away with a couple of rights near the end of the fourth; Gerena was hurt though pretended he wasn't. Mayweather took his eye off the ball and nodded, winked and smiled at Roy Jones in the crowd.

A tremendous right hand clattered off Gerena's head in the sixth, causing the crowd to gasp and analysts to salute his courage as he ploughed doggedly forwards. It was becoming batting practice for Mayweather, battering the challenger who seemed to be equally as content to take punishment as Mayweather was to dish it out and even in the seventh he stopped, held his hands out and in his broken English shouted, 'No punch!' at Mayweather. It would be his final act of defiance as by the time he returned to his corner Dr Flip Homansky had decided Gerena was in no way going to win and that he needed to be spared from being too macho for his own good.

Gerena had stood up to so much there were some who questioned whether Floyd's power matched his finesse. One writer commented that Mayweather's punches had been too fast to record. Regardless of that, Arum was chuffed once again. 'This will be the greatest boxer in the world,' he said. 'He may not be now, but will be in years to come. He'll become a legend.'

'Mayweather's the best, he was beautiful out there,' said the vanquished Gerena.

'He really surprised me when he got up from that second knockdown,' said Floyd. 'That was a good shot. He threw me out of my game plan. Remember, I've only been a pro for two and a half years.'

Arum once again beat the drum for Mayweather's future greatness. 'This young man will be,' he said, 'without any question, the premier boxer in the world. He may not be there now, but in the next couple of years he will be recognised as far and away the best pound for pound and I see him going into the pantheon of legends in the sport of boxing.'

As impressive as Mayweather might have been, there was only a small crowd of 2,072 back at the Mandalay Bay to see him. The De La Hoya-Trinidad superbout loomed large.

Boxing News said that the attendance 'shows that while Mayweather is fast becoming one of the best fighters in the world at any weight, he has some way to go before matching promotional stablemate Oscar De La Hoya as an attraction.'

Gerena's bravery would earn as many column inches as Floyd's skills but if Mayweather could nail down a fight with IBF champion Robert Garcia or Diego Corrales, who were due to meet a few weeks later, then he would be back in the news. He ruled out a fight with the smaller Hamed, saying, 'I can't make 126,' though he left the door open adding 'Anything is possible, but I could maybe fight Naseem at 128.'

Corrales annihilated Garcia in seven rounds, announcing

himself as a major player at super-feather, fixing his sights on Mayweather and knocking on the door of Mayweather's number-one spot.

Some felt Brazilian puncher and WBO ruler Acelino Freitas and Mongolia's WBA champ Lavka Sim were more likely targets. 'My goal is to unify the title,' said Mayweather. 'I love boxing. I do the right things. I couldn't be the champion without the people who are around me. It's been a hard but short road. The fighting's the easy part. Some days I don't want to run, but I know I want to keep winning and that's what drives me on.'

FIVE

SLAVE

A NEW MILLENNIUM dawned and Floyd Mayweather thought he was one of the biggest names in sport. HBO was blatantly keen to hold on to his young talent and offered him a $12-million-plus deal for six fights.

'That's a slave contract,' barked the youngster. 'Floyd Mayweather is a superstar,' he raged, fuming that he had not been offered a similar $48-million pact to the one that showman Naseem Hamed had earned.

Floyd later said that quote had been taken out of context, and that the full statement was 'That's a slave contract, compared to what Naseem Hamed is making.'

Promoter Lou DiBella, who was then a big-hitting executive at HBO, recalled some of the negotiations.

'At that point in time, honestly, Prince Naseem Hamed was a much bigger star,' he said. 'I was the one who offered Floyd the contract and I didn't appreciate the comment and I remember saying to Floyd Mayweather at the time, "We could walk down Times Square right now and most people aren't going to know who you are." Well guess what, he changed that, because he couldn't walk down Times Square now without getting mobbed and he's one of very few boxers in the United States in recent history that literally can't walk down the street without being recognised. That wasn't the case in 1999 but he's changed that. And that has nothing to do with whether he's lived the perfect life or he's the perfect guy or he's the most admirable guy or whatever, but he's certainly promoted and marketed himself into a superstar and his ability has differentiated him from everybody else. Anyone who thinks this is not the best pound-for-pound fighter in the world today is simply not paying attention. He absolutely is the best right now, but back then – in my mind – he was a little bit cocky with not enough reason yet. The truth of the matter is, you know what, maybe that comes with the territory when you're striving for greatness, maybe that's part of what got him to where he is. I think he believed more in his starpower than the people promoting him did at that time. He didn't have the Latino market behind him that De La Hoya, who at the time was the superstar, had. He wasn't Latin American; he was African American. But he believed more in his own starpower than anybody else and that, by the way, included me. Whatever you want to say, he got to that pinnacle, in boxing and economically. The man made over $200 million in one night, he's the highest-paid athlete in the world and by far the highest-paid athlete in the United States. This is despite any misgivings people have about him, despite the fact that he is a boxer and boxing is obviously not the biggest or most popular sport in the United States, but he achieved his superstar stature and a lot of it is through his own hard work and self-promotion.'

Whether or not he would have beaten Naseem Hamed had their sometime bout been discussed we won't know. With hindsight it might not have almost happened, but it was still close enough for the Las Vegas Hilton to open up a betting line, which saw them price Floyd as a 3/1 favourite. Of course, Floyd was never backwards in coming forwards and felt he was too big for the Englishman. 'I've got so many different moves I can use,' he said. 'I'm calling out Naseem Hamed. I'll take care of him. Five-foot-three, there ain't no way. Too short. Too wild. I'll see all that coming.'

He spoke to Sky Sports' reporter Adam Smith and was typically bullish. 'I remember interviewing him very early on and we talked about Naz,' Smith recollected years later as the head of Sky Sports Boxing. 'He told me that he would embarrass and destroy our "Prince".'

Now, though, Uncle Jeff was gone from the team. Floyd Sr, *Ring* magazine's Manager of the Year for the work he had done with his son in 1998, had been dumped as manager, though he was being retained as a trainer.

Their relationship, however, was disintegrating. In June 1999 it was reported that the young fighter had thrown out his father from his home in the Summerlin district of Las Vegas. A twenty-four hour eviction notice had been left on the door of the property. Then he apparently reclaimed a Ford Astro van his dad had been driving.

Holding the managerial reins now was rap impresario and fight-manager wannabe James Prince. He had started to pull up trees in boxing and was able to upset the establishment by signing a bevy of talented stars, giving him leverage across the TV networks. 'He has already blown Floyd's head way out of shape with his own record deal and a slew of bellowing flunkies,' said *Boxing News*. Then, as if it was the worst thing he could have done, Mayweather was condemned in the same piece for sporting a £300,000 watch, 'as if he's the Sultan of Brunei.'

Prince had helped Mayweather realise an ambition, setting up his own record label, called Philthy Rich Records.

'I think it turned people against him,' said Larry Merchant, when recalling the 'slave wages' comment. 'Whether he was deliberately or in a calculated way trying to get attention, that seemed to be the start of his campaign to create an atmosphere around him that would be good for him by shining a spotlight on him even if it was not particularly popular. And you know, he was booed in his hometown. There was also at that same time the issue with his father, in which he threw his father out of the house he had bought him and they were having problems and he brought in the guy from Houston, James Prince, who had never been in boxing. And he was paying him more than he had paid his father. In one sense it showed how ambitious and shrewd he was, that he saw a guy like Prince and how important music was in popular culture, the hip-hop world, and he wanted to be connected through this guy. The music world, like the boxing world, has a dark side and there have been many people from the music world who have jumped in to the boxing world and that's an interesting story in itself, when you look at Al Haymon, Shelley Finkel and others. And that was part of being savvy about whatever was going on and marketing himself in any way that he could. I think that was the low point.'

Prince was a big fish in a big pond. From Houston, the mogul behind Rap-A-Lot Records was a hip-hop heavy hitter. One writer called him 'Houston's OG [Original Gangster]' and 'arguably the most-feared figure in the history of Southern hip-hop.' The rumours that circulate Prince go far and wide, from his ability to make sure a rapper is safe in a rough section of Chicago to donating $200,000 to Al Gore's failed presidential campaign. It is fair to say his reputation preceded him.

Prince said Mayweather rejected the HBO offer before he was formally on board, though he bore the brunt of the criticism as the man managing Mayweather and his image. He did try to take credit for Mayweather's purse for his next fight, $750,000, potentially going over the $1 million mark, though Bob Arum disputed it was that much.

In the end, the finer details were not made public and it was left to HBO to state that they did not publicise their deals, with head of sports Seth Abraham saying their relationship with Prince was 'peaceful' and that Mayweather Jr 'holds him [Prince] in high regard.' He said that tension between a promoter [Arum] and manager [Prince] was a concern.

Mayweather's relationship with Prince appeared to be the catalyst for discord between Mayweather and HBO, Mayweather Jr and Sr, and Mayweather and his promoter Bob Arum.

The latter was certainly now strained.

'I would like to see a truce between Floyd and Top Rank,' said Abraham. 'Floyd is definitely in our plans for the future. I like to call him one of our jumbo jets, with Oscar, Naseem Hamed, Shane Mosley, Lennox Lewis: I would put Floyd in that group.'

'It wasn't like the waters were muddied,' DiBella added. 'It was [that] James Prince was involved and Arum was still involved.'

Concern was expressed that the external voices Mayweather heard were beginning to dominate. Prince was becoming a major player and Floyd was listening. The rapper had also signed WBA welterweight champion James Page and was thought to be making moves on former heavyweight champion Mike Tyson, who still had sway with a lot of young fighters coming through, particularly those into the same rap culture Tyson had once been immersed in. There was speculation Mosley and Zab Judah could join Mayweather in the growing stable. Both Page and Floyd had moved to Houston to train at Prince's facility, a 15,300-square-foot building called the Prince Complex.

The mogul was soon being featured in the boxing magazines as a 'mystery man, intruder and maverick.' He claimed to be a fight fan who wanted to 'live out a dream' and who was 'on a mission to bring dignity to the sport.'

In an in-depth interview with *The Ring* magazine, his first with the boxing media, he said, 'I don't know if I see myself as a threat to the people who run boxing, but I think they see me as a threat. I'm actually a threat to those who try to mistreat my fighters.'

He had first met Mayweather in 1996 and could now sense hostilities from his competitors. He knew some promoters and managers would not want to work with him. He and Floyd met again in 1999 through Tyson, at the Las Vegas Golden Gloves Gym.

He also refused to be blamed for the friction that had surfaced between Floyd and his father. Floyd Sr argued that Prince was already having a detrimental effect on his son's career. 'Ever since this man [Prince] came into play, things have gone downhill. The rappers are [Floyd's] crew now.'

Prince countered, 'I don't think, technically, they ever broke apart. In fact, I highly recommend Floyd and his father stay together. Let's get something straight: of all the bad things his father said about me, I never said a bad thing about his father. The only thing I ask is I just wish his father would respect my business position. In fact, he doesn't have to. I'm going to earn my respect from Floyd [Sr].'

Sr said, 'This situation between me and Prince, whose real last name is Smith, is incredible. Floyd meets him one night and two weeks later he signs a contract to manage my son. When Floyd has turned on his family the way he has, something is seriously wrong with this picture. James Prince has done nothing for Floyd but cause him to lose three or four million in purses, plus the respect of his family, friends and people around the world. Prince knows absolutely nothing about boxing – but he's obviously telling Floyd everything he wants to hear.'

Even Prince condemned Floyd Jr's choice of the word 'slave' when discussing the HBO contract. 'Floyd did absolutely the right thing when he made the decision to take charge of his business matters,' Prince said. 'That showed a lot of intelligence, foresight and courage on his part that he would take that step. But having said that, it's unfortunate that slave word came out. It wasn't a slave contract. If it had been up to me, I wouldn't have gone on record as saying that. And even though what's said is said, I think we can work out the situation with the people at HBO and have a perfectly fine working relationship.'

Prince denied that he was a wedge between the family and alleged that some of the boxing press were on Bob Arum's payroll, thus publicly taking the veteran promoter's side in the dispute.

It was revealed, though, that Floyd Sr had taken a ten per cent managerial cut while Prince was now being paid twenty per cent.

A May meeting to bring peace to the situation was later called a 'gross mistake by all parties.' Arum, his step-son and Top Rank vice president Todd duBoef, Mayweathers Sr and Jr and Prince met at the Strip's Barbary Coast Hotel and Casino but it disintegrated with the Mayweathers calling one another disrespectful and Mayweather Sr 'resigning'.

'I can't work for somebody who has such little respect as my son does. He isn't showing respect to anyone,' charged Sr.

The younger Floyd said the family fallout had been blown out of proportion. 'My daddy is the best man in the world, but he's never been my manager. I want to clear that up right now. My daddy's always got his ten per cent trainer's fee. I'm not undefeated and world champion for nothing. I'm smart inside and outside the ring.'

Floyd felt Arum controlled his father and that was why he, Prince and Sr could not sit down and talk it out. 'What I'm telling the world is that I'm happier,' he said. 'My father still thinks I'm a child; I have a son of my own. I'm happier now and I have more control over everything.'

Prince felt he was ready to shake up boxing's old guard. 'You have to realise,' he said, 'all of these guys have been controlling the industry for thirty years. All of them could hate me. I'm looking forward to the challenge. It's 2000, it's time for new players to take over. It's my time now.'

Ultimately, young Mayweather was frozen out of the picture due to his comments and attitude and sulked for six months before pleading to get back on the network. The problem was that while he was infinitely skilled, he couldn't draw flies to a carcass.

'With each succeeding victory,' wrote Las Vegas fight correspondent Jack Welsh for *Boxing Monthly*, 'the Grand Rapids, Michigan native's ego was soaring out of control, triggering unreasonable demands for mega-purses from Top Rank promoter Bob Arum who had shown him every consideration as a potential superstar . . . The irony of it all is Mayweather has made demands on Top Rank like he's the second coming of Oscar De La Hoya in ring talent and purses, all this from a super egoist who hasn't excited box offices, drawing only a combined 5,000 paid spectators to his last two fights.'

According to his father, his son had become 'too big too fast and the money had gone to his head. He's going to have problems ahead.'

There was a grey area between where Floyd was as a commercial entity, where he was a fighter and where he thought he was. In a *KO* magazine feature, Kevin Iole's article was headlined, 'Will Mayweather trip over his own ego? Even his own people are questioning him.'

Iole was asking Mayweather and Prince, who flanked him in a Vegas hotel room, how he would become an attraction. The Gerena fight had drawn a gate of $145,140 or, as Iole pointed out, 'roughly the same amount of money generated by the sales of a hundred tickets for an average De La Hoya fight in Nevada.'

Mayweather contended that he *was* becoming a draw, despite the numbers indicating otherwise. He said that, as a guest at the recent Mike Tyson-Orlin Norris bout, security guards had to protect him from the crowd around him.

By now, Mayweather had returned to the ring in training only and according to reports was schooled in a Las Vegas gym for six rounds by IBF lightweight champion Paul Spadafora.

Some insisted Spadafora won all six rounds, although Arum said not to read much into it as Mayweather had been inactive while the Pittsburgh man was approaching the end of camp to defend his crown. Top Rank's matchmaker Bruce Trampler said at the time that the gym scrap might have psychologically scarred Mayweather.

'I think we will have to wait and see what kind of impact it has,' Trampler said. 'But I know that some guys bounce right back and other guys, well, they maybe realise they're mere mortals and they're never what they were before. It could work both ways for him. Floyd's persona is ego-driven, and he's got the humiliation of the Spadafora workout where he got his ass kicked in front of his peers. All of his present problems stem from an inflated ego and sense of self-worth.'

When Floyd faced Gregario 'Goyo' Vargas for $750,000 in the last fight of his HBO deal in March 2000, the crowd at the MGM Grand in Las Vegas was again sparse. Only 5,121 were on hand – and 1,500 of those were complimentary – as they saw Mayweather deck Vargas with a sixth-round body shot before taking a clear verdict 119-108 (twice) and 118-109. Vargas, a former WBC champion at featherweight, was the man he was supposed to fight the previous May, when Justin Juuko was hired at short notice.

The day before the contest, at the rules meeting, Floyd Sr had been asked what colour trunks his son was going to wear, something ordinarily he would have known. He could not answer. 'That's how big the rift is between them outside of the ring and the gym,' remarked Larry Merchant as Mayweather made his entrance, flanked by Prince with Floyd Sr trailing.

The spectre of a possible showdown with Corrales, who was watching ringside after a third-round demolition of Derrick Gainer on the undercard, loomed as Floyd met Vargas in centre ring and started blazing away with his left hook and jab.

By round four, and with Vargas cut up on his scalp, a pattern had emerged. Floyd was too fast and too good. He even paused between punches to say 'Hi, Emanuel' to HBO analyst and Hall of Fame trainer Emanuel Steward, who was sitting ringside.

'He's hit him with everything but the stool,' said HBO's unofficial scorer Harold Lederman, who was lapping up Mayweather's performance. The dry Merchant said, 'I'm glad someone is enjoying this.'

Vargas tried to maraud forwards in the sixth, but the harder he fought, the better Mayweather was. The challenger tried to swarm Mayweather in the corner, particularly targeting the body. The crowd rallied and roared and then, as if to prove a point, Mayweather nailed him downstairs with a left hand and Vargas dropped to his knees.

Vargas smiled and shrugged in his corner. He was okay, but it must have dawned on him that his best was not going to be enough.

During the eighth, the HBO team began to ponder how a Mayweather-Corrales fight might go but in the ninth the fighters went toe to toe. 'This might be the most excitement we've seen in a Floyd Mayweather fight,' said Merchant. Mayweather, again concerned with what HBO thought of him, leaned over the ropes to tell Jim Lampley that he was making it more exciting, not Vargas. In the tenth, Lampley noted how Mayweather switched southpaw for the second time in the fight. 'Third time,' shouted Mayweather, taking his eyes off Vargas for a moment. 'Thanks for the correction,' shouted Lampley into the ring. Steward chuckled. He had seen a lot in his lifetime in boxing. He probably had never seen that before.

Going into the eleventh, Vargas's team told him he had won the last two rounds. Floyd Sr asked his boy for a big three minutes. Instead, Jr mostly circled the ring, stayed away from hostilities and was booed. The crowd had hoped for the type of action they had seen in round nine and ten, but Floyd had apparently shut up shop. He grimaced in the corner, perhaps indicating pain in his right hand as his father whispered quietly in his ear.

'I'll try to do it for you, Dad,' said Floyd Jr.

Regardless of what he was trying to do, Floyd largely moved and took potshots with his left hand, cruising through the final session and again boos rained down before the wide verdict was rendered in his favour.

And after he failed to dazzle, his old HBO adversary Merchant sneered, 'He doesn't look like any $12-million fighter to me.'

'On this display,' barked *Boxing News*, 'it was hard to believe Floyd was even the best super-featherweight on the show, what with Diego Corrales stopping Derrick Gainer.' They said Mayweather was not improving. 'Admittedly Floyd is only twenty-three, but when you run with your chin high, zip a jab at a time and are always bailing out, how can people possibly compare him with Sugar Ray Leonard?'

The post-fight Vargas report concluded with, 'Mayweather tried to put on a show, firing fast left hooks and uppercuts, but as the session wound down, amid more boos, it was questionable whether Mayweather would ever be box office.'

'At twenty-three,' considered the *Los Angeles Times*, 'Floyd Mayweather Jr has the talent to be a dominant fighter and the showmanship to be a crowd pleaser. But he's not as good as he thinks he is . . . Certainly not good enough to have turned down a six-fight, $12.75-million contract offer from HBO which did not include a bonus for pay-per-view revenue.'

'I went into the fight with both my [right] hand and wrist hurting,' Mayweather – sporting a lump beneath his left eye – countered, also citing inactivity for his drab showing. 'But I don't want to make excuses. I moved around more than usual because I didn't want to get hit. I was fighting with one hand. I need to go home and work on some defence with my father, talk about things with him and get ready for the next fight. I'm looking forward to fighting Diego Corrales in the future, you know. We can build that fight up and unify the titles.'

Mayweather Sr had his arm around his son during his in-the-ring post-fight interview.

'Everything that happened out of the ring was hearsay,' said Jr. 'I love my father and I will always love my father and I always want my dad to be my trainer and support me one hundred per cent. I love my father.'

Mayweather Sr said his son was hit a little bit more than they anticipated and that, perhaps in a shot at the new team, the sparring had not been right.

'This is my son and I love him,' he said. 'My blood runs through his veins. To me he's young, he's making mistakes but hey, we all make mistakes. He's going to make them, sometimes we pay more than the other guy. I hope and pray that everything will work out for him. This is my son and I love him and we will be together forever.'

Vargas reckoned Floyd showed a lack of courage.

'The long layoff affected me,' Mayweather went on. 'It affected my defence. I was hit too much. I want to fight in a month or a month and a half. Six months is too much.'

The Vargas fight drew a below average TV rating on HBO's *Boxing After Dark*. Floyd blamed the low attendance on the promoter. 'I sure can't fill seats when I'm not promoted, and I'm not promoted,' he alleged. 'People know me because of the show I put on. All the promotion I get comes from HBO. If Arum says I can't fill seats, then let me go. I can sit out my contract with Arum. I don't have to fight for two years, to be honest. I'm not desperate for money.'

Arum spoke in depth with *KO* magazine to put his side forwards. 'Floyd has a lot of friends that he listens to, who tell him he's the best fighter in the world and, therefore, should be getting the same money as Roy Jones and Oscar De La Hoya. They're giving him bad advice, and that interferes with our efforts to market him . . . If Floyd's going to listen to his little friends and not doing what he's supposed to do, it's going to prevent us from really marketing him the way he should be marketed.'

In the same interview, he said that Floyd had the potential to join Ray Robinson, Muhammad Ali and Ray Leonard as a legend. 'Floyd can be part of that group,' he said. 'But it's up to Floyd; he has to cooperate in the marketing effort. Oscar has been extremely popular because he's been able to draw on the Hispanics and we really believe that Floyd can be as popular as Oscar.'

Industry insiders wondered whether Arum actually believed the hype he talked about Floyd, or if the old promoter was just using sound bites to blow the Mayweather trumpet.

'To Arum he wasn't De La Hoya,' said one. 'Arum, I don't think, believed that an African American fighter who was so technical, not a huge puncher, despite how good Floyd was, I don't think Arum ever envisioned this level of success even though Arum was his promoter.'

Floyd's career was becoming about business and not the sport he'd taken part in as a child, as an amateur or even as a novice pro.

Arum was looking for a unification fight with the destructive Corrales for Mayweather, but Floyd wanted the right fight and the right deal for the right fight.

The boxing media was beginning to anticipate that clash, too. *World Boxing* felt Mayweather would win a tight decision, but speculated both might hit the canvas if they ever met.

They wondered if, at twenty-three, Mayweather was already on the slide after peaking against Hernández and Manfredy.

Regardless, the fight was one of the hottest matches in boxing.

'Bob is getting under my skin with this Diego Corrales stuff,' said Mayweather. 'I'm not letting Bob Arum control me no more and that bothers Bob. They want to control my friends and they control my father. I also had suspicions that people close to me may have been stealing. That's why they don't work with me anymore. Bob Arum wants that fight with me and Corrales. That puts money in Bob Arum's pockets, so for that reason I don't know if I want that fight. Bob Arum doesn't want me to have any money, because he's giving it all to De La Hoya. All I ask is he let me go. I'm not happy with Bob right now. I think he's doing everything against me.'

Meanwhile, the explosive Corrales had been carving his own trail through the super-featherweights in 2000. He'd stopped Justin Juuko in ten, then blitzed poor Angel Manfredy in three. Floyd Mayweather's inactivity and contractual disputes cost him the top spot in his division, with many awarding it to Corrales. That included *The Ring* magazine.

'Floyd Mayweather is all of twenty-three years old,' said *The Ring*, 'and he's already slipping. Maybe not in terms of skill or athleticism or potential to dominate the sport. But in terms of status, it hasn't been looking so pretty for 'Pretty Boy' of late. Ranked as high as number two, pound for pound by *The Ring* several months ago, Mayweather has dipped to number seven, simply by doing nothing. He's not even ranked in his weight class anymore.'

'I just need a couple of tune-up fights and get ready for Diego,' Mayweather said. 'I just need a lot of boxing to get me sharp.'

Even then, though, there were barriers to the match happening, not least Floyd's inactivity. Corrales had legal complications. He had been accused of severely beating his pregnant wife in July and a hearing had been set for October. His manager, Barrett Silver, said, 'We're not making light of it. It's a serious situation. But you must go forward with your life and that means making plans for Chico's boxing future. We will make every effort to make sure this fight with Floyd happens.'

HBO had withdrawn that big $12-million offer, with DiBella saying it made no sense to keep it on the table following Floyd's controversial statement.

But Floyd had leverage. He knew people wanted to see him fight Corrales. He also probably knew people would pay good money to see the gangly but explosive puncher knock him into next week, or at least bring him back down to earth with a bump. Instead, he signed a three-fight deal worth $2.25-million, which kicked off on an HBO show called *KO Nation*, a series aimed at younger fight fans. Floyd was going to fight Emanuel Burton [now known as Emanuel Augustus], a tricky, defensive and occasionally eccentric attacking-minded fighter. They were due to fight in Detroit's Cobo Hall [now known as Cobo Centre] eight months after the Vargas fight, with Mayweather making $250,000. *KO* magazine said Mayweather was 'on a salvage mission, attempting to regenerate interest in his stagnating career.'

'Floyd is taking a step back for a chance to take two forward,' said HBO's new boxing chief Kery Davis, who seemed to appreciate that Floyd was backing himself to be worth more than the $12-million-plus he'd rejected.

'The comment that was made, that's in the past,' Mayweather said. 'Everything is cool between me and HBO.'

'After this fight, I'm looking to fight again real soon,' Floyd added, ahead of what amounted to a comeback fight at the age of just twenty-three. 'I'm just glad to be fighting again. I just want to stay busy. I feel it's like this, I turned off the money and I'm the villain. This guy Diego Corrales allegedly cracks his wife in the ribs and she's pregnant and I'm the bad guy. The only thing I'm looking forward to doing is winning. Either people are going to see me win, or they're going to come out just to see me lose. The main thing is that they're paying to see me. In those seven months, I was talked about a lot, I know. People keep saying things between me and my father. That's all in the past. I don't like stories about myself. I give people quick and short answers, and somehow, someway they get twisted. My focus now is on fighting, and staying positive.'

Boxing writer Dan Rafael, then working for *USA Today*, said that Mayweather had risen quickly, facing stiff competition regularly, but admitted he was 'sort of forgotten' while Corrales, Freitas and Cuba's Joel Casamayor commanded more airtime in his absence.

Unsurprisingly, Floyd Sr had been axed from the entire team ahead of the Burton camp. In came his brother, Roger, to guide his nephew in and outside the ropes making the rift between the two Floyds the central piece of an increasingly ugly jigsaw.

International Boxing Hall of Famer and *Boxing Monthly* writer Graham Houston analysed the break up. 'The boxing trade has grown cool towards the fighter, who is widely perceived as having been disloyal to his father and whose attitude in general is thought to show an unattractive arrogance.'

Another writer said, 'Mayweather is running out of friends faster than a high school gossip queen.'

In an article in *World Boxing*, Arum reckoned that Floyd was 'impossible to deal with' and that 'he obviously doesn't have many friends among boxing fans, since his fights are selling like Confederate flags in Harlem.'

Sr could not stand Prince, nor did he understand his role in his son's career. He thought Lil Floyd was making a costly error and cited his own drug-dealing rap. 'I made enough mistakes for both of us,' he would say.

'James Prince is a terrible negative in Floyd's stalled career,' snapped Sr. 'Among friends, he is the only one who thinks the guy is a smart manager. I honestly think HBO taking that big contract away from my son at this present time is doing him a favour because he is turning into a much bigger monster than he already is.'

Only around seven hundred went to watch him headline against Burton at the Cobo Hall. The fighters had agreed to meet over the weight so Floyd's world title was not on the line.

'My first Mayweather fight was the one with Emanuel Augustus, who at the time was Emanuel Burton,' remembered ESPN's boxing writer Dan Rafael, who was reporting for *USA Today* at the time.

'He was given a slate of opponents to fight that October on *KO Nation* and Emanuel Augustus was the guy with by far the worst record, and they picked him and he gave Mayweather absolute hell.

'It was a good fight and it was funny because Augustus had this terrible record and the notion was that Floyd had put to bed some rough business times with HBO and he was coming back on their smaller programme which at the time was an afternoon show called *KO Nation*, which didn't pay as much money as the primetime shows. So for the network it was a big deal to get Mayweather, who was a big name at the time and a pretty big star relative to the fighters who had been appearing on that series. Part of the deal was [to] get him back in the ring on that programme and then get him back in the ring very quickly afterwards. So he fought Augustus in October, then he was going to fight Corrales in January.

'He has said over the years on a number of occasions, and I've heard him say it on conference calls, that Emanuel Augustus was his toughest fight and he gave him a tough fight,' said Rafael. 'Floyd was coming off, at that time, the longest layoff of his career of about eight months. For a younger guy he had not been out that long and Floyd broke him down and stopped him but it was a hard fight.'

There was two-way action throughout. Mayweather would strike with eye-catching blows; Burton would taunt him and then land his own shots. Floyd's punches were crisp, and he fired them more frequently, causing Burton to bleed from the mouth and nose in round four, yet Burton was strangely having fun. Mayweather fought with his back to the ropes and he did so with a thrilling panache. Burton stood between rounds. 'The fight's getting started now,' he was told before the fifth. 'We want to get inside. Now you go to work.'

'How do you feel?' Roger asked in the other corner. 'Good,' was Floyd's reply.

He was winning each round but Burton was throwing serious leather. He was Mayweathering Mayweather. In the fifth he took a big right and pretended to dip his knees, challenging Floyd to follow up with his showboating. Smiles lit up the arena. Floyd's nose bled but he was more accurate and Burton was paying a price for his aggression.

'He's bleeding too,' Burton was reassured in the corner, as he was warned not to blow his nose and told to work Mayweather's body more.

It was physical. It was hard. Burton tried to penetrate Mayweather's cross-armed defence in the sixth but was speared by straight shots. Burton goaded Mayweather to hit him in the next and Floyd accepted, but the underdog roared back as both noses poured crimson. Floyd switched southpaw, but this time there was no opportunity for dialogue with the commentators who noted his change in stance.

Burton took a deep breath at the end of the round. He was swelling below both eyes. 'He's ready to go,' said Roger Mayweather. 'He's ready to go. Keep doing what you're doing.'

A doctor was summoned to assess Burton's welfare in round eight, to Burton's bemusement, but after getting the all clear he planted his feet in the southpaw stance and tore into Floyd with both hands. Mayweather was still punching in bunches, Burton was telling him he hadn't hurt him. Ringsiders questioned whether Floyd's right hand had been broken and the bell ended arguably the most tumultuous round of the fight. Burton was told that if he did not change lanes in the ninth, his corner would stop the fight.

Mayweather opened the ninth by peppering his opponent with left hooks to the body and head. Burton was under fire and seemed to be hurt to the body when his cornerman Nelson Lopez ran up the steps and told the referee to stop the fight. Burton unsurprisingly disagreed with that decision.

Mayweather leapt onto the ropes and beat his chest at the crowd.

'One handed,' said some of the flunkies around Mayweather as Todd duBoef went into the ring to congratulate him. 'I hurt my hand,' Mayweather told him. 'I knew he was going to be tough. That's what I wanted though.'

'I felt I could catch him,' responded Burton. 'But every round he seemed to be going faster and faster. He's good. He couldn't stop me. The corner stopped the fight.'

As the verdict was announced, a disconsolate Burton – who had earned $20,000 the hard way – sulked into a white towel, which rested upon his shoulders. Mayweather had a diamond-encrusted crucifix hung off his neck as he accepted the crowd's cheers.

'That was real important to me,' Floyd said. 'Because Emanuel Burton was real tough and that showed I could fight under pressure. Both of my hands were messed up and I was still fighting. That fight showed Floyd Mayweather could brawl if he has to. I felt I did my job. The only thing I have to concern myself with now is staying away from the negativity. Too many people try to get into my personal life. But not too many people know what's going on in my personal life and that's the way I want to keep it. I'm always going to try and be private. I always have to have my guard up because I don't trust people. I had a little ring rust and it showed. But many are called and few are chosen. I feel like I am the chosen one. If I stay active, I blow everyone out of the water.'

Again, *Boxing News's* Jim Brady had massively cooled on Mayweather thanks to the tough time Burton gave him.

'Despite the never-ending, self-promoting hype, Mayweather is not a great fighter,' he wrote. 'He's good, he's fast – but great is an accolade reserved for the oh so few, such as Sugar Ray Leonard and Muhammad Ali.'

Boxing Monthly's Graham Houston also saw negatives. 'The downside is that he took rather more punches than we are accustomed to seeing him taking.'

Asked for his opinion, Floyd Sr reckoned his son had been hit too much while Roger countered that his performance gave the fans what they wanted, some action.

'My son, with me, you never saw him hardly get hit,' said Sr. 'But the other day he got hit more than he got hit in his whole career. Luckily the guy couldn't punch. My son needs me. But you know what? It's his call.'

Roger's take was different. Of course it was. 'I didn't see him get beat up. I didn't see him get wobbled. The reason he took punches is because he takes risks, but in order to be a great fighter you have to take risks. The different things that I do with Floyd as opposed to what his father does, I teach Floyd offence . . . Being more offensive minded, I think, is his best asset.'

Mayweather Sr was busy anyway, even without his son. He was working as a trainer to Oscar De La Hoya, who had flown the Top Rank nest and was setting up his own promotional empire, called Golden Boy Promotions.

Roger again contended the Burton fight and the excitement in it helped Floyd's career. 'Floyd is hotter now than he was when he made his exit from boxing eight months ago. When he beat Gregorio Vargas, he beat him easily but it was a boring, stinking fight.'

The Mayweather brothers, Floyd Sr and Roger, were each happy to disparage the other in the media.

Floyd Sr, never shy with words, would come out with lines such as, 'He's okay for the mitts, but ain't no trainer.' Then there was, 'Roger couldn't spell defence.' Then, getting more personal, he pointed to Roger's knockout losses, saying, 'He has a habit of over-training his fighters and he doesn't care about Floyd getting knocked out because he's used to sleeping in front of audiences.'

'The father don't understand what it takes to sell a fighter,' Roger shot back at his brother. 'I understand what it takes to sell a fighter, because I sold myself, that's why people still remember me today. You don't want people to remember you and say, "He was a great fighter, but he stunk." I want him to be one of the most talked-about fighters. When you see me in the corner with Little Floyd, you know you're going to get fireworks.'

Roger initially did not seem to want to get involved in a slanging match, but he eventually ended up talking down his brother's achievements as they went tit for tat. 'Who the hell has he fought?' Roger asked Graham Houston. 'I mean, which fights of my brother's fights can you remember?'

'Sugar Ray Leonard,' said Houston.

'That's the only fight anyone remembers,' Roger explained. 'He never even fought for a world title. Any day now I expect him to rewrite history and start telling people he was champ. I'm the one in the history books. How many world champions did he beat? Who is he to criticise me?'

Roger had long since given up his role as peacemaker between father and son. 'I used to come between them,' he said, 'But you ask our mother, this ain't no easy family.'

Mayweather Sr contended he had laid the foundations for Floyd Jr, training him through childhood and adolescence. Roger took the credit for developing Floyd Jr as a pro while Sr was locked up.

'My brother conveniently forgets I was the one who prepared Floyd for the Olympics, not the boy's father,' fumed Roger. 'I trained him for his first fourteen pro bouts. Floyd won the title in his eigteenth pro fight, so who laid the foundation?'

Jr, however, had distractions. Roger said he lacked the discipline to match his talent. 'You have to step lightly with Floyd. The one thing I know is he is very strong in his mind. If he doesn't want to do something he won't, whether it's good or bad for him.'

According to one writer, James Prince was pampering Mayweather because he liked to hang out with him. 'The wild parties Prince is legendary for are lethal for a fighter,' wrote another.

It wasn't lethal parties that fans wanted to see Floyd in; they wanted to see him in with a lethal puncher named Diego 'Chico' Corrales. It was one of boxing's must-have fights and not long after the Burton bout it was announced. Mayweather would face the division's axeman in a contest that was deemed 50-50 in the trade. Their rivalry boiled intensely. It was a genuine grudge.

There would be fireworks. There would be blood. Bad blood.

SIX

BATTERED WOMEN, BATTERED MEN

'I FEEL VIOLATED,' fumed Diego Corrales. 'He has gotten really personal with this, and it's gone way beyond athletic competition. Everything that is important to me or means something to me, he's attacked and questioned. He will have to pay for that. That will not pass unnoticed. It's not sport anymore. I will go at him with every strength and fibre of my being. If Floyd had just shut his mouth and just minded his own business, we would still have fought, but the passion wasn't going to be there like it is now.'

Mayweather had raised his rival's ire by repeatedly dragging Corrales's impending legal hearing about the alleged assault of his pregnant wife into the fight's build-up, with lines such as, 'I'm going to beat Chico like the dog that he is for all the battered women out there. It's really ridiculous. You have to be a coward to beat on any women. It's ridiculous to do that. If you want to fight, go in the ring. What's the matter with a guy who would do that to a pregnant woman? I'm going to abuse him as a favour to all the battered women in America.'

Corrales fired back, saying he was going to win for all of the battered fathers. 'As a person . . . it's a shame, a crying shame the things he's done, like kicking his own father out of his house. Something like that is uncalled for. Floyd's a guy who acts tough when he has seven or eight of his buddies around him. But this time it's going to be just him and me.'

According to fight insiders, the icing on the cake that saw the bout signed and sealed was when they ran into one another after Lennox Lewis defended his heavyweight titles against David Tua at the Mandalay Bay in Las Vegas. 'Several of Mayweather's posse cornered and tried to intimidate him [Corrales],' wrote *Boxing News*. 'Corrales claims Mayweather eventually showed up, words were exchanged, and Floyd took off his jacket as if to take the matter further. But the incident passed without fisticuffs.'

Of course, it did not help the manifesting bad blood when James Prince invited Corrales's wife, Maria, to sit ringside in Floyd's corner to see Corrales take the same beatings she allegedly had.

'I think Diego and Floyd developed a dislike for one another and I think it happened in the amateurs,' Ray Woods, Corrales's stepfather and trainer, recalled. 'They had some really competitive sparring matches in Colorado Springs and this time they were in the same weight class and Diego was coming up fast and Floyd started picking at him, especially when he got in trouble with his alleged beating of his spouse and it kind of just blew up from there.'

Both fighters had stories to tell and presented them through TV, radio, newspapers and the growing online boxing community.

Boxing websites were springing up left, right and centre, and many had an opinion on Mayweather himself, not to mention the fight. Thomas Gerbasi, one of the men behind houseofboxing. com, hosted a webchat with both fighters ahead of the contest. He had them on the phone for an hour each, answering his and the fans' questions.

'Mayweather Jr was loose, talking smack, and generally sounded like he was just happy to be alive,' said Gerbasi. 'It was a young kid before the biggest fight of his life and he didn't have a care in the world. If promoter Bob Arum and manager James Prince could bottle that Floyd Mayweather Jr up and sell it to the world, boxing might have its crossover star, and the SportsCenter addicts might be saying "Tiger Who? Kobe Who?" Or maybe Floyd Jr says it best. When asked what he needs to do to get to the level of a Woods or Bryant? More promotion. And don't talk about it. Just keep beating the best fighters they've got.'

Floyd was so animated on the line to Gerbasi that Dena duBoef, Todd's sister and PR guru at Top Rank, tried to cut Floyd off after several minutes. 'I'm not done yet,' said Floyd, who had more on his mind.

The fight was set for 20 January 2001, though the leadtime was far shorter than initially intended. They had been due to meet separate foes in a 17 February show, with Corrales challenging José Luis Castillo for the WBC lightweight title and Mayweather tackling another Mexican, Alejandro Lopez. The respective winners of those fights, and the assumption was it would have been Mayweather and Corrales, would then meet in the spring or summer, and most probably at lightweight after Corrales had moved up. However, after Roy Jones's contract expired with HBO and he began playing hardball over a new deal, HBO needed a date filled quickly, and Mayweather and Corrales felt there was no time like the present to settle their feud. Kery Davis, along with Ross Greenburg, had stepped in and taken over the boxing reins at HBO from Lou DiBella, who had started his own promotional company, and the departed Seth Abraham.

Arum – with superstar Oscar De La Hoya breaking away from him, albeit with the ageing promoter taking him to court – reckoned that Mayweather now saw an opportunity to be Top Rank's top dog, so had come back into the fold.

'Floyd called us and I think he finally understands that we and HBO really do have his best interests at heart and he's ready to start fighting again,' Arum said.

Some felt Arum was pushing the fight briskly forwards as the rivalry between the fighters was too strong and they could blow at each other at any time.

Ray Woods agreed. 'What I heard was every time Diego and Floyd laid eyes on one another, they got into it,' said Woods. 'I think before those guys went at it in the street I think Bob said, "Let's get on and do it before they do it for real."'

Opinions were split in the trade, with few united on who would win. It was one of those contests that sold for the storyline and that fight fans salivated over because it was two young, ambitious guys, approaching their prime and undefeated and the best two in the weight class. Corrales had vacated the IBF title to move up in weight (only to be enticed to stay), Mayweather, who in the build-up recounted how a sparring session in the amateurs with Corrales had been 'easy work', held the WBC strap. Floyd was 24-0 (18); Corrales had won all thirty-three contests with twenty-seven knockouts in the process. Floyd was twenty-three; Corrales was a year younger. The latter was a tall, rangy and terrifically heavy puncher, the former was smaller and an artful scientist. Floyd had speed. Corrales had power. If Mayweather was to take a heavy Corrales shot, from either hand, could he stand up to it? Would Mayweather be distracted by what was going on outside the ring? Would Corrales be able to keep up with the seemingly infinite skills of Mayweather, or the hand speed?

'Everyone is saying Floyd doesn't have his stuff right,' said Mayweather's old sparmate Paul Spadafora, the IBF lightweight champion, 'but if Floyd is Floyd, he'll win the fight easy.'

In fact, when put on the spot more people seemed to be coming down on the Mayweather side of the argument. HBO commentator Jim Lampley picked Floyd, so did ESPN's Brian Kenny and *Boxing News*'s Claude Abrams. Tommy Brooks, then trainer of Mike Tyson, tipped Corrales. 'He's too tall, powerful and may want it more,' he said.

'He [Floyd] showed he can fight if need be the case,' added Roger Mayweather. 'And I'm gonna tell you this, I've worked with Diego Corrales. He's going to box Diego Corrales early in the fight and he's gonna beat his ass down the stretch, too smart for him, too slick for him.'

French boxing journalist Thierry Chambefort visited Corrales in camp, on a secluded ranch fifteen minutes from Las Vegas. He was told Corrales would not do interviews but when Chico saw him they began chatting, the tape recorder rolling. He asked Corrales about the allegations he was facing. 'It's not true the way they put it,' he said. 'My friend was into drug abuse. I went back home and she put a gun on me. Also, I myself never had anything to do with drugs. I hate Mayweather. I have to look my opponents in the eye. My dad told me the eyes are windows to the soul and I believe that.'

Chamberfort was trying to delve beneath the surface of the two camps. He spoke to Zakeisha Jones, daughter of boxing referee Richard Steele, who said Floyd was acting too much, pretending to be someone he wasn't. 'He's recently been arrogant with people he's known for years,' she told the Frenchman.

On the first floor of Corrales's accommodation was a dartboard, with Mayweather's picture on it. 'This has nothing to do with "Chico", I installed it,' said Alex Ariza, a young Los Angeles-based Colombian who was working with Corrales on his strength, conditioning and nutrition as he tried to make 130lbs for a final time.

'I'll do whatever it takes,' said Corrales, of having to trim his six-foot frame down to just over nine stone once more. 'The belt is not important. It's whipping Mayweather that counts.'

'I'm going to bust him up good,' chirped Floyd.

'This has become very personal,' wrote *Boxing News* editor Claude Abrams, who hoped their feud would be settled at the final bell, whatever the fight's outcome.

The stakes were high. The winner was looking at a six-fight deal with cable giants HBO. The loser would get just one more guaranteed bout on the network. The main prize on offer was bragging rights.

There was, however, a healthy dose of mutual respect if you looked hard enough for it. 'Corrales is one of the best fighters out there,' said Mayweather. 'To be known fifty years from now as one of the greats, I have to get past him.'

'If I fall short in any area, Floyd will capitalise,' Diego admitted. 'I have to keep my head together and use my assets.'

Interestingly, Miguel Díaz, who had been in the Mayweather corner looking after cuts, was to be in the opposite corner on the night. He had chosen to remain neutral but his cut of Corrales's $1.4-million purse would have meant a $70,000 payday, as a co-trainer, while he would have made $34,000 as Floyd's cutman. Mayweather gave Díaz his blessing to follow the money.

Mayweather was making $1,775,000.

Grudge matches have always been better payers in boxing, and 8,126 fans were inside the MGM Grand in Las Vegas to watch. That meant, disappointingly, only around half of the seats had been taken.

For Corrales, who for three previous fights had struggled to make 130lbs and was keen to move to 135lbs, it wasn't about the money or the weight anymore. 'He will have to pay. Honestly, I would fight this fight for free. The way I feel about him, I will tear him up. I promise you that.'

From a fan's perspective, they were both bad guys. Mayweather was the arrogant punk, Corrales the alleged wife beater.

Mayweather couldn't understand that.

'I feel like it's this,' he said. 'I turned off the money and I'm the villain. This guy Diego Corrales allegedly cracks his wife in the ribs and she's pregnant, and I'm the bad guy. The only thing I'm looking forward to doing is winning. Either people are going to see me win or they're going to come just to see me lose. The main thing is that they're paying to see me.'

Like Mayweather, Corrales was at odds with his own management team of Cameron Dunkin and Barrett Silver. He would later sign with Prince.

Mayweather-Corrales made for a potent combination and ESPN writer Tim Graham was hoping they would both pay for past crimes on the night.

'I used to root for Floyd Mayweather Jr and Diego Corrales,' he began. 'They seemed like such nice young men. But when they fight each other in a 130-pound title bout Saturday night in Las Vegas, I'll be hoping for one of those blooper-reel double knockouts, where the two pugs abandon all defence, wind up with all they got and both land on the button . . . It's a shame one of these pukes will win.'

The tenor of the piece deteriorated, before he concluded, 'Sadly, one of these blockheads will not only win, but also increase his vast wealth because of it. No matter what happens in the ring, however, both of them are losers.'

At the weigh-in, however, there was concern from veterans in press row that Corrales, all 6 ft 1 in of him and still growing at twenty-three years of age, was no super-featherweight anymore. Ariza admitted it had been hard work getting him to hit the weight.

Graham Houston said he 'looked drawn and pale.' There was speculation that the morning he was due to step on the scales he was five pounds overweight, so his camp asked for a test weigh. Corrales stripped butt naked, security guards hiding his modesty with a sheet, and he was said to be a couple of pounds over. Two hours later – around ninety minutes of which were spent in a sauna – Diego returned and made 130lbs bang on. Mayweather did, too. Houston noted the opposite vibes from the fighters. 'Mayweather was positively glowing with physical well-being,' he wrote. 'His ripped abdominal muscles looking as though they were carved out of marble.'

There was talk that Mayweather might try to meet fire with fire. His estranged father said, 'I just hope my son remembers what his daddy taught him.'

Floyd insisted he felt more comfortable with his uncle Roger. He said his father had been too strict while Sr argued that outlook had garnered results. 'It was just like a boot camp. Do boxing and then go to your room,' Mayweather Jr reckoned. 'Now I feel like even when I'm training I still get a chance to live my life.'

Roger Mayweather's side of the story fit with Floyd Jr's. 'When he's out the ring, that's his business. When he comes in here [the gym] then I'm in control of him, what he should do, how he should do and what makes the fight easier for him.'

The Mayweather family, boxing's answer to a rolling *Jerry Springer Show*, was in turmoil. Uncle Jeff was now well out of the picture, having been ditched from the team.

'This kid should be a superstar because he has everything,' said Jeff. 'But Madison Avenue doesn't want to touch a guy who says a $12.5-million contract is a slave contract. There are a lot of bad connotations to that. But Floyd, I don't think, thinks about what he says sometimes. What he should have thought more about is what all this is doing to his family. He can achieve so much in this sport, but when boxing is all over and done with, he may not have one family member he can sit and talk to.'

Corrales was due in court just two weeks after the fight. Often the only place a fighter feels at peace, with no distractions, is in the ring. On 20 January 2001, nothing else mattered to the arch-rivals, nothing but blood and victory.

Corrales weighed in on the night at 146lbs, replenishing sixteen pounds in a day. Mayweather had added less than seven pounds to his frame.

Mayweather Sr was allowed backstage, and he smiled uneasily in his son's dressing room. Corrales was wearing camouflage fatigues and was given a good ovation by the crowd.

Two rappers who Mayweather had signed to his Philthy Rich record label escorted him to the ring.

The fighters touched gloves on the instruction of referee Richard Steele and soon the differences would be settled with punches rather than sound bites.

To start with, Mayweather shot out his trademark single punches, firing jabs into the pit of that lanky, weight-drained body while launching right-hand leads over Corrales's left hand.

Already in round two, Chico was starting to look one-paced and a left hook around the ear seemed to give him reason to slow down.

Before round three, Sr tried to get word to his son through a member of the ever-expanding entourage. 'Tell Lil Floyd to keep doing what he's doing and in round seven, eight or nine he will be ready to go.'

Meanwhile, in the third, Corrales swiped with the left, he swiped with the right, he missed with both and his head was then pumped back by a rapid-fire combination. Mayweather was boxing with an electric swagger. Corrales landed a sweeping left hook but Floyd took it well enough. Then he got back on his jab and started dictating the play again.

In round four Mayweather's continued movement meant Corrales could not set his feet to let his heavy shots go. He chased after Mayweather, eating leather after almost every step. There were a few boos as Mayweather did what Mayweather always did, dominated, though a Corrales assault that only saw him chew on another right hand promptly turned any boredom to excited cheers. With seconds to go in the fourth, Mayweather helped himself to more points and Corrales could only ruefully smile.

'Brilliantly executed fight plan by Floyd Mayweather,' said HBO's Jim Lampley in the fifth, as Floyd continued to dazzle. No single shot had hurt Corrales, but the cumulative effect was mounting. Corrales struggled like a drunken bull as matador Mayweather spun him in a corner to close the round. The feared puncher did not look so fearsome. Mayweather Sr rose from his seat and punched the air. 'Keep doing that, we're whipping his ass for real,' said Roger in the corner.

Mayweather stood inside and smacked away with left hooks upstairs in the next. Strangely, considering Corrales's legal position, Mayweather might have been the villain of the piece but the crowd was beginning to enjoy his pretty violence. He was landing blurring right hands and with twelve seconds left in the session he nailed the now impotent Corrales with a tree-chopping left that saw Corrales look beleaguered when he returned to his corner for a minute's reprieve.

Round seven opened and the cracks in Corrales soon revealed themselves. A lead left hook dropped him, the first punch of the session. 'There's a brilliant start to round seven,' enthused Lampley. Corrales was starting to look ragged and even more open for those spiteful lead hooks to the head and body, as well as Mayweather's signature right hands. With less than a minute to go Floyd's cobra-like left hook scored effortlessly again and Corrales was on the seat of his camo trunks once more, rolling onto his knees before rising at five. He crossed himself, looked at the giant screens above the ring to see how much time was left and steadied himself for Mayweather's furious two-fisted attack. Floyd bombed forwards and with seconds remaining in the round Corrales wilted again. He said he was okay to continue but there was an unenthusiastic look to him. Mayweather Sr proudly whooped and hollered ringside. The doctor checked on Corrales and asked if he wanted to continue. Miguel Díaz barked that if he didn't start throwing more punches they would pull him out. 'You fight, or we stop the fight. You got it?'

Corrales nodded softly.

Corrales opened the eighth trudging forwards and even scored with one of his better punches of the fight, a left hook, which only drew a smile from Mayweather. 'Corrales has been embarrassed here,' Lampley went on.

Diego showed courage to continually attempt to hack away but Mayweather was on a different level altogether. The Mayweather matrix puzzled Corrales. He couldn't figure out what to do. Nothing worked. The round-eight statistics showed that Corrales had thrown one jab and that had missed.

Corrales was plucky, but this wasn't about being plucky. This was supposed to be a superfight, the Sugar Ray Leonard-Tommy Hearns bout of its era. It was not. It was an exhibition.

'You need a knockout,' Corrales was told before the tenth. Mayweather was in retreat, setting traps as he tried to land the fight-ending equaliser. He teased Diego onto a right hand. The force of the blow was multiplied as a weary Corrales stumbled upon it and he went down again.

'He doesn't look like he has much left,' said Merchant, as a tired and thoroughly despondent Diego rose for a fourth time.

Two lead right hands later and Corrales's legs betrayed him for a fifth knockdown. Stepfather and trainer Woods could not watch it anymore and ended the slaughter.

Corrales was incensed. 'What the hell are you doing?' he yelled. 'What is wrong with you?'

'Yeah, he was upset,' Woods remembered. 'I don't have any regrets about pulling him out whatsoever. I don't think he was ever okay with it but let me tell you, from the start, Diego had caught bronchitis. He really had no business in the fight but we went on with it anyway and he was never in it. I mean, he got knocked down five times and I'd had enough of it. To be honest with you, he might have been angry but I thought maybe he was just frustrated and needed someone to lash out at because he wasn't even in the fight. How could you get mad with your trainer and you're not even in the fight? You're getting beaten all over the place – and he was already in trouble with the law. He was getting ready to go to jail and I think he just needed someone to lash out at. I guess I was the target. But he knew he wasn't in the fight.'

Mayweather wheeled away in celebration, pumping one fist off his chest, and he was hoisted into the air.

The two fighters embraced. Mayweather said they respected one another as fighters and they would go their separate ways. Corrales still raged at his corner.

Meanwhile, Mayweather Sr had made his way into the ring and he affectionately hugged his son and cradled his head. Mayweather Jr looked close to tears when they eventually let go.

'I loved Corrales, he was a warrior,' recalled Lou DiBella, who had his first HBO date as a promoter a week later when he showcased the Olympic debutants he signed from the 2000 Games. 'But the reason that fight was so remarkable was because he beat the shit out of Corrales and no one really expected that. I didn't expect that fight to be so easy for Floyd. I didn't expect it to be easy to that degree and that was a tremendous, memorable performance because people at the time thought Corrales was like a wrecking ball, and Mayweather made pretty easy work of him.'

The display was so good it convinced Hall of Fame referee Richard Steele to leave the sport at the top after thirty years. He had been the third man in the ring for more than 100 world title fights but said that during round six, Mayweather was so sublime he could not wish for a better fight to bow out on. 'Here was a kid putting on a boxing exhibition like I hadn't seen in years,' he said.

'Things were going so well and Mayweather was looking so wonderful. And I just said, "This is it." I was able to go out on the top of my game with no controversy.'

Corrales's prison sentence loomed large. He had not even been able to focus on the Mayweather fight, Woods reckoned.

He maintains that weight was not the issue.

'That's what they say but that wasn't really the problem,' Woods said. 'The problem was Diego was in trouble with the law. We were in training camp in the Prince Ranch in Las Vegas and Diego and his future wife would sneak out. We trained hard, we did everything we needed to do and Diego needed rest. But Diego and his future wife, they would sneak out after everyone had bedded down and they would sneak out into that night air, and it was cold, and he would eat, drink beer and smoke and do all the things he wasn't supposed to do. A lot of people don't know that. He was just being mean and rebellious. I even tried to call the fight off but nobody would have agreed with me. I even told my wife, "There's no way he's going to win this fight. He's not behaving properly." And it was all because he was in trouble with the law, getting ready to go to jail and he was just lashing out. Some people, when they get in trouble, they just self-destruct, they get worse, and he was one of them. Once he gets in trouble and he thinks everybody is mad at him he self-destructs and he gets worse. He was that type. Diego always wanted to get Floyd back into the ring but it never happened.'

Top Rank matchmaker Bruce Trampler, however, revealed that Corrales's pre-fight issues, with hitting the right number on the scales and trying to put the pending charges to one side had a greater effect on him than many thought.

'It could have been a tough fight but Corrales couldn't make the weight,' he conceded. 'He was trained at the time by Alex Ariza, who is not a good trainer, and Corrales was out and got drunk the night before and it wasn't the fight that most of us expected it to be.'

The statistics acutely reveal its one-sided nature. According to CompuBox, Mayweather had landed fifty-three per cent of his 414 punches, scoring with 220 of them. Corrales had found a home for just twenty per cent of his 205 attempts, meaning just sixty connected. Delving deeper into that set of numbers, Mayweather landed with forty-nine per cent of his 184 jabs, spearing Corrales with ninety-one in total. Corrales landed only seven of forty-seven and it was supposed to be one of his best weapons.

Corrales said he felt violated in the build-up. He had been by the time it was all over.

'I think it was the realisation that he was going to prison,' Woods added. 'We talked afterwards and I told him he needed to sit down and look at the fight and he would see I did the right thing for him. He was on the verge of getting hurt, bad. He had lost his strength, he'd lost the muscle tone in his neck and his head was bobbing all over the place and the vertebrae in his neck were shaking because Floyd was tattooing him. I told him, just like that. "Floyd was tattooing you and you was too weak to do anything about it."'

Mayweather, after thanking God, then spoke of his appreciation for his uncle and his father.

'Diego Corrales is a great fighter and he can be a champion if he moves up,' Floyd said. 'He's got a lot of potential. This showed who was the best 130-pounder in the world. He said he's the best, I said I was the best. It got a little personal but this is a business. I'm here to sell myself. I'm Pretty Boy Floyd, I say I'm the best pound for pound in the world so we came together to see who is the best. I would like to fight Prince Naseem. Hopefully we can meet at 128 or he can come up to 130. Or I can fight the winner of [Joel] Casamayor and [Acelino] Freitas.'

Even a few minutes after the fight had ended, and when Larry Merchant had finally got to Corrales, Chico was close to tears. He looked like a broken man, as though everything had come crashing down on him at once.

His voice cracking, Corrales said, 'He came out and he fought a good fight. I kept on trucking. I kept coming forward.

'He did what he was supposed to do, he boxed very intelligently . . . I'm still angry. I feel like a champion deserves to finish a fight on his feet or on his back, that's the way I wanted to go out. There's no way it should have been stopped. Nobody had the right to stop the fight. I don't care what their concern is. I am on my feet and I kept getting back to my feet every time. I shouldn't have been stopped. I don't know why they stopped the fight, there were two more rounds left. I could make it through two rounds.'

Merchant sensed Corrales's devastation and asked the man who had been, just thirty long minutes earlier, one of the sport's most dangerous men, whether he could ever rebuild. 'I don't know,' answered Corrales, a lump still in his throat. 'I don't know what I'm going to do. I've never planned after a loss, so I guess I will just go back to the drawing board and see what happens.'

Asked whether he would do better against bigger fighters who were not blessed with Mayweather's ridiculous speed, a crushed Corrales simply, meekly, said, 'I don't know. I don't know. Maybe. Maybe not. A lot of fighters find it hard to come back from the first loss. If I decide to come back, we will see how I rebound.'

Merchant felt Mayweather was never better as an attacking force than on that night. 'I think the Corrales fight was the high point of his career because Corrales was so well regarded, he was a good fighter and how he took him apart, when he had him hurt and had him figured out, how he went after him, it was incredible. Whereas when he became a welterweight his first, second and maybe third priority was don't get hit, don't take any risks, remove as much of the danger as you can from a dangerous game.'

Nigel Collins agreed. 'The Corrales fight was, as far as excitement was concerned, a devastating display of power, the pinnacle. Corrales was a tough customer, and he could punch. And there was a lot of anticipation and the way Floyd just took him apart, it was a savage display of punching and aggression and I don't think he's really equalled that since and then things started to change.'

'You can make the argument,' said Dan Rafael, when asked whether that was as good as Mayweather got. 'Some might look at later fights but for a long time, in my mind anyway, to me that's the standout fight because in all of his other fights Floyd was the favourite in them. I don't know what the closing odds were but there were a lot of people picking Corrales to win that fight, myself included. And he didn't just win the fight, he destroyed Corrales. He knocked him down five times. He made the corner throw in the towel. It was an absolutely brilliant performance.'

Years later, Ray Woods lamented Corrales's missed opportunity and maintains it would have been a different fight without the legal detractions. 'Diego, in my opinion – and people might not agree – if Diego was healthy and he was hitting on all cylinders and was in no trouble, in my opinion he would have beaten Floyd. In my opinion. That doesn't mean anything because that didn't happen. The fighter you saw in the ring that night with Floyd was a weak Diego. He was beat before he even got in the ring with Floyd. Let me tell you, in the dressing room Diego coughed himself out of air a couple of times, before we even left to go to the ring and I said, "Man, we ain't even going to make it out of here."'

He did, but his aura had been permanently shattered.

Victory earned Mayweather a six-fight deal with HBO worth $15-million. Not an overwhelming improvement on a 'slave contract' but enough for him to be proved right for backing his talents and enough for him to have proved the point he was trying to make all along.

Arum was suitably impressed by his immaculate display. Everyone was. 'I believe that, in the near future, he will be not only recognised as the best fighter in boxing but he will be the best attraction,' Arum said. 'That means making the most money.'

The promoter had lost Oscar De La Hoya, his superstar, and he lost the lawsuit with the exiting Golden Boy that confirmed the fighter's departure from Top Rank.

Maybe Arum felt his grip on Floyd was slipping so he tossed in verbal bouquets when he could. Maybe he wanted to downplay De La Hoya's departure. As Floyd listened to more voices, certainly those within Top Rank felt a shift in where his focus was.

'He pretty much kept himself to himself, whether he was with his father or Roger, whoever was in charge at the time,' remembered Bruce Trampler, 'And when he did sign with James Prince he became even more insulated from us.'

'Yes, Oscar De La Hoya was our superstar, but look, we have a whole group in the pipeline,' Arum said. 'I believe Floyd Mayweather is going to exceed Oscar in popularity and earning power. Yes, Oscar was unique, but Floyd Mayweather is going to be unique, too.'

When Arum said, post Corrales, that Mayweather could move up three weight classes to 147lbs and beat De La Hoya at welterweight many thought it was tongue in cheek or simply sour grapes. 'The crazy thing is, he might be right,' said *The Ring*.

Arum needed a star. Mayweather reckoned he was that star, and he had certainly shone against Corrales, even if much of the crowd had been supporting Diego on the night.

The Ring magazine debated whether Floyd would win supporters over with his ability, or alienate them with his arrogance. Nigel Collins' considered look at the aftermath of the Corrales fight was headlined, 'Pretty Boy Floyd, Superstar or Superbrat?'

He tried to get to the bottom of the 'sweet and sour' personality, the sweet being the post-fight huddle with his father and the new bond with Corrales, the sour being the pre-fight antagonism and the 'slave contract' barb.

'Is he the bright-eyed prodigy who won *The Ring*'s Fighter of the Year award in only his second full season as a professional, or the ungrateful malcontent who scorned a $12.5-million offer from HBO by calling it a 'slave contract?' Collins questioned. 'Or is he all of the above, a complex young man struggling to come to terms with exactly who he is and who he wants to be?'

Whatever the thoughts of Mayweather before the Corrales fight, that he came through it in such fine style and, ultimately, by showing some good grace afterwards, meant that his value as a commodity rose. The new, improved HBO contract showed that much but having opened 2001 with the Corrales win, it was going to be tough to follow that act, particularly as Naseem Hamed seemed to have little interest in the fight while Freitas and Casamayor were Showtime boxers, meaning their contests were staged on the airwaves of HBO's main rivals. As Mayweather had hammered his nearest rival into oblivion, it was difficult to see what he could haul out of his bag of tricks to continue the momentum through the year rather than spending a few more months either on the sidelines, treading water, or taking on competition that would not excite the paying public.

Now five years on from the Olympic Games in Atlanta, Mayweather was clearly the star of the American show. Any arguments about who was the best pound-for-pound fighter in the world now featured him, Mosley, Félix Trinidad and Roy Jones. De La Hoya was still the great earner.

Of the '96 squad, Fernando Vargas was rising well. Only twenty-three, he had given a good account of himself in a Fight of the Year contender with Trinidad. He was 20-1 (18) and had beaten good men like slick Winky Wright and Ghanaian banger Ike Quartey. Flyweight Eric Morel, with that fighter's curse of being small and thus often under the mainstream radar, was 29-0 (16) and the WBA champion.

Golden boy David Reid, however, had been battered into a painful defeat by Trinidad, was having multiple surgeries on that drooping eye and failing to adapt his amateur style to the pros.

Others, including Zahir Raheem, David Díaz and Rhoshii Wells were improving but remained untested. Lawrence Clay-Bey, the heavyweight, was thirty-five and struggling to make a mark, while Nate Jones had just lost to the decent though unspectacular Friday Ahunyana and another bronze medallist, Terrance Cauthen, was 18-1 (7) and on the road back after his first loss. One member of the team, Albert Guardado, had already retired, having won five of seven pro fights.

As was seemingly to be the case with Mayweather, any highs were followed by lows. The split with his father, despite the brief reconciliation on the night of the Corrales fight, now seemed beyond repair. Floyd Sr was training Oscar De La Hoya in Big Bear, California. But Sr was not happy. 'My son can go to hell,' he snarled. 'And you've never heard me say that. It doesn't matter, though, because he's the son of the devil anyway.'

'I've talked to my son twice since then [the Corrales fight] but it was all bullshit,' the father went on. 'There ain't nothing going on and there's been nothing going on since that day. He's a conniver, a liar and a hypocrite.'

Mayweather opted not to go into a remote training camp instead he chose to train in Las Vegas.

On fight night, as Floyd defended his crown against Carlos Hernández, the crowd booed and Mayweather squinted in agony. There was nothing overly complicated about El Salvador's tough Hernández, 33-2 (21), who fought out of the Bellflower suburb of Los Angeles.

But Mayweather's hands hurt so much when he fought the Mexican before 9,160 fans at the Van Andel Arena in Grand Rapids on 26 May that in round six, as he let his fists go against the WBC title challenger, he dropped to the floor in agony. He later said he had never felt pain like it, that it even shot up his spinal cord.

Don't think the fight was close; it was not. There was only one horse in it, but the horse was compromised from the start. Mayweather had needed painkilling injections in both hands prior to the first bell in order to make it through the fight.

Some gave Mayweather immense credit for winning while clearly in terrible pain. Others felt he was taking fans for a ride by competing while unable to put on the show they, particularly those who were watching him in his hometown, had paid to see. 'The performance was so bad it was like going to a Luciano Pavarotti concert and Vanilla Ice shows up instead,' wrote *Boxing News*. 'Five years after the Olympics and despite the absurd hype, Mayweather is not the fighter he is supposed to be.'

Nigel Collins, in the editor's chair at *The Ring*, was disgusted that Mayweather had decided to go into the bout with bad hands. He reckoned Mayweather, who was making around $2 million to Hernández's $210,000, and Top Rank should have reimbursed the fans who paid to watch the bout. 'It's an entirely different story when a fighter is injured during a bout, but when he enters the ring as significantly damaged as Mayweather, it's nothing short of consumer fraud,' wrote Collins. 'The fans in Grand Rapids who shelled out good money for tickets were ripped off, as were HBO's subscribers . . . Team Mayweather and Top Rank walked away with a handsome profit, but the sport that provided the payday took an unnecessary hit.'

Off the record, one promoter laughed at the time, 'HBO thought they bought a Rolex, but what they really got is a Timex.'

It had started well enough. While Michael Buffer introduced him, Mayweather – wearing white and red leather shorts – was finally greeted by a cacophony of cheers as he cupped his ears with his gloves, accepting the support like the wrestler Hulk Hogan used to.

The feel-good factor did not last. Hernández had brought in top Argentine trainer Amílcar Brusa – coach of that country's great middleweight Carlos Monzón – to shepherd him through the fight. But he typically found Floyd hard to hit. Mayweather worked the body with jabs and hooks, perhaps aiming those brittle hands into the tender target. He had some second round success with right hands, too, causing the crowd to become excitable and swelling to form above Hernández's eye.

The lead right seemed to have Hernández almost unravelling in the third but he stubbornly dug in and fired back and didn't take a backward step when Mayweather slammed in a succession of left hooks near the end of the round. Floyd was bleeding from the nose and Roger told him to move his head more while on the inside.

Floyd was more reluctant to engage in the fourth, throwing more single shots. He was working around the pain in his hands. He boxed southpaw in the fifth, too, trying to shield his left. But both were damaged and while his hands worked less, his legs worked more. Hernández plugged forwards and ringsiders were suddenly becoming aware that Mayweather's hands were a problem. In close, he landed right and left hooks but the pain was so excruciating Mayweather actually touched down, his gloves impacting on the canvas, so referee Grable initiated a count. Mayweather stood immediately, but used his right mitt to point to his left to explain away the so-called 'knockdown.'

He was warned for not closing his hands to punch in the next session, but the gap in class was so great that even though Hernández tried to push the pace of the fight he couldn't push closer on the scorecards. According to the stats, Hernández tossed sixty lumps of leather in Mayweather's direction and just thirty-one came back his way.

'My right hand is killing me,' Floyd told one of his seconds, Leonard Ellerbe, in the corner before round eight.

Floyd was reduced to darting in and out while in the left-handed stance in the eighth. The crowd were just about tolerating it but they had started to grumble and after he'd spent almost the entire ninth boxing as a southpaw the boos started to come as the discontent swelled. Hernández, with the swelling on the bridge of his nose turning into a horrendous knot, got physical in the tenth and was warned by referee Dale Grable for rough stuff, which included pushing Mayweather's head back in a clinch. He pushed his luck and was docked a point in the twelfth and final session for elbowing as he hacked away with both hands while Mayweather remained the most slippery of targets.

At the bell Mayweather saluted the crowd and grimaced as he walked to his corner. Hernández, with a forehead that would have made the Elephant Man envious, tried to claim some kind of moral victory by raising his hands. Mayweather's face contorted in pain as his gloves were removed.

'It was one of the hardest fights of my career,' Mayweather admitted, after the scores of 119-110, 117-110 and 116-112 were rendered in his favour, marking his seventh successful title defence.

'My hands have been messed up for the longest time,' said Mayweather, who acknowledged his hands had not properly healed after the Corrales fight. 'I wanted to give the fans a war for their money. But I couldn't give my fans a good fight because my damn hands are killing me. I wanted to get my knockout but I was hurt. I was hurt bad.'

Again, doubt was cast over his training set-up. 'By the tenth, it was obvious Floyd needed a better trainer,' commented *Boxing*

News. 'When your chin is high and you won't listen to your trainer between rounds, it is time for a taskmaster to take over.'

One writer even said that by round seven it was clear that Cuban southpaw Joel Casamayor, the WBA lightweight champion, would have his way with Mayweather and that he would be 'chomping at the bit for the fight.'

It was hard to know whether they actually thought that, or they had just taken Mayweather's antics, since snubbing the original HBO deal and joining with Prince, so personally.

It was the money issue that seemed to gall critics the most. When Mayweather said, 'I'm still learning,' it did not take a genius to see that over $2-million a fight was not apprenticeship money.

Mayweather had plenty of people around him, but one he confided in was Mike Tyson. The former heavyweight king was nearing the end of his tumultuous career, with Lennox Lewis lying in wait, but the likes of Mayweather and young up-and-comers including Fernando Vargas and Zab Judah all called on Mike for help and advice from time to time. Mayweather, who had asked to join in a Tyson photo shoot with him a couple of years earlier, explained that the ageing heavyweight gave him the kind of advice he could not get anywhere else.

'People have asked me why I'm associated with someone like Mike Tyson,' Mayweather said of the man who spent three years in prison in the 1990s on a rape conviction. 'People tell me he's an animal and a disgrace to boxing and all of this, but if that's the case, there are a lot of guys whose records are worse than Mike Tyson's. Mike Tyson's always been cool to me; he's always been a good guy to me. I never had a problem with him and everything Tyson has told me has been true. As a kid, I never thought I would know Mike Tyson the way I know him now. I just get in the car and just go over to his house; and he's always called me champ, even before I became a champ. Tyson is my friend and

I've never asked him for anything. What people don't realise is a lot of people try to get things out of Tyson. He would tell me, when I reached a certain level, I had to play the game. Tyson told me what life was going to be like for me when I was making certain money. What he said was true.'

Tyson had learned the hard way. When things had been bad for him, they were very bad. When things were bad for Mayweather they were very bad, too. He was due to meet Mexican Jesús Chávez in October but Floyd was sued by thirty-one-year-old Greg Bedford, who claimed the fighter broke a bottle of champagne over his head in a Vegas nightspot, Club Utopia, at 2 a.m. on 19 June.

Leonard Ellerbe, a friend of Mayweather's who had become a fixture in his camp, denied the charge on Floyd's behalf and met with Arum to discuss it.

'Leonard told a completely different story,' Arum said. 'Leonard said [Bedford] came up, grabbed Floyd's chain, there was a tussle and Floyd wasn't even involved in the tussle. I'd like to think I know when someone is lying to me. I'm inclined to believe Leonard.'

The suit alleged assault and battery with a deadly weapon and Bedford wanted damages amounting to somewhere between $750,000 and $1 million.

The police had no records of the assault though Bedford's attorney, John Moran III of Las Vegas, contended that officers had gone to the scene to investigate.

Arum said Moran had called Top Rank HQ the day before the lawsuit was filed to discuss a $350,000 settlement. Moran certainly seemed to think he was on to something. One writer reckoned Moran felt Mayweather was the new 'Baddest Man on the Planet' a tag he would have inherited from wild heavyweight Tyson.

He claimed that Mayweather, who had already been given a six-month suspended sentence as well as being fined a mere

$3,000 and given forty-eight hours of community service on a plea concerning domestic violence, was nothing but trouble. The allegation stemmed from an argument with his daughter's mother, Melissa Brim, who claimed he repeatedly punched her in the face. He entered a plea bargain and also wound up with two days' house arrest.

'Because of his money, Mayweather has never paid the consequence for the many incidents in which he has been involved,' Moran told the *Las Vegas Sun*. 'I've got three cases pending against him and I know of hundreds of Las Vegas Metropolitan Police reports with Floyd Mayweather Jr involved in unlawful conduct. There are countless incidents where he's brandishing a gun, beating somebody up or kicking somebody when they're on the ground. It's just that Metro doesn't have the money or the manpower to investigate them all. It really surprises me that the Nevada State Athletic Commission would allow and sanction a boxer to fight when he has already proved himself to be so unreasonably dangerous in public.'

Aside from Mayweather and the champagne bottle, Moran was also working on the civil suits brought by Brim, the mother of one of Mayweather's children, who was seeking $1 million on an assault and battery claim, and one that concerned Brim's father, James, and a separate assault and battery charge against Mayweather.

One instantly thought back to Mayweather's domestic violence charges at Corrales, who was now, finally, languishing in prison for fourteen months.

While Mayweather nursed his hands, utilising a doctor's advice of therapy and a new hand-wrapping method, the extraction of four wisdom teeth caused the delay of his next fight.

Jesús Chávez, who had won on the Mayweather-Hernández undercard, outscoring Juan Jose Arias over twelve rounds, found the original date of their proposed 6 October bout scrapped, postponed until 10 November. 'The dentist beat me to the punch,' joked Chávez, who felt victory was his destiny.

'He's been taking me very lightly,' Chávez said. 'It's insulting because I am the hungriest fighter in the division. I have heard from a number of people he wasn't training, that he wasn't even going to camp every day. If Mayweather thinks I'm going to cave in, if he thinks I'm going to go away because of these little games he's playing then he doesn't know who he's dealing with. I have more mental toughness than Mayweather can ever dream of having.'

Along with the civil cases being brought against Floyd, and the speculation that he wasn't training properly, Roger Mayweather told Graham Houston that his nephew's habits had started to change.

Apparently Prince had summoned Floyd to train at his gym in Houston but the fighter refused, opting to spread time between Vegas and another gym in Phoenix.

'He's looking good but he doesn't take care of himself,' Roger said. 'Floyd lacks the discipline. He got the desire but he's young and he thinks all he needs is his power and his speed. He lets himself get out of shape in between fights. He still hasn't learned it's real hard on the body when you do that.'

Chávez had not lost a fight in six years, had gone unbeaten in thirty-one and had been in and around the top of the division for three years.

The usual pre-fight pot was stirred. Chávez said he did not believe Mayweather was one of the sport's premier fighters. 'He is overrated,' said the challenger. 'He is considered one of the best fighters pound for pound in the world but I do not consider him like that.'

'I'm the best athlete in the world hands down,' Mayweather shot back. 'You got athletes like Kobe Bryant; he can have an off night and still be the great Kobe Bryant. Tiger Woods can lose ten golf tournaments and still be the great Tiger Woods. In boxing, if you have an off night, they'll eat you up and destroy you. Your payday drops, you lose your contract. But right now, I am dominating everyone they put in front of me and doing it with ease. I'm not bragging or boasting; it's the truth. [Chávez] said I was overrated. On November 10, I am going to give him a chance to show I am overrated. Jesus can pick which way he wants to go out; on his face or on his back.'

Around 7,000 showed at San Francisco's Bill Graham Civic Auditorium to find out and they saw that Floyd was back to his brilliant boxer-puncher best. Chávez became the twentieth stoppage victim in Floyd's twenty-seven fights. The audience was rewarded with a performance that just about justified the fight's billing as the biggest in the city since Dick Tiger outfought Gene Fullmer in Candlestick Park in 1962.

Mayweather started with a violent majesty, boxing beautifully, punching spitefully. Chávez had no answer, but under instruction from trainer Ronnie Shields he tried to peg Mayweather to the ropes in the second. He tried to get rough, crowding Floyd, though he was starting to take right uppercuts to the head and body. Mayweather's counters were exquisite and he always seemed to make Chávez pay for every attack he tried – or even thought about.

Through the middle rounds, Chávez seemed to be trying all out to land with heavy shots while Mayweather was boxing within himself and still managing to contain the WBC top contender's assaults. In the fourth, as Chávez beavered away with dozens of punches, Mayweather's guard stayed high and his body swayed, meaning almost nothing connected. Chávez could not have hit Mayweather's chin with a handful of sand.

The pro-Mexican crowd booed the one-sided nature of the contest as Mayweather opted to outfight Chávez rather than outbox him. He could do either. As Mayweather moved even more in the sixth, Chávez – looking increasingly cumbersome –

missed more. He was warned for shoving Floyd as his frustration grew evident. There was more booing. Fans wanted war, not a pure boxing treat. When Chávez connected with a good right early in the seventh it only prompted more boxing in reverse from Mayweather, which only allowed the crowd to become more vociferous about the lack of two-way action. Chávez, though, was slowing.

He did not lack for courage or fitness, but he needed more than that. He went all out in the eighth but with a minute left in the ninth Floyd smashed away with a volley of hard shots and Chávez could do nothing but walk onto them. The crowd now roared at the action, they were witnessing a real fight, the perfect blend of skill and will.

Mayweather went to skip back to his corner. Chávez stumbled towards his. 'You're looking good, baby,' said cutman Cassius Greene, working on the swelling over Floyd's right eye. 'Every time you hit him downstairs you hurt him.'

Meanwhile, on the other side of the ring, Chávez was asked some hard questions. 'Are you going to agree with me or not?" asked trainer Ronnie Shields, preparing to stop the fight. 'You're getting hit too much now.'

Chávez, who had been battered, nodded hopelessly. He knew he could not win. It was over.

As the news spread, Mayweather leapt onto the ropes to accept the loud boos. He then made a beeline to the HBO team where he told Lampley, Merchant and George Foreman that he had made Chávez punch himself out and then taken him apart. That was about right.

Floyd went across to commiserate with another vanquished challenger and Chávez stood from his stool for an embrace. The punchstats, and not everyone takes them as gospel, were extraordinary. CompuBox counted Chávez throwing 925 punches and Floyd taking aim 456 times. But they reckoned

Mayweather landed 197 against Chávez's 182, meaning Floyd connected with forty-three per cent of his attempts while Chávez, who lost for the second time against thirty-five wins, managed a paltry twenty per cent. Mayweather, said *Boxing Monthly*, had reduced him to 'a bemused target.' Chávez, they went on, 'was starting to get hammered.'

It wasn't long after Chávez had been disposed of before the next Mayweather foe was being discussed. *KO* pondered who would win if Floyd stepped up to lightweight to challenge quality Mexican José Luis Castillo. There was even speculation Mayweather might move up to light-welterweight, two divisions north, to face Australia's Kostya Tszyu, but the heavy-punching Russia-born champion was a Showtime fighter, so that bout always seemed unlikely.

Either way, it seemed that not only had Mayweather run out of creditable super-featherweights, but he had grown into a heavier division. 'I'm a lot stronger at 135 and 140 pounds. For this fight, for the last four days I couldn't eat no food,' he said. 'The only thing I could do was eat a little salad and a little fruit. I couldn't drink no liquids at all for four days. My weight went up once I started training so I had to monitor my diet.

'I took my time and let my experience work for me,' said Mayweather. 'I knew he'd be strong in the early rounds but I also knew that if I went to the solar plexus he'd weaken and then I would come on with combinations in the later rounds.'

'I'm happy with my performance,' responded Chávez. 'Floyd is the better fighter. I gave it my best shot and hope there'll be better times. My trainer felt the fight should be stopped because I was getting hit. I agreed with him. Safety should come first. I knew I had to bring it to Floyd. Now I'm his number one fan. I'll think about things and then come back.'

Chávez continued with his successful career. He won the IBF lightweight title four years later, toppling Atlantic City's

Leavander Johnson, who sustained fatal injuries in the fight. Chávez fought seven more times after that, but his heart was no longer in it. In 2015, he was working as a case manager for a non-profit organisation in Dallas, dealing with at risk kids. His involvement in the sport was over. 'I fought some really, really good fighters,' said Chávez, who also traded punches with world champions like Michael Katsidis, David Díaz, Humberto Soto, Érik Morales and Carlos Hernández. 'He [Floyd] is definitely on top. I would say he's the best based on his record, absolutely. I fought some pretty tough opposition afterwards and on my way up to fighting Floyd. He was defensively the best fighter I ever fought. If you look at the style and the way that I fought Floyd it was pretty much the blueprint on how to fight Floyd. I would do exactly the same again; I just wish that fight had not been stopped so prematurely. Absolutely I'm proud to have fought one of the best fighters in the world. Yes, I'm proud to say I lost to the best.'

Floyd felt he now needed to box more frequently. 'I'm still young, only twenty-four,' he said. 'Everyone on the pound-for-pound list is over thirty.

'This is my last fight at 130,' he confirmed. 'I can't make the weight no more. I'm looking forward to moving up to 135 and fighting Paul Spadafora, José [Luis] Castillo and hopefully going to 140 and fighting Kostya Tszyu.'

There were issues with that, of course. HBO had looked out a 20 April date for him as he eyed Mexican Castillo, the WBC lightweight champion who was regarded as the best in that division. Mayweather, though, said he wanted a warm up at the higher weight and identified the shop-worn Alejandro González only for HBO and Arum to reject that idea. They wanted a more formidable opponent.

Yet while Mayweather said one thing he left open the possibility of doing another. He showed up at the post-fight press conference after Brazil's Acelino Freitas outscored Cuba's Joel Casamayor to be regarded as the number two super-featherweight, behind Floyd.

'I'd knock either one of those guys out in the first six rounds,' he said. 'I could have beaten Casamayor in my tenth pro fight. Corrales would kill either of these guys. They're not in that league.'

'It's easy money for Floyd, that's what it is,' said Prince, if Floyd was to stay down to face the big-punching Freitas. 'We'll have to see where we go but if they want to give Floyd a ton of money to take a serious ass-whipping, we'll go along with them.'

That Freitas was contracted to Showtime and Mayweather to HBO made that fight virtually impossible.

There was nothing left to prove at super-featherweight but there was much more to gain – and much more money to make – by moving up in weight. The question was, who would he set his sights upon.

SEVEN

WINNERS AND LOSERS

JOSÉ LUIS CASTILLO thought he had beaten Floyd Mayweather and he was not the only one.

'Quick, call 911,' wrote Jim Brady, who felt the new WBC lightweight king was over-hyped. 'There's been a stick up. Unfortunately, cops didn't arrive at the MGM Grand fast enough, or José Luis Castillo might not have been robbed of his WBC lightweight title.'

'That's not the fight we saw,' said Jim Lampley, after the verdict was rendered and a stream of boos cascaded into the ring.

At the end of the night, Castillo was hoisted high and carried through the MGM Grand Casino on the shoulders of his fans celebrating his 'victory.'

Only he had not won.

That was not the point. Many in attendance that night felt he had. The media was split, however, and the judges – more importantly – unanimously felt Floyd Mayweather was the rightful winner.

Was the supposedly great Mayweather not great? Or was he just not a lightweight?

Castillo had not just won a round or two, he had pushed Floyd to the absolute wire.

Kevin Iole, writing for *KO* magazine and with the feeling Mayweather had won a close fight, said bluntly, 'It was hardly the dominating performance many had expected.'

On the contrary, Castillo had made such a fight of it that Bob

Arum fumed at the decision while the HBO commentary team scratched their heads at the scorecards.

The crowd, well, they jeered.

Of the judges marks of 115-111 (twice) and 116-111, George Foreman said, 'I hope he [Floyd] said thank you.'

Some agreed with the officials. Marc Ratner, the executive director of the Nevada State Athletic Commission, said, 'I thought Floyd fought one hell of a defensive fight. It was one of Mayweather's finest defensive performances. Maybe his best.'

You can't please all of the people all of the time.

Boxing News reckoned Mayweather showed more cowardice than craftsmanship.

'He looked like a schoolboy in a playground scrap who was constantly "bailing out" for fear of getting hit,' wrote Brady.

For once, the CompuBox statistics were not lopsided in Mayweather's favour. Castillo apparently landed a higher percentage of punches, scoring with 203 opposed to Mayweather's 157 at an accuracy of forty per cent to Floyd's thirty-five.

The fight and the feeling afterwards did not help Floyd's popularity.

His debut at the weight had been eagerly anticipated and ESPN's host of *Friday Night Fights*, Brian Kenny, captured the mood of hardcore fans when he said, 'It's a great fight because I think Castillo is the real lightweight champion and I commend Floyd for calling him out right away. Instead of picking on someone he can beat easily, Mayweather is going after the real champ in that class.' He felt Floyd would stop Castillo late, his speed being the difference.

Steve Forbes, IBF super-featherweight champion, thought Mayweather would win on cuts. Jesse James Leija, cousin of former Floyd foe Louie, tipped Floyd to win by decision as did rising lightweight Francisco Bojado. In fact, few picked Castillo; it was more about Mayweather having another chance to prove that he belonged on top of the pound-for-pound lists.

If he impressed against Castillo, he could perhaps reach the top of that illustrious pile, even by default. Félix Trinidad had been upset by old middleweight Bernard Hopkins in September 2001, ending the Puerto Rican's sizzling streak, and Mosley had finally been scalped, defeated by Vernon Forrest in January 2002 in a stunner, even though Forrest had beaten him in the amateurs.

Regardless of his pound-for-pound rank, Mayweather was on 'superstar' wages. He was being paid $2.2-million while the champion, Castillo, was to be paid $1.1-million.

'This is the opponent I've been waiting for,' said Castillo. 'I can, and I will, prove to the critics that I am the true champion. Lightweights hit harder. Let's see if he can take it.'

Mayweather, who through his career had sparred middleweights and even bigger men, thought he was too versatile and Castillo was too straightforward to topple him.

He had also made further changes to his team. Cutman and ex-boxer Cassius Greene was at the weigh-in but he had been replaced by veteran cornerman Rafael Garcia. Garcia's job was also to bandage Floyd's troublesome hands – in the gym and for fights – while dealing with any cuts or swellings that might appear in the fight.

Greene was disappointed but had been around long enough to know how the game worked.

'They could have kept us both and paid us both,' he said. 'It ain't all that much money. But I'm still cool with Floyd. It's all love, baby.'

Although the boxers both weighed in a pound or less under the 135lbs lightweight limit, Mayweather tipped the scales at only 138.5lbs on fight night while Castillo weighed over the welterweight limit at 147.5lbs, nine pounds heavier than Floyd.

Castillo, a 5 ft 8 ins Mexican from Sonora, served a five-year apprenticeship as a sparring partner to the great Julio César

Chávez and had risen to the top of the ladder by defeating Stevie Johnston and then drawing with the gifted American in the rematch. A six-round warrior-like stoppage of former WBC champion César Bazán backed up his credentials while Mayweather's stand-out victories over Hernández, Manfredy and Corrales had been diluted since with a few lacklustre showings.

Perhaps that was why, despite those three brilliant performances, Mayweather still toiled at the box office.

There were just 6,920 curious enough to see if he could top the lightweight lists after moving up from super-featherweight.

'There are only a few thousand people here to see a fighter regarded as one of the best of the world,' said Larry Merchant, as Mayweather made his entrance.

Reports indicated that ticket sales had been exceedingly slow. Arum had admitted that the crowd had been 'papered', with discounts and giveaways to try to fill the place up. Hundreds of tickets were doled out for free to servicemen and women at the nearby Nellis Air Force Base. Mayweather even publically spoke of his disappointment that a banner or poster with his likeness on did not drape down one side of the MGM, as it had done for Britney Spears when she performed there. That would have cost Top Rank around $150,000. He again said Arum was not doing enough 'to get my face out there.'

Arum responded with the usual vigour, saying, 'About three years ago, we had Floyd positioned to become Sugar Ray Leonard. And then, he kind of lost his senses. You can't talk to the kid. He sits there quietly and seems to listen, but you can tell it's not getting through. He keeps saying these outrageous things and getting into the middle of trouble, and that turns people off. How does he expect us to be able to promote him when he won't cooperate? He brings up De La Hoya, but De La Hoya was extremely cooperative and worked to become one of boxing's top gate attractions.'

Chants of 'U-S-A', most likely from the military personnel who had bagged free tickets, were matched by the Hispanic cheers of 'Me-hi-co' as Mayweather's speed put him in an early lead and allowed him to draw a trickle of blood from Castillo's nose.

Floyd, who had asked his corner to massage his shoulder in between the first and second rounds, boxed southpaw in round two. As their feet tangled, Castillo fell to the deck but it was ruled a slip. Both reeled from a head clash moments later.

All three judges gave the first four sessions to the challenger.

Mayweather was moving a lot but Castillo, by the fifth and sixth, was closing the gap. There was a hard straight right that caught Floyd on the ropes and as the seventh ended the crowd erupted as Castillo poured on an assault with a left to the body and an overhand right.

'Show me something then,' shouted Roger Mayweather as Floyd sat on his stool ahead of the eighth. There was more success for the champion in the next round, Castillo landing hefty blows up and downstairs, but he was docked a point by referee Vic Drakulich at the close of that session for hitting on the break as he caught Floyd with a left hook while the official tried to separate them.

Castillo came out firing in the ninth as both fighters jostled for control. Again, at the end of the round, as the bell sounded, there were afters. This time it was Mayweather who landed a left, clearly once the bell had sounded.

Drakulich seemed to think long and hard about deducting a point. Colour commentating for HBO, George Foreman urged him to. The referee did not.

Floyd was landing with left hooks and jabs, fending Castillo off with jabs but he could not slow the marauding Mexican in the tenth. As they battled in close, Mayweather seemed to try to line up Castillo for a right hand by placing his elbow against the champion, and that cost the American a point. 'Watch that elbow,' ordered Drakulich.

There was some delightful close-quarter warfare in the eleventh. Neither retreated, both stood and delivered. There was not much to choose between them but that was probably the hardest round of Mayweather's career to date.

Castillo's left seemed to stray south of the belt line a couple of times in the final session but neither Mayweather nor Drakulich made anything of it. The fighters tore into each other through the twelfth as if everything depended upon it and still there was little between them. The crowd roared on every attack, every punch. They dug in all the way to the bell and even a little beyond before Drakulich could pull them apart.

Merchant, Lampley and HBO's resident judge Harold Lederman all thought that Castillo had done enough. Lederman thought Castillo had won seven rounds, Mayweather four and one session was even, which would have meant the champion would retain by a margin of 115-111.

But when Michael Buffer announced the scores, boos erupted. Castillo threw his arms into the air. Floyd was raised onto a teammate's shoulders and paraded around the ring – clutching onto his WBC belts. The least popular person at the party looked up to the heavens and thanked God.

In the ring, Merchant got his teeth stuck into Mayweather, asking him whether he felt it was close and if it had been the 'easy' fight he had forecast.

'You've got to realise, I beat this guy with a messed-up arm, but I don't have no excuse,' he said. 'If he wants a rematch we can do it again.'

'I thought I won the fight, unfortunately the judges didn't agree with me,' said a clearly deflated Castillo. 'At one point he hurt me with a left hook but I think I hurt him a lot more.'

'I disagree with the way the scoring went,' said Arum. 'It's not that I feel Mayweather didn't win, but not by this margin. This is ludicrous.'

While some cried robbery, and Merchant asked Castillo whether Mayweather had received the decision because he lived in the city and was fighting at 'home', Foreman looked at the flipside and said it was what Mayweather's career needed, that a rematch would make him into a pay-per-view star. That opinion might not have been wholly shared and there were plenty who felt adding the lightweight crown to his burgeoning belt cabinet had caused Mayweather's reputation more harm than good.

Leonard Ellerbe, while examining Floyd's left shoulder in the dressing room post fight, made the new champion whimper as he pressed on the injured area.

He said he'd damaged it two days before the fight, when he slammed a hard shot into a heavybag. He reckoned it had hindered him from throwing his right hand. An orthopaedic surgeon diagnosed it as a strained rotator cuff that would cause pain and discomfort but not require surgery.

'Mayweather did good at the beginning,' agreed Castillo. 'But it is a long fight and I was there for the whole time. And when I was doing all that work, what were the judges seeing?'

'He's a strong guy,' Mayweather admitted. 'But he fought a one-armed fighter and he still lost. I showed a lot because I fought a great champion with one arm and I still won.'

Jerry Roth, one of the judges who marked it 115-111 for Mayweather, said the punchstats did not tell the story of the fight.

'Every time I saw Castillo get aggressive, Mayweather's movements seemed to confuse him. That to me was not effective aggression,' he said.

Oscar De La Hoya, watching from home, believed Castillo deserved to win. In the build-up, Mayweather had spoken of his desire to one day move up to welterweight and tackle boxing's 'Golden Boy'.

'Mayweather's not going to get anywhere by complaining and by wanting to fight me and saying he doesn't receive enough money and this and that,' said De La Hoya. 'Just keep on winning in the ring, do the best you can do, and keep on smiling and be a good person outside the ring, and the fights will come.'

Brady felt Mayweather was a long way from stardom. 'Superstars are supposed to be breathtaking,' he said, 'Mayweather isn't. He's 28-0 (21) but he's no Sugar Ray Leonard or Roy Jones. At twenty-five, he's never going to be.'

Castillo wanted to go again, though doubted he would get the opportunity. 'He did the talking and I did the fighting, and the people told you what they thought. I hope he is a man of his word and we have the rematch. I will do the same thing. I understand him and his style and I know how to beat that style. I already have beaten him, I'll just have to do it again. And I won't waste it if I get it. The judges should be impartial but I'm going to get a rematch. I got it from Bob Arum himself.'

Mayweather said immediately he was open to another match with Castillo and the WBC issued a statement supporting a second contest.

'He was a class guy and gave me a shot when he didn't have to. And the one thing about Floyd Mayweather, I don't duck nobody. I want the best, and if people think this guy is one of the best I'm happy to do it again. I'm more than ready.'

By way of protest, *The Ring* – who called for an immediate rematch – named Castillo as their Fighter of the Month and as a consequence, Mayweather fell to seventh in the publication's pound-for-pound list. They said he would have to do better than in the first fight to avoid slipping further down the ratings.

Nigel Collins, the magazine's editor, sent a direct message to Mayweather through his column and addressed Floyd's issues in and outside the ropes.

'Do the right thing,' wrote Collins, who called the scorecards 'predictable'. 'Give Castillo a rematch – and keep your hands to yourself outside the ring. That way, maybe they won't be so sore when you get another chance to prove yourself against Castillo.'

In the same issue, Mayweather again appeared in the 'Outside the Ropes' section, usually reserved for fighters in trouble away from the ring, gym gossip or law suits. It reported how, after Mayweather pleaded guilty in the Las Vegas Justice Court to two counts of domestic violence and one of battery for alleged attacks on Melissa Brim, the mother of one of his three children, that a third conviction in a seven-year period could see him imprisoned. *The Ring* reported that another domestic violence charge, brought by Josie Harris, the mother of Mayweather's other two children, was dropped as part of the plea bargain.

Collins recalled Floyd's name often cropping up in the 'Outside the Ropes' section. 'I had a philosophy when I was writing *The Ring* and it was not to go out of my way to publish bad stuff about a boxer,' he said. 'Obviously there was some stuff you couldn't avoid and we covered it and I had no qualms about it. But rather than a running a series of features about the difficulties Floyd was having, when he wasn't going to jail we put it in that section "Outside the Ropes" and there was no shortage of material.'

With regards to their pound-for-pound list, Hopkins was up at number one; Jones sat at two despite nondescript wins against overmatched challengers; Mexican featherweight Marco Antonio Barrera was third; Forrest was now fourth and set to fight, and defeat, Mosley again; Trinidad had fallen to five, one spot ahead of Mosley; while Kostya Tszyu, De La Hoya and heavyweight Lennox Lewis closed out their top ten. Castillo was twelfth.

Mayweather, of course, had an opinion, and told Thomas Gerbasi that Jones might be one of the best but he should be higher up the list than the Pensacola man based on the opposition he had faced. 'Roy Jones and me are two different fighters,' said

Mayweather. 'I'm fighting real opponents; I'm not fighting cab drivers. I'm not saying he can't beat top-notch opponents, but I'm fighting the top-notch guys in my weight class. You can't compare the two. I think Roy Jones is one of the best; he's a helluva fighter, but it would be a lot more exciting if he had some competition.'

In June, Diego Corrales was released from jail in Tracy, California. He had spent an extra three months behind bars because he had not always been 'a compliant prisoner'.

He began sparring the day after his release, having been unable to do any at all while in jail. He was twenty-four, was going to be managed by James Prince and said he would fight at lightweight if the right challenge came up. There was only one bout he wanted.

'If I'm physically able, it will be at 135lbs because of who the champion is there. The motivation is Floyd. I intend to get back to where I was, and then some,' he said.

However, Floyd was focused on facing Castillo again and he was given credit for that. Top Rank publicist Lee Samuels said Mayweather wanted the rematch, then he hoped to settle the score of *that* sparring session with Paul Spadafora before facing Tszyu. The rematch seemed destined for the STAPLES Center in Los Angeles before Mayweather worked his magic to get it in Vegas on a bill that was topped by the world heavyweight title fight between Wladimir Klitschko and Jameel McCline.

Eight months after Mayweather and Castillo fought on 20 April 2002, they were matched once more. It was 7 December and both had something to prove. Mayweather claimed his shoulder was fully healed. Castillo said he would finish what he had started. There was a widespread feeling that Mayweather could up his level of performance from the previous fight while Castillo had fought near his best and, at twenty-eight, had little room for improvement.

Originally the date had been set for 5 October, but tendinitis in Castillo's left ankle, which left the deposed champion unable to train, forced the bout's delay.

Mayweather could have done with the extra time, too. In September, Josie Harris, the mother of two of Floyd's children, claimed that a vehicle owned by Mayweather tried to run her car off the road in Vegas.

Mayweather's attorney, Richard Wright, said Floyd had been in the passenger seat. That 'incident' came after his March suspended sentence for domestic violence and misdemeanour battery.

Mayweather, wrote Graham Houston, was on a charm offensive going into the Castillo rematch, even putting his arm around Castillo during the weigh-in the day before the fight. Was he grateful the Mexican had garnered him another big payday, this time $2.4-million? Was he playing up for the cameras, or had the two forged a fighter's bond that can only be formed in the ring? It was certainly a long way from the Corrales hostilities.

That some in the media felt Castillo won still rankled Pretty Boy.

'I don't go by what the media says,' Mayweather told fight writer Gerbasi from his training camp in Las Vegas. 'They're always trying to be negative and going by things they don't know nothing about. But I'm not really worried about that. I'm going to be the same old Floyd and do what I've got to do. People are just waiting for my downfall. They want to see me lose. Everybody at the top has lost at the top of their game. I'm not gonna lose. I'm gonna keep working hard, and doing what I've got to do. The money is good, but there's no limit to what I'm worth. The sport is cool, but it's a job now. I already fought a hundred fights for free [in the amateurs]. Now as a professional, this is my reward.'

Floyd's grandmother, Bernice, told Sky Sports commentator Ian Darke that the brash fighter was better off trying to make friends rather than enemies. 'I think he must have listened,' she said. 'I told him, you can't go on upsetting people like this. It's not the right thing to do.'

Floyd only partially listened. He skipped the Thursday pre-fight press conference, which left Arum red-faced trying to sell a fight with just the one boxer, and not the champion at that. 'Does this make sense?' asked Arum. 'I feel sorry about this, I really do. I've promoted Floyd Jr since the beginning of his career and I want to apologise for him. Siegfried and Roy 'disappeared', him, I don't know. If I could give you an answer [as to his whereabouts] I'd give it.'

Arum had wanted the fight to go pay-per-view from Los Angeles. Floyd felt that with a large Mexican contingent in the crowd he would not get a fair shake. Arum said he also wanted New York. Floyd wanted Vegas. Larry Merchant wondered how Arum could make him a global star if he wouldn't leave his own home state. 'So how's he going to become this national figure if he's stuck here in Las Vegas and never gets out of town,' said Merchant, as Floyd made his way to the ring at the Mandalay Bay for the second Castillo fight.

Even in Vegas his reception was, at best, indifferent, when he was announced to the crowd of little more than 6,500.

Mayweather got down to boxing from the start, moving when Castillo tried to close the distance and scoring with lead left hands, jabs and hooks.

Floyd clinched when the challenger attempted to hold him in the second and he speared Castillo to the body with jabs. Already, as round two closed, Castillo was beginning to look impatient and frustrated.

When the bell sounded to end the third Castillo landed his best shot of the fight so far, a clubbing right. Floyd told him it was late but then extended his fist, touched gloves and returned to his corner.

The Mexican's corner implored him to throw combinations ahead of the fourth. Floyd was told to keep his jab working. Castillo was more aggressive in the next but paid for getting in too close, too recklessly with a bloody nose.

Ahead of the sixth, Roger said Floyd could either use his left jab or lead right to score points and then took time out to speak to referee Joe Cortez, asking him to keep an eye on any low punches Castillo might throw. He was concerned that Castillo was hitting his nephew on the hips.

With the bout halfway and the seventh about to start, Castillo was advised to charge Mayweather. It seemed desperation was already kicking in, even though some felt Castillo had done better work in rounds four and five and was well in the fight. Merchant was scoring it 3-3 and in the seventh, as Castillo again pursued Floyd, the champion took a moment to wink ringside at Larry.

There was now blood from the nostrils of both fighters. Castillo was having success with the overhand right and body shots in his best spell of the fight.

Floyd seemed to do enough to win the eighth, landing with some good rights and once again becoming more elusive but Castillo was sharper in the ninth as the bout hung on a knife edge.

'He's winning rounds with that lousy jab he's got,' Castillo was told in the corner. 'Come on, don't tell me you can't do it.'

'I can,' he charged back.

'Then do it!'

Floyd was again more precise in the eleventh, countering well, and Castillo's body language lacked positivity. He trudged forwards rather than think or fight his way in. The blood now poured from his nose, but he finished the round stronger than he started it.

Still, Castillo seemed to think it wasn't close. 'I can't get his style,' he said to his team. 'He's very elusive.'

With a round to go, Mayweather was well up on many cards, his lead unassailable. As the bell signalled the end of the fight, Castillo barrelled forwards and lobbed over a right hand. Their feet tangled and Mayweather skidded back onto his trunks. The crowd roared. Perhaps some in the cheap seats thought Floyd had been bowled over by the right. He hadn't. Floyd finished the fight on the seat of his pants and then concern switched from the ring to the judges.

Would they see Mayweather the winner based on his boxing and moving, or would they sympathise with Castillo for the verdict he did not get in the previous fight? It seemed an easier contest to score. Mayweather had not done a great deal more, but Castillo had seemingly done less this time.

The tallies of 115-113, 115-113 and 116-113 were fair and might have even been complimentary to the runner-up, Castillo.

This time the media's verdict, the scorecards and the punchstats were all in Floyd's favour. Mayweather landed seventy-four of 164 power punches – a rate of forty-five per cent – and 162 of 399 total punches, a much more stellar forty-one per cent. Castillo's frustrations lay with scoring just 101 of 427 power shots (twenty-four per cent) and 137 of 604 total punches (twenty-three per cent).

Mayweather had said it would be easier, he did not say anything about it being more entertaining. 'My plan going into this fight was just to box, to box more, be smart and [throw] no power shots,' he said.

'I thought Mayweather gave Castillo a twelve-round boxing lesson,' wrote Graham Houston in *Boxing Monthly*. He felt Floyd had played it safe to win on points rather than chancing his arm at a stoppage victory.

Unimpressed veteran historian Bob Mee, writing for *Boxing News*, agreed. 'The twenty-five-year-old American posed, defended, held on the inside and threw single punches instead of committing himself to hard work.'

Mee said he basically 'fiddled Castillo out of the fight' – in laymen's terms he did just enough to win without doing anything more.

'I think Castillo was ready to go in the later rounds but my left hand was hurt,' Floyd said. 'I think in the fifth or sixth, so I wasn't able to set up combinations like I would like to set up later on in the fight. So I just boxed and used my defence at the end.'

Mayweather called himself 'the black sheep of boxing,' and then said he was fighting against the odds. 'I feel like everybody is against Floyd Mayweather,' he reckoned, when Merchant asked him to clarify his statement.

'I couldn't find him all night,' Castillo confessed. 'I couldn't figure him out. He fought a more intelligent fight. I never felt I did anything this time.'

'This time nobody can say it was controversial,' said Arum. 'It was a clear-cut victory.'

But tensions between fighter and promoter had resurfaced with Floyd's no-show at the presser to promote the fight.

'Bob Arum is my promoter – I have nothing bad to say about him. He's a great promoter,' Floyd said.

Arum seemed resigned to losing Mayweather, who was now twenty-five-years-old and 29-0 with twenty stoppage wins. Floyd had said he was so fed up with the business he might retire. It all seemed a long way from sleeping next to a trophy in a Red Roof Inn.

Houston wondered if only the very best fighters would bring the best out in Mayweather. 'There don't seem to be many of those around for this extremely gifted young champion,' he wrote.

The Ring felt that Mayweather was still an exciting fighter, just not against Castillo. They pondered the impact moving up in weight had, allied with hand injuries, and wondered whether

Floyd's power was diminishing. Of a possible eighty-two-scheduled rounds in his last seven fights, he had boxed seventy-six of them, even if Burton, Corrales and Chávez were stopped later in their respective contests.

Neither Mayweather nor Klitschko electrified that night. The big Ukrainian heavyweight got by McCline in ten sessions without setting the world alight. Critics said McCline froze. Others just thought he was not that good.

'I think that, in hindsight, the big fight for him was the Corrales fight,' Merchant recalled about Floyd years later. 'That and the Castillo fight – which many people thought he lost – when he tried to fight instead of box and he found that against a stronger, more experienced opponent and champion that was risky. And I think based on the Corrales fight and the Castillo fight and so on he was an outstanding lightweight and maybe in hindsight that's where he was at his best, just like may fighters who later in their careers move up in weight. Some of them prosper and can even be better than they were in the lower weight classes but I think Floyd was better as a lightweight.'

'It was a close fight,' DiBella said of the first Castillo match. 'I didn't think it was controversial, but then you saw what happened when they fought again, he eliminated any doubt with the rematch.'

Mayweather had righted a supposed wrong, avenged a defeat that did not exist – and that many had not seen in the first place – but it seemed that anything less than the dazzling standards he had set against Hernández, Manfredy and Corrales would be seen as failure. He had become a victim of his virtuoso successes.

And when Larry Merchant asked him whether he would test himself against two of the better lightweights, Juan Lazcano and Stevie Johnston, of course he said yes. But he actually fought Victoriano Sosa next. Then Phillip N'dou. Then DeMarcus Corley. Then Henry Bruseles.

For now, Lazcano and Johnston were due to face one another to decide who would meet Mayweather, who was to fight Sosa at the Selland Arena in Fresno, California.

It was hardly a boxing Mecca. Whether Floyd was in exile of not, it did not matter. He still wasn't putting bums on seats. Not the sort that tallied with the money he expected to make anyway.

There were 7,225 on hand to see him improve to 30-0 with another twelve-round win. That meant around 4-5,000 seats remained empty. The Las Vegas casinos couldn't be persuaded. Madison Square Garden in New York couldn't care less after he snubbed an opportunity to fight the Castillo rematch there.

This was not what the big time was about. Only 400,000 lived in the town and local promoter George Chung had to do the ring announcing when the original guy did not show.

Sosa had twice knocked down Paul Spadafora, the IBF champion and one-time Mayweather sparmate. But he'd lost a decision. It was supposed to be interesting to compare how Mayweather and the southpaw Pittsburgh champion did against the same opponent.

The difference was that Sosa, a cousin of baseball star Sammy, and 35-2-2 heading into the fight and ranked by all four governing bodies, could not land the type of shots that had troubled Spadafora. Floyd was too defensively sound. That defensive outlook contributed to the crowd cheering Sosa's offensive efforts. Floyd, as Floyd did, caught the hard shots either on his arms, gloves or elbows. At a point in round seven, Sosa tried so hard to connect that he wound up on the deck.

Punchstats don't tell a whole story, far from it, but that Sosa had scored with just seventy-nine of 565 punches at fourteen per cent, and just twelve per cent of the 182 jabs, told its own tale. Mayweather was up to sixty per cent of 246 jabs and prior to the bout had been speaking about his interest in facing Oscar De La Hoya all the way up at light-middleweight, three division's higher. That was the type of fight he could use to earn the fame and riches he so desired.

The Sosa fight was not. Again, nursing a swollen left hand afterwards, Mayweather said it was more likely he would face someone like Lazcano, the WBC mandatory challenger, and then he would possibly meet the winner of an interesting-looking bout between Paul Spadafora and Leonard Dorin.

'He was easy work,' Floyd said rather disparagingly of Sosa. 'He threw more shots, I landed more shots. He was strong in rounds one through six, then he tired.'

Sosa, astonishingly, felt he had won. So did those in the Fresno nosebleeds who could only see a whirlwind of Sosa's gloves without seeing that they were actually missing. Either that or they just wanted him to win. That was always possible.

Sosa was a decent, compact fighter who had enjoyed landing some solid shots in the fight, but he wasn't on Mayweather's level.

'I got robbed,' he reckoned. 'I hit him whenever I wanted. I did what I wanted to do. I want a rematch right now. I beat him. Here in California, I guess you have to kill someone.'

Mayweather pocketed $1.8 million for his 'easy work.' The scorecards reflected that, too, with two judges marking it 118-110 and the third scoring it 119-109.

The crowd was not thrilled. They booed even as Floyd left the ring. Mayweather felt it was racial. 'Sosa's a Hispanic fighter and most of the fans here are Hispanic,' he said. He thought the main thing, anyway, was winning. Industry experts believed he needed to reassess that outlook.

The lightweight division failed to inspire, though, which is why Mayweather kept an eye on old Top Rank stablemate De La Hoya. Aside from Lazcano and Johnston, you would struggle to make a case for any of them having half a chance with Floyd.

Spadafora might have more than held his own in sparring with Floyd, but his form was dipping. Little-known WBO champion Artur Grigorian never fought outside of Germany. Dorin might enter the fray if he could unseat Spadafora, but really the marquee matches weren't there.

And after the Sosa fight, Bob Mee, for *Boxing News*, wondered what Floyd could possibly bring to the table to tempt the big names, including Oscar.

'On the evidence we saw here,' wrote Mee, 'he would have nuisance value against the light-middleweight No. 1 but that's about it . . . He could take on Mayweather, but what would he gain from it? De La Hoya is interested in his place in history now. That will not be advanced one jot by beating a lightweight – and were the unexpected to happen and Mayweather to fiddle him out of a decision, the "downgrading" would be dramatic.'

Mee bumped into Sosa in the hotel later and said the Dominican challenger had appeared to accept that he had lost.

All eyes were now back on Mayweather. He'd apparently plateaued, even while defeating decent opposition.

'Four of Mayweather's last five fights have gone the full twelve rounds,' Mee added. 'And although as usual he emerged unmarked, it may be that this type of performance may be what he will provide from here on in. But if he is to sustain interest, and serious paydays, he has to find a way of producing more drama than he managed here.'

Outside the ring, however, there was still plenty of drama. Jeff Mayweather was nowhere to be seen, Floyd Sr a distant memory.

'My father is jealous of me,' Mayweather Jr told the *New York Times*.

'His career never took off. He knows as a fighter he was never as good as me. In fact, he was never better than me at nothing.'

'The Bible says, "Honour thy father and thy mother," and three years ago he kicked me out of the house for a man named James Prince, who has made $3 million from my son while I made $75,000,' Mayweather Sr countered.

Now, though, Prince was also exiled from the group after his contract ran out on 16 October, though Floyd's ex-manager was not a man to be told he was no longer invited to the party.

It was 11 September 2003, and Floyd was working out in the Top Rank Gym in Las Vegas. Prince, smarting from the contractual battle that was going on, had not wanted out.

On that day in the gym, several men showed up and worked over Leonard Ellerbe and camp member Thomas Summers. Both were reportedly hospitalised and Mayweather, watching in shock from inside the ring – so it is understood – could do nothing.

The story was never confirmed by Mayweather's side, though Arum would later say Floyd had been left shaken and Mayweather apparently told duBoef, 'These are bad guys, you have to help me save my family.'

Arum offered a letter of credit to help him with Prince.

'James don't take no letter of credit,' Floyd replied.

Over the years there's been talk of guns being involved during the incident; only a handful of people know what happened.

One of boxing's best pound for pound best fighters of the modern era, Bernard Hopkins – who spent several years in jail for armed robbery and understands a bit about the flip side of the law – believes he knows.

'Hey, listen, at the end of the day, when I look at guys, and some rappers that I ain't going to mention, that talk about gangsta, talk about street, talk about going to jail, talk about being hard on the street, that reminds me of Floyd Mayweather. Floyd Mayweather is no tough guy. And Floyd Mayweather can tell you about, and Ellerbe can tell you about when a couple of guys came up in Top Rank's gym and they was taking two to three weeks to scrub blood out of the stains of the carpet that was in there. Where was the gangsta then? See, they know I know.'

Larry Merchant had also heard various things. 'He [Floyd] admitted later that he had made a mistake. And there was that infamous incident at a gym when Mayweather tried to finesse a contract with Prince and delay a fight and Prince apparently, presumably, sent some tough guys to the gym who apparently inflicted some damage on some of Floyd's cronies. And much later Mayweather said, "I made a youthful mistake." I don't know if in the long run it was a mistake or not, because he went on from there and if he learned from it, good for him.'

Top Rank had apparently given Mayweather $610,000 to settle with Prince, in cutting the Texan a twenty per cent slice of Mayweather's $3.05 million purse for his next fight, against Phillip N'dou.

'Bob Arum, what he has done for me personally the last couple of months, I can't do anything but praise him,' said Mayweather.

Even if it was only temporary, Arum felt Mayweather had realised the error of his ways. 'What happened was an aberration. He made a mistake,' said the promoter. 'We tried to warn him about the mistake, but he went ahead with it and now it's over. I think he realises we were always supportive of him and appreciates us more now for our efforts.'

Prince had been with Mayweather for three years. Because the N'dou fight came after the end of the contract, he would not have been entitled to the slice he took. There was, of course, plenty of speculation about why it was paid but Floyd's camp was silent. 'I choose to be mature about the situation,' he said. 'Some people can be forty years old [Prince was thirty-nine at the time] and not be mature.'

By the time they parted ways, Floyd had made $16.8 million, meaning Prince would have been paid $3.56 million.

'I brought James Prince into the game,' said Floyd. 'I helped him build an empire, as far as boxing goes. As far as my music, I got no help. Will that slow me down? Will it hold back Philthy Rich Records? No. I'll make my mark. James Prince got what he wanted. I got no help. But I'm not mad about it. I choose to be mature about the situation, be a man, make my own decisions. I'm free now.'

Loyal Leonard Ellerbe became an advisor. Mayweather had hired NRaGE Sports Management, based in Hatboro, Pennsylvania, as his new management team. Lew Hendler, co-owner of NRaGE, said they were looking to 'follow a George Foreman model' with Floyd. 'I don't know if I want to change Floyd, but I want to encourage him into addressing areas where his image could be viewed positively. The legal issues, we'd like Floyd to put behind him. As far as the press, we intend for him to be more accessible. We're looking to involve him in events, whether they are for charity or as a spokesman for a product. Over time, we'd have his recognition level and fan base go beyond boxing purists.'

South African Philip 'The Time Bomb' N'dou came next in the ring in November. That same high drama did not follow. Even the expectation of Mayweather being at his best began to ebb away, though he was at least able to paint such a pretty picture on the ring canvas that he well reminded even the staunchest critics of his qualities. N'dou, like Mayweather, was a featherweight in the 1996 Olympics. He had lost to the eventual gold medallist, Thailand's Somluck Kamsing, in the second round of the event. Facing Floyd, he walked to the ring on the back of twenty-one consecutive wins, twenty of them early, and members of his entourage shouting the clichéd 'And the new' in optimistic anticipation of his triumph.

Unfortunately for the challenger, it was Floyd's best display since Corrales and 9,080 fans (of whom 7,200 paid making $443,000 at the gate) in Grand Rapids lapped it up. N'dou lapped up plenty of punishment before he was stopped in the seventh.

The crowd, who gave Floyd his kindest ovation in some time, were satisfied. Mayweather had boxed with a fur trim on his black shorts, while N'dou wore tassled trunks. They donned similar colours but the disparity in speed was glaringly obvious from the start. The champion was able to land solid right hands over N'dou's tardy jab.

Floyd dominated. N'dou tried to chase him down but was just getting picked off.

In the fifth, some felt it should have been stopped but N'dou roared back with both hands. He fired dozens of blows but Mayweather's shoulder-roll was ridiculously sublime and almost impregnable despite more than 100 punches coming his way. It was a spectacular three-minute show.

Mayweather had said he would try to get the job done in the sixth and he nearly did. N'dou was down from a big right although referee Frank Garza ruled it a slip. 'How on earth is that a slip?' screamed Lampley on the HBO telecast.

Mayweather knew it wasn't so rushed in to finish the job.

The South African was chewing on flush shots, testing out the durability of Mayweather's hands, and still trying to land his own blows with only fractional success.

'You're getting hit too much, we can't let this happen. This is your career,' said veteran trainer Tommy Brooks, who had been drafted in by South African coach Nick Durandt to help the team prepare for Mayweather.

Durandt said he was giving his man another round. Mayweather was not so generous. Halfway through the seventh and decisive round, Mayweather cracked N'dou with three consecutive lead rights and he finally crumbled onto his front.

Durandt tried to communicate with N'dou to tell him he would stop it. The fighter, of course, implored him not to. But Durandt climbed the steps. He'd seen enough and Garza waved it off.

'Terrific fight, terrific performance by Floyd Mayweather,' gushed Larry Merchant, finally. He was not the only one.

The absence of Prince had softened the portrayal of Mayweather in some media outlets. Floyd also said his long-term partner, Josie Harris, was changing him as a person and she'd even got him involved with the local church.

'I'm not out to get the fastest car or more jewellery,' he said. 'I've been there. When I retire, I want to have boxed everybody. And it won't matter if I wasn't a knockout artist. All I ever claimed to be is a winner. An ugly victory is better than a pretty loss, but my last two fights at home weren't pleasing, so I really want to put on a show.'

'I'm very proud of Philip,' said Durandt. 'We're going home with our heads held high.'

Ultimately, though, Floyd was judged on what he did in the ring and after battering N'dou he was hot once more.

He said he wanted to fight Arturo Gatti, moving up to light-welterweight in what would be his first pay-per-view date, rather than meet the likes of Casamayor and Freitas who he said did not want to fight, or not on their terms anyway. There was talk by Arum of moving Floyd up to welterweight to face Antonio Margarito, another Arum-promoted fighter. The De La Hoya fight, well, Floyd was just waiting for Oscar to nod in his direction.

Ellerbe and Floyd just kept talking about 'big fights.'

Kostya Tszyu, the world's leading 140-pounder was with Showtime, so that seemed unlikely. Ricardo Mayorga, at welter, was rumoured but also deemed unlikely because Don King – Arum's arch enemy – promoted the crazy Nicaraguan.

Gatti's manager Pat Lynch said they had no interest in Mayweather. Certainly not in 2004. All the while, the spectre of a huge leap up in weight to take on De La Hoya loomed large and the boxing media was intrigued. Not only did they want to see how Floyd would fare with someone so much bigger, but the plot twist of Mayweather Sr training Oscar to fight and beat his own son was almost beyond Hollywood.

Outside the ring there were more distractions, however, with pending court dates in Nevada and Michigan. One was for allegedly striking Josie Harris. The other was a 'misdemeanour assault and battery' charge relating to a bar fight in Grand Rapids. Ellerbe told *The Grand Rapids Press*, 'It's obvious that Floyd is a target.'

Floyd's hot streak in the ring, however, continued into May 2004 when he met DeMarcus Corley in Atlantic City. It was not Gatti, but it was his debut up at light-welterweight. Washington DC's Corley even buzzed Mayweather in the third round of an exciting, crowd-pleasing fight.

Corley had not boxed in almost a year since disappointingly losing to Zab Judah. But he had been sparring good fighters and therefore active, to an extent.

The New Jersey fight fans reserved the right to judge. Just 6,103 attended Boardwalk Hall and 'there were acres of empty seats,' according to Jim Brady.

The former WBO light-welterweight champion came into the ring for Mayweather wearing a gas mask. The fight was billed as a WBC title eliminator. Southpaw Corley was being paid just $150,000, a marginal amount compared to Mayweather's $3-million plus.

Unlike against Judah in his previous fight, though, Corley showed up ready to rumble and was not intimidated.

The left-hander boxed and traded punches, giving a good account of himself throughout the early rounds. After three sessions he was well in the contest and his corner tried to let him know.

'He don't want to fight, he wants to stand on the outside and potshot. Fight this motherfucker. Fight,' he was urged.

Corley was fired up and came out smoking. He nailed Mayweather with a right hook that staggered Floyd momentarily. The crowd gasped. There were excited and concerned screams ringside. Corley had him on the ropes and began working over his body. Mayweather would not be upstaged and with ninety seconds to go in the round he pinged in a wicked right, which was the punch of the fight. Now it was Corley's turn to duck and dodge but he could do so only for so long before shipping a similar right and then caving to the floor. It was not ruled a knockdown. He rose, shaking his head, then landed a big left of his own as the two tore into one another again. It was a scintillating round.

Mayweather was getting tagged far more than many had anticipated but in the eighth he broke through with left hooks and right hands and Corley staggered to the canvas for the first official knockdown, even though it was his third visit to the mat.

Corley battled back but slipped to the floor again before the end of the session. He was tiring, but still dogged in his attacks. Again he was on his knees in the ninth as Mayweather tried to catch him with a left hook but Floyd seemed to realise it was only a slip and tried to assist Corley back to his feet. The crowd applauded his sporting gesture.

The tenth had barely started before Corley was back on the deck. Floyd caught him with a right uppercut, then landed a blistering fusillade of hooks and Corley's legs buckled. Mayweather continued to boss the session.

'This motherfucker's dead tired,' Ellerbe told Floyd between rounds. Corley's resolve remained steadfast through the final two rounds but the result was predictable, a wide win for Mayweather: 119-107, 119-109 and 118-108.

'He's magic out there. He's electric,' conceded Corley's trainer Don Turner.

Corley said Mayweather had the opportunity to 'make a noise' at 140lbs.

'A true champion will fight through anything,' said Mayweather, who claimed his shoulder and hand hurt again.

'He landed some solid punches. He's a good puncher, but I wasn't hurt at all. I beat the best at 130. I went to 135 and beat the best, and now I'm moving up to 140. The only thing I want to do is to fight the best.'

'Talent alone is never enough,' headlined the report in *The Ring*. 'Maybe someday Floyd Mayweather will finally get it. "Pretty Boy" may eventually realise it's not talent alone that attracts huge pay-per-view numbers and sellout crowds. Maybe someday, a box office stampede will occur and Mayweather's face appears on a fight poster, and when doors fling open droves upon droves of fans will come streaming in to watch one of the best pound-for-pound fighters in the world,' wrote Joseph Santoliquito. 'But that day has yet to arrive.'

The HBO team wondered how Floyd could now cross over into the mainstream. Merchant said there was no way he could reach De La Hoya's level but did not rule him out of becoming an attraction in his own right, if he could take part in big fights.

The bout was the last for Mayweather under his contracts with promoter Bob Arum and HBO, although each had the right of first refusal for his next fight. Mayweather's stock was just right for any renegotiations.

He was now regarded as, pound for pound, the sport's number one fighter by *USA Today*. *The Ring* had him at number two, behind Bernard Hopkins, but they were certainly the top two.

Mayweather, of course, felt he deserved to be number one.

'There is no way you can rank Bernard Hopkins above me in the pound-for-pound rankings,' Floyd contended. 'All he did was beat two small men, Félix Trinidad and Oscar De La Hoya. Those are two small men that came up to his weight class that he beat. When you rank fighters on pound for pound you have to rank them on how many weight classes they can go to and dominate. This is my third weight class in seven or eight years that I will have dominated and next year I will be at welterweight and dominate welterweight. The guy who was at the top [Roy Jones] and already beat Bernard Hopkins has been knocked out, so how can you rank these guys in front of Floyd Mayweather – pound for pound – when I win on a constant basis and have been a world champion since 1998. In the year 2008, I will have been a champion for ten years.'

A week before Floyd topped Corley, the great Roy Jones had been brutally defeated by Mayweather's old Olympic teammate Antonio Tarver, starched in two rounds.

For *The Ring* in 2004, it was not just about whom of Mayweather's contemporaries he could beat, but where he might stand among the best lightweights in history. William Dettloff tossed Mayweather into a host of dream fights against some of the best lightweights of all time, reckoning Floyd would top Joe Gans, Pernell Whitaker, Carlos Ortiz, Joe Brown but lose to Benny Leonard, Bob Montgomery, Tony Canzoneri, Beau Jack, Ike Williams and Roberto Durán. That was elite company to be considered alongside.

There were lucrative options that were more realistic although the oft-discussed bout with sparring rival Spadafora was off the table. The 'Pittsburgh Kid' had his own legal troubles after allegedly shooting his fiancée in August 2004. He would not box for two years and never reclaimed his titles or form when he did eventually return to the ring.

Mayweather had come through his own set of legal troubles.

In mid-June, Floyd was convicted on two counts of battery, for punching Herneatha McGill – a friend of Josie Harris – and Karra Blackburn at the Ra nightclub in the Luxor Casino on 1 August 2003.

The women alleged that Mayweather had punched McGill on the cheek, and then struck Blackburn on the back of the head as she went to help McGill from the floor.

A one-year jail sentence was suspended, although Mayweather

had to have 'impulse control' counselling and either pay a $1,000 fine or serve 100 hours of community service. Mayweather said he had not even seen the two women he had been accused of punching that night but Nevada judge Deborah Lippis was not convinced and even said she was "shocked" at the lies she believed he was telling.

'You may be a terrific and famous fighter, but that doesn't make you a god,' Lippis said.

Of course, many felt the women were out for money. Neither required medical attention and both contacted a civil lawyer.

'I don't want to sue Mr Mayweather,' McGill said. 'I just want Mr Mayweather to leave me alone.'

Back inside the ring, as 2005 opened, 21-2 (13) Puerto Rican Henry Bruseles was not anybody's number-one choice to fight Mayweather but the Caguas man, who could boast being a friend of fast-rising light-welterweight Miguel Cotto, had put almost thirty rounds in the bank in training with his pal as he prepared for Floyd and their match at the American Airlines Arena in Miami. *Boxing News* said that with 4,000 seats full the venue was 'mostly empty.'

Juan Lazcano had turned down a fight at light-welter with Floyd, opting to stay at 135lbs for the vacant world title bout at lightweight against José Luis Castillo.

'The size of the crowd is not what Floyd would have been looking for,' announced Lampley, as Floyd walked to the ring, 'But maybe the worm is turning on his public appeal.'

Merchant could not recall a fighter with so much talent who had made less of an impact at the gate. No national sportswriter was on hand to cover the fight, which would decide the WBC's number-one ranked contender.

'Bruseles was a hot prospect a few years ago but he never fully realised his promise, nor has he fought a serious fighter, which begs the questions: why is he fighting one of the most gifted fighters in the world?' queried Merchant. 'Well, maybe the women Mayweather usually spars with weren't available.'

Jim Brady, who referred to Mayweather as one of the sport's most 'highly touted and over-hyped fighters', chimed in during his fight report, 'Mayweather is unbeaten in thirty-three fights but that is not including the two lovelies he was convicted of cracking in a Las Vegas nightclub in 2003.'

Against Bruseles, Mayweather won in the eighth of a scheduled twelve-rounder to improve to 33-0 (22). He was on his way to a third title in a third weight class.

The crowd booed in the third round, with Mayweather in the ascendancy. He again used his quickness to boss the contest, leading with jabs and single right hands. It was straightforward stuff. He fought on the inside in round four, and convincingly held the upper hand in that department, too, even rattling Bruseles with a sharp right and, moments later, with a left hook.

As soon as the round finished, Floyd and Roger had a heated disagreement in the corner. It took Floyd twenty-five seconds of the minute-interval to eventually sit on his stool. Even then, the fighter seemed to be neglecting to listen to the trainer's instructions.

He peppered a wobbling Bruseles with rights throughout round six, even taking the time to tell HBO's Jim Lampley – talking US football on commentary with Roy Jones – that he predicted the New England Patriots would win an upcoming match as Bruseles tried to press the action. Mayweather was winning every session at a canter. Again there seemed to be tension in the Mayweather corner before round seven but it was the last opportunity for any discord between sessions.

Thirty seconds into the eighth, Lampley called up from ringside, 'Eagles or Falcons, Floyd?'

'I like Michael Vick,' the fighter replied, referring to the Philadelphia Eagles star.

Mayweather then speared his Puerto Rican prey with lefts to the head and body and with less than a minute to go in the round, stepped in with a right into the pit of Bruseles' stomach, causing him to drop.

Mayweather jived on his feet as Bruseles made it back to his and tried to renew hostilities but he was down once more under pressure as the clock ticked by.

Referee Jorge Alonso waved the fighters back together but as he did so the ringside doctor stood on the apron and called off the contest with five seconds to go in the round.

The crowd seemed confused by the ending but the disparity in quality and class between the fighters was obvious. Mayweather had closed the show, landing twenty of his final twenty-nine blows.

He held his oldest daughter, Iyanna Mayweather, in his arms in the post-fight interview with Merchant.

'I knew eventually the shots would break him down and I was going to drown him in deep waters when it got late,' said Mayweather, who denied there had been any kind of dissension with his uncle.

'I trained hard for this fight. It was no dispute, we were just having fun. [Roger] is the best trainer in the world and we know it.'

'I told him to go to the body and close the show,' explained Roger Mayweather.

'He was tough but I knew I'd get him,' Floyd continued.

Everybody else knew that, as well.

The Bruseles fight was a mismatch.

'I feel real good right now,' Mayweather went on, looking towards the Gatti bout.

The New Jersey warrior, however, was apparently now only a stepping stone for Floyd, not an end target.

'I'm told that [Shane] Mosley and [Oscar] De La Hoya are going to 147,' Mayweather added. 'I plan to join them there.'

Whether he would or not remained to be seen.

Brady felt he would not. He also clearly did not take to Mayweather's personality. 'Showing enormous ego that hasn't been borne out of what he has done in the ring, "Pretty Boy Floyd" even rattled on in the third person, sounding like a man who is so in love with himself that he dreams of dying in his own arms.' He wondered why HBO gave him passes to fight the likes of Bruseles, particularly when there seemed to be so many attractive alternatives.

If Floyd wanted to be pay-per-view it would not happen against the Corleys, N'dous or Bruseleses of boxing. Gatti had box-office magic, though, and Floyd hoped some of that would rub off on him. He wanted to be on pay-per-view. The time was now.

EIGHT

BLOOD, GUTS AND THE $600,000 SKIRMISH

'GATTI WILL GO and say how much he did for the sport,' charged Floyd Mayweather. 'All he did for the sport was make the ring mat bloody. You can tell this guy's taken a lot of punishment. He's had so much plastic surgery he's starting to look Japanese.'

Mayweather was finally going to be co-headlining a pay-per-view – with a lot of help from the Canadian gladiator – so he took the trash-talking up to a new, vile level.

The difference between slating a wife beater like Corrales and a people's champion like Gatti was, at times, shocking to hear.

'I'm not going to let some guy beat my brains out,' he went on, referring to Gatti's back catalogue of brutal wars. 'The name of the game is to hit and not get hit. The less you get hit, the longer you last in this sport. I'm not in this sport to see how many big punches I can take. That's what he does. I'm a major-league hitter. This guy is minor league.'

He went on. And on.

'He's a C-plus fighter. He's a street bum. I'll walk right through him; I don't have any respect for him.'

On the grounds that poor taste and grudge matches sell, he continued at every opportunity, saying Gatti – who was putting his WBC light-welterweight title on the line – was not on his level and that he should not even be in the same ring as Floyd.

'Arturo Gatti is a heavybag with legs. He's so slow it's ridiculous. When he punches, I can turn, say "hi" to my mom, talk to the TV people, turn back and still beat him to the punch.'

All 12,675 tickets at Atlantic City's Boardwalk Hall, a Gatti stronghold and his fifth consecutive sell-out in the venue, were gone in minutes. Was Mayweather a box office draw, or were they all paying in the hope of seeing their hero shut the braggart up?

The vast majority of pundits and experts predicted a Mayweather whitewash. Emanuel Steward foresaw a Mayweather victory by stoppage, so did HBO's unofficial scorer Harold Lederman, while former Floyd foe DeMarcus Corley was in a minority picking Gatti.

Despite the widely held view that it could even be a mismatch, it was 2005's big summer bout in boxing.

Top Rank's Bruce Trampler felt sure it would be Mayweather's long sought-after breakthrough fight.

'The kid started out on fire,' said Trampler. 'But as we all know, he made a few foolish statements that he wishes he could take back and he's done a few things that have slowed down his ascent. Floyd always felt that he was entitled to certain things, that he had certain things coming to him because of his talent. But he didn't understand how the marketplace worked. He didn't understand that HBO doesn't have to pay him any more than what they've paid him, because the next option is Showtime and they can't pay as much as HBO. Will this be a breakthrough year for him? He's going to have to demonstrate on pay-per-view that he's a draw. He's had a few chances to fight on pay-per-view in the past, but he hasn't rolled the dice. This time he has, and it may pay off for him. We'll have to see. The Gatti fight could be the springboard, but Floyd will have to do all the right things outside the ring and do all the right things inside the ring if he's going to reach that next level.'

Incredibly, shortly after turning pro, Mayweather had prophesied that he would defeat Genaro Hernández, Azumah Nelson and Gatti. The great Nelson had by now retired,

Hernández had been vanquished and Gatti was no longer a dot on the horizon. He was next.

Mayweather had lambasted the champion for bringing his private life into their pre-fight build-up. Floyd had posted a no-contest plea to the Grand Rapids misdemeanour charge – resulting from a bar fight – and regretted doing so.

Main Events, Gatti's promoter, had insisted Mayweather clear up the Michigan incident – where he had allegedly kicked a bouncer in a bar – before the promotion could move forward.

'I'm truly upset because I would have fought my Grand Rapids case,' he explained. 'I knew I was not guilty. I put that on my kids' lives. I was not guilty. But I pleaded no contest just to get this fight. I'm mad that I pleaded no contest. I didn't want to do that. I was not guilty. I didn't want to do that. So he's going to pay for that.'

Floyd was placed on a non-reporting probation, ordered to take part in eighty hours of community service work and pay a $500 fine, for which he peeled ten fresh bills off a 'fist-sized money roll' and paid on the spot. 'There will be no jail time for troubled Floyd Mayweather,' said the 'Outside the Ropes' section in *The Ring*. 'At least not yet.'

That was Mayweather's fifth misdemeanour conviction in three years and he had a domestic violence charge still hanging over him. He denied that.

'If a women gets crazy, gets drunk, tears stuff up in my house, stuff I've worked hard for, and I grab her to hold her, if you want to call that hitting a woman then I hit a woman,' he told the TV cameras in a build-up show for the Gatti fight. 'But I'm not going to let a woman break my stuff, tear my stuff up because there's been blood, sweat and tears to get to where I'm at.'

Ivan Goldman, commenting in his column in *The Ring*, pulled no punches.

'As I write this, braggart, whiner and documented serial woman-beater Mayweather had just gotten off with community service after pleading no contest to kicking a bouncer in a joint in Grand Rapids, Michigan. And he wonders why he can't get a shoe named after him.'

It is fair to say not all of the media was on board.

Mayweather, though, seemed to be a magnet for trouble. 'Vegas is everything,' he said of the place he'd lived for almost a decade. 'When I say everything, twenty-four-hour gambling, twenty-four-hour clubs, twenty-four-hour strip clubs . . .'

The gangster-rap image he'd chosen, of fast cars, jewellery and mink coats, and a record label that seemingly was going nowhere, rubbed plenty of people up the wrong way.

He said it was hard to keep a girlfriend because he liked to go to strip clubs so much. 'That's just me,' he explained. 'That's what I like to do. I'm not sugar-coating it. I love strip clubs.'

Floyd did not show at an arranged press conference to announce the Mayweather-Gatti fight after Arturo defeated Jesse James Leija on his way to confirming the summer bout. That was on January 29, but in March, when Gatti and Mayweather were supposed to kick off their own press conference, Gatti was nowhere to be seen, citing a stomach virus and then hastily arranging his own press conference for the next day. Mayweather called it 'disrespectful'.

'That's funny to hear Floyd Mayweather talk about being disrespectful,' laughed Gatti.

In fact, the fight nearly did not happen and the date had to be shifted from early to late June. 'At one point I didn't think it was going to happen,' admitted Pat Lynch, Gatti's long-time manager and friend. 'I think we had a deadline on the table, then the deadline passed and we thought the fight was dead. And I received a call I think twenty-four hours later saying he [Floyd] had signed and the fight was now on. Because we had moved on I remember speaking to Arturo and saying, "Floyd never came in and signed a contract so we are going to have to move on and go in another direction," and then later we were told he had signed and it was finally done. It did take time to get it completed.'

Gatti was in the midst of a career renaissance. It coincided with besting Micky Ward in two of three simply stunning ten-round battles and hiring Buddy McGirt to train him. He'd become more boxer than brawler, though he was still prepared to go into the trenches. McGirt had also recently coached Antonio Tarver to topple Roy Jones, so he was looking to scalp a second high-profile pound-for-pound opponent.

Floyd, of course, had other ideas. He said the fight might not go three rounds.

'Back in 1997, when I first called Arturo Gatti out, guess what – I know when I have a guy beat,' he said. 'I know when a guy is tailor-made for me. I know when I have a guy who has a certain style I can punish. A guy flat-footed, all those big, wild shots, bleeding like that, going down from body shots, all kinds of guys knocking him down. I'm going to punish a guy like that. I can outbox the guy. I can outslug the guy. I've been world champion so many years. Nobody has beaten me. There's no way to beat me. There's at least six ways to beat Gatti, because he's been beat six times. And I'm going to show you the seventh way. Ain't no way, in the fight game, a guy with six losses is going to beat me. Period. Ain't no way in hell.'

Mayweather was making $3.1 million to start with, plus add-ons depending on how well the bout did on pay-per-view. The champion was making $3.5 million, and would earn every dollar in blood.

Gatti, 'The Human Highlight Reel', was introduced to the ring by Michael Buffer as the 'blood and guts champion of the world'. Here, Arturo was clearly cast as the good guy.

Mayweather knew the money would be made if he played 'the heel', a wrestling term for bad guy or villain.

Boxing writer Ron Borges felt that came naturally to him.

'The only thing pretty about "Pretty Boy" Floyd are his smile and his boxing skills,' wrote Borges. 'He's worked overtime to make himself about as repulsive a human being as possible. He can't act even remotely like he understands the meaning of the word "class" except when he's in the ring.'

The respected doyen of boxing scribes, Thomas Hauser, said Mayweather was the new Mike Tyson, or at least 'a poster boy for bad behaviour.'

'I don't want nobody to judge me on what I do outside the ring,' Floyd said.

Gatti had been no saint. He'd been involved in some drink-driving incidents, had experimented with illegal substances and was hardly whiter than white. His father told him he could not be both a fighter and a rock star. He had to choose. He needed to change his lifestyle and put fighting ahead of partying.

But because he had paid some heavy dues in giving fight fans so many wars, he was given a pass in that respect. He also seemed to have grown out of those troublesome days.

He was nearer the end of his storied career than the beginning, and Lynch knew more than just his title was on the line against Mayweather.

Gatti, who could sell out the Boardwalk Hall against almost anyone, was risking his future against Mayweather and his team was aware of it.

'He did,' Lynch added, 'and we wanted to make sure that we were compensated for making that fight. So what we did is negotiated with HBO that if Arturo lost to Mayweather we didn't get the one fight on HBO we demanded we got two, and we got that in the negotiation. So we knew that win or lose we at least had two big paydays with HBO, not just one.'

Gatti was seen as the bigger man, too, even though Floyd was an inch taller. Mayweather had turned pro at super-featherweight, or 130lbs. Gatti had turned over at 126lbs, featherweight.

Still, there was a clear difference in being able to outbox gritty Micky Ward and trying to outbox Floyd. Gatti had lost to far, far lesser boxers than the complete fighter he was facing.

And Roger Mayweather was equally spiteful with his pre-fight patter. '[Floyd] don't need no strategy to fight Gatti. Close your eyes and throw your hands, and you'll hit him in the fucking face.'

Gatti would have to try to turn it into a battle. Mayweather prophesied running 'boxing circles' around the hardened veteran, who'd had so many tough fights he could come apart at any time if the old adage of a boxer 'getting old overnight' was to come true.

Mayweather's comments understandably rattled Gatti, who lived and trained out of Jersey City, New Jersey. 'I've never been in a fight where my opponent is talking like he is,' Arturo said. 'He has no class, to speak about another fighter like he does.'

The best that Gatti – who traditionally did his talking in the ring – could muster was to say that Floyd was a little boy who deserved a spanking.

During fight week the boxers were to hold separate scheduled news conferences over lunch in New York.

Mayweather crashed Gatti's gathering, and started calling him a 'bum' and a 'paper champion'.

By now he was using every opportunity to tease Gatti about making weight, as Gatti was known to struggle cutting the pounds off in fight week. So Floyd loaded his plate with food.

'It got to the point where we didn't put them together until the weigh-in,' Lynch explained. 'We didn't do a press conference together, we did separate press conferences. Arturo didn't even show up to the first one, that was the one to announce the fight, we did our own the following day. When we did ours the week of the fight, Arturo got to ours a little late so we got started late and then Floyd actually came in at the end of our press conference and there were a few words there, as we were leaving the building. There was a lot of trash-talking leading up to that fight. Arturo was annoyed by it. He really was. It aggravated him and that's why, speaking with Kathy Duva [head of Main Events] and Bob Arum, we thought it was best we didn't put them together until the weigh-in. I think it [the talk] was to sell the fight. I was annoyed by it, don't get me wrong, because we had not been in a situation like that. Arturo was a gentleman and he always took the high road no matter who he fought. I don't think we'd had bad words with opponents in any of the previous fights we had. That was really the first one. Looking back on it now, it probably helped the pay-per-view.'

At the lunch, Gatti fumed and stormed off, grabbing a microphone on his way out and saying, 'I'm going to knock you the fuck out Saturday night.'

Gatti's old opponent Micky Ward was now part of his camp and inner circle and had agreed to walk his friend to the ring. He was around Gatti during fight week, and noticed how Mayweather attempted to push his buttons.

'You've got to understand that's just Floyd,' said Ward. 'The thing about him . . . I hate people who talk a bunch of crap and all that, I don't like it but believe me, if you can back it up you have all the right in the world to say whatever you want.

'He's earned it and now he's TBE [the best ever], he's one of the best ever. He really is good.'

Gatti wanted to make Floyd dig deep and test his heart. Fight fans wanted that too. They wanted to see the substance behind the style. Gatti had the power; Floyd had the speed. And so it was called 'Thunder and Lightning', though Gatti felt he was being underrated as a technical fighter, that he was skilful and talented.

Gatti was the warrior, yet Mayweather wanted that tag for himself. On the night he came out wearing a gladiator's gold suit, being carried on a throne in one of boxing's more elaborate ring entrances. He was held aloft by costumed gladiators, hired from nearby Caesars Palace as 'Another One Bites the Dust' echoed around the arena.

Boos filled the air once Floyd settled in the ring, waiting for the champion.

Gatti, hanging fire for a signal to walk to the ring, jumped out of his skin when the flames burst into the air around him and the pyrotechnics went live to mark his arrival, but he masked it by shadowboxing intently before striding out to his trademark ringwalk song, ACDC's 'Thunderstruck'.

Gatti was given another unpleasant shock in the very first round. Mayweather's speed and velocity had already made an early impact but as they came in close Gatti pulled up, seemingly on the assumption that referee Earl Morton was about to call 'break.' That judgment never came and Gatti, standing with his hands by his side, gave Floyd an opening. Mayweather uncoiled like a cobra, darting in behind a left hook and landing a free shot, dropping Gatti into the ropes for a count. It was a disastrous moment for the champion. Gatti remonstrated with Morton but he'd forgotten the crucial first rule of boxing, to protect himself at all times.

'With less than a minute gone, this fight was over,' wrote Jim Brady. 'Even the most ardent Gatti worshipper knew it.'

That included Lynch. 'We were never, never in the fight and I did not expect that because we had a tremendous training camp, but Arturo never got off,' he said. 'There are no excuses, Floyd was just a better fighter and Arturo would be the first one to tell you that. His hand speed was incredible, his quickness, it was amazing. At one point, Arturo put his hands down and Floyd cracked him, which was a legal punch – don't get me wrong –

because Arturo said after the fight that one of the first things you are taught is to always keep your hands up. He didn't do that. After that, forget it. We had no shot whatsoever.'

The beating continued through round two. It was both systematic and horrible. Usually rounds that include a knockdown are scored 10-8. Mayweather took the first by that margin and even though there was no knockdown, some scored the second the same way – it was that lopsided.

Arturo's eye was swelling badly in the third. By the fifth, the left was going. Yes, he had taken beatings before. He had even taken them and won. But he never even crossed the starting line on that glum night on the New Jersey shore.

The crowd soberly chanted 'Gatti, Gatti,' praying for a miracle they seemed resigned to not witnessing.

Mayweather sliced away with both hands. Blood leaked from Gatti's increasingly bulging face. His features were red raw. It was like watching a butcher at work, softening up the meat before making the final cuts.

After round six, and as Floyd went back and sat on his stool, Roger turned to the probing camera and said, 'I told you, he [Gatti] is going to get his ass whipped, on HBO.'

The question was not now whether Gatti could turn things around or produce a big shot to clutch a dramatic win. The question was how much longer was he going to be able to see through those closing eyes and how much longer could he possibly last.

'Why would anyone continue,' asked Lampley at the end of the session, with Gatti more forlorn and beaten than ever before. Colleague Roy Jones had talked about referee Earl Morton stopping the fight and Gatti was in a defensive shell as the bell sounded to end another three-minute beatdown.

As soon as he sat on his stool, Gatti found his head cradled by trainer Buddy McGirt. 'I'm stopping it,' said his coach. 'I'm stopping it.'

'One more,' pleaded a wincing Gatti.

'No, no more,' replied McGirt. 'Your eye is closed. I'm not going to let you get hurt. I love you too much.'

No one needed to see any more.

'I was very happy when Buddy stopped that fight because he was taking a lot of punishment,' sighed Lynch retrospectively. 'It wasn't one of those Arturo fights when you felt it could change at any time if Arturo just catches him. You could see really from the opening bell that we were outclassed. We knew it was a difficult fight but we definitely thought we had a shot to win the fight. No doubt about it. Buddy McGirt was confident about it. We knew we were in with a great fighter, we obviously never thought it would be that one-sided.

'I didn't think Arturo was going to lose that decisively. I really thought it was going to be a more competitive fight, I was disappointed, as was he.'

Micky Ward agreed. 'He gave it his all but he was just in there with a young superstar. There was no shame, he got beat by one of the best to ever live, he was that good. You could just see the greatness. Back then, I knew Floyd was a really great fighter, I didn't realise how great a fighter was until I saw him there. It was his ring generalship and his smarts, and people don't think he can punch hard but he can hit pretty hard. He's got some pop in his punches.'

Gatti's remodelled face backed up that assertion.

Mayweather knelt on the canvas and burst into tears in an extraordinarily emotional reaction.

The crowd didn't care. They were concerned for Gatti.

Punchstats showed Gatti landed forty-one blows in the fight, averaging less than seven punches per round.

Hauser called it 'target practice' and a 'slaughter'. You'd be hard pushed for better descriptions.

'The great ones always rise to the occasion,' said Arum.

Hauser captured the mood that night, the evening the Atlantic City faithful saw their hero get absolutely routed. 'It's hard for people to watch a fighter they care about lose,' he wrote. 'And harder still to watch him get beaten up. When both happens, it's worse.'

Mayweather was simply better, younger, faster and stronger.

David Mayo wrote that, 'Gatti had a puncher's chance but no chance to land a punch.'

'He was just too fast,' sighed Gatti, who said he wanted a title shot in his next fight, and he would move up to welterweight for it. 'He was harder to hit and quicker than I thought he'd be. Everybody told me he had fast hands, but he's very fast with his upper body, too.'

'He was a tough guy, a strong guy, but he never laid a hand on me,' said Floyd, who added that he felt under more pressure to perform than actually win. 'This is a brutal sport. This is not like tennis or golf, it's not a gentleman's sport, it's a brutal sport. I don't hate Arturo Gatti. He gave it his all. I respect him as a fighter. At first, I didn't respect him, but that's just talk. They're just things we say.'

McGirt added, 'Floyd told me at the first press conference that he was just doing what he had to do to sell this fight. I wasn't mad at him. After the fight he was a gentleman. He thanked Arturo. He even thanked me. He felt he had to be the villain and he did what he had to do so I'm not mad at him one bit.'

'This is one of his most dazzling performances,' gleamed Roger. 'Floyd is used to big fights. I'm not surprised what happened. He thought he was the champion coming into this fight.'

Floyd had shown power, ability and talent. But he said that something was more important than that – staying unbeaten.

'Don't ever underestimate the power of being undefeated,' he said. 'After God and my family, staying undefeated is the most important thing in my life. It's something I'm not giving up easy.

No one who fights me, or is thinking about fighting me, should ever forget that.'

Whatever Floyd had said before, you could not argue with him now. *The Ring* magazine surmised that 'Mayweather should be fighting wolverines or alligators; he's too good for other humans.'

They now had Mayweather as the number one pound-for-pound fighter, partly because of the Gatti annihilation but mostly because Jermain Taylor had outpointed Hopkins.

Dan Rafael, covering the fight for ESPN, was not shocked by the acute dissection he witnessed from ringside.

'Honestly, I did [expect it],' he said. 'And that's hard to say because it's no secret Arturo Gatti is my all-time favourite fighter. I have a charcoal painting of him hanging in my office, I named my cat after him, I was friendly with Arturo before he passed but you have to be able to separate your personal feelings from your boxing intellect and my personal feelings and my boxing intellect said Gatti would give it everything he has but he has zero chance to win this fight. Most Floyd fights are one-sided. This fight was more one-sided than even the typical one-sided fights he puts on. It was an absolute beating and I'm glad Buddy McGirt stopped the fight when he did.'

Meanwhile, there were still many who felt Mayweather's claims of wanting to fight the likes of De La Hoya and Mosley were outlandish and unrealistic. Eric Raskin wrote in *The Ring* that 'De La Hoya's never going to fight him. Oscar has everything to lose and nothing to gain fighting a blown-up lightweight, especially one who has never proven to be much of a box-office draw.'

'I know HBO invested a lot of money into me,' said Mayweather, who with Gatti had been sold into 340,000 homes on his first pay-per-view outing, making $15.3-million in revenue. 'I told Kery Davis [vice president of HBO Sports] I'm not going to let him down.'

'Floyd is probably the closest thing to an unbeatable fighter today,' said Emanuel Steward. David Mayo added that the six Gatti rounds had quite possibly been the most one-sided in pay-per-view history.

Zab Judah, a New Yorker from Brooklyn, immediately said he was interested in a fight with Mayweather. Floyd had previously said he would not face someone he considered a friend – unless the price was right. Now there was a chance it could be right.

Ricky Hatton, fresh off a huge win over the leading light-welterweight Kostya Tszyu in Manchester, had flown to the US to watch Gatti-Mayweather. For a while, he and Gatti appeared to be a matchmaker's dream. Now, the talk was of Mayweather against Hatton, the exciting, ticket-selling conqueror.

As always, speculation about potential opponents fluttered. There was even some chatter about a Corrales rematch, though Puerto Rico's Miguel Cotto was not deemed seasoned enough. A 12 November clash with feared brawler Antonio Margarito was put out there. With Margarito being promoted by Arum that was potentially an easier match to make, though the Mexican's WBO title did not give him any significant leverage. Mayweather said he preferred Hatton in November and tried to shoot holes in the Mancunian's win over Tszyu by saying his Gatti victory was a win for boxing while Hatton's had been one for wrestling.

'I only want to fight big fights,' Mayweather reiterated. 'I want to be on pay-per-view until the end of my career. I know this is the beginning. I think I put on a hell of a show and I showed the people that I deserve to be on pay-per-view.'

Leonard Ellerbe, advisor to Mayweather and also involved in his strength and conditioning, said the Gatti fight was 'Floyd's platform to become the pay-per-view star that he's always wanted to become.'

Las Vegas would now surely have Floyd back. The fickle nature of the business meant those who'd closed their doors on Floyd in

2002 would not only open them for him, but that they would try to coax him back through them.

And he still held dear the idea of facing De La Hoya.

'He says he won't fight me because of my dad,' Floyd said. 'Because my dad is his trainer, but this is business, man. I would love to fight De La Hoya. I think we've got the chance to make crazy numbers. I've got a chance to make twenty-plus million. He's got the chance to make thirty-plus million. At the end of the day, you've got to look at it like this . . . it's business.'

Even so, De La Hoya had bigger fish to fry since his audacious attempt at Bernard Hopkins' middleweight world title, which had ended in defeat inside nine rounds.

He was contemplating a comeback, but at light-middleweight. Mayweather had really only made his mark at light-welterweight, a full fourteen pounds less. But he took steps towards De La Hoya five months after smashing Gatti by moving up to welterweight.

He was testing the 147lbs water against a skilful but past-his-peak Sharmba Mitchell at the Rose Garden in Portland, Oregon, in front of 5,881 fans, although only 3,749 of those paid their way in. Just $346,402 was made at the gate. And it was not Vegas, although there was a reason for that.

Top Rank had surprisingly won a bid to stage the heavyweight title fight between Vitali Klitschko and Hasim Rahman. They were going to put it on pay-per-view, thus filling one of their few box-office slots later in the year. Mayweather was thought to be in the running for the 12 November date – but they had chosen to stage the heavyweight title fight. Floyd thought he was box office gold after the Gatti fight, but he was back on regular HBO against Mitchell.

Mayweather-Mitchell was not a popular match. Nigel Collins, writing in *The Ring*, said, 'Unless everybody came to their senses in the interim, it should be over by now.'

He said what others thought, that if Floyd wanted to prove

himself he should do it against the best. Having awarded Mayweather his Fighter of the Year honours in 1998, he had expected a slew of those titles to follow. They did not. 'His career has lacked consistency, getting bogged down by legal difficulties, layoffs and meaningless matches,' Collins continued.

He felt that HBO giving fighters contracts rather than actually buying fights allowed inconsequential matches like Mitchell and Bruseles to happen in place of more appropriate headline fights. He had a point.

'Mayweather is used to being coddled by HBO,' he wrote. 'And if it doesn't stop, we're eventually going to look back on his career the same way we are now looking at [Roy] Jones' – great, but nowhere near as great as it should have been.'

There had been speculation that Mayweather could meet Cuba's Joel Casamayor in Memphis, too, but Floyd and Top Rank again quarreled over the direction of his career, which resulted in having his future contractual obligations rewritten. Floyd still had two years left to go with them.

That meant it was in their best interest to throw him in with anybody and everybody, whether it was Hatton, De La Hoya, Winky Wright or the winner of the upcoming fight between old target Shane Mosley and Olympic teammate Fernando Vargas. He turned down Margarito and entered long discussions with Wright before nixing that proposed fight, but in the background talks with Zab Judah were gathering pace. He and slick southpaw Wright bickered over who would take the lion's share of a $15-million pie, in a fight that would likely have been dire to watch.

The Top Rank-Mayweather relationship was gradually disintegrating. In September, a couple of months before the Mitchell fight, the promotional giant filed lawsuits against anyone and everyone it suspected of trying to entice Mayweather away. Mayweather and his new advisor, Al Haymon, were recipients, so were HBO, its parent company Time Warner and Goossen-Tutor Promotions.

A month later, the suit was settled out of court and a two-year contract renewal between promoter and fighter was agreed. Fight dates were arranged with HBO and the agreement with Goossen saw them snare some of the foreign TV rights to Mayweather-Mitchell.

Dan Goossen maintained that he had not tried to poach Mayweather, he'd just heard he was a free agent.

Unfortunately for Top Rank, Klitschko-Rahman was a non-starter after the giant Ukrainian suffered a career-threatening knee injury in training. It was then that rumours abounded that Mayweather was looking for an alternative promoter, finally, after years of feuding. There had been a visit to Don King in Florida earlier in the year.

'I was amazed, as I listened to him, at how much he really hates the guy [Arum],' King said of Mayweather, though it should be added that King had endured his own long-running feud with Arum.

'He only wants big fights, so let's go for it,' said Todd duBoef. 'We're ready. Let's do it.'

'All I want is fights that can make me a legend,' Mayweather said. 'I only want the biggest fights against the biggest opponents, in the biggest arenas, with the biggest pay-per-view numbers. I've been saying that for the longest. I told everyone I was the best, pound for pound, until they finally figured out I was right. I told everyone I would be the last one standing with an undefeated record at HBO, until they finally figured out I was right. Now I'm telling everyone that you will only see Floyd Mayweather in big fights, history-making fights. To make the most money and reap the biggest rewards, other fighters will have to go through me. You mark my words; you'll see that I'm right.'

Mitchell in Oregon was merely a detour to the world's best. It was also promoted by Goossen-Tutor, Mitchell's side, with Top Rank having no involvement for the first time in their nine years with Floyd.

Interestingly it did involve basketball legend Michael Jordan. The former Chicago Bulls hero was in attendance because Nike's Jordan line appeared to be interested in aligning themselves with Mayweather, who walked to the ring with a white Nike Air Jordan headband on. They had paid a high five-figure fee to hold the event in Portland – not one of boxing's capitals – but the money went straight into Mayweather's side of the purse split, meaning he got a record $4.3-million sum. Without the Nike money, the promotion would have suffered a significant financial shortfall.

Mitchell, who'd suffered from long-standing knee injuries, had also moved up in weight. He was a former WBA light-welterweight champion who'd been mixing in top class for several years. A southpaw, he'd lost in three rounds to Kostya Tszyu in November 2004 and, at thirty-five, he was no longer operating at his best.

Mayweather-Mitchell was a non-title fight because it was at welter, Floyd's debut at the higher weight. It turned out to be more of a showcase at 147lbs than a meaningful contest. Floyd proved he was just as fast and spiteful with seven extra pounds at his disposal.

Again in the opposite corner was Buddy McGirt, who was working with Mitchell.

The straight right hand is always a useful weapon against a southpaw and Floyd enjoyed early success with it. Mitchell was floored by the shot in round three, standing and shrugging his shoulders as though there was nothing he could have done to prevent it.

Michael Jordan made his way down to the ring in round four and with a minute to go in the session Mitchell was trapped on the ropes and shipping punches. Floyd's dominance continued in the fifth, fighting out of both orthodox and southpaw stances, and in the sixth Mitchell was floored as Mayweather reached in with a right to the body.

Mitchell tried to rise in time, and he did beat the count, but referee Richard Steele – who had come out of retirement following his decision to quit after Mayweather-Corrales – felt Mitchell was in no state to continue. His verdict was met with little resistance.

'It wasn't a big crowd, but those that were here appreciated what they saw,' said Lampley.

Mayweather thanked Nike and advisor Al Haymon. 'We want to fight Zab Judah,' he said. 'I've been asking Zab Judah, I would love to fight him. Winky Wright is a good fight for me, Oscar De La Hoya . . .'

'His speed was amazing,' praised Mitchell. 'He's a great athlete and a great fighter. I was able to get away with a few little tricks that might have surprised him, but wouldn't advise too many people to mess with him.'

'I was a little anxious,' Mayweather said. 'I was trying to perform better than in the Gatti fight, but that was a flawless performance so it's hard to better that. Every performance I try to better myself. I still have room for improvement. You never stop learning. I just want to get better as a fighter and a person.'

Referee Steele thought Mayweather looked as though he was a cross between Sugar Ray Robinson and Sugar Ray Leonard.

Mayweather was nearly twenty-nine. According to David Mayo, writing in *The Ring*, 'The window on his prime years slowly could begin closing soon, particularly as his weight also escalates. He doesn't want to be fighting for paydays when he's Mitchell's age.'

Zab Judah had a fight coming up with Carlos Baldomir, a tough but straightforward Argentine. It made sense that, as the welterweight champion, Judah should be targeted. Hatton was again in the frame, and Mayweather was open to that because Ricky was the man to beat at light-welterweight, having unseated the great Tszyu. A night after the Mitchell bout, Hatton defeated Carlos Maussa in Sheffield to claim the WBA title Maussa had beaten Vivian Harris for. That made Hatton the IBF and WBA ruler.

But speaking for Mayweather, Leonard Ellerbe reckoned the Manchester idol had to still prove himself. 'Hatton needs to come to the United States and establish himself here first,' said the advisor. 'Hatton isn't on the level of Castillo. Really, outside of Kostya Tszyu, who has this guy beaten? With all due respect to Kostya Tszyu, Kostya Tszyu is not Floyd Mayweather.'

De La Hoya appeared to be coming round to the idea of the Floyd fight, too. He'd said he was possibly looking for two career-ending paydays in 2006, with Mayweather the finale. He seemed to like dangling the carrot for Mayweather, who knew he would make more money for that than any other match by a long, long way.

His father, De La Hoya's trainer, thought it represented a high risk for his fighter.

'Little Floyd is a sharpshooter right now,' he said. 'I really wouldn't want Oscar to take that fight without being more active. I'm not saying Oscar can't win – he's a lot stronger than little Floyd and he can knock anyone out at 147 with one left hook. But he would be going in there with a sharpshooter who is at the very top of his game. To do that, you have to be at the top of your own game, and Oscar hasn't been active enough.'

It certainly was not the joke attraction it had seemed when De La Hoya was thinking of going up to middleweight while Floyd was only a lightweight. The gap was closing and though De La Hoya's prime was over his great marketability remained intact.

Mayweather and Judah had said for years they would not fight one another because they were close. They nearly did not fight each other at all, not because they were friends but because Judah dropped the ball – and his WBC title – in what was supposed to be a routine warm-up fight against Baldomir. Coming off a loss against an average if gritty Cinderella champion like veteran Baldomir was hardly the thing giant promotions are made of.

Of course, many felt Baldomir was more worthy of a Mayweather fight than the Las Vegas-based New Yorker Judah, though in boxing there is no need to let a loss get in the way of a potentially more lucrative fight. 'You get what you negotiate not what you deserve,' could be one of boxing's mantras. And in another pitiful example of the sport at its most putrid, Judah still held onto his IBF title because Baldomir would not pay the sanctioning fee, meaning Mayweather would get the chance to become a champion in a fourth weight class.

Friends or not, Mayweather typically went in hard with the pre-fight patter, digging at Judah's surprise loss. 'I've been here before, I know about big fights,' he said. 'You'll never see me in the ring unprepared. Zab is strong and fast, but he's got no chin. No way he'll be able to take my punches.'

'Floyd and I have been friends for a long time,' said Judah, in the rare position of underdog for him. 'And we talked about fighting for almost as long. That last fight [with Baldomir] wasn't me. Everybody knows that. I've been waiting for a fight like this my whole life.'

Both were boxing bad guys. Their personas and entourages evoked images of rap, gangsters and a little bit of boxing. Judah had been one of the sport's brightest prospects and most talented champions, then he ran into Tszyu and was swatted in two rounds.

Yet he infamously thought he was okay to continue having been floored three times with the same punch; after being ruled out by referee Jay Nady he launched his corner stool in Nady's direction and then shoved his gloved fist into the official's neck.

That ugly indiscretion had cost him $75,000 and a six-month ban in Nevada. But a career renaissance had been sparked when he travelled to St Louis to gain a revenge nine-round stoppage win over Cory Spinks to reclaim his title. Still, he was never at the races against Baldomir and dropped the belt he had done so well to topple Spinks for.

Floyd was now 35-0 (24). Judah was 34-3 (25). The bout also pitted long-time promotional rivals against one another. Mayweather, still unhappily with Top Rank, was going up against one of Don King's stars.

Judah represented Floyd's first fight back in Sin City in almost four years, since the second Castillo fight. That was astonishing given it was his hometown, and where Top Rank were based, just a few minutes from the Strip.

Judah did not give interviews pre fight. He also failed to appear on the line for an international conference call.

He had a lot on his mind.

Before the Baldomir loss, Judah's guarantee was going to be $3 million. That instantly fell to $1 million. In fight week it was revealed that he had a debt to the IRS and his own promoter Don King went public to say the fighter owed him seven figures. The Baldomir loss had hit the promotion hard. Mayweather's earnings dropped from $6 million to $5 million. Caesars Palace and Wynn Las Vegas wanted $600,000 less of tickets. Arum also cut the top ticket prices from $800 to $700, although HBO kept the pay-per-view at $44.95. Judah's flat fee went down, but he could make decent money if the fight cleared $7 million in profit as he was still due some of that upside.

'If this fight goes through the roof,' said King, 'and Zab makes enough to pay me the money I loaned him, I don't think I'd even have to argue about that, he'll pay me. Because why wouldn't you pay a bank that let you have money with no collateral, and no future, really, other than what I believed you could do? Then, when you win it, you pay it back. There's an obligation to pay the loan back.'

Mayweather and Judah might have been professional rivals, but Floyd sided with his New York friend on the matter, saying King should have kept their agreements and deals behind closed doors.

It seemed the shock-haired promoter talking about his client's private affairs finally alienated any chance he had of working with Mayweather. 'I don't like that King is out there telling his business,' he said. 'King is the one telling people Zab is in the hole with him. He's telling Zab's personal business, starting after the Baldomir fight when Zab disrespected his promoter on TV, and King said he didn't understand why Zab was acting like that, because he was a million in the hole to him. The biggest mistake Zab has made in his career is leaving Shelly Finkel to go with Don. I can't see how you would do that. It's like trying to get in a room that everyone is trying to get out of. It's like a smoky room with a lock on that everybody's trying to get out of and Zab's trying to get in. It doesn't make any sense.'

Floyd was seemingly giving up the ghost with flogging the Philthy Rich Records horse and for the first time in years did not have it emblazoned across the back of his fight robe.

Judah won the first round on two of the three judge's scorecards. He took the next, too, and caught Floyd walking in with a short southpaw right hook that caused Mayweather to touch down with his right glove even if Richard Steele did not call it a knockdown.

It was not an official knockdown, but Steele could have called one. The two tried to counter one another. Finally Floyd was in with somebody who could challenge him for speed.

His father and trainer Yoel, in the corner, told Judah at the end of the third that Mayweather could not hurt him. He was implored to throw more punches. 'The more you hit him, the more he's going to run,' Yoel advised.

'Keep doing what you just did,' said Roger to Floyd. 'He can't fight going backwards anyway.'

Judah winged in some useful left hands early in round four. He thought he had Mayweather hurt and followed up. The crowd went nuts at one particular straight left. Mayweather responded by softening Zab's body with rights.

'Keep punching to the body, the body shots are slowing him down,' Ellerbe told Mayweather.

In the other corner, father told son to be bold and more confident, to throw more punches in the belief that would cause Mayweather to retreat. CompuBox had totalled Zab's efforts and reckoned that after four rounds he had landed fifty-seven per cent of his power punches, but he had only thrown forty-four of them. Mayweather had thrown twice as many.

Floyd took over in round five, continuously landing single shots and slowly deflating Judah's body. Although Judah scored with another long left by the end of the round, when he tried to talk smack to his friend it seemed he had become emotionally involved in the contest. He was growing frustrated. Mayweather, cool, pressed his lips together, knowing he was in control of the physical and mental battles going on.

'Zab, he's nothing, but you can't let him dominate you,' said Yoel. 'He's going to potshot you all night.'

Judah's face was swelling. An iron was pressed against his right cheek to calm the pressure.

His priority was to defend in round six, costing him that session as well. Mayweather's own caution was replaced by a familiar swagger in the seventh and that was a bad sign for Zab. He had been opened up, sporting a bloody mouth and nose. Judah was not a sitting duck, but his foothold in the fight had slipped. He threw just eight power punches in round seven. He was effectively being shut down.

He became more aggressive near the end of the eighth but he

could only fight in spurts. They talked to each other in there. Mayweather later said they were saying the same thing, calling one another 'bitches'.

'The body shots are going to shut his ass down and make him quit,' predicted Roger.

'He don't want no more,' said cutman Rafael Garcia.

They all looked expectantly over to Judah in anticipation of a white flag. Round nine was all Mayweather and the question was whether Judah would fold physically or mentally. He was shipping an incessant stream of right hands.

Yoel Judah was increasingly frustrated and animated in the corner, shadowboxing how wanted his son to fight – only more furiously.

His charge, who was only able to finish the rounds with any kind of fire, nailed Mayweather in the groin with a scooping left uppercut with ten seconds to go in the tenth. Mayweather dropped. Judah caught him with a right hook behind the head as he did so and backed off.

Mayweather wobbled and rose wincing as he tried to gather himself.

In steamed Roger, who angrily confronted Zab. Leonard Ellerbe bowled in. Steele held the uncle back, but Judah went after him. They swung at one another. In poured Yoel Judah and within seconds the ring was filled with both sides, police officers and security personnel pushing and shoving amid carnage and chaos. For a while, Roger tried to choke Zab in a corner before being hauled off him.

'There are some hotheads in there,' said an excited Lampley.

Of all the pre-fight arrangements, the call to increase security was perhaps the most important, with more than thirty Las Vegas Metropolitan cops on hand to calm the storm.

It was several minutes before order could be restored, allowing the fighters to touch gloves and the remaining five seconds of the round to be played out. No further leather was landed, legal or otherwise.

It had been an ugly, deplorable scene. Referee Steele must have wondered why he'd bothered coming back after deciding to leave officiating after Mayweather-Corrales.

'Floyd, Floyd,' chants filled the arena, partly in appreciation for his skills and partly because Judah had raised his hand for the villain role by striking low.

By comparison, almost nothing happened in the penultimate round. Judah was content to survive, Mayweather equally happy to coast.

Judah put up his best effort since the early rounds in the twelfth, but that only ended with Mayweather inviting him in to try more offence.

On the bell, Floyd ran to a corner and leapt onto the ropes, saluting the crowd. Yoel and Zab embraced. Judah's face was marked up, Mayweather looked as though he was ready for a GQ shoot.

The scores of 117-11, 116-112 and 119-109 told the story, that Mayweather had well won despite enduring some sticky rounds early on. Judah had his moments, but it had still been pretty easy for Pretty Boy.

Mayweather said he knew his opponent was a frontrunner. 'He's strong for the first six rounds, and after that, he gasses out,' he explained to Merchant. 'I was relaxed, keeping my composure. We were relaxed and I was going to take my time and if we hadn't had that confrontation in the ring the fight would have been over. The confrontation put me out of my zone. [After that I was going to] just box the last two rounds and take the victory.

'I don't want to say nothing about Zab. He's a great fighter. I respect Judah, I respect his camp and tonight he made me respect his fight game.'

'I make no excuses,' said Judah, who said he was not a dirty

Above: Floyd Mayweather Sr (right) lands a right against Jose Baret on his way to an eight-round victory in New York's Felt Forum in 1983. *Getty Images*

Above left: Roger Mayweather lines up Fidel Avendano at the Inglewood Forum in California in a bout he would eventually lose on points. *Getty Images*

Above right: Oscar De La Hoya celebrates after defeating Jeff Mayweather at the Las Vegas Hilton on 13 March 1993. *Getty Images*

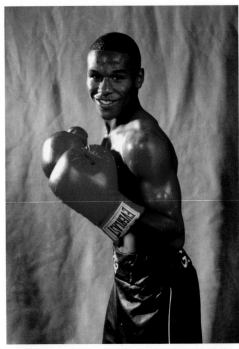

Left: A young Floyd Mayweather Jr poses for the camera in 1990. *Getty Images*

Below: Floyd Mayweather catches amateur rival Augie Sanchez with a right hand in Augusta, Georgia, on his way to a third-round decision win on April 19, 1996. *Getty Images*

Above: Serafim Todorov (left) is the last man to defeat Floyd Mayweather, after outscoring him in the semi-finals of the Atlanta Olympics in 1996.

Below: Mayweather fires a right hand at tall Tony Pep in Atlantic City in 1998 as he nears his first world title fight. Mayweather won on points. *Getty Images*

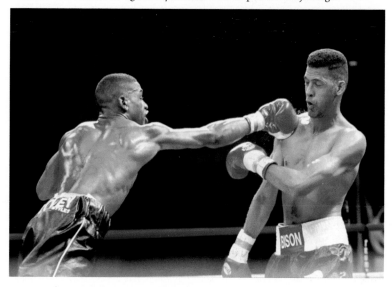

Above: In 1999, Oscar De La Hoya and future professional rival Floyd Mayweather point to the plaque of then joint promoter Bob Arum at the International Boxing Hall of Fame in Canastota, New York. *Getty Images*

Below: Mayweather aims a left at Carlos Gerena at the Mandalay Bay in Las Vegas in September 1999. *Getty Images*

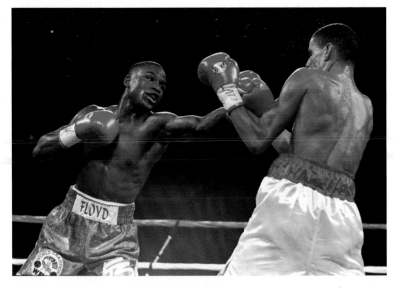

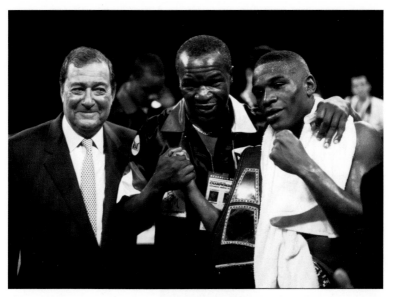

Above: Promoter Bob Arum, Floyd Mayweather Sr and Jr celebrate a points victory over Mexico's Goyo Vargas at the MGM Grand in Las Vegas. *Getty Images*

Below: Floyd (left) poses with manager James Prince and former WBA welterweight champion James Page in 2000. *Getty Images*

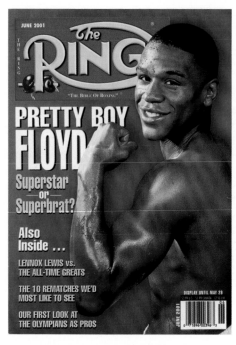

Left: On the cover of *Ring Magazine,* June 2001. *Getty Images*

Below: Bitter rivals Floyd Mayweather and Diego Corrales finally come to blows in their long-awaited grudge match. Corrales was sent to the canvas five times and stopped in the tenth round. *Getty Images*

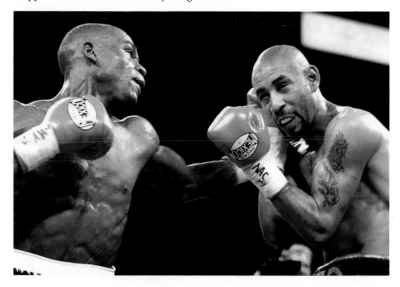

Above: Jose Luis Castillo pushes Mayweather as close to defeat as anyone, but ultimately would lose twice to Floyd. This is from their second fight. *Getty Images*

Below: Mayweather pounds away at Arturo Gatti during a one-sided rout on the Atlantic City Boardwalk in June 2005 in his first pay-per-view main event. *Getty Images*

Above: There's chaos as Roger Mayweather jumps into the ring after his nephew was hit below the belt by Zab Judah in their welterweight title fight in April 2006. *Getty Images*

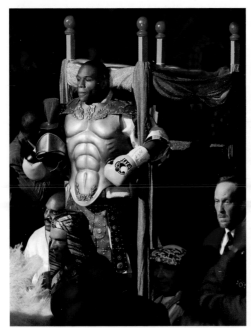

Left: Mayweather is carried to the ring ahead of his title fight with Argentine Carlos Baldomir in November 2006. *Getty Images*

Above: Leonard Ellerbe (right) looks on as Mayweather weeps at his post-fight press conference after his convincing win over Baldomir, declaring he will retire after his next fight. *Getty Images*

Below: The feud ignites as, finally, Oscar De La Hoya and Floyd Mayweather agree to fight in a bout that had been in the offing for years. *Getty Images*

Above: De La Hoya is the aggressor, Floyd the more accurate technician. The judges were split, with Mayweather taking a tight decision win in a huge money-spinning fight in Las Vegas in 2007. *Getty Images*

Below: Mayweather and his crew show the spoils of his career after the split decision win over De La Hoya. *Getty Images*

Right: Floyd begins his journey into the mainstream with a run on the hit TV show *Dancing with the Stars. Getty Images*

Below: Britney Spears, Sean 'Diddy' Combs, 50 Cent, Paris Hilton and Floyd Mayweather attend '50 Cent Hosts Party at The Hard Rock' on 8 September 2007 in Las Vegas. *Getty Images*

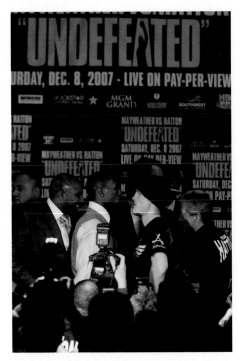

Left: Ricky Hatton (right) might have been joined by more than 25,000 British fans to support him against Mayweather but it was not enough to inspire him to victory. *Getty Images*

Below: Previously undefeated Hatton goes down and out as referee Joe Cortez signals the end of his December 2007 loss to Mayweather. *Getty Images*

Right: Mayweather takes centre stage at WrestleMania XXIV as the 'Big Show' hoists him up for a choke slam at the Citrus Bowl in Orlando, Florida. *Getty Images*

Below: For years, fans speculated who might win between Mayweather and Shane Mosely but in 2010, when they eventually met, Floyd was far too good, despite having to see out some rocky moments in round two. *Getty Images*

Above: Some felt Miguel Cotto (left) would not provide Mayweather with much of a challenge. Instead, the gallant Puerto Rican pushed him hard in a thrilling fight in Las Vegas in May, 2012. *Getty Images*

Below: After pleading guilty to attacking his ex-girlfriend while two of their children watched, Maywether is led away in handcuffs at the Clark County Regional Justice Center as he surrenders to a three-month jail sentence. *Getty Images*

Above: Floyd Mayweather lands a right as he dazzles on a huge night in Sin City, dominating young champion Saul Alvarez in the MGM Grand in 2013. *Getty Images*

Below: The action is limited as Mayweather (left) and Pacquiao finally meet in the ring on a record-breaking night in Las Vegas in 2015. *Getty Images*

Above: Mayweather and Conor McGregor stop in Toronto as part of a four-city tour to promote their 26 August 2017 clash. *Getty Images*

Below: Mayweather is patient against McGregor, but ultimately breaks him up in the richest fight in combat sports history. *Getty Images*

fighter and had no deliberate intention to aim low. 'Mayweather's a good fighter, he's quick. He's got good hands. He is a great defensive fighter, he has a tight defence.'

'I knew Judah would come out on his toes and be strong,' Mayweather continued. 'He brought his A-game and so did I. I hurt my right hand, but those things happen in big fights. Me and Zab took care of things like businessmen. What happened, happened. We're friends and fought through our problems. It was a great fight, that's all I can say.'

'Things got a little carried away,' replied Judah. 'That's not my style to try and hit him low. We had a great round going, why would I mess that up? It happened and I apologised. It's just two fighters in there. Everybody's emotionally involved in this whole thing. But when somebody takes it upon themselves, from the outside, to come in and make their own consequences, I don't think that's the right thing to do.'

In the ring post-fight, Don King, was already saying that Mayweather should have been disqualified. No one important was listening.

'Once you get on the apron, the fight is a disqualification,' King hollered with his familiar bombast. 'It should be total disqualification. There was a third man in the ring chasing the fighter during the round. The fight is over when the man stepped on the apron, and this man came all the way into the ring. We got to do this again.'

By the letter of the law in Nevada, 'The referee may, in his discretion, stop a contest or exhibition if an unauthorised person enters the ring or fenced area during a round.'

It was Steele's call and he let it go on.

The commission, though, made those involved pay heavily for their indiscretions.

Roger, who had lit the touch paper, was fined the entirety of his $200,000 pay packet and banned for a year.

Zab and Yoel Judah were slapped with fines and suspensions. The fighter had to pay $250,000, the whole slice he was making of the $1 million that Top Rank had paid promoter Don King for his services. The Nevada State Athletic Commission also banned him for a year. The black mark against him from the melee after the Tszyu fight was held against him, making him a repeat offender.

Yoel also had his licence revoked for a year. His fine was $100,000. He said he felt the penalties were harsh and unfair.

'They came down hard on us,' he told Dan Rafael. 'It was bad. They said they were trying to make a statement.'

'I thought it was crazy,' concurred Zab. 'I don't think it was fair. A lot of BS was involved. I thought I'd get a $100,000 fine and maybe a four-month suspension. I was very surprised at how harsh they were. They gave me the maximum out of everyone and Roger [Mayweather] started the whole thing.'

Ellerbe, who was suspended for four months, also copped a fine of $50,000, meaning the combined fines heading in the direction of the NSAC totalled $600,000.

'They all apologised, and I think it was sincere,' said Marc Ratner, in one of his last significant calls as the chairman of the Nevada State Athletic Commission before he left boxing for the Ultimate Fighting Championship.

'It was tough day. Everyone handled it very professionally. None of the licensees left smiling. The commission felt that it wanted to send a very strong message. This incident was so close to a full-scale riot that innocent people could have gotten hurt or maimed. The commission felt very, very strongly that this cannot happen again.'

'Roger was very apologetic,' said Todd duBoef. 'It's a sad day for Roger, who is one of the good guys in boxing. But he committed a deplorable offence and he is being punished for it.'

Roger, who sent a letter of apology to the commission,

appealed the verdict but Nevada's stance was unwavering. The Judahs unhappily took their punishments on the chin.

Floyd came out of it all well. Finally he was starting to draw, his marketability was closing the gap on his skill level. He had made another career-high purse and the De La Hoya fight now seemed plausible.

Zab, however, had lost two fights consecutively for the first time in his career.

'Can't cry over spilled milk,' he sighed. 'I'll just move on and pray for better things.'

Judah-Mayweather did slightly better than Mayweather-Gatti had on pay-per-view, 10,000 more at 350,000. It generated $15.7 million in revenue. There was a good live crowd, 15,170 at the Thomas & Mack Center. Singers, actors and other celebrities wanted to be seen there. Floyd was in a strong position. He was also about to go it alone.

Top Rank were spinning plates. They'd recognised that the Hispanic demographic was hugely profitable and were building slow, tough welterweight Antonio Margarito into a star who was hard to match.

Mayweather had little inclination to fight him, even though the $8 million on the table would have been a career-high purse. The risk was relatively high, the reward potentially very low. Top Rank kept offering it to Floyd. He still had his heart set on De La Hoya as his top target and he asked Bob Arum for $20 million to make it happen.

Arum didn't see how those kind of figures could possibly add up so a few weeks after the Judah fight. Mayweather paid Arum $750,000 to release him from his Top Rank contract.

It made him a free agent.

Arum revealed that Mayweather had turned down Margarito for 12 August on HBO pay-per-view.

'I did hear from him,' he told ESPN. 'He decided not to fight this summer. I made him a tremendous offer. I think Margarito is the riskiest fight for him of anyone out there.'

Many felt Floyd was dodging the Mexican hard nut, who looked like a bad guy from a Tarantino flick, but Leonard Ellerbe insisted that was not the case.

'Floyd is not 100 per cent healthy,' Ellerbe said, adding that Mayweather's hand had been bruised in the Judah fight. 'His hand is not broken. It's bruised, but it's a bad bruise. He wants to go into any fight 100 per cent healthy. If Antonio Margarito happens to be the best available option when he is healthy, so be it. We are not turning down Margarito. I want to make that crystal clear. When and if he is the best available option for Floyd's next fight, that's the direction he will move in.'

Unlike their earlier split, Arum said there were no hard feelings this time. 'We intend to be back together. Everything with this was honourable and good. I had offered him numbers [for a multi-fight contract extension] that were liveable. His expectations are in the stratosphere. He was entitled to buy me out, and he did. We decided this was the best way to handle it.'

He told Kevin Iole at Yahoo, 'The big divide between Floyd and ourselves, with me, it was really the age difference. Floyd was asking me to reach out on his behalf more to the African-American community. I was familiar with the African-American community, but it was a different community. It was the community of the [Muhammad] Ali times and the [Joe] Frazier times and older people like myself. What Floyd was talking about, which I later realised, was the hip-hop generation, which I couldn't connect to. I didn't do what Floyd asked me to do because I didn't know how.'

Mayweather never looked back and the snowball – which would become a financial avalanche – began to roll.

'When I became my own boss, I could do things the way I felt they should be done,' Mayweather said. 'I don't think it

I made him a tremendous offer. I think Margarito
fight for him of anyone out there.'

Floyd was dodging the Mexican hard nut, who
ad guy from a Tarantino flick, but Leonard Ellerbe
vas not the case.

ot 100 per cent healthy,' Ellerbe said, adding that
hand had been bruised in the Judah fight. 'His
roken. It's bruised, but it's a bad bruise. He wants
fight 100 per cent healthy. If Antonio Margarito
e the best available option when he is healthy, so
not turning down Margarito. I want to make that
When and if he is the best available option for
ght, that's the direction he will move in.'

ir earlier split, Arum said there were no hard
ime. 'We intend to be back together. Everything
honourable and good. I had offered him numbers
fight contract extension] that were liveable. His
re in the stratosphere. He was entitled to buy me
id. We decided this was the best way to handle it.'

vin Iole at Yahoo, 'The big divide between Floyd
, with me, it was really the age difference. Floyd
e to reach out on his behalf more to the African-
mmunity. I was familiar with the African-American
but it was a different community. It was the
f the [Muhammad] Ali times and the [Joe] Frazier
der people like myself. What Floyd was talking
I later realised, was the hip-hop generation, which
nnect to. I didn't do what Floyd asked me to do
't know how.'

r never looked back and the snowball – which
e a financial avalanche – began to roll.

ecame my own boss, I could do things the way
uld be done,' Mayweather said. 'I don't think it

fighter and had no deliberate intention to aim low. 'Mayweather's
a good fighter, he's quick. He's got good hands. He is a great
defensive fighter, he has a tight defence.'

'I knew Judah would come out on his toes and be strong,'
Mayweather continued. 'He brought his A-game and so did I. I
hurt my right hand, but those things happen in big fights. Me
and Zab took care of things like businessmen. What happened,
happened. We're friends and fought through our problems. It
was a great fight, that's all I can say.'

'Things got a little carried away,' replied Judah. 'That's not my
style to try and hit him low. We had a great round going, why
would I mess that up? It happened and I apologised. It's just two
fighters in there. Everybody's emotionally involved in this whole
thing. But when somebody takes it upon themselves, from the
outside, to come in and make their own consequences, I don't
think that's the right thing to do.'

In the ring post-fight, Don King, was already saying that
Mayweather should have been disqualified. No one important
was listening.

'Once you get on the apron, the fight is a disqualification,'
King hollered with his familiar bombast. 'It should be total
disqualification. There was a third man in the ring chasing the
fighter during the round. The fight is over when the man stepped
on the apron, and this man came all the way into the ring. We
got to do this again.'

By the letter of the law in Nevada, 'The referee may, in his
discretion, stop a contest or exhibition if an unauthorised person
enters the ring or fenced area during a round.'

It was Steele's call and he let it go on.

The commission, though, made those involved pay heavily for
their indiscretions.

Roger, who had lit the touch paper, was fined the entirety of
his $200,000 pay packet and banned for a year.

Zab and Yoel Judah were slapped with fines and suspensions. The fighter had to pay $250,000, the whole slice he was making of the $1 million that Top Rank had paid promoter Don King for his services. The Nevada State Athletic Commission also banned him for a year. The black mark against him from the melee after the Tszyu fight was held against him, making him a repeat offender.

Yoel also had his licence revoked for a year. His fine was $100,000. He said he felt the penalties were harsh and unfair.

'They came down hard on us,' he told Dan Rafael. 'It was bad. They said they were trying to make a statement.'

'I thought it was crazy,' concurred Zab. 'I don't think it was fair. A lot of BS was involved. I thought I'd get a $100,000 fine and maybe a four-month suspension. I was very surprised at how harsh they were. They gave me the maximum out of everyone and Roger [Mayweather] started the whole thing.'

Ellerbe, who was suspended for four months, also copped a fine of $50,000, meaning the combined fines heading in the direction of the NSAC totalled $600,000.

'They all apologised, and I think it was sincere,' said Marc Ratner, in one of his last significant calls as the chairman of the Nevada State Athletic Commission before he left boxing for the Ultimate Fighting Championship.

'It was tough day. Everyone handled it very professionally. None of the licensees left smiling. The commission felt that it wanted to send a very strong message. This incident was so close to a full-scale riot that innocent people could have gotten hurt or maimed. The commission felt very, very strongly that this cannot happen again.'

'Roger was very apologetic,' said Todd duBoef. 'It's a sad day for Roger, who is one of the good guys in boxing. But he committed a deplorable offence and he is being punished for it.'

Roger, who sent a letter of apology to the commission,

appealed the verdict but N
Judahs unhappily took thei

Floyd came out of it all
his marketability was closin
made another career-high p
seemed plausible.

Zab, however, had lost t
time in his career.

'Can't cry over spilled mi
pray for better things.'

Judah-Mayweather did sl
had on pay-per-view, 10,0
$15.7 million in revenue. Th
the Thomas & Mack Center
wanted to be seen there. Flo
also about to go it alone.

Top Rank were spinning
Hispanic demographic was
slow, tough welterweight Ar
hard to match.

Mayweather had little in
the $8 million on the table
The risk was relatively high,
Rank kept offering it to Floy
Hoya as his top target and
to make it happen.

Arum didn't see how tho
up so a few weeks after the
$750,000 to release him fro

It made him a free agent.

Arum revealed that May
for 12 August on HBO pay

'I did hear from him,' he

this summer
is the riskies

Many fe
looked like
insisted that

'Floyd is
Mayweather
hand is not
to go into a
happens to
be it. We are
crystal clear
Floyd's next

Unlike t
feelings this
with this wa
[for a mult
expectations
out, and he

He told
and ourselv
was asking
American co
community,
community
times and
about, which
I couldn't c
because I di

Mayweat
would becor

'When I
I felt they s

happened overnight. The only thing I kept doing was I kept pushing myself and I kept believing. Like I said before, I had a brilliant team outside the ring. We had a great game plan. The game plan was for them to take care of business and make sure I was comfortable outside and I would go in and execute the game plan on the inside. That's what we did.'

Ellerbe, who became the CEO of Mayweather Promotions, agreed. 'They [Top Rank] did a lot of great things building Floyd. They did it the conventional way, the old-school way. Floyd just wanted to think outside the box and do it his way.'

He was now also being represented by the William Morris Agency, a Hollywood-based outfit whose clients included basketball legend Magic Johnson, golfer Michelle Wie and tennis star Serena Williams. Oh, and Oscar De La Hoya. Lon Rosen was his agent.

'We're working very closely with his management and himself and we're going to develop an overall strategy,' announced Rosen, who said he was going to look for opportunities for Floyd in both the endorsement markets and in the entertainment industry. 'We're very confident that he can succeed. He was very impressive in the meetings we've had with him. He's got a great personality. He speaks well. He's a good-looking guy and he's got a great mind on his shoulders. He knows what he wants.'

'It just takes time,' Mayweather said. 'I'm not going to be boxing forever. But now that I have my team in place, there's a lot of things other than boxing that I feel I can do.'

'I believe people in the urban, African-American market appreciate someone's brilliance,' said Todd duBoef, Top Rank's president. 'Whether it's Denzel Washington as an actor, P Diddy as a musician or Floyd as a fighter, they appreciate brilliance. There was just an outpouring of response to see Floyd perform. It's like seeing Louis Armstrong perform. That's how they look at it.'

De La Hoya seemed to be growing keener. Hatton had signed a three-fight deal with HBO that was apparently designed with a grand finale against Mayweather. Mosley had to take Mayweather seriously as a potential opponent. Then there was Baldomir. He was no pound-for-pounder and certainly not an all-time great but he had beaten Judah, who had given Floyd problems.

'If Oscar is willing to step up and fight Floyd, we'll fight him at whatever weight he's comfortable with, so there are no excuses,' said Ellerbe.

De La Hoya had returned to emphatically defeat Nicaraguan nutter Ricardo Mayorga with a blistering performance. At light-middleweight. Floyd still wasn't that big yet. 'Who says he has to weigh 154,' queried Ellerbe. 'Floyd can change weight divisions as the situation dictates. The name of the game is skills. And there isn't anyone in any of those three weight divisions [from light-welter to light-middleweight] who has the skills to beat Floyd – not one.'

Mayweather had almost stopped calling out opponents and mentioning names. He wanted to be the draw. He was letting his fighting do the talking.

'I don't think he was mature enough to do it before,' said Arum. 'Now he understands and he's acting like a business guy.'

'The fights are all lined up,' said Ellerbe, about the possibilities. 'Margarito, Oscar, Ricky Hatton, Shane Mosley, it doesn't matter. They all have to go through Floyd. This is the second part of Floyd's career. In this part, he takes off both inside the ring and outside.'

Rugged Carlos Baldomir was not the opponent that box-office blockbusters are made of, but having beaten Judah and then defeated a returning Gatti he was the linear champion, he was the man who had first beaten Judah and the Gatti win inside nine rounds only solidified that position. He was a hard man. 'Moving him back is like trying to push around a building,' wrote Ivan Goldman in *The Ring*, adding 'This is a guy who was groomed for obscurity but refused to accept it.'

Goldman praised Mayweather, too, saying that hitting him clean was like 'trying to catch the world's most athletic flea.'

Predicting that repeated Mayweather wins would help him cross into the mainstream, the writer also noted how Mayweather was becoming boxing's man to fight. 'He has reached a stage in his career that Oscar De La Hoya has enjoyed for years,' he wrote. 'Everyone wants to fight him. He attracts so much cash, and beating him would be so prestigious, that it's worth the risk.'

Mayweather appeared on that issue's front cover, dressed like a 1920s gangster and holding a Tommy gun.

The winner and loser would both have plenty of opportunities. The welterweight division was awash with talent and danger lurked throughout the top ten. Tall, southpaw puncher Paul Williams had routed Sharmba Mitchell. Another lefty, Puerto Rico's Carlos Quintana, was on the rise. There was Hatton, moving up from light-welter and capturing the WBA title from Luis Collazo, who remained a player. There was Miguel Cotto, De La Hoya, Mosley and Margarito, but who only brought a high risk against a low reward into the equation.

Either way, Dan Goossen, now working with Mayweather and taking the opportunity to speak on the Baldomir fight, said that Mayweather had instructed him to make the biggest and best fight he could. 'The key here is taking on a man based on what he has done recently. Floyd is dealing with a dangerous, big, strong and determined champion in Baldomir,' said Goossen. 'There's only one other fight that would have been better in my eyes for Floyd, and that's against Oscar De La Hoya. Anyone who ridicules Floyd from here on out, and what he's done against some of the names on his résumé, doesn't know what they're talking about. Floyd's overcome a long line of tough, tough challenges. But because of the way he handles these guys, fans want to see someone who has a shot at beating Floyd Mayweather. This is a fight that catapults Floyd to a new level of greatness. Their styles match perfectly. It's what everyone wants.'

'He's the champion, the real welterweight champion,' confessed Mayweather. 'But I'm the best fighter in the world. He might be the Cinderella Man but I'm Pretty Boy Floyd: HBO's own, the one and only, the greatest fighter in the world.'

Baldomir was thirty-five but in the form of his life. He hadn't lost a fight in nearly eight years and had scored nineteen wins and drawn twice without losing in that period. He'd beaten Judah in New York when he was only supposed to have a walk-on role, and then he'd stopped Gatti in front of another sold-out Atlantic City crowd when they thought their hero would be manoeuvered into a fight with Cotto. Some took the Santa Fe star seriously as a threat to Mayweather, others saw him as an accidental winner over an unmotivated Judah who was already thinking of Floyd, and a Gatti who'd seen much better days.

For a contest that was dubbed 'Pretty Risky', Baldomir-Mayweather, which took place at the Mandalay Bay in Las Vegas, was decidedly unspectacular. In fact, Dan Rafael – on the boxing beat for ESPN – went so far as to write, 'The fight was not competitive for a single moment as Mayweather overwhelmed the plodding Baldomir with his speed.' He said Mayweather 'toyed' with Baldomir in a fight 'devoid of drama.'

Floyd had weighed in a pound under the limit at 146lbs. Baldomir was bang on 147lbs. On fight night Mayweather had gained three pounds, Baldomir walked into the ring a whopping fifteen pounds heavier, fighting in essence as a middleweight. The extra poundage did not help him.

Floyd came to the ring in a gladiator's golden body armour, carried upon a throne with a helmet under his arm. It certainly was not to Larry Merchant's taste, who shook his head and tutted at what he saw.

After hitting the usual lines about tough competitors and durable guys, Mayweather finally admitted in the post-fight press conference, 'It was a cakewalk if you want to know the truth.'

Two of the officials scored every round for the American – 120-108, one judge saw Baldomir win two rounds, losing 118-110.

'Maybe Mayweather should have fought with one arm tied behind his back?' continued Rafael. 'It might have made Saturday night's fight a little more interesting.'

Many of the 9,427 in attendance left before the final bell because the result was not in doubt. Of course, uncle Roger was missing. Not only did he have to sit it out because of his suspension but he had been jailed for six months for a battery conviction.

Mayweather did not need him for Baldomir. Nor did he need it from stand-in Leonard Ellerbe, who assisted in Roger's place through training camp and on the night.

'Being around the sport so long, I should be able to go out there and handle myself for thirty-five or forty minutes without my uncle in my corner,' Mayweather had said.

'When it's all said and done, a trainer can't fight for a fighter. When it comes down to skills and smarts, it's about what a fighter knows. I know what it takes to handle things by myself because I've been here before in so many championship fights. I just went out there and put on a boxing clinic. I feel like down the stretch I would've got the knockout, but I hurt my hand. Look at what I did tonight, I had a shutout. I can win under any circumstances, and I am here to stay.'

Baldomir knew he was second best by some margin.

'I didn't fight my fight,' he conceded. 'He was too fast. I couldn't catch him, and when I did, I just wasn't strong. I felt sluggish.'

The Argentine had been cut outside his left eye and on the nose in round one and it did not get better for him at any point in the fight. Indeed, the action was so similar through the middle rounds that the HBO crew began hypothesising what might happen if Mayweather was to fight De La Hoya.

'I don't see anybody on the edge of their seats,' said Merchant of the Baldomir fight. 'I don't hear anybody roaring. It's just a wonderful exhibition, but where's the drama.'

His team speculated, accurately, that Mayweather had hurt his right hand as he was throwing it so sparingly. They wondered whether he was boxing almost one-handed because that is all he needed to beat the Argentine champion or if it was injured again. After round eleven, and with the result and method of victory beyond any doubt, golfer Tiger Woods joined hordes of others heading for the exits to beat the traffic or get to the tables at the Mandalay Bay first.

In the corner, Ellerbe asked for three minutes of 'smart boxing.' Fireworks were not permitted. Boos followed through much of the last round as a contest with little sparkle fizzled completely out.

Mayweather, speaking to old adversary Larry Merchant, said he felt his right hand hurting halfway through the rout. Merchant then asked Floyd whether, with the crowd booing and leaving after the tenth and eleventh rounds, people had been entertained.

'You always give me a hard time,' Floyd snapped, turning on Merchant. 'You don't ever give me the credit I deserve. You're good at commentating so stick to commentating; let me do the fighting. I'm the best at what I do, that's why I'm with HBO. HBO is my family, HBO is my home; like I said before, you can learn boxing from "Pretty Boy" Floyd, you're just a commentator, stick to commentating.'

'That's what I'm doing and I'm asking you a question,' Merchant retorted.

'Don't always be a critic and be so negative, let's be positive. I got the victory tonight under any circumstances so all you can do is respect me for that. You're hoping and wishing a fighter can beat me. I'm the king of the throne. I'm here to stay. I can win under any circumstances.'

He then tried to battle it out with Merchant for airtime, telling him to let him do the talking. Floyd went into a monologue to camera and said Merchant was just a commentator who knew nothing about boxing. Their exchange was more captivating than the last six rounds of the fight it had followed.

'Well, we finally got some drama,' said Lampley, tongue in cheek, when the camera panned back to him.

Some felt Mayweather's clinical performance had been simply brilliant. Others were left wanting. 'Truly, Mayweather is a marvel,' wrote Eric Raskin in *The Ring*. 'He is a once-in-a-generation boxing artist. He is a special athlete. And he is, at times, a colossal bore.'

Mayweather's incandescent rage had softened by the time he arrived at the post-fight presser and the emotion had switched from anger to sadness.

He dolled out watches to several media members who had assembled to listen to his thoughts.

Maybe he did not know what he had to do to be appreciated. Was he growing bored with his own dominance? Was he satisfied with five titles in four weight classes? Whatever it was, he again threatened retirement. Cynics were not buying it. He maintained it was on his mind.

'All I have is one more fight and that's it,' he insisted. 'Then I'm walking away.'

He, along with many others, hoped that fight would be against De La Hoya.

'I think he will get in the ring with me after tonight,' Floyd reckoned. 'If he wants to, he knows how to reach me. If De La

Hoya really wants to fight me, I'll tax that ass too. Oscar said he wants to leave fighting the best. I know we'll make the De La Hoya fight happen. We still got another big fight to do, but if it's not on my terms it won't happen.'

He said he would remain involved in boxing in some capacity when he hung the gloves up, starting up Mayweather Promotions and working with advisor Al Haymon to expand his outside-the-ring business empire.

He also talked of going back to school to earn his GED, having dropped out of school in twelfth grade to focus on making the Olympics.

'I love the sport,' Mayweather said softly, as he wiped away tears at the post-fight presser. 'One more fight and I'm through. I don't need boxing. I'm not in it for the money. It's about legacy. I'm rich and I've accomplished what I want. I'm leaving on top. That's what it's about. I'm not hurting for money, for nothing. I love my family. They tore my name down, tore my family down and I still rose to the top. I thought about retiring after the Zab Judah fight. The sport has been great to me. When I die, my legacy will live on. One more fight and I am through. Boxing's got me from the ghetto to the suburbs. I got a lot of money. I couldn't spend it in a billion lifetimes. It's about being a legend in the sport, and I am a legend. I accomplished what I wanted to accomplish in this sport. I won the titles I wanted to win.

'I don't need no five-star restaurants. You can give me McDonald's and I'm cool with that. Give me Pizza Hut.'

During the press conference he leaned on HBO boss Kery Davis for moral support, even weeping on his shoulder at times. Davis was taken aback that Mayweather, finally crossing over into the mainstream, was talking about walking away.

'Obviously, whatever he wants to do, we will always wish him the best,' he said. 'We've had a great relationship. We'll wish him the best with whatever he wants to do with the rest of his life. But he's certainly at the top of his game right now, so him leaving the sport at this point would certainly surprise anyone. But I'm not fighting anybody. Nobody is hitting me. I would never try to talk anyone into doing what they don't feel like they want to do anymore.'

There was no question, though, that HBO was now sold on making De La Hoya-Mayweather – 'The Golden Boy' versus 'Pretty Boy' – a massive fight. It could even set some records. There was immediate speculation that there could be as much as $50 million to divide between the two fighters. Just how big it would be was down to the fighters and how they would sell it, and themselves.

NINE

GOOD VERSUS BAD

THE WORLD AWAITED.

Or so the tagline insisted.

In 2007, Oscar De La Hoya was still king of the pay-per-view mountain and so De La Hoya-Mayweather was his project to announce.

'It's official,' read a statement from Oscar's Golden Boy Promotions. 'The fight will happen May fifth.'

Mayweather had long wanted to use De La Hoya as a springboard to fame and greater fortune and now was his chance.

Insiders were split as to who would win, wondering if Floyd was too youthful and fast or whether the old glamour boy would be too big and experienced.

Regardless of the outcome, the world knew it was Floyd's big opportunity.

'Even casual observers in the boxing community understood "the fight" meant Floyd Mayweather Jr would finally get his dream bout jackpot,' wrote *Boxing Digest*.

'This is the fight I've been waiting for,' Floyd confirmed. 'To show everyone that I'm one of the greatest.'

There was speculation that the contest could earn Mayweather, who turned thirty in the February before the bout, as much as $20 million.

HBO, who would broadcast the fight in the USA, announced a pioneering show called *De La Hoya-Mayweather 24/7*, a series they would go on to utilise in future years for major fights.

It was a four-part documentary that took the audience behind the scenes of the training camps, introducing the fighters and those in their families and entourages to the fans. The content was gritty, the delivery and production high-end and polished.

The first thing Floyd said on the show was, to the camera, 'Look me in my eyes Oscar, I'm going to beat your ass.'

That set the tone for what was to follow.

De La Hoya had been the network's cash cow, appearing twenty-nine times on their airwaves. Floyd was now on twenty, though his relationship with them had, of course, endured many issues.

De La Hoya was the betting underdog when the odds were announced. He had become a part-time boxer, fighting just fifteen rounds in three years and, at thirty-four, could no longer claim to be in his prime.

He did not need the money and with a history of big fights extending back to a 1992 Olympic gold medal in Barcelona, four years before Floyd took a shot at the same colour medal in Atlanta, he was asked if he should still be fighting.

'I just decided,' he said, 'I'm going to continue fighting as long as my reflexes, my speed and my timing are all intact. I'm going to keep going and take advantage of my youth while I have it. I decided to fight, and I'm going after the best.'

The last time he had fought a pound-for-pound ruler he was stopped by a Bernard Hopkins body shot in a bold attempt for the middleweight title. This time someone was moving up to fight him, as Mayweather aimed for another title in a fifth division, challenging De La Hoya for the WBC light-middleweight title he had smashed Nicaraguan Ricardo Mayorga for a year earlier.

De La Hoya, the old fighter-salesman, knew how to market an event – by saying it was not just any ordinary fight.

'Motivation is oozing out of me right now,' he said. 'I can say that I'm treating this as the biggest fight of my life. I've never sparred with him. I've never seen him train. We're gonna meet up for the first time and it'll be something else. I can't wait to give a spectacular performance. I mean, I'm gonna be a machine by May.'

The weekend of 5 May, Cinco de Mayo, had become one of boxing's annual dates for the diary. De La Hoya, in particular, had built a foundation on having his big fights on the Hispanic holiday as the TV and live audiences would potentially be bigger, with families or groups of friends all chipping in to share the pay-per-view cover price during barbecues or social gatherings.

'I don't have to prove anything to anybody but myself,' said Floyd. 'And I've already done that.'

The plot was not as thick or muddy as it might have been.

De La Hoya said he would not be working with his regular trainer, Floyd Mayweather Sr. Instead, he hired the services of Los Angeles trainer Freddie Roach in the build-up and on fight night.

De La Hoya had a history of changing coaches, having already worked with Robert Alcazar, Emanuel Steward, Gil Clancy, Jesus Rivero and Floyd Sr.

He explained, '[Floyd Snr] looked into my eyes and told me "I'll train you to beat my son". It's just not in my nature to get in between family.'

Floyd Sr had also apparently put a $2-million price tag on his involvement in the fight, which De La Hoya baulked at.

It was not wholly amicable as both told their sides of the story.

'If they want me to work against my son, then they're going to have to pay me,' Mayweather Sr told the *Las Vegas Review-Journal*. 'My son and I, no matter what's gone down between us, he's still my blood. Hey, I'd work for Oscar if the deal is right, because that's my job and boxing is just a sport. But if you want me to tell you how to beat my son – and I'm the only one who can tell Oscar how to do that – then you need to pay me.'

He said he was offered a $500,000 fee and the same again if De La Hoya won. He called that 'insulting'.

Roach was to be paid $1.3 million but Oscar said the decision was not a financial one.

'It had no impact whatsoever,' added De La Hoya, who felt uncomfortable with the Mayweathers' family situation and did not want to become involved in it.

'It was a very touchy subject. When I was making my decision, at first, I said, "Yes, he is going to train me and he can do it." But after thinking for days and weeks and months, I said to myself, "This is his son. Is he going to be as passionate as I am in the gym?" I want to knock this guy out. I asked myself all these questions. How am I going to feel in the gym? Will it feel awkward? I didn't want to feel distracted, like, "Wow, here's the father training me to beat up his son." I finally figured we have to get someone else. I think it turned out better for everyone, including Floyd Sr.'

He had not worked with Roach before, though Freddie had become boxing's 'go-to guy', working with the likes of Virgil Hill, Mike Tyson and his Filipino protégé Manny Pacquiao.

'I started training in October,' said De La Hoya. 'I've done a little bit of weight training, a lot of flexibility work. I want to make sure that I'm really, really fast. I know I have the power at 154 but I want to be fast and explosive.'

The returning Roger Mayweather was in Floyd's corner, fresh from his six-month jail term on an assault charge. And before long, Floyd Sr was back in the fold as an uneasy peace was temporarily restored.

'Floyd Sr is my father,' said the welterweight king, 'I respect him as my father. But Floyd Mayweather right here is going to do what he wants to do.'

Sr seemed to understand it had to be that way. 'It's Floyd's fight. Whatever he decides he wants to do, it's fine with me,' he said.

It was not harmonious, though. Brothers Roger and Floyd were not on speaking terms and Floyd Sr ended up leaving camp when he decided he was not getting the respect he was due.

'Even though he's acting like a jerk, I still love him,' said his son. 'He's still my father. I don't want to go through the rest of my life beefing with my father. That's not a good feeling and I feel that's childish and one of us has to be the bigger man so I let him know that I love him.'

'I'll be honest with you,' Sr said, who had seemed pleased to be reconciled at first, even if it was only as a peripheral camp figure. 'I don't know this kid now. I don't know him.'

Elsewhere, Floyd was spending time with his celebrity pal rapper 50 Cent while training in his own gym in the Chinatown part of Las Vegas.

He had also taken on another pair of hands for camp, too, working with Nate Jones, his former Olympic teammate, who held the body belt for him.

'He's matured, he's older,' said Jones, who had fallen on hard times. He had just fifteen dollars in his account, was depressed and gaining weight. Then Mayweather called to help him out.

'He's had a great career, I had an okay career,' said Jones. 'We met many years ago and became best friends. We had a lot of fun, he never turned on me, I never turned on him.'

'He's a close friend of mine,' Floyd agreed. 'He's been a friend of mine for ages, since we were seventeen. We went to the Olympics together, he won a bronze medal. His career didn't really get off the ground but I love him so much.'

De La Hoya worked out for eight weeks in Puerto Rico, and drafted in two-time conqueror Shane Mosley for some sparring.

'Floyd's approach is business as usual,' said Leonard Ellerbe. 'He's always in the gym anyway. Obviously it's the biggest fight in Floyd's career. De La Hoya has fought the best of his era but he'll be totally surprised with what he has to deal with. Floyd's the complete package. The best Oscar has faced.'

'I have to mug him,' Oscar told the press. 'My biggest concern is my footwork. I have to cut off the ring, make sure that every move he makes, I'm right there in his face with a controlled distance. I mean, I don't want to smother the guy. That's a mistake a lot of fighters make with him because he has that sneaky defence. The way you break through that defence is get your distance and pick your shots. I mean, double and triple left hooks are really gonna be key. And the jab.'

Those were all Oscar's bread-and-butter shots anyway. A superb, accurate jabber – a rarity in boxing, De La Hoya was a left-handed fighter who boxed in the right-handed orthodox stance – Oscar's real power came in his star-studded left hook.

'Oscar's a good fighter,' Mayweather admitted, 'But there's nothing he can do that I can't deal with. I'll be doing all the things he can't handle. After this, everybody will know about my skills.'

Of course, it was not just about the fight. It had been about the deal to get it done. Negotiations went backwards and forwards for weeks. There was also then an eleven-city media tour, which started at the Waldorf Astoria in New York City.

Within moments of arriving, Mayweather stripped his top off to show the press that he was already in fantastic condition, displaying abs of marble. It prompted Oscar to get involved in a showboating contest and while the Golden Boy lifted his shirt to unveil a six-pack, it was comparatively fleshy.

He said he weighed 162lbs, so only eight pounds over the limit, though Floyd's team insisted he would come in well below the division's upper bracket.

When the fighters squared off, Floyd dusted off his shoulder and called Oscar a bitch. 'I'm top drawer, I'm going to beat you, I'm going to beat you until you respect me. I'm going to beat you until you call me pretty,' he gassed.

He shoved Oscar. De La Hoya responded in kind as it threatened to escalate.

The next ten stops on the tour saw neither man calm down. Oscar told the *24/7* cameras that Floyd had stolen boxing kit from a bag he carried with him – 'Do something about it,' Floyd dared him – and then, in another stunt, Floyd brought a chicken in a cage to a press conference with the label 'Golden Girl' on it. He then took the chicken from its temporary hold and talked smack to it in front of the cameras, pretending it was De La Hoya.

All the while, the Golden Boy seethed in a quiet, professional manner. 'I've been at many big fights,' he said. 'It's not going to work.'

'I respect Oscar as a man before I respect him as a fighter,' replied Mayweather. 'It takes two to make a mega-fight. He's a champion and I'm a champion; that's why we're making this fight.'

'I respect Floyd as a fighter, I do,' countered Oscar, who appeared to getting wound up by Mayweather's dismissive outlook on his career. 'But come May fifth, when I touch you, you're going to hurt for a week. And believe me, come May fifth I'm going to give you something to cry about.'

He was referring to Mayweather's tears at the Baldomir post-fight presser and continued, addressing the unbeaten star's trash-talk, 'It doesn't bother me. It's just funny to me. I see a kid in there who is nervous and he just keeps talking and talking because he is so nervous. I've been there. I've done that. When you're up there on May fifth it's a whole different story. You can't be talking up in the ring. It's going to be a long, tough, gruelling fight for him.'

'Thirty-seven have tried, thirty-seven have failed,' was Mayweather's simple riposte. 'If you want the fake shit here it is.' He said that pointing at De La Hoya's WBC light-middleweight title. 'If you want the real shit, it's here,' he added, pointing to himself.

'This is a fight Floyd's been wanting for his whole career,' said Ellerbe, as the mood between the fighters grew ever more frosty. 'This is a fight the whole world's been waiting for. Oscar thinks he can win in his mind, but deep down in his heart he knows what he's up against. How are you going to outbox the best boxer in the world? Come on, let's be realistic.'

Mayweather said it would be his last fight, that he would call it a day at 38-0.

Others questioned whether De La Hoya was still ambitious and if he had the hunger that saw him rise so briskly up the ranks, even scalping Floyd's uncle, Jeff, in only his fifth pro fight, stopping him in the fourth round of eight scheduled sessions.

In June 2002, Mike Tyson's forlorn challenge of Lennox Lewis garnered almost two million buys on pay-per-view. Early financial projections for De La Hoya-Mayweather saw that number smashed.

The previous record for a non-heavyweight fight was the 1.4 million De La Hoya's fight with Félix Trinidad had drawn in 1999.

The pay-per-view was set at $54.95 in the USA, fifty dollars on closed circuit, and the fight was to be shown in 176 countries. Tickets opened at $150 and went up to $2,000 for ringside seats. They went on sale on 27 January at 10 a.m. Pacific Time and were all gone in three hours.

It generated a record-breaking gate of $18,419,200, eclipsing the $16,860,300 total set by Lennox Lewis-Evander Holyfield II in 1999.

There was money everywhere.

Mayweather was the villain of the piece. Of course he was. 'You can't be two good guys, I chose to be the bad guy,' he'd said on *24/7*.

He knew that flashing his increasing wealth would rile fans and get them to root against him. So he exhibited his cash at every opportunity.

But Floyd did not purchase just any bling. He became a student of jewellery, fast cars and clothing designers. The *24/7* cameras also picked up on his penchant for carrying wads of cash everywhere he went and his increasing love of gambling. At the time, he had a $34,000 bet on Allen Iverson's Denver Nuggets winning their next game.

He learned how the other half lived. In an interview with Thomas Hauser, the author wrote that 'Mayweather is the new poster child for boxing bling-bling'. Hauser revealed how, 'On the road, an assistant carries the jewels that Floyd isn't wearing in an unobtrusive black leather attaché case. If one asks to see what's inside and Mayweather is in the mood, the contents are revealed. Like a pirate reaching into a treasure chest, he brandishes myriad gold chains, pendants, watches, bracelets and rings. Most of them are gold and platinum, embedded with large-carat diamonds.'

At the time, Mayweather's prized possession was a 'Ferrari horse', which was designed for him by a Las Vegas jeweller named Mordechai.

The horse had blocks of black, white and yellow diamonds totaling more than 600 in all and 120 carats in an invisible setting. It took three months to make and cost Floyd around $150,000.

'I know all about jewellery,' he told Hauser. 'People say I'm cocky and arrogant, but I say, in reply, that I'm confident and slick. Sure, my lifestyle is flashy and flamboyant. There can never be too many diamonds.'

While the *24/7* cameras played up Mayweather living large, Floyd maintained there was substance behind the wealth. 'That *24/7* show only showed one side of me,' he insisted. 'I'm a decent guy. I love my family and fans.'

Veteran fight scribe Jeff Ryan, in *The Ring*, summed up how Mayweather came across to many, intentional or otherwise. 'The HBO reality show, *24/7*, revealed Mayweather to be an idiot around the clock. He showed off how much money he had by stacking piles of it on the table and then arrogantly flinging hundred-dollar bills at the television camera. He got in De La Hoya's face at press conferences and tried to provoke confrontations. No matter what setting it was in, Pretty Boy unleashed the f-word with such regularity, a CussStat computer would have been required to keep count. Basically, he came across as a punk.'

What the show did do, though, was give Mayweather an identity to the wider public, one he could utilise and something they could like or loathe. He was no longer just a talent. He was a personality and the street kid from the dysfunctional family was promising to batter the family man who had won a gold medal at the Olympics in memory of his late mother. It all helped Mayweather go mainstream.

'Cocky, rude, unpleasant, Floyd's pantomime bad guy act sailed close to the wind of bad taste at times,' wrote Glyn Leach, the late editor of *Boxing Monthly*. 'And, given the propensity to misbehave of his recently released trainer/uncle Roger Mayweather, there was a very definite tinder box element to the "Pretty Boy's" faction, even without the will he/won't he element of father Floyd Sr's potentially fractious reintroduction into the fold.'

The *24/7* show also made celebrities out of the likes of Roger and Floyd Sr, and added to the burgeoning fame of trainer Freddie Roach. Fans with cameras and Sharpies, wanting their own slice of the drama during fight week, surrounded them all.

The fighters stripped for the weigh-in the afternoon before the fight and the scenes were chaotic. Around 6,000 (with around a further 2,000 left kicking their heels unable to get in) attended the MGM Grand Garden Arena, the fight venue, to watch the fighters tip the scales. It was the biggest crowd recorded for a Vegas weigh-in, with some fans queuing in line as long as six hours to make sure of their spot. There were more than 1,000 media members in town to cover the show.

Mayweather weighed only 150lbs, four pounds under the 154 limit that De La Hoya tipped exactly.

Larry Merchant, opening the telecast for HBO, was asked who would win.

'If I were a betting man, Mayweather,' he said. 'But if I lost my money, I wouldn't be unhappy.'

Everyone likes an underdog, but the Mayweather-Merchant dynamic had unquestionably hit a low point with the post-fight Baldomir Q and A.

Floyd walked to the ring in glittery Mexican colours and wearing a sombrero, which was on backwards. One report suggested the thick white, green and red jacket he wore was bulletproof. Jim Lampley, for HBO, said the Mexican theme was probably worn in tribute to his uncle and trainer Roger, the one-time 'Mexican Assassin.' Merchant and Emanuel Steward felt he was taunting the crowd.

For Floyd, it was probably more a point of riling the Mexican-American fans on hand to support De La Hoya by using his rival's gimmick, the same way he flipped the gladiator script on Arturo Gatti by wearing that elaborate costume.

It was, in Las Vegas, Cinco de Mayo weekend, and Mayweather wanted everyone to know that he would soon change the date to Cinco de Mayweather.

Friend and entertainer 50 Cent rapped him to the ring.

Merchant took the time to offer Mayweather some praise.

'Give him credit,' he said. 'Way back when he was fighting in the 130s he started brewing up a fight with De La Hoya. We all thought it was just so much talk and [he was] looking for headlines but he dreamed it, he fantasised it and he made it happen.'

In the ring, with De La Hoya's Mexican tunes filling the arena, a topless and ready Mayweather bounced on the spot near De La Hoya, who was seemingly trying to deny his rival's existence by turning his back and fixing his gaze as he danced.

Referee Kenny Bayless was on hand, just in case they tried for an early start.

Marc Anthony sang the USA National Anthem.

Michael Buffer introduced the protagonists and told the 16,700 in the MGM Grand audience, and the millions watching around the world, that they were ready to rumble.

Mayweather was booed. De La Hoya, ever the Golden Boy, received a warm and motivational ovation.

The fighters touched gloves and returned to their corners. Roger Mayweather used his last moments before the opening bell to tell Bayless that De La Hoya's groin protector was too high over his shorts. There was no reaction.

A star-studded crowd including John Madden, Tom Jones, Matthew McConaughey, Jack Nicholson, Jim Carrey, John Cusack, Wesley Snipes, Will Ferrell, Magic Johnson, Ron Howard, Senator John McCain, Mary J Blige, Usher, Leonardo DiCaprio, Sean 'Puffy' Combs, Tobey Maguire and dozens of other A-listers from the worlds of sport and entertainment took their seats.

The world waited no longer. The new biggest fight in boxing history was about to begin. And the MGM Grand hit fever pitch.

Within a minute De La Hoya set his stall out. He bowled in an overhand right and crashed in left hooks to Mayweather's side and head. He attempted to bully Pretty Boy. Nothing landed cleanly but the bigger man was trying to get physical and make his mark.

Mayweather snaked out jabs, Oscar continued trying to hook downstairs and was warned for straying low with another by Bayless.

The old champion boxed sharply in the second, too. Crisp right hands found Floyd's whiskers, though Mayweather rolled them to reduce the impact. Still, Oscar tracked him to the ropes and was busy landing clusters of shots. He banged away on the gloves, arms and shoulders, looking for a way through and scoring occasionally.

Chants of 'Os-car, Os-car' filled the arena.

Floyd lost the round but in the corner Roger said, 'He's just walking in, he ain't doing shit. Keep the jab working, keep the feints working.'

De La Hoya trapped him against the strands again early in round three. The crowd erupted as he burst through Mayweather's defensive gates with a right hand, forcing the favourite to lean backwards over the ropes before composing himself and returning fire.

As the session progressed, Mayweather scored with more and more jabs. He then started to get his lead right hand increasingly involved.

Again De La Hoya let the leather fly in round four. With Floyd employing his usual tight defence, Oscar hacked away at his body with multiple left hooks. Mayweather's shots were more accurate, but De La Hoya was throwing far more.

Floyd landed his best punch of the fight so far in the fifth, when a right hand round the side of Oscar's left thudded onto the older man's head.

Oscar caught him with a glancing left hook in retaliation as the action picked up. Mayweather picked off the onrushing Golden Boy with two sweet right hands with a minute or so to go in the round and there were more still before the session closed.

Roger Mayweather continuously told his nephew that De La Hoya would slow in the later rounds.

'Be you,' he said, moments before round six opened. 'That's all you have to do is be you.'

Rounds six and seven were close, though De La Hoya, as he did in big fights, was starting to fade.

An exciting exchange opened the eighth, with Oscar jabbing Mayweather into reverse and Floyd landing right-hand counters. De La Hoya also made himself a more elusive target as the session closed. It was a good, close fight. It was not a fight of the century and it was not a barn burner, but they were two excellent fighters boxing well. There was almost nothing in it.

In the ninth, Merchant turned to his broadcast colleague Emanuel Stweward and asked if Mayweather could be considered an all-time great if he only threw one punch at a time. 'Well, I've never been saying he's great, he's considered pound for pound, but the Ray Leonards and comparing him to Ray Robinson? No. But he's a good fighter.'

'You're whuppin' his ass,' said Roger, 'Don't go to the ropes, tie him up in the middle, other than that, whup his ass.'

The tenth was tedious for De La Hoya. He was caught cleanly a few times but unable to get any traction on his own shots. The tide of the fight seemed to be turning irrevocably into Floyd's favour. There were boos as Mayweather put some daylight between them in the eleventh. Oscar was slowing and other than a right hand near the end of the session, he was beginning to look deflated.

'He's already frustrated, now go to work on his ass,' said Roger.

'You're not even breathing heavy,' countered Roach to his charge, trying to encourage Oscar to go hard for the final three minutes.

But De La Hoya, although still determined, was at times a sitting duck in the last session. He paced forwards but Floyd was too swift of hand and foot, catching him when he could with clinical retaliatory blows or moving off before Oscar could let his hands go.

Both fired fast, heavy punches with ten seconds to go in the fight, all the way until the bell. Oscar jumped on the ropes to a huge ovation from the fans.

Then a quiet murmur went around the arena as the crowd awaited the judges' decision.

The first scorecard, belonging to Tommy Kaczmarek, read 115-113 to De La Hoya. Mayweather's face contorted in disbelief. The next judge, Chuck Giampa, marked for Mayweather 116-112. Jerry Roth's final card, 115-113 for the winner by split decision, informed the crowd that Mayweather had won and there was a new WBC world light-middleweight champion.

It had been close. Two of the officials awarded Oscar the last round, and if Jerry Roth had agreed with his colleagues and also scored that session for the man from East LA, the fight would have been a draw. Plenty of the ringside press scored only narrowly in Mayweather's favour. A smaller number, including *Boxing News'* Claude Abrams, saw the fight as a draw.

Mayweather Sr found his way into the ring and spoke with De La Hoya, who had given him a $2,000 ringside seat to take in the fight.

Cries of 'bullshit, bullshit' from De La Hoya's fans filled the air, but he had lacked the energy, movement and speed towards the end of the contest to give himself the best chance of victory.

'It was a hell of a fight,' said Mayweather to old sparring partner Merchant. 'We gave the fans a hell of a fight tonight.'

He pulled Roger in to get some credit, maybe incensed by his father's continued relationship with De La Hoya, and Roger stated, 'I said he'd whup his ass, and he whupped his ass.'

'He was throwing a lot of punches but they weren't landing,' said Floyd. 'If you check the punchstats [which showed him connecting with 207 punches to Oscar's 122] I outpunched him, I outboxed him, it was easy work like I told you guys it was going to be. He was rough, he was supposed to fight, ten-time world champion in six different weight classes, but he couldn't match "Pretty Boy" Floyd tonight.'

Floyd said the closeness in scorecards was because it was a Golden Boy Promotions show.

'That's what you call a masterpiece of boxing,' he added. 'He's one of the best fighters in our era and I showed you what I could do to one of the best fighters in our era.'

He then thanked his father and, clearly getting irritated once more by Merchant's line of questioning (particularly when the grizzled interviewer asked Floyd why it wasn't a massacre like he predicted it would be), confirmed he would walk away.

'I'm still retiring after this fight,' Mayweather said. 'I've proved myself in the sport, six-time world champion in five different weight classes. They said I couldn't do it. I weighed 150 yesterday, came into the fight weighing 148 and you saw a welterweight beat a junior-middleweight today.

'I have nothing else to prove. I've made a ton of money in the sport, these years are valuable to my children. I'm moving on to bigger and better things.'

No one believed he was going anywhere, not after the biggest win of his career. He knew nothing but boxing. There were rivals like Miguel Cotto and Paul Williams, both unbeaten, on the horizon, and Margarito loomed large.

'I felt I won,' said De La Hoya, who admitted Floyd was very fast. 'I felt I landed the harder punches, the crisper punches. Every time I would hit him I hurt him and I was pressing the fight. You've got to beat the champion decisively and if I didn't press the fight there would have been no fight.'

Floyd Sr was interviewed in the ring and he said Oscar deserved to win if it was based on him making the fight, but his son should have won if it was based on single shots. 'I thought it was a close fight,' he said, sounding extremely conflicted.

'Who won, Oscar or Floyd?' pressed Merchant.

'If you're going on the points system then you're going to have to give it to Oscar.'

'The crowd was for De La Hoya,' snapped Floyd Jr. 'He chose the [Reyes] gloves, the site and the weight class. There were 16,000 rooting for him. I probably had two or three hundred fans. But popularity and fame don't win fights. He's a good fighter but I outboxed him easy. I'm not Superman; I can't win every fight by unanimous decision.'

'You have to respect the judges,' said De La Hoya, who accepted defeat gracefully and shook Floyd's hand and embraced him at the post-fight press conference.

'I don't feel like a loser because I did what I had to do. Mayweather's a fast fighter, talented. But my jab failed me. But it also has to do with Floyd's style.'

'As of now, I'm sticking to my word,' Mayweather said, confirming his retirement. 'I don't know what the future holds. I've done everything I wanted to in this sport. I beat the best from 130 to 154 and made a lot of money. You can't stop God's work. What's meant to be is meant to be. Right now I am officially retired.'

'Floyd didn't dominate or defeat De La Hoya in a manner that would leave us, the watching public, thinking he could have done likewise with former greats Sugar Ray Robinson or Sugar Ray Leonard,' wrote Claude Abrams in *Boxing News*. 'But that's not to denigrate his fabulous achievement of becoming a "world" champion at five weights, the only man to do so without ever losing.'

There was another slap in De La Hoya's face. Mayweather relinquished the WBC light-middleweight title he won from him and said he would hold on to his WBC welterweight crown. He had gone up in weight, defeated the man he had envied so much early on in his career, and now no longer needed him.

Even though it was close, there was little clamour for a De La Hoya-Mayweather return. Oscar had again failed to defeat an A-list fighter in his prime, although the fight had done huge business.

It generated 2.45 million pay-per-views, smashing the Lennox Lewis-Mike Tyson record, and it cleared $136 million in domestic revenue. Those figures helped De La Hoya to become the all-time leader in pay-per-view sales, with 12.8 million career buys – and once the cash-registers from the fight stopped ringing and the pay-per-view percentages were added on Oscar took home $52 million and Floyd earned $25 million. It was the biggest payday in history for two boxers.

Oscar, however, was all but done as a prizefighter. A year later he unspectacularly outscored Steve Forbes and then he was demolished by Filipino Manny Pacquiao, stopped in eight emphatic rounds by the little typhoon from the Pacific.

The East LA idol was past his best when he fought Floyd, and three years later he said he knew it during the fight. He reckoned Floyd was the best he fought in his career, giving his rival plenty of credit considering that he'd shared a ring with Pernell Whitaker, Julio César Chávez, Bernard Hopkins, Shane Mosley and Félix Trinidad.

'Skill-wise, ring generalship, he knew how to control the ring,' said De La Hoya. 'He's always in control, he's very skilled.'

And he hadn't come far from blemishing that otherwise unbeaten record of Mayweather's. 'I would have given myself a draw, at least,' he said. 'I kind of felt I could have pulled it off. Obviously I was at the end of my career and so when you can't do it anymore then you have to hang them up. At the end of the sixth round, I felt that was the end of my career. You know, physically you just don't feel it.'

'We had a really good training camp for that fight,' remembered Freddie Roach, despite De La Hoya later claiming he had coached him to be a one-dimensional fighter for the contest. 'I thought it was a very close fight. You could have given him [Oscar] the edge in the fight but Mayweather came on a little stronger in the last six rounds.'

What would the master tactician have done differently, if he could have made De La Hoya-Mayweather again?

'It really wasn't a case of doing something differently because he [Oscar] stopped throwing the jab and he started following Mayweather. We were working on cutting the ring off quite a bit in training camp and he kind of lost sight of that and what he did in the first five rounds, which was cut the ring off and keep him right in front of him. As soon as he started following him, the jab came up short, it didn't work anymore and it gave Mayweather the advantage. I would have liked to have had more time to work with Oscar on cutting the ring off and I think that would have been the key factor in the fight.'

Oscar had done as well as any fighter had over six rounds with Mayweather. It was as close to a blueprint as anyone had left, with the possible exception of José Luis Castillo in their first fight.

'Yeah,' Roach agreed of the success De La Hoya had enjoyed and whether that was a way that Mayweather could be beaten. 'If people would realise how to cut the ring off and keep a guy in front of them. But ring generalship really isn't taught that much in training anymore, you know? I see so many guys just following people and walking into bad positions. It's something Eddie Futch taught me very well when I was very young, it was one of the first things he taught me – how to cut the ring off and control the fighter. If I could have had more time with Oscar, I think it might have been better.'

Just two days after the money-spinning event of the year another old Mayweather rival, Diego Corrales, was killed in a motorbike crash.

The world no longer awaited De La Hoya-Mayweather. It was not overly impressed, either, although Mayweather did not care.

Nigel Collins, for *The Ring*, accurately said that the fight, which was not quite lost in the immense hype, was 'Respectable enough to appease if not enthral.'

248

In *Boxing Monthly*, Glyn Leach felt that while De La Hoya made the fight what it was – half decent to watch – Mayweather deserved credit for standing and fighting often. 'On the wider scale it is to Floyd that boxing owes the most thanks,' he wrote. 'The bad boy came good.'

The world was now more interested in finding someone who could scalp him and a young gun from Manchester was talking up his chances. And people were listening.

TEN

DANCING WITH THE HITMAN

FLOYD MAYWEATHER WAS primetime. He was entertaining the crowds with his fancy footwork and had an audience of millions.

But he wasn't boxing. He was on the popular ABC show *Dancing with the Stars* and paired with the striking Ukrainian-born American Karina Smirnoff.

He was becoming more than a boxer.

David Mayo, who had covered Floyd's career for years for the *Grand Rapids Press*, said Mayweather was on the crest of a wave.

'Four years have passed without legal incident or significant oral blunder,' he wrote in *The Ring*. 'During which his boxing career exploded, placing some media and fans in an unusual position. They find themselves behind the curve on one of their own.'

Mayweather had crossed into the mainstream, finally, and his 'retirement' was short-lived, even by boxing's ambiguous standards. He was preparing to fight again.

Ellerbe said he worked for a year to get his friend on the show. 'When he wins this thing, he'll be bigger than life,' said the advisor. 'And he'll raise the profile of boxing with him. He is the face of boxing. This is a whole new challenge for Floyd.'

Evander Holyfield, a famously wooden previous participant on the TV show, thought it was a bad idea to attempt to juggle dancing and boxing.

'I definitely wouldn't be thinking about trying to do that,' said the former heavyweight king. 'They worked me harder than boxing. Dancing is a good workout, but it's stressful on your mind to learn different dances.'

Little more than a month after Floyd Mayweather outscored Oscar De La Hoya, Manchester's marauding Ricky 'the Hitman' Hatton cut José Luis Castillo in half with a body shot in Las Vegas.

The Mexican dropped to the floor, breathless and groaning.

It was the same man who many still reckoned had outscored Mayweather in their controversial 2002 meeting, and the one who still gave him plenty to think about in a rematch.

Yes, it was an older version who crumpled so devastatingly before Hatton but the fourth-round finish was emphatic, thrilling and a legitimate statement of intent. Like Mayweather, Hatton had entered the ring wearing a Mexican sombrero, albeit in the colours of his beloved Manchester City football team, but rather than trying to wind up Castillo's crowd, it was a nod of appreciation to those who'd long said he fought like a Mexican. And besides, Mexican great Marco Antonio Barrera, the ageing legend who'd formed a friendship with the Manchester idol, walked him to the ring.

'This fight tonight, I think you saw more action in these four rounds than you've had value for money in Floyd's whole career,' Hatton told the HBO cameras post fight.

'When Hatton made the comment in the ring that he made on HBO,' recalled Leonard Ellerbe, 'Floyd looked at me and said, "Make the fight fucking happen."'

'Ricky Hatton has talked non-stop about fighting me for two weeks,' Mayweather charged. 'He has disrespected me and my accomplishments in the ring and I take that very seriously. I'm going to give him the opportunity to step up and fight the best in the world, but I don't think this punk will take the challenge. Does he really want to step in the ring with the best fighter of this era and embarrass himself? Being the coward that he is, I doubt he will get in the ring.'

Ironically, Oscar De La Hoya's impressive Golden Boy Promotions were going to promote the fight. Hatton was their client and their company was booming, with other stars like Barrera, Shane Mosley and Bernard Hopkins all flying the GBP flag.

Mixing dancing and boxing was going to be precarious, particularly because Floyd was due to fight Hatton on 8 December, just a fortnight after the 24 November season finale – if he made it that far.

'I'm dedicated to the sport of boxing,' Mayweather said. 'I still love the sport. My retirement was short-lived, so there was no time for a party, but you live and learn. It's unreal, everything I've been through in my career. People say I'm big-headed, people say I'm cocky. But I just think I'm the best in the business and I think I have the best team in the business. Without all those pieces in place, I wouldn't have an opportunity to do something like *Dancing with the Stars*.'

And Mayweather had other out-of-the ring plates spinning. He was making gradual progress in the music business and had helped with the promotion of a recent Beyoncé tour. That came courtesy of his link-up with manager Al Haymon, a concert promoter who – behind the scenes – was becoming a boxing bigwig. He certainly had Mayweather's ear after they first began working together, around the time of Floyd's no-contest plea to the misdemeanour battery incident resulting from a Michigan bar fight. Haymon had not left his side since.

Floyd talked up the Hatton match during a five-day cross-country tour to promote the event. It started in Los Angeles.

'Give me some of that face-to-face action,' implored Mayweather, when the two came head to head for the cameras.

'You know you fightin' the best, right? You willing to die?'

The mid-September 2007 tour went to Grand Rapids, to New York and also to London and Manchester in the United

Kingdom. There, Floyd tried to get the passionate Hatton fans to start singing 'There's only one . . . Mayweather,' rather than the usual rendition of 'There's only one Ricky Hatton', a song they'd been familiar with for years. They booed the bad guy.

'By the time the Manchester one came round,' recalled Hatton's then-trainer Billy Graham, 'I think Ricky was getting a bit sick of him. It was pouring with rain and Floyd was probably the most vociferous that I remember him on the tour. It was all the banter and animosity between the two fighters, but there was nothing directed at me. I'd seen it all before, I'd expected it. I'd been watching Floyd forever and I'd been in loads of similar situations. I found it quite amusing. I found Floyd quite amusing. I knew what he was about. Floyd wasn't scary; he wasn't intimidating. He wasn't like a Mike Tyson. Kostya Tszyu was a scary fighter, even though he was a very polite man. When you thought about losing – because you always know in any fight there's a chance of losing – I didn't see it being dramatic. It wasn't scary. His skillset was daunting, but he's not a scary fighter, he wasn't a scary guy. Off camera, when Ricky wasn't there, he was polite. I think there was mutual respect. I certainly respected him as a fighter.'

Wearing a Manchester United jersey, to incite Hatton's Manchester City supporters, Mayweather held up his middle finger to the huge crowd that had swelled to see the fighters.

'He gave me a load of abuse,' Hatton recalled of the media tour, which saw Floyd chipping away at Hatton constantly until the Englishman rallied his supporters with a number of expletive-ridden chants on his home turf. 'We went to New York, Michigan in his hometown and Las Vegas, Los Angeles, and I took a bit of stick but I think I got my own back in Manchester with the four-letter rant I did on Sky Sports, when nobody told me it was live! I think I got under his skin in Manchester and apparently he was on the train with Oscar De La Hoya afterwards who said,

"You should have seen Floyd ranting and raving about the stuff you were saying. Oh my god." I said, "Well, I'd put up with his shit for the last few days so he could have a little bit back."'

The fight would not be won or lost on the road, or in the media beforehand.

'I'm ready and I'm always ready,' promised Mayweather. 'That motherfucker ain't on my level.' He seemed to believe that was the case in and out of the ring. He took the opportunity to remind people what he was worth; listing the price tags of the jewellery he wore.

'You see me, 250,000 on the wrist, 300,000 on the pinkie, 600,000 on the neck . . .' he would say.

Typically witty, Ricky bluntly mocked him. '"Look at my ring, look at my chain, look at my tailor-made suit – $3,000." Who gives a shit?'

'Technically there is no better fighter around,' admitted Hatton. 'Even though his performances bore most people to tears. He has so much talent but I don't sit up until four in the morning to watch him in England, because he'd only send me to sleep. Has he seen my fights? I lay everything on the line. I don't fucking run away like he does.'

Mayweather and Smirnoff were eliminated from season five of *Dancing with the Stars* in week four, on 16 October. Funnily enough, while filming in Hollywood, Mayweather – preparing for Hatton – trained at Freddie Roach's Wild Card Gym after hours, with Roach opening up for him to accommodate Mayweather's taste for late-night workouts.

'He wanted to use my gym from like one o'clock in the morning to something like three, or twelve to four and I told him no problem,' said Roach. 'I had a guy living there at the time [an ex-pro named Shane Langford] and Floyd was very respectful and he was here for seven or eight days and there was no problem whatsoever.

'Me and him are okay with each other. He's respectful to me and I'm respectful to him, he's a good fighter and all that. I wish maybe he was a better role model but that's not my choice, it's up to him. I've known him and seen him in gyms in Las Vegas since he was five and he was in the gym with his dad. I like him. He's a good guy.'

Back in Vegas, Floyd drafted in old rival Carlos Baldomir for sparring. He was also having paraffin wax treatments on his injured hands and joints, as he tried to eke out of his career a few more fights.

Around 14,000 tickets were snapped up in half an hour when they went on sale, the rest following shortly after.

The *24/7* series portrayed Hatton as a charming, funny man of the people who was exceptionally close to his family. Floyd was the money-orientated egomaniac and a disruptive centrepiece in a family at war.

'I think that's what made it such an occasion,' assessed Hatton. 'We were both undefeated, it was the United States versus Britain, the bad guy versus the good guy, the *24/7* programme I think is the best you could watch. Mine and Floyd's was extra special because we were just so different.'

The *Mayweather-Hatton 24/7* ended up winning Emmys for outstanding camerawork and an award for outstanding journalism.

The state of the feuding Mayweather family, with both Floyds again not speaking, was a fixture of the series. 'I would love to have a relationship with my son,' said Sr. 'But I think my son's a little bit too big for me.'

'He's stuck in his ways,' claimed Jr. 'He thinks he can talk to fighters any type of way, he's not going to talk to me any sort of way.

'He used to beat me when all I wanted was that one-on-one time and that's probably why I take it out on my opponents to this day. I'd do anything for my mother. I'd give my life for her. Ask me if I'd die for my dad. I'd die with him. But for my mother I'd die for her. My kids? I'd die for them. There's a difference. No one will ever understand Floyd Mayweather. Never. They can't walk in my shoes.'

Hatton was 43-0 (31) and twenty-eight years old. The downside was he was at his absolute prime as a light-welterweight, seven pounds beneath where he would challenge the American. In his only previous contest at the weight, he had won the WBA welterweight title with a razor-thin decision over decent Luis Collazo. Hatton had endured real difficulties in an incredibly physical and draining battle.

Mayweather-Hatton was called 'Undefeated', because their combined record was 81-0. Mayweather was a 2-1 favourite. He was making $11 million plus add-ons depending on how well the pay-per-view did. Hatton had a $6-million guarantee but had managed to retain the upside of the pay-per-view generated in the UK, where it would be screened on Sky Box Office.

'Hatton's a good fighter but he's not versatile,' Mayweather professed. 'If he really does come after me it will be over quick. After I beat him in the USA, I'll beat him over in England. It will be the same thing as with all the fighters once they get in the ring with me. He's never seen anything like what I've got.'

Mayweather hit his par-for-the-course trash-talk. Billy Graham felt the sound bites were used to market the event, without real malice.

'I think he's trying to sell a fight,' Graham reckoned. 'But, like anything else, you're a product of your environment and of your upbringing, aren't you? I think he says quite a few things, especially in the early days, that he regrets once he's said them.'

The perennially down-to-earth Hatton was still pinching himself about the magnitude of the event awaiting him. 'I wasn't sure this fight would ever happen,' he said. 'It's a mega-fight, my wildest dream to go up against the best pound-for-pound fighter in the world. I fully respect his ability and his record, but if Floyd thinks he's going to get me upset he's wasting his time. I'm going to stay in his face. No one gave me a chance against [Kostya] Tszyu either. I feel I've already proved myself, but I want to show what I can do against the very best.'

In fight week, Golden Boy Promotions head Oscar De La Hoya visited Hatton at the gym to wish him well.

'I took this belt of his boss,' said Mayweather, apparently still with beef towards the Golden Boy. 'He said his boss had told him how to beat me, only thing is, I beat his boss.'

It was believed that with the Hatton fight and his TV appearances, Floyd might earn more than $35 million for the year, which could place him as high as second on the sporting rich list for the year, behind De La Hoya.

The fight-week grand arrivals were colourful. Hometown fighter Mayweather, surrounded by several huge bodyguards, was greeted by thousands upon thousands of Brits chanting, 'Who are ya? Who are ya?'

Then he started singing 'There's only one Mayweather' to antagonise them. He tried further still, by telling the media that the British fans had come over to be a part of the Mayweather experience.

'The fans make you,' said Hatton later. 'So don't shield yourself away. You don't need five bouncers pushing people away from you, that's why I've got 33,000 people wanting to come and watch me and he's got thirty-three.'

Mayweather began calling Hatton a midget to the media.

Yet because there were still many quality welterweights competing, it was thought that the Hatton fight would not be Floyd's boxing farewell.

Ivan Goldman, writing in *The Ring*, maintained that Floyd still had boxes to tick before the fans would take to him. He needed to beat the top welterweights like Miguel Cotto, Paul Williams, Antonio Margarito and Shane Mosley – and even Joshua Clottey and Kermit Cintrón – and he needed to throw punches in combination, not just one or two at a time.

'That's right "Pretty Boy",' wrote Goldman. 'You're telling us you're the greatest ever, greater than Joe Louis, both Sugar Rays, Muhammad Ali, etc. Well, those guys fought everybody.'

Roger Mayweather reckoned the list of possible opponents meant his nephew would have possibly another five fights before retirement.

'The reason I say that is if he gets by Ricky Hatton, there's still Shane Mosley out there,' Roger explained. 'There's still Miguel Cotto out there. There's still a De La Hoya rematch out there. If Kostya Tszyu comes back and got a couple of wins, he could even be in line. Floyd is still only thirty years old. There are a lot of fights out there for him.'

The weigh-in was unprecedented. More than 7,000 fans – many of them from the UK and queuing through the casino since dawn – packed into the MGM Grand Garden Arena for the mid-afternoon event.

Thousands more could not get in and the atmosphere was electric, better than for many Vegas fight nights.

'There's only one Ricky Hatton,' reverberated around the venue with a band beating drums and blowing whistles.

After they weighed in – Hatton at 145lbs, Mayweather on the 147lbs limit – they went nose-to-nose and started pressing foreheads into each other. They had to be separated and a fired-up Hatton peeled away and punched the air as he encouraged his supporters, who had jeered Mayweather throughout.

Hatton grabbed the microphone from MC Michael Buffer and screamed to his fans, 'Who did you come to see? Floyd?'

They booed violently.

'Me?'

They cheered euphorically.

'Who's taking the belts?'

'You!' they roared as one.

'I'm not worried about that,' Floyd told Sky Sports reporter Ed Robinson about the reception he received. 'I'm Floyd Mayweather.'

Some felt Hatton had been too fired up, that he'd lost his cool.

'If I'm honest, it did get to him at first,' Graham remembered. 'I think a few things were getting to him by then but he wasn't fucked up. He still believed he would win; it wasn't like he was freezing. I think he'd had enough [of the build-up] by then. For him, it must have been a very long build-up. He had a lot to put up with with Floyd. And with almost anybody something will get to you in the end. I might have been a tiny bit concerned with how he was at the weigh-in. I know it registered.'

'You can't argue with his record or what he's done but all good things come to an end,' Hatton said, after tipping the scales. 'On Saturday night it comes to an end. It will be an eight or nine-round stoppage for Ricky Hatton.'

Mayweather's trainer and uncle Roger opined, 'We've had Rocky one to six – we ain't gonna have a Rocky seven.'

As referee Joe Cortez went to see Hatton and his team before the fight, giving him his instructions in the dressing room, Billy Graham took the chance to say to the official he'd heard that Mayweather's camp were concerned about his charge wrestling with Floyd.

'There's been quite a lot said about Ricky grappling inside,' Billy said. 'He's been accused of being a dirty fighter inside. He isn't. He's an inside fighter. He's clean, but he's an aggressive fighter. We just want a fair shake. I wouldn't have even brought it up only their camp has been complaining.'

'Okay,' said Cortez. 'One thing right now, I will let the fight take its course. However, I will only come in if something is not being done by the rules.'

Although only 16,000 could get into the venue with tickets, around 30,000 Brits flooded Sin City and had to watch on closed circuit television in the other casinos on the Strip. Famously, they drank many bars in Las Vegas dry.

Tom Jones had sung 'God Save the Queen' and for the most part Hatton's fanatical supporters were a credit to Hatton, but when they booed the US national anthem, sung by Tyrese Gibson, with the fighters waiting to walk to the ring, the Americans seemed surprised.

Another star-studded audience was on hand. Tiger Woods, David Beckham, Mark Cuban, Will Ferrell, Tommy Hearns, Jude Law, Sugar Ray Leonard, Lennox Lewis, Wayne Newton, Wesley Snipes and Denzel Washington were among dozens of A- and B-listers who wanted to see the collision.

Mayweather walked to the ring to 'Born in the USA', the Bruce Springsteen classic, and he was accompanied by three of his fellow competitors from *Dancing with the Stars*, Mark Cuban, Wayne Newton and Hélio Castroneves.

Hatton, with the crowd offering a boisterous rendition of 'Rule, Britannia!', got off to a solid start and landed a couple of jabs, with one even capturing Mayweather off balance.

'Ricky started fantastically and he did what we wanted to do,' remembered Graham. 'The screw shots to the head and the pit of the stomach are the favourite punches I like Ricky to throw for opening somebody up. He did it right at the start, unsettled him, knocked him back, took him by surprise. I didn't want him to do just traditional shots, but sneaky stuff, threading shots through small gaps and stuff like that. I knew that just typical pressure was going to be fun for Floyd, but Ricky wasn't a typical pressure fighter. That's not how he operated. It was sneaky shots to vital areas and things like that. As he started off, I wanted him to carry on like that. Indeed, I thought he would have.'

But from early on in the fight it became clear that referee

Cortez was looking to break up the boxers at the soonest opportunity.

'Even though he was known for his speed,' Hatton said of the gifted American, 'I thought I might be one of the quickest he'd fought, with me coming up from the weight below. And I think I gave him a lot of problems. I think HBO had me winning three of the first five rounds but right from the outset – I don't want to say the reason I lost to Floyd Mayweather was the referee – but any sort of chance of me winning that fight I think it was gone. I'm a very rhythmic fighter, I fight in a rhythm, I like to slip in and slip out and move in and when I get close I rarely hold because I'm looking to get into the body and hurt people.'

Mayweather was calm as the challenger pressed him. He caught an over-excited Hatton with some cutely timed counters.

'Relax, relax,' ordered Graham, in the Hatton corner.

'All he's doing is looking for that body shot,' Roger told Mayweather.

Hatton came out like a bullet in the second. His typical relentless pressure had ground down the excellent Kostya Tszyu in Manchester a year and a half earlier. But Floyd's balletic footwork made him difficult to pin down and he caught Hatton lunging in with a left hook. The action appeared relatively smooth, but into round two referee Cortez decided to call time and have a word with them about tidying the fight up. It was unnecessary. 'There will be a row about this later, I'm sure,' said Sky Sports commentator Ian Darke as Cortez again needlessly intervened.

Cortez called a second time out, with both boxers warned about point deductions.

'He was fucking disgusting,' Graham said of the official. 'I don't know if he had that mindset from the start. I cringed when they [the fans] booed the national anthem. I think it's very impolite, I don't like all that stuff and I thought, "Fucking hell, you can't be doing this."

'Whether they might have affected him [Cortez], I don't know, but what he did was unbelievable, breaking them inside every single time. And he was letting Floyd get away with all kinds of stuff on the inside, constantly letting him get away with it. I don't blame Floyd for what he did. You do anything the referee will let you get away with. You do anything to win, so I would never get angry at the boxer for that. It was still a good fight but we were fighting Joe Cortez as well.'

'I think a lot of people enjoyed the Ricky Hatton experience in Las Vegas for my fights,' said Hatton. 'I don't know that the Americans liked it. We sort of took over Las Vegas, we were in the bars singing songs like "You're supposed to be at home," "God Save the Queen," all this. If you're from Las Vegas you might have thought, "Who's this lot?" And at the weigh-in I was saying, "Who've you come to see?" geeing the crowd up, and I think, although the Brits loved it, I don't think they did in Las Vegas and it was a Las Vegas referee and it was Las Vegas' favourite son in many ways. It just didn't look right to me.'

The pattern of the contest remained similar. 'Listen, all he's going to do is pressure you, he can't fight,' said Roger.

Hatton attempted to chase him down. Mayweather tried to land dazzling counters as Hatton moved in. All the while, Cortez got involved each time the fighters came close in a bizarre refereeing performance.

In the third, Hatton was cut by the right eye as Mayweather landed his best flurry of the fight. 'It's fuck all,' Graham informed him.

Mayweather had a superb round in the next, scoring with his usual straight rights and also picking him off with left hooks.

'Keep doing what you're doing,' said Roger. 'He can't outfight you or outbox you.'

Graham warned Hatton that he needed to work his way in to attack.

They both held and punched in the fifth. Cortez was constantly talking to them and often separating them.

The tide swept permanently in Mayweather's direction in the sixth. Hatton landed a left, a right, then flurried downstairs, forcing Mayweather to put his head out of the ring, under the top rope. As he did, Hatton attempted to club him with a right and Cortez took a point away from the Englishman. The shot had not landed.

When the official went to get the fight back underway, Hatton turned his back and bent over, offering Mayweather a shot – or something else altogether. Hatton had lost his focus. He was Mayweather's now. Floyd waffled him with a hard left hook with a minute to go while the British contingent started another football chant, 'The referee's a wanker.'

Boos echoed around the arena as the session closed. They were for Cortez.

'I'm going to start taking some points,' the referee began, when he visited Hatton's corner.

'You already have,' snapped Graham.

'There's only one Ricky Hatton,' sang the crowd, trying to rally an increasingly disconsolate challenger. The American commentary team had Hatton a point up, their British counterparts marked him a point down, but Floyd finished the round strongly, with a flashy left and right as Hatton tried to walk him down.

There were plenty more right hands down the pipe in round eight as Hatton was shipping more and more punishment. Then Mayweather started to work over his body and Ricky walked into a bomb of a right hand that caused Hatton to hold. The Manchester star was in dire trouble with thirty seconds left in the eighth. He had to dig deep to both stay in the fight and on his feet.

'I was still firing back,' said Hatton to Cortez, when he came to see him and warned that he might stop it between rounds.

'I thought, "You're joking",' Ricky said in 2015, when he recalled that section of the fight. 'I didn't think I was taking that much. It was as if they were looking for an excuse, not letting me near him and then looking to stop me.'

Graham thought that was the final nail in the coffin. 'Floyd got Ricky on the ropes and he was giving him some stick, probably the most stick he'd given him during the fight and there are times you can't fire back as much when someone's unloading on you with much more than a single because it's pot luck who lands. So he was under a bit of fire but it's the biggest fight on the planet. And when Ricky had the chance he came back, and for the last ten seconds Ricky was throwing shots. Joe Cortez came over in the fucking corner and said, "If you don't fight back I'm going to stop it." It didn't warrant anything like a stoppage and Ricky was firing back in the last sequence yet he still came over and said that to him, and that's when I knew.'

Mayweather was now looking majestic, controlled and boxing at his own tempo.

Hatton started the tenth looking fresh and on his toes but within a minute he strode onto a left hook, was sent headfirst into a cornerpost and then planted onto his back. Weary, he staggered to his feet and tried to cling on for a breather but Mayweather chucked in some left hooks and Hatton fell backwards. Down. Then out.

'When he walked onto the left hook and he went down I knew he was a beaten man, mentally,' said Graham, who felt that psychologically Cortez had done a thorough job of discouraging Hatton. 'It was a good shot. I couldn't see [properly]. That corner was the worst one I'd ever worked in. I had a big, fat guy sat there and I'm sure he was in TV and I had murders with him. I had to keep jumping from one side of the corner to the other side to be able to see. I suspected Ricky was mentally beaten when he went down and I was thinking about throwing the towel in – I'd got hold of the towel – and then all I could see from the corner was his feet and I could see the feet tottering and then he appeared on the canvas.'

'I started losing my cool and getting frustrated,' admitted Hatton, 'And what happens when you do that against a fighter as good as Floyd is you get knocked out. I'd worked so hard in the early rounds, it wasn't necessarily how hard the punch was that knocked me out, it was a little bit of fatigue that had set in because of all the hard work I'd put in and it was a wonderful check hook he nailed me with. I wasn't going to beat him on skill. I wasn't going to beat him on speed. What I was going to beat him on was work rate and aggression and I kept the work rate high trying to get to him and when I got to him I got broke [by Cortez] and I was very, very fatigued by the time Floyd knocked me out. He's not the hardest hitter I've ever boxed with but I was starting to flag down the home straight.'

Mayweather jumped onto the ropes in the corner and saluted the crowd. Heartbroken Hatton was helped back to his feet and pressed his lips together as he had to accept his first defeat. Mayweather came to sympathise with him, kissed him on the head and embraced him. The enormity of the loss hit Hatton hard, who seemed a world away from what was happening in front of him. Mayweather then consoled Billy Graham.

'There's only one Ricky Hatton,' chants filled the arena again, but it was Mayweather who was being paraded around the ring. Then he and Cortez posed for pictures together.

'I took my time. I fought inside and outside,' Mayweather said. 'A true champion can adapt to anything. I already knew coming in it was going to be a rough night and that it was going to be tougher than most of my fights. I didn't prepare halfway. I had a great training camp. Ricky Hatton is one tough fighter. He's still a champion in my eyes. He's one of the toughest competitors I ever faced, he kept coming and I see why they call him the "Hitman". He's one hell of a fighter. I just took care of business and did my job.'

'What a fluke that was,' Hatton joked instantly to Merchant, before telling Sky he slipped and it wasn't a knockout. 'I thought I was forcing it but he's very good at making you miss and slipping and sliding. He was better inside than I thought and he got me.'

Hatton said he would fight on; Mayweather talked about taking a break from the sport again.

He thanked Haymon, Golden Boy Promotions and Leonard Ellerbe and insisted he wouldn't call out any welterweights, be it Cotto or Mosley, and it was his time to become a promoter. He said he had nothing else to prove.

'I won't let the sport of boxing retire me, I will retire from the sport.'

Hatton was angered by Cortez's performance and to this day says that while he might not have beaten Mayweather, the referee's actions cost people seeing the best of him.

'He's very clever,' Hatton said of Mayweather. 'He picked up a couple of shots and that was that. I was forcing it and I was doing well. I should have been a touch more careful. He knocked me out, but he wasn't the hardest puncher I've ever fought. He's very accurate. Knock me down; I keep getting up. Ricky Hatton is still going to fight.'

It turned out the Englishman was well behind on the scorecards, despite his early successes. Two judges only gave Hatton round five, with final tallies of 89-81, while the third official gave him the third and fifth sessions, marking 88-82.

'I'm not possibly saying Ricky Hatton is a better fighter than Floyd,' said Graham years later, after his professional relationship with Hatton had ended. 'Floyd's defeated, continuously through his career, great fighters and the majority of the time he's made it look easy. Ricky couldn't do that. I just thought we had his number. We planned it alright and Ricky was carrying it off alright but the referee just made a mockery of everything because I think possibly we could have beaten him without Cortez, but I'm certainly not saying Ricky was a better fighter than Floyd. Listen, I don't give a fuck what anybody says, Ricky would have beaten him at light-welter, I don't care what they say – unless Joe Cortez was in the ring.'

'They say the art of boxing is to hit and not get hit, well Floyd has got it off to a tee,' Hatton admitted in 2015. 'A lot of people have tried to emulate his shoulder-roll style, and some are pretty good at it but nowhere near as good as Floyd. He's a very good all-rounder. He always finds a way to win no matter what style opponent he is in against. He is good from a distance where he can back off, shoulder roll, get low, use his ability and speed but he can look after himself in close, like he did against me. He was a very good all-rounder.'

'The name of the game is to box and give me a good, clean fight, no rough tactics inside and no excessive holding,' Cortez later said. 'Sometimes there's too much holding. We don't allow that in boxing. Here in the United States there's rules, certain guidelines and processes we follow as referees in officiating a fight. There are some fighters that fight a lot on the inside and there's too many rough tactics and wrestling on the inside, we don't permit that. We try to keep boxing as clean as possible.

'I'm very pleased with the way I handled it [Mayweather-Hatton]. I didn't get any complaints from our commissioners or our boxing writers in the United States. I understand Ricky's excuse and I respect him for that. I think he was a great boxer and a great human being and I think he's one of the nicest guys I've seen in boxing.

'I've done about four of his [Mayweather's] fights. I have refereed better fights and better fighters in the past. He's one of the great fighters in boxing but I refereed many other fights that have been much more exciting than his fights. I think Floyd is a great asset to boxing. He's one of the good ones. I have given Floyd some warnings, in reference to some styles he was fighting. I've given him warnings for holding, coming up with the elbow, and maybe I said it once and I didn't have to say it again. He's been very respectful. I've had no problems with Floyd Mayweather and I've disqualified a lot of fighters in the past.'

Mayweather always praised Hatton for the effort he put in during their fight. 'He has the heart of a lion,' said the American. 'The crowd pumped him up. But the crowd didn't bother me. The boxers are the only ones who can be the judges. We decide who wins and loses.'

The year 2007 had been a breakout one, finally, for Floyd. The Hatton fight made him in excess of $20 million, adding to the approximately $30 million he earned against De La Hoya.

His reputation in boxing soared further still. 'He [Floyd] nullified a man who had won all forty-three fights and, deservedly, earned the reputation as the best body attacker in the business, while making him look ordinary,' wrote Claude Abrams in *Boxing News*. 'That reinforces the huge body of opinion that Mayweather's abilities are, to put it mildly, exceedingly special.'

'I never got to know him personally,' confessed Hatton, whose team performed a masterstroke of tying up all of the revenue from the UK pay-per-view on Sky. 'I've read a few quotes where he spoke very highly of me and then a few quotes after the fight where he spoke really badly of me. I don't really know if it's for the cameras, but he could be an absolute gentleman. He seems to have mellowed as he's got older, as he approaches the end of his career. But it doesn't matter how much money you've got or how many belts you win, when you retire one thing that remains is the love of the fans. I have that in abundance. I wonder if Floyd thinks that, after everything he's done, he doesn't want to retire with people hating him, so I think he might have calmed it because he might be approaching retirement and he might want to be remembered as not being the bad guy.'

The *Dancing with the Stars* jaunt had contributed to Floyd Mayweather becoming a mainstream star.

The likes of Cotto, Mosley, Williams and Margarito all waited in line. But they did so in vain.

After defeating Hatton on 8 December 2007, Mayweather did not fight again for twenty-one months and he announced another retirement on 6 June 2008.

'It's not like it used to be,' he said. 'I think I liked this sport better when I was fighting for free. When you're young, you don't have concerns, so you're not worried about nothing. I mean, you never know what can happen in boxing. A lot of times, you worry about certain things like, if I die in the ring, what's going to happen with your family? When I didn't have no kids to live for, I really wasn't worried about nothing. I was like, I don't care what goes on. If I die, so be it. Now that I'm a lot older and a lot wiser, it's more like I've got something to live for. I've got some people who love me. So that worries me a lot, because I feel like my job is like a cop. One shot can end your whole career.

'I don't want to talk now about boxing again,' he continued. 'I need to see if I want to come back. What else is there for me to prove? These guys can't beat me. I'm the best.'

ELEVEN

THE MONEY ERA

THE SEVEN-FOOT, five-hundred-pound giant declared he was ready to fight.

He scooped up the injured, masked Mexican by his neck and threatened to bury him in the centre of the ring.

It was not boxing; it was professional wrestling and it was on a World Wrestling Entertainment pay-per-view called *No Way Out*.

The Big Show hoisted up Rey Mysterio, goading Floyd Mayweather – who was ringside – and prompting the boxer to crash over the security barrier, vault over the top rope and intervene.

Big Show shoved him away and Mayweather was held back by his entourage. The giant stooped to his knees and dared Mayweather to hit him. Floyd jumped in, landed a blizzard of shots and hightailed it from the ring.

The bloodied behemoth gave chase but Floyd was long gone as he sprinted from the arena.

This was sports entertainment, scripted for the audience in WWE programming. That encounter, and the subsequent challenge from the Big Show to the boxer on the *Raw* television show the following night, led to Mayweather being matched with the Big Show at *WrestleMania XXIV*, the WWE's annual showpiece extravaganza.

'I'm sorry things had to happen that way, but I'm the best fighter in the world,' Mayweather, in character for the WWE, said. 'And when I get called out like that, I have to retaliate.'

The Big Show's own sound bites were entertaining, if you could take them for the scripted comedy they were supposed to be. 'The only way you could hurt me was on my knees, and even on my knees, I'm still bigger than you,' he joked. 'You know if I wanted to, I can take you out in two minutes. You don't believe me, you have doubts? Why don't you take me on one on one? You're 39-0, why don't you try to make it 40-0? Think about it, what do you say?'

Mayweather said yes. He wanted to be more famous.

It was also set to earn him up to another $20 million.

'It's entertainment,' he explained of his involvement, in a more sensible interview. 'You have a chance to just be you and do what you want to do. Wrestling takes care of business right on the spot. Whatever they say they're going to do, they do it right on the spot. There's no waiting three, four, five months. Quick results, quick money. Quick big money, too.'

The Associated Press covered a mock news conference for the 'fight' at the STAPLES Center in Los Angeles.

'Mayweather incited the couple hundred of already hyped fans by whipping out a thick wad of cash and repeatedly tossing $100, $50 and $20 bills into the crowd that had nearly as many women as men,' read their account.

'A mad scramble ensued, with a light pole nearly getting knocked over and two small children caught in the chaos. One lucky man emerged from the pile-up clutching six $100 bills.'

The 'fight' was held on 30 March 2008, at the Citrus Bowl in Orlando, Florida.

It was another high-profile venture into that lucrative mainstream market for Floyd, introducing his extravagant ways to a young demographic that might not have been familiar with him through boxing.

Nearly 75,000 were in the arena for *WrestleMania*. Millions more watched around the world.

It was billed as a 'no disqualification match' and Big Show ambled around, trying to pin Mayweather in a corner. Floyd 'hit' him in the torso with both hands but they did not dent the giant. At one time, the wrestler grabbed Floyd by the hand and motioned to stamp on his gloved mitts, but Floyd pulled clear.

Moments later, after he'd been hoisted onto the top ropes, Mayweather punched his opponent away and then put him in a sleeper. The façade continued, in WWE style, with Mayweather clattering the Big Show with a chair several times, then nailing him with a low blow and, finally, brass knuckles, to secure victory. Floyd 'Money' Mayweather, as he was introduced, had won by knockout after the referee counted ten over the fallen Big Show.

It was pantomime, but it was lucrative pantomime.

A couple of months later, he retired from boxing. He was thirty-one years old, he was unbeaten in thirty-nine fights. There were challenges still out there, a bustling welterweight division to clean out, but the fire was waning.

'This decision was not an easy one for me to make, because boxing is all I have done since I was a child,' read a Mayweather statement.

'These past few years have been extremely difficult for me to find the desire and joy to continue in the sport. I am sorry I have to leave the sport at this time, knowing I still have my God-given abilities to succeed and future multi-million dollar paydays ahead, including the one right around the corner [a mooted De La Hoya rematch]. But there comes a time when money doesn't matter. I just can't do it anymore. I have found a peace with my decision that I have not felt in a long time.'

The 'retirement' lasted far longer than many had imagined. His self-imposed twenty-one-month exile came when he had reached the pinnacle, on the back of the two biggest nights of his career and four of the biggest events of his life. His dominance atop pound-for-pound lists was indisputable. He was at the peak of his powers and just walked away.

When he eventually returned, he said his body had needed a chance to heal and that he had needed to find himself as a person.

'Boxing was still in me,' he said.

A three-city press tour in May was scheduled to promote an 18 July 2009 bout, although a rib injury Floyd suffered put that date back to 19 September.

'I knew he was going to come back anyway,' said Roger. 'He came back because he missed the sport. He loves the limelight. Any athlete that's good or great, they all come back.'

Floyd felt boxing had missed him.

'When I left the sport,' he started, 'it's like the sport was hurting without Floyd Mayweather. What was lacking in the sport of boxing when I was gone? Charisma, flair, flashiness. I'm an entertaining risk-taker, that's what I do.'

He did admit, though, that he missed the sport, too.

'I'm boxing because boxing is something that I love to do,' he continued. 'The things I miss about a mega-fight is I love contact; I love hand-to-hand combat. I love hitting the pads, the bag, but the main thing I love the most . . . contact. When I see blood, it makes me hungry. I guess [when] I see blood I'm like an animal, I go for the kill, and my sport is either kill or be killed.'

Opponent Juan Manuel Márquez, who for more than fifteen years had been trained by the great Mexican coach Ignacio 'Nacho' Beristáin, talked up his chances, saying he would bring Hispanic fire to the party. He was fighting for the fifty-sixth time, had won world titles in three weight classes and was one of boxing's pound-for-pound best fighters. The problem was, he'd only boxed as high as lightweight and he had not won either of arguably his two biggest fights against a man called Manny Pacquiao, who in Mayweather's absence from the ring, had inherited the pound-for-pound title with a series of destructive wins as he rose through the weights. He'd laid waste to David Díaz for the WBC lightweight title, sent a beleaguered Oscar De La Hoya into retirement with a dominant eighth-round win and then he spectacularly shelled Ricky Hatton in two shocking rounds, laying out the 'Hitman' – who was ironically being trained by Floyd Mayweather Sr – cold.

Mayweather-Márquez was signed off to be at a catch weight of 144lbs. That meant Márquez would be putting on weight, coming up from 135lbs, while Mayweather would have to be three pounds lighter than he had been against Hatton almost two years earlier. Márquez, a married father of three who turned thirty-six while in training camp, said it was the most important bout of his career as he was fighting the best in the world. 'It's a weight that's not mine, but I will reach it,' he said.

The press tour saw the fighters travel from Los Angeles to New York to London, England. Mayweather was attempting to capitalise on the notoriety he'd assumed in the UK by taking out Manchester's favourite son, Hatton, and people wanted to see him.

Thousands went to East London to watch him train, and Sky Sports' head of boxing Adam Smith fondly remembered the bedlam. 'The rammed Peacock Gym stays with me,' he said. 'There were people hanging off the viaduct just for a glimpse of him – he was the biggest attraction since [Mike] Tyson came. Leonard Ellerbe told me recently that he has such a huge British fan base that he just loves us. Almost more than the Americans.'

For once, Mayweather's lavish lifestyle was not the sole focus of his character on *24/7*, but his charity work also received some coverage.

He was filmed at the Nevada Partnership for Homeless Youth, giving a motivational talk to teenagers. Then he and his ever-burgeoning team handed out food parcels to hundreds of hungry residents in run-down areas of the city.

'The true Floyd Mayweather, the person, these are the kind of things he likes to give back to his community to show he really appreciates being in the position to give back,' said Ellerbe.

It was not long, though, before the cameras were back on Floyd in his element, showing them around his new pride and joy; the 22,000-square-foot Big Boy Mansion, his new home.

'I deserve to live like a king,' he said to the TV crew. 'I fought my way to the top. I deserve the finer things in life. I truly do.'

Reports circulated that he owed the IRS more than $6 million in back taxes dating back to 2007. Ellerbe denied that and Mayweather said he had a good relationship with the IRS.

'He wasn't broke,' said his father, 'but he had a money problem.'

Either way, he had another eight figures coming his way from the Márquez fight.

He had also resolved the issues with his father after the best part of a decade-long separation. Roger said he and Floyd Sr had mended fences, with Sr saying he didn't need to train his offspring, he just needed to have a relationship with him. He was, however, a voice in the camp.

'Roger is my trainer and he's going to get what he deserves,' Floyd said, 'But my dad's going to get some money, too.'

'Me and my dad are cool,' he went on. 'My dad is spending quality time with me.'

His father responded, 'Sometimes you have to break up to make up, and make it better the second time round.'

'Good is one thing, great is another,' said Roger of their joint target, Márquez. 'He's good. Floyd is great.'

In the lead-up to the Márquez fight, however, Floyd was again involved in the wrong sort of headlines after he was questioned about a shooting in the parking lot of a roller rink. His Rolls-

Royce was reportedly at the scene. He told HBO he was innocent until proven guilty and that he wished they would find the perpetrators. HBO's *Mayweather-Márquez 24/7* reported that police had found handguns and ammunition following searches of Mayweather's house and car.

Roger was again in trouble, too. In August, it was alleged that he choked a female boxer, Melissa St. Vil, who was staying in an apartment he owned. Roger claimed he was struck on the head by a lamp as he tried to evict her and that he held St. Vil off around the throat. 'I didn't hit her, she's a woman,' he said. 'I could hit her, but I didn't.'

'If the police didn't come when they did,' St. Vil told VICE Sports, who taped a mini documentary with her, 'I wouldn't be here right now. He was choking me from the back and punching me so the more I was trying to wrestle him off me, because I was on the floor and he was on top of me, the more I was moving and my heart was slowing down, I just felt like my brain was about to explode. I couldn't really breathe, I just felt my heart was beating slowly, slowly, slowly . . . Then, police came in at gunpoint, had him let me go, I was on the floor, blood was coming out of my mouth. I was real light-headed, it was crazy.'

Roger would eventually agree a deal with prosecutors to keep him out of prison. He pleaded no contest to two charges of misdemeanour battery, but St. Vil felt he deserved a stiffer penalty than a $1,000 fine, a year's probation, domestic counselling and fifty hours of community service.

Veteran boxing writer Michael Marley, never one to mince his words, was surprised at the leniency of the sentence. Writing for the *BoxingScene* website, he said, 'Defendants with the last name Mayweather can get special treatment when it comes to felony criminal charges for beating up women in the Las Vegas courts.'

Roger's brother, Floyd Sr, also had his own issues. He had been diagnosed with the incurable lung disease sarcoidosis, which had taken the life of comedian Bernie Mac. He coughed a lot as a consequence. His son was pleased they had built bridges. They both regretted time lost, too.

Meanwhile, in the Márquez camp, for all of his traditional training philosophies, Mexico's future Hall of Famer was filmed drinking his own urine.

'I've done it for the last five or six fights with good results,' he insisted. 'I also drink my own urine because that's where a lot of the proteins and vitamins are, it's part of your vitamin intake and why not drink them again instead of wasting them?'

Mayweather Jr, who saw the episode of *24/7* that captured Márquez's bizarre ritual, of course spent plenty of time in what was left of the fight's build-up mocking the Mexican at each opportunity.

Floyd's Vegas exile was well and truly over. The casinos now wanted his fights. This was his fifth consecutive outing in his hometown but there was curiosity about how he would draw at the box office. Márquez was good, but Hatton, De La Hoya and Gatti had all done their fair share on pay-per-view against opponents other than Floyd. Mayweather had needed those three to generate big numbers.

Márquez had loyal, hardcore and knowledgeable fans but even after almost two years out, Mayweather was the dominant A-side.

Now celebrities were even going to watch Mayweather train. Actor Eddie Murphy swung by the Mayweather Boxing Club in Chinatown in Vegas to watch the master at work.

Hundreds flocked to his gym. It became a Las Vegas hotspot in its own right. Hundreds made the pilgrimage hoping to get an autograph, a picture, meet a Mayweather – any one of them – and say they had been in or around the place where the man himself trained.

Of course, media members knew where to go for their stories. The likes of Floyd Sr, Roger, Nate Jones and countless others were always on hand. Fences had been mended with Uncle Jeff, too, and he coached fighters at the gym.

Floyd always trained; it was just a matter of going at the right time to see him. One photojournalist who visited was Irishman Eoin Mundow. He had covered Mayweather around the time of the De La Hoya fight, when Floyd was a star in boxing but not in the mainstream. 'He was very approachable,' said Mundow.

'He wanted to speak to the press, because it was his big opportunity to shine and he played up to the cameras but he came off as a good guy, a nice guy. Then, after that, the beast, as it were, took over. '

Things were now different.

As Mayweather prepared for his comeback fight, Mundow headed to the gym and experienced an altercation that he would remember as 'surreal'.

'I went out on a whim to take pictures but it was very hard to take pictures of him because he had become a big star, the ego had taken over and whatnot,' Mundow recalled. 'I did a feature in his gym with some of the kids and I had kind of a minor altercation with Leonard – I didn't do anything – but I think everyone was just trying to protect Floyd and the egos just got in the way. It is interesting to see how Floyd's metamorphosed over the last eight years or so.

'So I went to Floyd's gym and at that time you could still just walk in. Roger was there and I had a chat with him and Zab Judah was there, so I took pictures of Zab training and hung out there for three or four hours. I was hanging out on the off chance Floyd would show up and I was just about to leave and I felt a tap on my shoulder from behind, and it was Floyd who had just walked in the gym. There was myself, another English guy who was looking to become a trainer in Vegas and Roger, and when Floyd heard me speak, he said something like, "Fuck you Brits."

'I've got an English accent but I'm Irish. He said, "It's the same thing. When you came over here you burned our flags and booed our national anthem." He was playing. I wasn't scared but I think he was just trying to show me up in front of his friends, so I just said that I was Irish and not English and he said it was the same thing. I said if I was English that made him a Mexican, to which Roger and Zab Judah laughed at him, and he didn't like that. Then I thought, "Oh jeez, what have I gone and done?"

'He went off around the gym, did a few chin-ups in the background and I stayed there for about another half an hour. Floyd went outside as I was leaving the gym. He was with Zab Judah and Zab had given him a present of a bright yellow Lamborghini for fighting him in the first instance, I think the car was worth a quarter of a million dollars or something. So I went up to him and said, "Can I take your picture," because that was the goal. Then, him and a friend asked for my ID and there was about twelve or thirteen of his entourage in the car park, and I was on my own. So I gave him my press card, and then they started passing the press card from Floyd to his friend, back to Floyd and it was like piggy in the middle. In the end I got the hump with him. So I grabbed Floyd by the bicep, which was quite firm, and said, "Stop fucking around," basically, to which he sort of flipped out. I think he did it because I touched him and he was in front of his entourage. Then he changed. He went into a big thing about, "Take your hands off a nigger . . . If you came to the hood you'd get a cap in your ass." All that sort of thing. It was a bit surreal because it was me and about fourteen other blokes. His friends were in the background shouting, "Go on Floyd. Go on Floyd." I think more than anything he's just used to people saying yes to him. I don't think he really knew what to do in front of his friends, because no one puts their hands on him or says no to him. Maybe I'd have been a rich man if he knocked me out! It wasn't a case of me trying to be macho. I'm not professing to be the toughest guy in the world, but growing up in south London you learn to stand your ground. And I was a bit pissed off because it was all a bit juvenile, passing my press pass from one to another.

'Floyd's not a gangster at all. I've been in situations before when I know I'm in trouble and I know I'm not going to be grabbing anyone. He's a professional boxer and yes, he could knock me out and beat me up. But I didn't feel intimidated. There was [Mike] Tyson back in the day, and I met Bernard Hopkins when he knocked out Joe Lipsey. I met him and his mates and he scared me to death. I wasn't going to fuck around with him. Floyd is like a little boy in comparison to that. I think he plays the gangster. Not very well. Maybe I shouldn't have done what I did. Unfortunately it takes away from what he is, which is a brilliant fighter.'

After all that, Mayweather relented and let Mundow shoot some pictures of him in the Lamborghini.

'When I went back to London I mentioned it to a couple of people who said, "Bullshit, of course that happened",' Mundow added. 'I think he leads a very weird existence in Las Vegas. He travels more now.'

What was a noteworthy experience for Mundow would probably have hardly registered in a day of the life of Floyd Mayweather.

Besides, he had a fight to prepare for.

'The weight is made, I'm comfortable, I'm happy,' said Mayweather. 'Actually, I'm right where I need to be if the fight was today.'

That was a couple of weeks beforehand, but when he tipped the scales the day before he and Márquez met in the ring inside the MGM Grand Garden Arena, he did not make the agreed 144lbs.

Márquez, who had toiled to put on weight, and who'd even fought down at super-featherweight since Floyd's last fight, made it up to 142lbs but did not look as chiseled as he had in the lower weight classes.

Mayweather came in at 146lbs, thus meaning he had to pay Márquez $300,000 for each pound he had come in over weight. He also had to pay the commission a fine. Or so that is how it looked. It soon came to light that the contract had been changed so he would be able to weigh up to the welterweight limit of 147lbs, meaning he would not have to pay a fine to the Nevada State Athletic Commission, he would just have to pay Márquez for not making right on the original agreement.

Many thought the size disparity between the two could be the difference.

Internet fight writer Steve Kim went so far as to say, 'Mayweather should get no credit whatsoever if he wins.'

Signs of Mayweather's crossover appeal were everywhere on fight night. He was walked to the ring by WWE superstar Triple H, making his outing relevant to the wrestling fans he'd wanted to bring on board. Sky's Adam Smith could see that he'd become the main man.

'I remember looking around me at ringside,' he said. 'There was Leonardo DiCaprio, Angelina Jolie, Jack Nicholson, P Diddy, Arnold Schwarzenegger, Meg Ryan and [Tommy] Hearns, [Ray] Leonard – you name it. He attracts the triple-A list.'

He had also lost the 'Pretty Boy' tag. He was introduced by Michael Buffer as Floyd 'Money' Mayweather. It was a new chapter in his career. It was the money era.

Floyd dominated the opener and, almost halfway through round two, he stepped in with a pernicious left hook that felled Márquez.

Mayweather was sharp throughout while Márquez was comparatively cumbersome. It turned out to be the first lopsided loss of the decorated Mexican's career. 'I think the difference was 20lbs in there,' said Márquez, who still held WBO and WBA belts at lightweight, afterwards.

Mayweather refused to get on the scales on fight day, so we will never know what the final disparity was.

'Márquez is as tough as hell,' said Floyd. 'I hit him with some shots and thought "this one will get him" but he kept coming. When I dropped him, I was like "Let me see if I can finish this guy off," but I couldn't.'

'I gave it my all,' said Márquez. 'If I'd maybe had one or two more fights at the weight, I may have been better, but Floyd is also very fast and a very good counterpuncher.'

For all the talk of size, and the playing field not being level, the gap between the fighters in speed and skill was also great. Size might have aided Mayweather's dominance; it was not the sole reason for it.

'Next time out,' wrote one critic, 'hopefully he'll pick on somebody his own size.'

'Márquez is tough as nails,' Mayweather reiterated. 'He's a great little man. He was really hard to fight and he kept taking some unbelievable shots. He's a great small man. Don't forget, I came from a small weight class too, so I know when you're in front of a great fighter. I think he brought his best tonight. I've been off for two years, so I felt like it took me a couple of rounds to really know I was back in the ring again. I know I'll get better.'

'He surprised me with the knockdown,' Márquez said. 'He hurt me in that round, but not any other time. I don't want to make any excuses, but the weight was the problem. He's too fast. When I hit him, he laughed, but I knew he felt my punches. We tried to work the speed, but the difference was the weight.'

Inevitably there would be a scramble to meet Floyd as he now equalled the 'money' in any fistic equation. He was where De La Hoya had been. Shane Mosley rumbled to the front of the queue, possibly in premeditated fashion borrowing something from the WWE, by confronting Mayweather in the ring afterwards. It was thought Haitian Andre Berto and even Pacquiao were also possible opponents.

Interestingly, Floyd was not too concerned that – according to some boxing writers – Pacquiao had moved ahead of him in the pound-for-pound lists. 'That is just about opinions,' said Mayweather, who made around $30 million after add-ons against Márquez's $3.2 million. 'They say it's Pacquiao and that's fine. I think I can do better next time now I've shaken the cobwebs.'

Sky's Adam Smith was still high on Mayweather, despite Floyd admitting to being a little rusty. While some called Mayweather's performance – in front of an audience of 13,116 fans at the MGM Grand and a very respectable 1.08 million on pay-per-view – an exhibition, Smith labeled it 'punch perfect.'

'It was out of this world,' he said. 'I always had a really soft spot for Márquez and he couldn't lay a glove on Floyd. Everyone was banging on about the weight difference but that's not what mattered – it was simply one of the most brilliant performances of his career.'

Max Kellerman was covering the post-fight interviews for HBO and went head to head with Floyd.

It did not take him long to raise Floyd's ire when he asked about the selection of Márquez as the opponent.

'I'm gonna do that talking, you do too much talking,' said Floyd.

Kellerman wouldn't allow it and signalled for the camera to pan back to Lampley and Emanuel Steward.

The post-fight exchange between Mayweather and Mosley, scripted or not, segued into the build-up to their fight on 1 May 2010 – ten years after boxing experts had wondered who would win between them when they were both in or around the lightweight division. Was it ten years too late? Floyd, now thirty-three years old, was still top of the pound-for-pound pile, a position Mosley had held briefly in the early 2000s.

But Shane's career took a downturn when he lost twice to the very good Vernon Forrest, then suffered another pair of losses to Winky Wright. He had scraped two controversial decision wins over Oscar De La Hoya (certainly the second fight was especially controversial) and he'd been defeated at welterweight by Miguel Cotto in December 2007. Inactivity followed, with two fights in two years, but he scored one of the best victories of his career with a nine-round thrashing of Mexican Antonio Margarito.

A plaster-like substance was found hidden in Margarito's hand wraps in the dressing room. His hands had to be rewrapped and some say it completely threw him out of his stride for Mosley, who simply hammered him. The controversy stayed with Margarito, tarnishing his earlier wins – particularly a spectacular come-from-behind beatdown of Cotto.

Unfortunately for Mosley, he did not fight between defeating Margarito in January 2009 and meeting Floyd in May 2010. He was thirty-eight and clearly not same fighter he had been in his absolute prime, about ten years earlier. He'd been due to fight Andre Berto in January, but after the horrific earthquake in Haiti, where Berto was from, the younger challenger withdrew from the contest.

Mayweather's team had other plans, too. They had opened negotiations with Manny Pacquiao, but a row over the type of drug testing that would be used saw the carpet pulled from underneath that mouth-watering showdown. 'If Manny Pacquiao can take a blood and urine test then we have a fight,' Mayweather said. 'If not, no fight.'

Pacquiao said he would not do bloods because he didn't like needles, which seemed strange coming from someone adorned in multiple tattoos.

So Mayweather-Mosley was on tap, and a decent enough alternative.

'Mosley is one of the best welterweights of this era,' said Mayweather, 'and I'm one of the best fighters who ever lived. And when you bring those two fighters together you get a hell of a fight.'

Hostilities started early, on the stage of the press conference to announce the fight when the dapper fighters began shoving one another.

There was another *24/7* series, and HBO also introduced a new show called *Face Off*, in which Mayweather and Mosley sat face to face to discuss their fight with just commentator Max Kellerman between them.

There was an interesting exchange between them when Mosley recalled a conversation they shared as young pros at the Olympic Auditorium in Los Angeles. Shane was already an established star and he said Floyd told him, 'I think you're a great fighter and I want to be just like you when I get up in the ranks.'

Mayweather remembered it differently. 'I never wanted to be like no fighter, I wanted to be the first Floyd Mayweather. But like I said before, you're going to have to make me respect your fighting skills.'

With time to let Mosley's claim digest, Mayweather became more and more outspoken.

'Shane, I barely know who the fuck you are,' he said. 'What the fuck do you mean, I want to be like you? How do I want to be like you? Come on, man. I'm the face of boxing. I'm the cash cow. Who holds the record for pay-per-view? Me.'

'Your biggest payday is facing me. Without me, you're not getting shit. I made more money in my last two fights than you made in your whole career. Shane Mosley says Floyd Mayweather fights for money. You fucking dummy. I'm a prizefighter, that's what I'm supposed to fight for. A prize.'

Mosley, on the other hand, wanted to fight to prove himself and solidify his position as an all-time great.

Training, as always, in Big Bear, the Californian said, 'I'm fighting right now because people are saying these guys are better than me, and I don't believe that. I'm just as fast as he is, I'm stronger than he is, my arms are longer than his. I can hit him before he hits me. This is a real fight.'

Mayweather insisted his opponent was driven by money. 'You dumb motherfucker,' he said to Mosley via the *24/7* crew. 'You're almost forty years old. You better be fighting for a cheque you stupid motherfucker.

'He says he don't fight for money, he's forty years old but he don't fight for money? I'm thirty-three, I don't fight for legacy. I don't fight for none of that. I fight for that cheque. I'm in that cheque-cashing business. Vernon Forrest fucked you up. Winky Wright fucked you up. Miguel Cotto fucked you up. "Money" Mayweather, I'm going to fuck you up some more.

'Shane wants to be me. He wants to live in this lavish house. He wants to be fly like me, drive fly cars, have pretty watches, hang in Dubai. Like I told Shane, "We'll get you a job. We'll let you hold my feet while I'm doing sit-ups. Something like that."'

The fight was being promoted by Golden Boy Promotions in conjunction with Mayweather. Mosley had gone into business with De La Hoya, so he felt Floyd owed him more respect when talking finances.

'I'm a partner in Golden Boy, so basically I'm writing his cheque,' he said.

'Man, you know how these bitches are in the sport, total disrespect,' Mayweather, who now was protected around the clock by a security detail of muscle-bound giants, continued. 'The kid has no class, no style at all.'

Floyd felt he was no longer just the best of his era. He felt he was the best fighter of all time.

'I think the gym is packed the way it is every day because I'm a part of history,' he said. 'You can't stop God's work. I truly believe I'm the best. I know I'm the best. I've got to be a damn fool to give the sport thirty-three years of my life to say there's another fighter better than me. Someone can say, "Oh, he says he's better than Muhammad Ali." "Yup, I'm better than Muhammad Ali." "Sugar Ray Robinson?" "Yup, I'm better than Sugar Ray Robinson." I would never say another fighter is better than me. Absolutely not.'

'I'm a machine,' Floyd went on. 'Because I can generate the most [money]. Not Oscar De La Hoya, not Shitty Shane – with the nose job. Me. Classy, clean cut, straight shooter. I approach everything in life like this. If you say, "Fuck me," I say, "Fuck you". You don't like me; I don't like you. Don't disrespect if you don't want to get disrespected. Period.'

Away from the ring, Roger had been diagnosed with diabetes. Floyd admitted his uncle was slowing down but with Jones holding the belt and thus sharing the workload, Roger could focus on pad work and strategy.

Floyd, of course, concentrated his early assault on getting into Mosley's head.

In 2003, Mosley had testified in the monumental BALCO scandal and admitted that he had unknowingly taken designer steroids before his rematch with Oscar De La Hoya in 2003.

'I got here through hard work and dedication,' Mayweather said at one of the press conferences. 'No HGH [human growth hormone], no steroids. Hard work.'

Hard work and dedication had become his mantra. He would shout, 'Hard work', and his acolytes would reply with, 'Dedication.'

'I can't say how many fights Shane has won in the past because we know in the past Shane was using drugs,' Mayweather said, detracting from Mosley's record. 'That is something we do know.'

'That was seven years ago,' Mosley responded. 'It has been dealt with.'

As a consequence, and partly in line with his demands for the Pacquiao fight, Mayweather called for Olympic-style drug testing to be used ahead of the fight with Mosley, monitored by USADA (United States Anti-Doping Agency).

'This win will be the icing on the cake,' Mosley told the media when he looked back over his career. 'Oscar was in his prime, Margarito was on the big stage, now there's Mayweather and then I'm going to fight Pacquiao.'

Mosley, after seventeen years as a pro, said he was in the best shape of his life and that he was ready to go. He was not concerned about ring rust or inactivity. He also was unfazed by being the underdog, as he was against Margarito, and there was plenty of late money on him in Sin City. He bullishly predicted a knockout. 'That's what I go for, that's why the fans love me,' said Mosley, who had not lost in his three previous fights at the MGM Grand. And *The Ring* magazine still had him ranked at number three pound for pound, with Floyd at two and Pacquiao in pole position.

That said, the gulf between two and three was significant, considering Mayweather opened as 4-1 favourite.

And Floyd knew it. His smack talk was ratcheted up. 'I'm doing Shane Mosley a favour, I'm letting him share a ring with greatness. He's just a desperate fan.'

It was a star-studded night in Vegas, the big celebrity guns were out in force for Floyd once more, with the likes of Michael J. Fox, Jamie Foxx, Eva Longoria, Will Smith, Arnold Schwarzenegger, Mariah Carey and Mark Wahlberg all wanting a piece of the action. Controversial R&B artist Chris Brown sang the national anthem.

His uncle and father both joined Floyd on his ringwalk. Roger was still head trainer.

The audience did not know that within minutes Mayweather would be dramatically dazed, tremendously confused and clinging on precariously to his unbeaten record.

A minute into the second round a speedy and ambitious Mosley threw a jab into Floyd's chest and then cracked him with a tremendous right hand. Floyd instantly, cleverly, claimed him and held on to buy time. He was in a shocking fog, his guard was high, he attempted to shoulder roll, he tried to smother Mosley and then 'Sugar' Shane delivered an overhand right that could have felled a tree. Mayweather, his legs buckled, was in dire straits. It was a very real crisis and with a minute to go Mosley tried to get it wrapped up inside two rounds.

'Mo-sley' chants rang out around the MGM with many patrons on their feet, mouths open.

Back in his corner after the trauma of the session, Floyd looked stoic on his stool.

'Don't worry about exchanging with that motherfucker,' shouted Roger Mayweather. 'Box him. You'll beat him easily if you box him. Box.'

Mayweather did that. He made some cautionary adjustments, stepping back each time Mosley stepped forwards while landing his trademark potshots with left hooks and right hands, earning him the round and establishing control by slowing the pace of the fight.

For HBO, Emanuel Steward believed Mosley was starting to look old in round four. He was certainly throwing less and the success in round two already seemed like a long time ago.

Mayweather was looking stronger and Mosley was not coming close with the type of right hands he had landed in the second, Steward reckoned

'It ain't gonna be no hard fight if you keep boxing the motherfucker like this,' said Roger. 'Boxing is a thinking man's game.'

The dye was cast and the pattern of the fight remained the same. Mosley's moment had come and gone and he was fed a steady diet of right hands over his left lead. Mayweather was not blowing him away, but he was winning well and that was beyond dispute.

'It looks like you're fading on me,' said trainer Naazim Richardson in Mosley's corner before the eighth.

In the next, Mosley was warned by referee Kenny Bayless for some rough stuff and when Shane and Floyd touched gloves Mayweather cracked him with a left hook and right hand.

The crowd erupted. Mayweather and Mosley talked shit at each other.

Mosley began looking dejected. He wasn't just losing. He had already lost. Richardson threatened to 'do something you don't want me to do' as he spoke about stopping the contest.

Weary Mosley had nothing left and Mayweather had no real inclination to put a full stop on the performance, thus it fizzled out with Mayweather taking, for many judges, each of the last ten rounds of the fight.

'It wasn't even a tough gym workout for the most part,' said Steward.

'Another technical mismatch,' added Lampley.

Mayweather's dominance was once again charted by his advantage according to the CompuBox statistics.

He landed 123 of 267 power shots (at forty-six per cent), while Mosley scored with just forty-six of 169 (twenty-seven per cent). In total, Mayweather had connected with 208 of 477 punches – an impressive forty-four per cent – but Mosley managed only ninety-two of 452 (twenty per cent).

'The fans wanted to see a toe-to-toe battle, they didn't want to see me moving,' said Mayweather, who spent about as much time moving as engaging. 'They wanted to see me moving forwards so that's what we did tonight.'

The usual accolades were dished out in Mosley's direction: 'He was a tough customer,' and a 'Hell of a fighter,' Mayweather nodded approvingly.

'Sometimes you get hit by big shots,' Floyd said to Merchant when asked about that hectic second-round assault. 'You've got to suck it up and keep fighting hard like a warrior.'

The contest, drab though it turned out, delivered at the box office. It drew in a sterling 1.4 million buys – $78.33 million in pay-per-view revenue – and a crowd of more than 15,000 saw the live gate generate more than $11 million.

When Floyd Mayweather had halted Roberto Apodaca in the Texas Station fourteen years earlier he made $2,500. That long, winding road had now taken a stop at Mosley and Floyd had earned $22.5 million, which was going to grow to around $40 million with box-office additions. Mosley made $7 million and also took home a share of the television upside.

Of course, a Pacquiao fight would cause those numbers to pale into insignificance.

'Do you believe that you can find a compromise to make a deal to fight the fight everyone wants to see with Manny Pacquiao?' enquired Merchant.

'If Manny Pacquiao wants to fight, it's not hard to find me,' responded Floyd, before referring back to the drug-testing conditions. 'All I want to do is be on an even playing field.'

Pacquiao's stance was that he would take part in any commission testing, but he would not do it under Mayweather's say-so.

'If he takes the blood and urine tests, we can make the fight for the fans,' Mayweather added. 'And if he doesn't, we don't got no fight.'

Floyd insisted he would continue to take on the best and as Merchant turned to Mosley, Floyd told his opponent, 'You're a helluva fighter. You're a tough motherfucker.'

Mosley admitted he had been looking for the big single shots, having landed those terrific right hands early on.

'I couldn't adjust,' he shrugged. 'He adjusted and that's why he won the fight.'

It seemed there was only one fighter left to fight.

Margarito had destroyed Cotto. Margarito had been trounced by Mosley. Tall southpaw Paul Williams, whose career briefly stalled with a loss to Puerto Rican Carlos Quintana, was now campaigning at middleweight. Hatton was gone.

But Manny Pacquiao had brutalised Cotto in twelve rounds. He was also about to lay waste to Margarito. He'd taken care of dangerous Ghanaian Joshua Clottey, too. Between them, Floyd Mayweather and Manny Pacquiao had pretty much cleaned out boxing from 140lbs to 154lbs.

The next logical step was to fight one another. Simple.

TWELVE

IMPRISONED

THE MAYWEATHER VERSION of the *Jerry Springer Show* was on again. At the Mayweather Boxing Club, and in front of the *24/7* cameras no less, Floyd Jr started giving his uncle Roger all of the credit for training him, while Floyd Sr listened in. Sr couldn't stand it, and said he got both Roger and his son into the sport.

'Jealousy don't get you nowhere,' Jr answered back.

'What jealousy?' barked Sr.

'Hands down the best trainer right here,' said Jr, pointing to Roger. 'You're not even close to him. Not even close. Tell me what champion you've got right now. Don't no one want to be with you.'

Jr started saying that Sr's former charges, Oscar De La Hoya and Ricky Hatton, had left him. Sr tried to disagree, claiming he'd walked away from Oscar. Tempers were beginning to flare. Roger, his health and eyesight failing with diabetes, sat stoically on the ring apron.

Then Jr turned nasty.

'We don't want nobody in the way interfering when we work,' he said. Sr was outraged.

'Get out of our way,' shouted Jr.

'Get out of your way?' his father responded.

'This is our gym,' his son stated.

'I don't give a fuck about this gym, are you crazy?'

'Why are you here? Nobody asked you to come here.'

They went head to head in an ugly showdown of egos, and it looked like it could have become physical before Jr was ushered away.

'Don't fuck with me, motherfucker. Come on,' yelled his father.

It was not over.

Floyd returned. 'Get the fuck out my gym,' he told his dad.

'Put me out your motherfucking gym, punk,' was the response.

It went back and forth, with both winding each other up further and further still. 'I'll beat your motherfucking ass,' shouted Sr. 'Forty-one and one.'

'You couldn't fight worth shit,' his son snapped back. 'You weren't nothing but a motherfucking cab driver. You weren't shit as a fighter so how are you going to be something as a trainer. Get the fuck out my gym. Faggot. Get this fucker out of my motherfucking gym.'

Later, to camera, he said, 'Roger Mayweather made the Mayweather name and I took it to the next level. When it's all said and done there's only two Mayweathers that motherfucking count: Roger Mayweather and Floyd. And I'm not no motherfucking Junior.'

When asked what happens next between him and his father he said, 'What's next is September 17. I don't have to fight my father. I don't have to speak to him in life. I don't care, I'm fine, with or without him in my life, I'm fine.'

Floyd Mayweather Jr had been out of the ring for fifteen months but was preparing to meet WBC welterweight champion Victor Ortiz. The Los Angeles youngster, a southpaw, was a Golden Boy fighter and they handled the promotion of the show at the MGM Grand.

'During his time away from the ring, Mayweather has had multiple run-ins with the law,' said the narrator on *24/7*, explaining that Floyd was a defendant in six pending legal cases.

'My mentality is like it's always going to be,' he said, addressing the cases. 'Fuck it. It's going to be what it's going to be. If I'm innocent, leave me alone. If I'm guilty, do what you got to do. It's lies, lies. Period. Lies. When it's all said and done, it's bullshit.'

Mayweather said he had the best team that money could buy, that he had paid millions in legal fees.

'It comes with the territory,' he added, acceptingly. 'People are money hungry, what else can I say? That's what's been going on the last fifteen months.'

There had been other headlines, too, including when he was filmed in a nightclub setting fire to $100 bills, which Ortiz described as 'pure ignorance'.

He'd also got engaged to Shantel 'Miss' Jackson, a girl he'd met five years earlier in Atlanta.

Ortiz got the call for a couple of reasons. Firstly, as the champion after defeating Andre Berto, he brought a title to the table. Secondly, he had a hell of a backstory and that was going to allow the good guy-bad guy dynamic to sell in the programming of *24/7*.

Ortiz, a handsome fighter who had quit in his first acid test, when he bailed out halfway through a thriller against Marcos Maidana, said he no longer cared what people thought about him following his surprise submission. He was pilloried for it in the boxing media. There was not just a question mark as a consequence; there was a black mark.

But it was his life story that really sold him as an opponent because that, and his Hispanic bloodline, meant Mayweather could tap into a lucrative market. And 17 September marked Mexican Independence Day weekend. Mayweather was selecting his dates as well as he was selecting his opponents.

The Ortiz story was this: his mother left when he was seven, his daddy went shortly after. He grew up through his teens in foster care. Then he found boxing and after a successful amateur career rapidly became one of the bright hopes of Golden Boy Promotions.

Unfortunately for the Golden Boy, not long before the Ortiz-Mayweather bout Oscar De La Hoya admitted that pictures of him in women's lingerie, which had appeared online years earlier – and that he'd denied – were genuine and that he was struggling with addictions to drink and drugs. He also revealed that he had suicidal thoughts. That gave Mayweather carte blanche to haul his old rival over the smack-talking coals.

'De La Hoya, wearing drag, doing coke,' he said, before questioning why Ortiz would still idolise the Hall of Fame fighter. 'He look at him like a god, are you fucking serious?'

Of course, Ortiz's deprived upbringing became one of the centrepieces of the build-up and while Mayweather would have known about it beforehand, he acted as though it wasn't a useful subplot, when he must have known it was.

'We're tired of hearing about the same story every week,' he said. 'Of course, I've had a very, very rough life. They make it seem like I just woke up and I was a multi-millionaire. My father been to prison, my mother left, my mother's been on drugs, my father was a drug dealer, so I've been through it all. We lived seven deep in one bedroom but I don't talk about that on the show.'

There had been drama the day before the fight when Ortiz and Mayweather went head to head and jaw jacked at the weigh-in. Mayweather pressed a finger into Ortiz's neck, and then held him by the throat in an ugly confrontation that somehow did not quite spill over.

As interesting as the mix in characters was, on fight night the difference in quality was clear from the opening bell. Ortiz was peppered by right hands and Floyd had never looked more comfortable.

Less than a minute into round four of their bout and Ortiz

was warned for coming in headfirst by referee Joe Cortez. About sixty seconds later, he again tried to burrow forwards, his cranium banging in Floyd's face. There was no official warning.

'Or-tiz' cheers filled the arena. He tried to put on pressure but ended up gobbling up around fifty per cent of the right hands that were coming his way.

With fifteen seconds remaining in the round, Ortiz became overexcited, had Mayweather on the ropes and lunged in with his forehead.

They were separated and the clackers sounded to inform the fighters there were ten seconds left in the fourth.

Ortiz bizarrely went to embrace Mayweather, as if to say no harm had been done. He kissed him on the cheek. Cortez grabbed the champion by the arm and paraded him to the judges, instructing them to deduct a point. Ortiz reached out and touched his left glove with Mayweather.

'What's wrong with you, man?' yelled Cortez. 'Don't be doing that.'

Cortez waved them back in, Ortiz again tried to embrace Floyd but this time Mayweather struck. He sunk in a left hook and then cracked him with a right hand and Ortiz dropped heavily onto his back.

Cortez picked up the count. Ortiz tried to gather his senses and rolled onto his hands and knees. But his senses had gone when he gave Mayweather a free shot and it took more than ten seconds to find them before he could get back to his feet.

It was all over.

Flash back to the Ortiz-Mayweather *Face Off* show when Mayweather had gone out of his way to tell Ortiz not to switch off.

'If you make any mistakes you have to pay,' he told the younger man. 'If you make any mistakes, you have to pay.'

Ortiz had made a cardinal boxing error; he had not protected himself at all times. He'd also taken their quarrel to the streets, which is where Floyd settled it.

Mayweather might not have fought in sixteen months but he knows an opportunity, in or out of the ring, when he sees one.

Ortiz claimed he was hit with sixteen elbows in the fight, with Mayweather turning over his hook into an elbow strike each time – but he described it as 'a learning experience.'

He could have learned by watching the tapes of Mayweather against Gatti and Mosley; he would have seen that Mayweather will always take advantage of an unguarded target if the fight is on.

Floyd was vociferously booed during his now infamous post-fight interview with Larry Merchant.

What he'd done was not sporting, but it was legal.

'I got hit with a dirty shot, it's protect yourself at all times,' he said. 'I hit him with a left hook-right hand, and that ended the bout.'

'For you, it was just an automatic response, let's get on with the fight?' enquired Merchant.

'It's protect yourself at all times. We ain't here to cry and complain over what he did dirty or what I did dirty. I was victorious. If he wants a rematch he can get a rematch. He couldn't take brutal punishment like that for twelve rounds. If he did, he would never be the same again in his whole career.'

Merchant then started his next line, saying Mayweather – who was looking agitated – had been more aggressive than normal in the fight. Mayweather cut in and seemed to pick up from their Baldomir run-in years earlier. 'You don't never give me a fair shake,' snapped Mayweather to his interviewer. 'So I'm going to let you talk to Victor Ortiz. I'm through. Put someone else up here to give me an interview.'

'What are you talking about?' replied Merchant, who was eighty years of age at the time.

'You never gave me a fair shake,' Mayweather shot back. 'HBO need to fire you. You don't know shit about boxing. You ain't shit. You ain't shit.'

'I wish I was fifty years younger, I'd kick your ass,' said Merchant.

'You won't do shit,' said Mayweather, as he moved off and left Merchant to Ortiz.

Years later, and with Merchant in semi-retirement, the flashpoint is still one of the moments in a long boxing career that he is most asked about.

'I've always felt that it was a natural counterpunch, that I was not smart enough to plan anything like that,' he said of his decision to answer back to Floyd. 'It was just spontaneous. I don't second-guess myself. I had done countless interviews, both as a writer and as a broadcaster, and it's not always a popularity contest. Sometimes you get in there and a guy has been fighting for an hour or he's been running up and down some field or court for hours and it doesn't always make the athlete happy, they think we should just appreciate them and be part of their entourage, so this wasn't the first time, in all the years that I'd been doing this, that something like this had happened. Bernard Hopkins and I went at it one time and we had a serious argument at a fighter meeting, when he attacked Emanuel Steward. It was before one of the Jermain Taylor fights, maybe the first one, and Emanuel didn't agree with him on something and he attacked Emanuel [verbally] in a vicious way almost and he and I stood up and we had a real confrontation over it. I told him I wasn't going to sit there and listen to him do that to a colleague and friend of mine. The night after the fight we had to do a tough interview about the fight and some of the stuff that had gone before, but when it was all over Hopkins said to me, "Larry, you and I should take this show on the road." There are many variations of how athletes or fighters feel about how you question them. This was the first time that someone had challenged me personally and so I felt that maybe there were some people who thought it was not professional. Okay, I get it. But under the circumstances I just felt I stood up and defended myself and I will let other people decide whether it was the right thing to do or the wrong thing to do – or however they see it.'

By then, Merchant was splitting shifts with Max Kellerman but he was also always supported by the powers that be at HBO.

'Because of Mayweather's economic clout, I think there may have been some people in the executive suites who initially might not have appreciated the whole thing,' he reflected. 'But in the immediate aftermath, suddenly for a week or two I became this kind of celebrity, which to me was a laugh, because I never thought of myself as anything but a guy who was a commentator and the fighters and the fight were the star of the event, certainly not me. And I found it all quite startling that cameras were in my face in airports and restaurants and that an hour afterwards there were T-shirts selling on the internet – "Mayweather versus Merchant" – and I had a grandson who was telling me I was trending past Justin Bieber [on Twitter]. First I had to be told who Justin Bieber was, then I had to ask what this trending was! I just smiled at the whole thing and just said, "Well, I'm just another guy in Floyd Mayweather's movie." And that's the way it turned out. But I do think that later, when Mayweather was in play in terms of who he was going to sign with next [between HBO and Showtime] and all of that, I found myself being pleased that I had left HBO months and months before that was decided so that I was not an issue – it was simply all the money one network was throwing at him. They felt it was like signing a star in football or baseball for maybe more than his actual worth because of the value he brings your franchise. At the end of the day, I think he had the last laugh on a lot of people, with how big a pay-per-view star he became, and it's there for everyone to acknowledge.'

As big a star as Floyd was, Manny Pacquiao was still seen many as the best fighter in the sport.

He had also been doing well on pay-per-view, with his bouts against De La Hoya, Miguel Cotto, Antonio Margarito and Shane Mosley – whom he'd convincingly outscored – and the third fight in his rivalry with Juan Manuel Márquez all topping a million buys.

The world clamored for Mayweather and the Filipino to meet and they again negotiated. While Pacquiao had bowed to the Olympic-style testing demands, there were too many finer points that could not be resolved.

Mayweather took to social media, challenging Pacquiao publically via Twitter.

'Manny Pacquiao I'm calling you out,' he tweeted. 'Let's fight May 5th and give the world what they want to see.'

Pacquiao and his team – he was promoted by Top Rank – believed they were worthy of an equal share. Mayweather thought otherwise.

'He asked about a 50-50 split and I told him no that can't happen, but what can happen is you can make more money fighting me than you have made in your whole career,' Floyd said. 'I also let him know I'm in control on my side but he needs to get on the same page with his promoter [Arum] so we can make this fight happen.'

Pacquiao was offered a flat fee of $40 million. The fight was worth several times that so he turned it down.

He also had some leverage as he had initiated a defamation suit against Mayweather after his rival implied that Pacquiao's impressive rise in weight and subsequent success was due to performance-enhancing drugs.

The case was eventually settled – with details remaining confidential – and the Mayweathers said in a statement that they 'wish to make it clear that they never intended to claim that Manny Pacquiao has used or is using any performance-enhancing drugs, nor are they aware of any evidence that Manny Pacquiao has used performance-enhancing drugs.'

Frustratingly, the boxers ended up going in different directions again but both needed to fight. Mayweather opted to meet Puerto Rico's Miguel Cotto, the sport's third biggest franchise behind Floyd and Pacquiao, while Manny was matched with undefeated Californian Timothy Bradley.

Mayweather tweeted after the announcement of his next bout, 'I'm fighting Miguel Cotto on May 5th because Miss Pac Man is ducking me.'

Mayweather and Cotto were two of boxing's biggest names from the last ten years. Cotto set up camp in Orlando under trainer Pedro Diaz, his second contest with the same coach after a spell of three trainers in three years.

'We know we are going up against a great fighter,' said Diaz, a doctor with a PhD in Pedagogical Sciences. 'But we also know we will win.'

'I'm glad Miguel Cotto's trainer is a doctor,' joked Mayweather, 'so when I open his ass up, he can close his ass up. I'm the doctor and I'm going to operate on May fifth.'

Mayweather said he saw Cotto as an undefeated fighter. Yes, his 37-2 (30) record was not perfect but in the trade there was speculation that Margarito had used 'loaded' gloves to stop him, while he dropped down to a catch weight to suit Manny Pacquiao in his other defeat. He'd brilliantly avenged the Margarito loss in his previous fight, too, stopping his bitter Mexican rival in New York's Madison Square Garden in December 2011.

Cotto said the Mayweather fight was the biggest and most important of his career.

'I am here to fight the biggest names in boxing,' said Cotto, a three-division champion. 'I've never ducked anyone or any challenge in front of me. I have accepted everything to give the fans what they like – great and exciting fights. That is what the sport of boxing is all about, making the fights that the fans want and deserve to see. On May fifth, stay tuned, because I will convincingly beat Floyd Mayweather.'

Making the third defence of his WBA light-middleweight title, it marked the first bout of the Puerto Rican hero's career that was not being promoted by Top Rank; his contract with them had expired after the Margarito rematch.

'Miguel Cotto, he earned it the hard way,' explained Mayweather, who said he would not conduct any post-fight interviews with Larry Merchant after the contest. 'He didn't do fights at catch weight, he didn't piggyback off Floyd Mayweather's name, like Pacquiao did, he earned it – just like I earned it. He's a quiet killer. Miguel Cotto is tough, he's going to come to fight. Miguel Cotto is a world-class fighter who can never be taken for granted and continues to prove he is one of the best in boxing.

'Forty-two have tried, forty-two have failed,' Floyd added, wheeling out some old, dependable if gently moderated lines. 'He must know I'm not like no other fighter. I can give it and I can take it. I've been here before; I know what it takes. We chose him because he's solid. We want top competition and he's one of the best fighters out there.'

Cotto also still meant big money.

By now, Mayweather had taken to calling his entourage The Money Team – TMT. He had merchandise made and a TMT clothing line created. The crew included advisor Al Haymon, Mayweather Promotions CEO Leonard Ellerbe, trainer Roger and others who worked in the Mayweather Boxing Club including Jeff Mayweather, strength and conditioning coach Bob Ware, Nate Jones, former WBC super-featherweight champion Cornelius Boza Edwards and former WBA light-heavyweight champion Eddie Mustafa Muhammad. There was veteran cutman Rafael Garcia, publicist Kelly Swanson, his enormous and fast-growing security detail, assistant David Levi, a personal barber, marketing coordinator Nicole Craig, and a stable of hungry fighters who could fill spots on local shows in Vegas or on his undercards. The Mayweather Boxing Club became an orphanage for fighters from around the world. Londoner Ashley Theophane, Romanian Ronald Gavril, Sweden's Badou Jack, an old friend from the amateurs, Ishe Smith, and a host of young American talent were on hand to run, spar and train with Mayweather whenever the opportunity presented itself.

'We have so many people on this staff and on this team I don't even know everybody now,' Floyd said.

'All those people in the gym?' asked one of them. 'Floyd takes care of almost every one of them in one way or another. He's generous to a lot of people.'

Then there was rapper 50 Cent, real name Curtis Jackson, who was always around. 'It works because neither of us needs anything from the other,' 'Fiddy' said of their friendship.

For Mayweather's thirty-fifth birthday, the entertainer had an open-wheel Formula One car designed and modelled for him, costing around $500,000.

Floyd no longer looked up to leading fighters or sporting figures and hoped to emulate them, but said he admired great entrepreneurs, like Bill Gates, Mark Cuban, Warren Buffett and Steve Wynn.

Cotto and Mayweather met for HBO's *Face Off* show. There was a healthy dose of mutual respect, though Floyd broke from the conversation a few times.

He had a $100,000 bet on a college football game and wanted to know how it was going. As things stood, he was going to be up more than $80,000 from his bet on one half of the match.

Max Kellerman asked Cotto what he thought of Mayweather's gambling. 'He has what he has,' Cotto answered. 'He works for it. He can do whatever he wants.'

The fight was called *Ring Kings*, with Cotto the light-middleweight ruler and Mayweather the pay-per-view boss.

Seemingly as ever, though, Mayweather faced obstacles out of the ring.

He had been sentenced to eighty-seven days in jail at the Clark County Detention Center in Las Vegas after a plea deal stemming from domestic violence charges in connection to a September 2010 incident with Josie Harris, mother of three of his children.

Despite having that hanging over him, the Nevada State Athletic Commission granted him a licence to fight.

Perhaps more incredibly, the sentencing judge said Mayweather was allowed to go to jail in June rather than on 6 January to allow the Cotto fight to happen.

He would have to hand himself over on 1 June. Las Vegas had been hit heavily by the double-dip recession. Even those who ran Sin City couldn't put a stop to – or didn't want to put a stop to – Money's earning power. Through fight week trade, the ailing economy would have missed out on a \$100 million bonanza.

The commission had drilled Mayweather about his legal case and he said that he'd not struck Harris and that he opted to make a plea so his children would not have to testify in court, because two of them had been present during the alleged incident.

He said he'd restrained Harris, whom he claimed was under the influence of drink and drugs.

'I feel I'm automatically guilty without getting a chance,' Mayweather told the panel. 'I could have fought the case. I chose to take a plea bargain.'

He had been going to weekly counselling sessions, as ordered by the court, and he had completed the community service he'd been asked to do.

'If I could go back to the time when that happened, would

I do something different? Absolutely,' Mayweather told the commission.

'The only reason we are considering this today is because we respect the judicial system and the court granted you a deferral of your [report to jail] date,' chairman Raymond Avansino said. 'We wanted to be certain that you are committing to the commission you will serve that time beginning on June 1.'

It meant that Mayweather would have time to heal and recover from the 5 May Cotto fight, if it was a physical tussle, and he would be behind bars when Pacquiao fought Bradley on 9 June.

'In life there's obstacles,' Mayweather said. 'When it comes to June first, I have to accept it like a man.

'I'm thankful that the judge didn't stop me from making a living. Boxing's what I do. Boxing is what I love. June first is just an ordinary day. I'm not worried about it, I don't even think about it. I take the good with the good and the bad with the bad. Can't nothing stop me.'

Leonard Ellerbe reckoned that Mayweather was being the bigger person by putting in the plea. 'All you can do is respect a man for not wanting to put his kids through a difficult process,' said Mayweather's right-hand man. 'Things aren't always what they seem. I have the advantage of knowing what the facts are in this particular case and the public doesn't have that information. He's stepped up and he did what he needed to do to protect his family.'

Then there were the other family members to consider. After eight months of not talking, and with the HBO *24/7* cameras back in the gym, Mayweather Sr saw his son for the first time since their fall-out.

A half-hearted embrace meant they were both prepared to move forwards. 'We beef a little bit but it's alright,' said Jr. 'Next week we'll be arguing, he'll be trying to take over the gym.'

Then, of his trainer, Floyd said, 'My uncle Roger is a great person. Unbelievable. That's my uncle. I love him. I'd do anything for him.'

Roger, explaining how their relationship as coach and pupil had worked for almost sixteen years, said, 'I'm not his daddy. I don't tell him what to do. I ask him what to do. I want the best for him, whether him and his daddy get on or not, I want the best for him.'

'If he wins, I win,' said Senior. 'He's Floyd Joy Mayweather Junior. I'm Senior.'

Floyd Jr told the world that he made *24/7* the success story that it had become, that his character was earning the show high ratings. He also factored in his dysfunctional family set-up, but knew he was the star of the show.

Boxing fans, however, were growing weary of the real-life soap opera and the repetitive nature of seeing family fall-outs, wedges of money, flash cars and everything else. After episode three of *Cotto-Mayweather 24/7*, Floyd told the world he had become disappointed with the series, too.

'I want to apologise to all my fans and viewers who watched *24/7* last night,' he wrote on Twitter. 'I wasn't pleased with this weeks [sic] episode of 24/7. Me and my film team are providing Bentley Weiner with exciting content which she is not using. We really needed the producers from *Mayweather-Hatton 24/7* to come back to HBO give the fans and viewers more excitement.'

Mayweather felt he was serving up what people wanted to watch even though he admitted, to Max Kellerman, that the real Floyd Mayweather was not the character on *24/7*.

'When it's lights, camera, action, it's time to give the fans entertainment,' he said, of the persona he had developed. 'The fans want to be entertained. When I'm home I'm like anyone else. Normal. I spend time with my children and I'm always watching sports.'

Mayweather was also using social media to engage with fans,

talk about how he lived and spent his money, and comment on things he liked or disliked. A keen basketball player, who often had pick-up games with members of his Money Team in training camps, Mayweather had friends who played in the NBA, and was unafraid of passing comment.

One post that got noticed was a tweet in which he shared his opinion of fast-rising basketball star Jeremy Lin. 'Jeremy Lin is a good player,' he wrote. 'But all the hype is because he's Asian. Black players do what he does every night and don't get the same praise.'

His comments were not well received and he was asked to explain them in an interview.

'Anything that Floyd Mayweather says is blown up crazy,' he stated. 'I'm far from racist. It is what it is, I said what I said – so be it.'

Three years earlier, when Pacquiao was starting to blaze that colourful trail to Mayweather's doorstep, Floyd posted a Ustream video that was widely condemned online for 'racist content'.

'I'm on vacation for about a year, about a year,' Mayweather said as he recorded himself. 'As soon as we come off vacation, we're going to cook that little yellow chump. We ain't worried about that. Once I kick that midget ass, I'll want y'all to jump on my dick. So ya'll better get on the bandwagon right now because once I stomp the midget I'm going to make the motherfucker cook me a sushi roll and cook me some rice. All "Poochio" can do is keep making $6 million.'

The video was about ten minutes long and Mayweather again went down the performance-enhancing drugs route with his rival, saying he would fight Pacquiao 'when he gets off the power pellets.'

The whole thing was bizarre and in incredibly poor taste, but the comments on Lin instantly took the media back to the Ustream video Mayweather had posted.

Anyway, that the Cotto fight was taking place was virtually a subplot given that the world's wealthiest athlete would have to spend near on ninety days in prison.

Floyd opened up as a 6-1 betting favourite. Cotto had been on the receiving end of the brutal, draining losses to Margarito and Pacquiao, and he'd been involved in numerous physical wars over the years, with the likes of Joshua Clottey, Mosley, Judah, Ricardo Torres and DeMarcus Corley.

He was younger than Floyd, at thirty-one, but he had a high mileage. If Floyd could go through the gears, some felt Cotto, good as he was, might unravel.

Thousands of fans again showed up just for the weigh-in at the MGM Grand, the fight venue.

And it might have been a few years too late, but now Mayweather had an entire advert draped down the side of the giant green building, just as he'd wanted in the early days.

Floyd weighed 151lbs, three pounds under the division limit. Cotto was on the money at 154lbs.

A long staredown was mostly spent with Cotto's stone face looking emptily into Mayweather's excited eyes while Floyd chewed gum. Finally words were exchanged, then the two were split up.

Mayweather reckoned Cotto looked drained but said he felt comfortable coming in lighter.

Both fighters had agreed to random blood and urine testing, which Mayweather had demanded of his recent opponents, and Floyd's crossover appeal into the mainstream was completed with a ringwalk that saw him accompanied by rapper and friend 50 Cent, pop icon Justin Bieber (brought in as he was idolised by one of Mayweather's daughters) and wrestler Triple H. It was quite a crew.

Mayweather might have edged round one but Cotto fought hard in the next. He targeted Floyd's body, had success with

Mayweather on the ropes and managed to buoy the crowd with his pressure. Floyd fought back well, though, and the buzzing audience anticipated the makings of a good fight.

Trainer Diaz told his charge to be more active.

Mayweather, wearing red leather trunks, countered some body shots with a straight right hand early in the third but Cotto's own right hand, to the body and head, also found a scoring home. Floyd's nose started to trickle blood.

Mayweather had the better of the fifth but Cotto spent most of it in his grill, drawing more blood from his nostrils.

Cotto's jab was a factor in the sixth and he turned over a smart hook that sent Mayweather's head back and caused the former "Pretty Boy" to smile. Cotto then started to use the ring, countering Floyd's attacks.

'That motherfucker's running,' said Roger, sounding surprised.

Cries of 'Cot-to, Cot-to' filled the MGM Grand cauldron. Mayweather's mouth now had blood leaking from it and Cotto again tried to soften Mayweather's body, with a right and a left.

There was a welt by Cotto's left eye, but he was known to bust up during fights.

Mayweather was in the lead but there was all to play for. They both swung and landed right hands early in the eighth and Cotto then piled in behind both piston-like fists as he crowded Mayweather in a corner. Floyd fired back with uppercuts. The action was spicy. It was one of the best Mayweather fights in years, if not of all. The crowd ate it up the whole way through round eight and it was a big, big round for Cotto. Floyd's nose was a mess. Some ringsiders, including HBO's Harold Lederman, had scored three consecutive rounds for Cotto.

'When was the last time that happened?' asked Jim Lampley, glued to what he was watching.

Mayweather began to break through with left uppercuts in the ninth and Cotto's work rate dropped. That was the same over the final two sessions, meaning the result was not in doubt on the scorecards. A sizzling straight right-left uppercut dazed Cotto in the twelfth and last round, sending his eyes momentarily into orbit, and served as a punctuation mark on Floyd's performance.

The fans had value for money.

Two judges scored it 117-111, the third marked 118-110, all in Mayweather's favour.

'You're a hell of a champion,' Mayweather told Cotto. 'You're the toughest guy I ever fought.'

Lampley handed over to his broadcast colleague Larry Merchant, who was in the ring. Merchant kicked off, addressing the audience. 'To end the suspense,' he began, 'I want to let you all know that Floyd graciously came to me yesterday, and apologised for the incident last September and I accepted it and thank you for doing that.'

Mayweather said it was okay.

Merchant asked whether Floyd was prepared to go from his chaotic life of luxury into a lonely cell. Mayweather said he was blessed, despite his upcoming prison stay. 'When June first comes, only thing I can do is accept it like a man would do.'

He said Bob Arum was stopping the Pacquiao fight from happening. 'Let's give the fans what they want to see, Mayweather-Pacquiao.'

At the post-fight press conference, Mayweather looked like he'd been in a fight. There was fresh blood on his lip and swelling around both eyes. He was a wonderful boxer and remarkable talent, but he had shown he could fight his ass off when he needed to.

'He's a tough competitor,' he said of Cotto. 'He came to fight; he didn't just come to survive. I dug down and fought him back. When you fight on pay-per-view, you have to give the fans what they want, and that's excitement.'

'The judges said I lost the fight,' groaned Cotto. 'I can't do anything else. I'm happy with my fight and performance and so is my family. I can't ask for anything else.'

Neither could the powers that be. The fight generated a whopping 1.5 million pay-per-view sales, making more than $90 million from that revenue stream alone. A further $12 million was made at the gate from more than 14,000 ticket sales, with ringside seats costing $1,500.

'I could have boxed him and moved,' maintained Mayweather. 'But we're in a recession and you guys spend your hard-earned money, so I wanted you to see a good fight.'

Mayweather's $32-million guarantee swelled to more than $80 million. Cotto was rewarded with a career high $8 million.

On the undercard, Saúl Álvarez, a young, ginger Mexican talent, scored a breakout win with a commanding victory over the fast-fading Mosley. Álvarez, a wildly popular prospect – known as 'Canelo' – tossed his name into the Mayweather sweepstakes.

It had been Floyd's sixth consecutive fight at the MGM Grand, and Cotto's eighth fight there overall.

Prison time loomed but the money kept rolling in.

'Love him or hate him, he's the bank vault,' said Ellerbe. 'Love him or hate him, he's going to make the bank drop.'

ESPN picked up a story on Floyd's wealth.

'He is a one-man conglomerate,' they wrote online. 'With a net worth – not counting cars, jewellery and houses – estimated at $100 million. Unlike manager- and promoter-dependent fighters, Mayweather dictates his share of fight revenue and his opponent's. He controls the gate receipts by setting ticket prices at the MGM Grand; for his May fifth light-middleweight title fight against Miguel Cotto, they range from $200 to $1,500. He negotiates directly with HBO to set the price for the pay-per-view broadcast. HBO is advertising the fight for a "suggested" retail price of $59.95 . . . It costs roughly $10 million in fees

– site rental, infrastructure, promotions – to put on a big fight. Mayweather Promotions essentially fronts the money, paying Golden Boy on a per-fight basis to handle logistics. As Ellerbe describes the relationship, "If you run a construction company, you have to hire someone to pour the cement".'

'In everything he does, Floyd's betting on himself,' Ellerbe added. 'He puts up the money, bets on himself and hits a home run every time.'

Mayweather was blazing a trail unlike anything that had been seen in sports. He called all of the shots. He dictated to networks, to fighters, to staff, to executives and promoters. It was his way or no way.

But less than a month after the Cotto fight he surrendered himself in a courtroom to start his prison term, 'For a hair-pulling, arm-twisting attack on his ex-girlfriend, Josie Harris, in September 2010 while two of their children watched.'

He was handcuffed behind his back and led away.

The domestic battery charges he pleaded guilty to allowed him to avoid trial. He could have received as much as thirty-four years if he'd been convicted.

Yet on 3 August, almost two months later, it was over. He had around thirty days deducted from his sentence for good behavior and 'work time'.

'Money' Mayweather was a free man. And he'd never been more powerful.

THIRTEEN

DEALS, DOMESTICS AND THE ONE

FLOYD MAYWEATHER WAS leaving network giants HBO and heading 'across the street' to their arch-rivals Showtime.

The shockwaves reverberated in the news in financial and sporting sections of websites and newspapers.

It was an astronomical, pioneering deal that saw the rich get richer and the balance in power in the sport shift from one company to the other.

Mayweather had spent almost his entire career with HBO and their parent company Time Warner, but his six-fight, thirty-month Showtime/CBS contract worth a record $200 million was going to open on 4 May against Robert 'The Ghost' Guerrero.

'This historic deal reflects a global superstar who is head and shoulders above his peers,' Leonard Ellerbe told ESPN's Dan Rafael. 'HBO, they made a great offer, but the Showtime PPV/CBS offer was substantially greater in every facet, from top to bottom.

'So bottom line, HBO was outgunned. They came to a gun fight with a knife. At the end of the day, it's business. Floyd has had a fantastic relationship over the last sixteen years with HBO but he's moving on.'

'It was a very detailed process,' Showtime Sports general manager Stephen Espinoza said of the deal. 'We put forth a very aggressive offer, and I know Floyd spent a lot of time with Al Haymon poring over the details. Ultimately, I was able to bring a lot of the [Showtime and CBS] assets to the table, and with so many of our platforms stepping forward to support it, this was a deal he couldn't refuse.'

The partership was announced in February 2013. What made it all the more extraordinary was that Mayweather was about to turn thirty-six and arguably should have been a decade beyond his prime.

But prison had added an element of suspense. Yes, it turned out to be just seventy days, but would it change him? Would it affect him as a fighter, or as a person?

He certainly did not enjoy it inside.

Eight days after entering prison he found himself back on top of many pound-for-pound lists as the Manny Pacquiao fight went up in smoke. The Filipino was upset on points by Timothy Bradley.

Even though a vast majority felt Pacquiao won, he was defeated on the scorecards. It caused a stink, rightfully, but the lure of two fighters at their peak meeting to decide who was the best of their time had gone. Part of what had sold Pacquiao was his devastating momentum, and that had dissipated.

Floyd couldn't watch the fight as he had no television in his cell. He also could not celebrate when *Forbes* named him the highest-paid athlete in the world, topping a rich list that included Tiger Woods, David Beckham, Kobe Bryant and, of course, Pacquiao.

Mayweather appealed to prison authorities about the food and water on offer in jail. He was also concerned at the lack of space he had to exercise, in a cell that measured just ninety-eight square feet, claiming it would affect his health and fitness. It certainly was not the Big Boy Mansion.

Las Vegas Justice of the Peace Melissa Saragosa said that Mayweather was just fine where he was and ruled on 13 June that, while he was not happy, Floyd had enough space and time for physical activity and that he was only not eating properly because he chose not to eat the meals provided. Rather sarcastically, chief prosecutor Lisa Luzaich, said, 'It's jail. Where did he think he was going? The Four Seasons?'

Yet he was kept separate from the 3,200 other inmates, with police saying his high profile meant he needed protection.

Meanwhile, Leonard Ellerbe was working hard on the outside. He told writer Donald McRae that when Floyd was released he could go on to become the first athlete to make a billion dollars.

Ellerbe, who was originally from Washington DC but moved to Vegas in 1997 and had devoted fifteen years of his life to Mayweather, was keen to point out the Floyd he knew was not who audiences watched on TV.

'"Money" is just a persona,' he insisted. 'And it attracts controversy and appeals to fans. That's Floyd showing his genius. That's Floyd doing a bank-drop. He uses that Money persona and at the bank he shows them cheques with amounts they've never seen before. That's what Floyd does. He's a record breaker.'

On 3 August, when Mayweather was released from prison, onlookers reckoned he looked fit and well. He wore a Miami Heat baseball cap, a grey hoodie over his head and a posse of around twenty friends and family members greeted him. His twelve-year-old daughter Iyanna was there, so were Ellerbe and 50 Cent.

He did not speak to the assembled media, but got behind the wheel of a blue Bentley sedan and left.

In the months that followed he said little about his time behind bars. Then he struck the Showtime deal, while confirming that he would fight Robert Guerrero on 4 May – Cinco de Mayo weekend.

Fight week was again chaotic. Guerrero was a three-weight champion but he'd cut a swathe through mediocre opponents, winning fringe titles. Mayweather was still the WBC welterweight champion, having defeated Victor Ortiz for the championship. Guerrero held that body's interim title.

Mayweather, however, openly began to reflect upon his time in prison to reporters after the pre-fight press conference.

'What was I doing?' he said, when asked how he spent his prison time. 'I was locked up, I was in the hole, and I was doing 1,300 push-ups a day. That's the only thing I can do. I'm locked up twenty-three hours a day, I get to come out one hour, and on weekends I don't get to come out at all. So out of seven days a week, I only get to come out of my cell five hours. It was rough.

'I was just thankful to everyone who wrote me letters, and to the fans that wrote me. There were about 100,000-200,000 letters. A lot of letters I didn't get, a lot of them I did get.

'Even if someone took time out to make a negative comment, they took time out of their life to write about me. Whether it's positive or negative, thank you. I had your attention at that particular time.

'I was doing counselling also when I was incarcerated. One of the stories that was told to me by my counsellor was hostages were put in boxes and the boxes were like coffins. Those hostages were going crazy in the boxes but one hostage learned the language of the guards who was guarding the boxes. He befriended them, learning their language. What happened was, while the hostages were in the boxes, one of them made friends with roaches and survived in his box for a long period of time. My mentality was that if he could make friends with roaches in a coffin or a box and survive for a long period of time, I can do time in administrated segregation and last seventy days. So that's how I got through it. But I was also fighting other cases while I was incarcerated, so my lawyer [Shane Emerick] would come two times a day every day to talk to me about my different cases and go over paperwork. Some days I would break down, not in tears but just break down because my body was deteriorating. I was surviving on candy bars, soda and potato chips. I didn't eat the food because I just didn't trust it. I didn't feel comfortable or I didn't trust it. He [Emerick] would come to me every day, he would pray with me every day and he knows my whole life story. I told him everything. He's like one of my best friends. I was doing fan mail, 1300 push ups every day, and that's basically all I was doing.'

Had he learned his lesson?

'You can never learn nothin' from losing your freedom,' he continued. 'But the main thing is, you appreciate other things in life. You appreciate the small things in life. Just seeing trees and walking down the street, and just seeing people walk by, you appreciate certain things like that after losing your freedom.'

Mayweather said he made no friends in prison.

He also claimed that despite having an increasingly lengthy rap sheet he could be considered a positive role model.

He said he had grown more mature. He had children who were in their teens. His outlook had changed.

'I'm older now,' he said. 'So I look at things a different way. You got class and you got trash, and I never got no piercings or tattoos. I carry myself in a classy way, and after my career is over hopefully I can do commentary and help keep the sport of boxing alive.

'I don't care what you see on rap videos, sagging your pants is not cool. Piercing in your ears is not cool. I just teach them different things. Always have manners. Always be respectful and always be appreciative and thankful for what you do have.'

He was thankful to have his father back in his camp. On Valentine's Day, Mayweather sent a tweet out saying he would be training under Floyd Sr for the Guerrero fight.

'I'm happy to be working with my father,' he said. 'I'm working with my father and Roger but on fight night my dad will be in my corner.

'My dad is sick and if I never made up with my father and something harsh happened, because anything can happen – he's older, he's lost a lot of weight from being sick – it would hurt me, not speaking to him. It would hurt me very, very bad for him not to have a relationship with his grandchildren. That's very important to me. "Why are me and you arguing? We are both in this sport to be the best, why not work together?" The team is stronger together than apart.'

Mayweather was faced with an unusual confrontation a couple of days before he and Guerrero were going to fight at the MGM Grand.

Guerrero's father and trainer, Ruben, who'd added an explosive, outspoken element to the build-up, took to the microphone and began an undignified gutter rant about Mayweather's run-ins with the law.

'We're going to beat up that woman beater, the one that beat up his wife, man,' shouted a charged Guerrero Sr, pointing at Floyd. 'He beat up his wife in front of his kids. You guys like that shit? Like this guy? Woman beater. He must have learned that from his dad. Woman beater, baby. We're going to beat that woman beater. He's going to get it from a real man. We're going to beat that woman beater.'

A shocked Oscar De La Hoya arrived at the podium to replace Guerrero as a shell-shocked media looked on and Guerrero Sr continued to rant and rave in the background. He later tried to goad Mayweather Sr into hitting him.

Although Floyd Sr was back in his son's corner, the fighter had kept him off the dais at the press conference in case he was provoked. Mayweather Jr's own calmness surprised many.

'I keep my dad under control,' he said. 'I'm trying to avoid anyone getting hurt.'

He also claimed he was not bothered by Guerrero Sr.

'I don't have to fight his father,' he explained, saying he was simply texting Miss Jackson throughout the outburst. 'I'm here to fight the fight.'

'I was young,' he said, reflecting upon the time when he might have taken the bait. 'I'm a lot older now so I'm a lot wiser now. I know what I bring to the table. When I was young, you'd see a wild Floyd Mayweather, but I'm a lot older now. My kids are teenagers now so I can't be conducting myself in a disorderly fashion. I'll still trash-talk sometimes and give the people excitement, but there's a time and a place for everything. I don't have to sit here and bad-mouth his father, because only God can judge me.

'If I did or didn't do a crime, I served my time and I love my children and I have nothing negative to say about the mother of my children.'

Josie Harris, however, had plenty of negative comments to make about him.

Three days before the fight, British journalist Martin Rogers, who spoke with Harris about her time with Mayweather, wrote a story for Yahoo!Sports. He'd spent three hours with her; she had been moved to act after Showtime's documentary, *30 Days in May*, seemed to downplay Mayweather's involvement in the incident that saw him imprisoned. Mayweather, as part of the Showtime deal was an 'Executive Producer' of the show. He had the same role in Showtime's new *All Access* series, the network's version of *24/7*.

If Mayweather and his team tried to make it out as no big deal, there was another side of the story.

In an article titled, 'Behind the police report' Harris told her vivid version to Rogers.

She backed it up with a doctor's report and handwritten statements from Mayweather's then eleven-year-old son Koraun.

On the night in question, 9 September 2010, police had already been called to Harris's home after a verbal dispute between the two but, at 5 a.m., Mayweather returned to Harris's property.

Harris told Rogers she was asleep on the sofa but woke up to see Mayweather with her phone, shouting at her about messages she had received from NBA star C.J. Watson.

Mayweather was engaged to Shantel Jackson but the Yahoo article claimed he did not want Harris seeing other men while living in a house he owned.

'Are you having sex with C.J.?' Mayweather yelled, according to the arrest report.

'Yes, that is who I am seeing now,' she answered.

The document then says he grabbed Harris by the hair and punched her in the back of the head 'with a closed fist several times.' He then pulled her hair and twisted her left arm.

'From there it was just . . . bad,' she told Rogers. 'I was powerless. He was holding me down. I couldn't fight back. The kids were screaming and crying, "You're hurting my mom."'

Then Mayweather shouted, 'I'm going to kill you and the man you are messing around with,' she told police. 'I'm going to have you both disappear.'

She thought Mayweather was trying to break her arm and screamed at the children to call the police or get the security guard.

Koraun's handwritten statement told how he had seen his father 'hiting' [sic] and 'kick' his mother.

The picture is unpleasant. 'There is no telling,' said Harris, over what might have happened had Mayweather's friend James 'P-Reala' McNair not been on hand.

'In the heat of the moment you are upset and enraged and you pick up a lamp . . . He could have hit me in the head in the wrong place . . . I could have died. He would've been on murder charges. I could've grabbed a knife from the kitchen, stabbed him – anything.'

McNair appeared in *30 Days of May*, and said, 'The only people who truly know the truth is Floyd and Josie. But when

I was there, from what I saw, I don't see a reason why he should be jail.'

Harris is preparing a book about her complex and volatile relationship with Mayweather, which extends back more than ten years. Rogers called it 'a love story, albeit a dysfunctional one torn apart when the boxer's gravitation toward celebrity culture became an occasional habit that morphed into a permanent lifestyle.'

Yet Harris still feels a loyalty and bond to the father of their three children, through it all. She said they still loved one another, and also revealed that they had been intimate since his release from prison. She admitted he is a 'doting father'.

Harris also talked to Rogers about Mayweather's gambling, saying he bet 'risky amounts.' One time, she recalled going to a casino to settle a $700,000 wager.

It was a much more innocent time when they first started dating, all the way through to 2006 when he bought her a $500,000, twenty-five-carat diamond ring. Following the September 2010 incident, she sold it to make a fresh start in California with the children.

Harris, however aggrieved she has been, still looks out for Mayweather and wants others to do right by him.

'He has told me people have stolen from him, his house was robbed and they thought it was an inside job,' she explained to Rogers. 'The people who are just leeching on . . . I didn't like that. I wanted Floyd to run his business like a company. You [should] clock in and clock out and get a salary, not, "I'm going to buy you a Rolex or a car." Is it a charity? A very lucky-ass charity. They are getting an extreme donation.'

She and the children had therapy after that September night and she explained to Rogers in a later interview that she'd suffered physical abuse from Mayweather on 'six occasions.'

She said she still suffered anxiety when she had to see him, though that was becoming less frequent because he used a jet service to ferry the kids between his Las Vegas home and Harris's, about fifty miles north-west of Los Angeles.

Harris's first interview with Rogers came out the week of the Guerrero fight on the Yahoo website.

Despite it being an exclusive, it did not get a great deal of attention.

'It was the great untold story of Floyd Mayweather,' said Rogers. 'You know what it's like with boxers these days, they have these *All Access* shows, or *24/7*, and all that sort of stuff and what else is there that we haven't heard? We all know he likes money. We know he likes to walk around with hundreds of thousands of dollars in a bag, counting it out on his bed or throwing it around in a bag. We know he likes going to strip clubs, expensive cars and spending millions of dollars on cars. That's not new to me. If I was telling that story it was giving readers something they hadn't seen. The reason was twofold. One, I felt it was an important and compelling story, and those are the type of stories that I tend to gravitate towards – they have a human rights element to them. I'm not a typical reporter in that way. My job, that I'm paid to do, isn't just to go to events and write about who won and by how many goals, it's how to find different elements to the lives of these athletes that people love watching. And that was the one that stood out. And the more the Mayweather camp and Mayweather tried to gloss over what happened it became even more compelling and it was important, I felt, that people knew about it.

'I went to see her, and she copied the documentation that was used in the story and the police report, the hospital report and all that kind of stuff. She goes back and forth. There are days when she's really quite angry and hurt about how Floyd continues to treat her and the things he says in public and so on, and then she still feels sorry for Mayweather and the situations he gets himself into. It's a very complex relationship.

'Being famous shouldn't protect you either from the law or the way you should be judged in the public eye and if you've done something wrong and violent towards a women then you deserve to be treated like any other guy who does that, whether they're famous or they're just a guy on the street.'

Mayweather, now thirty-six years of age, was accumulating a high mileage of wear and tear outside the ring, more so than inside the ropes. Reporters in town for the Guerrero fight noted how he had aged since the Cotto battle a year earlier.

Victory over Berto, as it had done for Victor Ortiz, had earned Guerrero the shot. They shared a war, with Berto going down twice as Guerrero triumphed on the scorecards.

Equally as important to Mayweather, however, was a ready-made 'good guy-bad guy' subplot.

Guerrero's childhood sweetheart and wife, Casey, had endured a long battle with leukaemia and he had been by her side throughout her brave fight. She was in remission. It might sound cold, but it was a story and laced the build-up with human interest, too.

And Guerrero, not Mayweather, had also attracted the wrong type of headlines when he jeopardised the bout after being arrested at John F. Kennedy International Airport in New York, charged with carrying a .40 caliber Smith & Wesson semi-automatic handgun and three unloaded magazines.

The gun was not loaded, but New York laws require them to be licensed in the state, whether it was licensed elsewhere or not.

Floyd showed up three hours late to film the fight commercial with Guerrero, which saw them go face to face in front of a green screen. 'It's your biggest payday and it's your only payday,' asserted Mayweather, getting in Guerrero's face.

'We didn't have a press tour, but when we get our photo shoots, he was definitely running his mouth,' recollected Guerrero. 'You just have to block him out and move on with your business, or else you'll get caught up in his games. That's certainly something you want to avoid.'

Guerrero had said before facing Mayweather that there were signs the veteran's legs were starting to slow. The southpaw from Gilroy was confident, but he'd never been on a stage this big.

'They say it takes two fighters to make a fight of this magnitude,' Mayweather stated. 'That's not true. I'm at the level now where you can give me anybody, you could give me a cab driver and I could still do crazy numbers.'

It was the Floyd Mayweather show, Guerrero had just been hired for a walk-on part; although Floyd fell short of a Mike Tyson-like boast, with the former heavyweight champion sending out the same message when he said he could sell out Madison Square Garden masturbating.

But the audiences were growing, even just to watch him work out in the gym.

'I just tell my team this, when we come here to do work and people are looking for autographs and stuff, they've got to get that later on, I've got to focus on my job,' he said. 'It's so crazy. I go to the boxing gym and I box in front of two hundred people. I spar in front of two hundred people every day so I'm accustomed to a crowd every day. They're making noise like a crowd, clapping like an audience, so it's basically like a boxing match every day in my gym.

'A lot of people don't know that a lot of my family work in the gym. My mother's two brothers run the boxing gym, my father's two brothers and my father train fighters in the gym. We're one big family.'

Showtime's Jimmy Lennon Jr, with his 'It's Showtime' catchphrase was in. HBO's 'Let's get ready to rumble', Michael Buffer was out due to the switch in networks.

Music artist Lil Wayne rapped Floyd Mayweather to the ring for the Guerrero fight. The boxer had fallen out with old pal 50

Cent, though both remained tight-lipped about why they had gone their separate ways.

Mayweather did not need him. He posted a virtuoso performance to dominate Guerrero and beat him on points, 117-111 on all three cards.

For some, Guerrero won only a round. For the judges, he won three. But the ones he did earn he only nicked while Mayweather dominated his by and large. He pasted him in the eighth and eleventh sessions in particular.

It was a display of boxing in its purest form. Guerrero had been unable to get untracked and in round eight there was a smattering of boos as Floyd dissected him with right hands.

What prison sentence? What inactivity? None of it mattered. Floyd Mayweather was thirty-six and he had never looked better.

From a crowd of 15,880, many started leaving in round eleven and twelve. The result and method of victory was not in doubt. There was no mileage added to Mayweather's ring age.

'A lot of people thought the layoff would be a problem but it wasn't,' he said. 'Tonight was just a stepping stone. I've got five more fights and then I'm through with the sport.'

There was a school of thought that after getting hit more by Cotto than anyone else in years, Floyd Sr, the defensive specialist, might add to his son's longevity.

'In camp we had great chemistry,' said his son, who showed off a swollen right hand, which he said was damaged from halfway. 'Everything played out like it should have. It's always great to work with family. No family is perfect but my life is always on camera. He is set in his ways, I am set in mine and we are always going to have differences of opinion.'

'My son came to the gym and told me he wanted me to train him,' said Sr. 'It wasn't a problem. I went to the gym and he was boxing this big old guy and someone else and they were hitting him quite a bit and I told him, "We ain't going to take no punches. We ain't going to do that." And in two days he wasn't taking any punches, he was capitalising and counterpunching. He just got better and better.'

'I landed some good shots on him,' Guerrero contended. 'He's a great fighter. He's slick and quick.'

'Honestly, Floyd could have danced the whole night,' Mayweather Sr said. 'There wasn't anything he couldn't do in there tonight.'

'He ran like a chicken,' contested Ruben Guerrero. 'I thought we were going to go toe to toe with him.'

'I just remember Floyd being super-fast, unlike any fighter I've ever faced,' Guerrero recalled, with the fight long since gone. 'He's got a long reach and it's very hard to get off your punches against him. I think that I should have boxed more, instead of trying to push the fight. He tried to go toe to toe with me, thinking I was a small guy coming up a weight, but I hit him with a nice body shot in the second round and he started to move a lot. He never engaged.'

Like many others, though, he is proud to say he fought boxing's main man of recent years.

'I humbly say yes,' he added. 'Considering the fact that I did better than a lot of future Hall of Famers did against him. Twenty years from now when you look back on history, and you look at the scorecards, I did better than Shane Mosley, Miguel Cotto, Juan Manuel Márquez, Arturo Gatti, Ricky Hatton, and Diego Corrales.'

Instantly fans wanted to see Mayweather take a sterner test.

Saúl 'Canelo' Álvarez, the up-and-coming Mexican, had won the WBC light-middleweight title from Austin Trout on a show at the Alamodome in San Antonio, Texas, and in front of almost 40,000 fans. That confirmed Álvarez as a bona fide draw, and there were not many of them left for Floyd to fight. Trout-Álvarez was originally heading onto the Mayweather-Guerrero undercard, but when Mayweather did not agree to a written guarantee that Álvarez would get the next shot at Floyd, on 14 September, the Mexican star decided he would top his own bill. It was a shrewd move.

He was twenty-three years old, thirteen years Mayweather's junior, had a near-on eighty per cent knockout ratio and was a natural light-middleweight. He had won forty-two times, drawn one fight and was unbeaten.

He was just eight years old when Mayweather won his first world title, against Genaro Hernández, all those years ago.

If the Pacquiao fight still couldn't be made, and it seemed further away than ever after the Filipino was crushingly knocked out in six rounds by old rival Juan Manuel Márquez – who had finally grown into the welterweight division – Álvarez was the man many wanted Floyd to test himself against. It appeared Mayweather-Pacquiao, which had looked unlikely anyway, had been torpedoed for good.

Mayweather did not seem bothered that a career-high payday for him had been blown to smithereens, however. He later took to Instagram to post a video of the devastating knockout blow that had laid Pacquiao out to the tune of Queen's 'Another One Bites the Dust'.

With the losses to Bradley and Márquez, Pacquiao's stock had not been so low in years. Not only did 50-50 seem like a pipedream, so too did the $40 million he had already declined. Mayweather held all the cards, again, but with Golden Boy Promotions anointing Álvarez as the next big thing – a cross between the great Julio César Chávez and commercially lucrative Oscar De La Hoya – the young star was on the cusp of landing the big one.

People wondered if Canelo would be the one to beat Mayweather, thus the fight – when it was signed – was called 'The One'.

An eleven-city media tour kicked off with traffic stopping in the heart of Times Square, New York, and then across the United States and into Mexico.

De La Hoya was again on the road with Mayweather. He said he'd given Álvarez the blueprint for how to defeat Floyd based on his efforts in the first-half of their fight. That he didn't get the job done only served to make Mayweather grin at his old foe. 'As far as Oscar [goes], he's jealous of me,' said Floyd. 'The Golden Boy is extremely fake.'

'When someone jabs and pokes at me,' countered De La Hoya. 'Especially a guy that I fought, deep down inside of me, yes, I want you to lose, because it's personal to me.'

Mayweather pointed to the Golden Boy fighters he'd beaten and said De La Hoya had given them all the blueprint, and they all lost, whether it was Hatton, Mosley, Márquez, Ortiz or Guerrero. 'Also he will try to give Canelo the blueprint, and he will lose,' Floyd smiled.

The Mayweather-Álvarez fight was signed at 152lbs, two pounds under the light-middleweight limit Álvarez fought at. Mayweather's team called the opposition camp 'inept' for offering terms at catch weight, thus playing straight into their hands.

Fight week was ridiculously busy. Vegas was alive and fight fever took over Sin City. Hardcore boxing fanatics and casual fans all wanted a piece of it. The temporary shop in the foyer of the MGM Grand was constantly busy. At times, there was a lengthy, roped queue for an hour or more to get in there to buy fight merchandise.

For a week in September, boxing had seen nothing like. Typically, as with any major boxing event, it was called 'the fight to save the sport.' Sadly for De La Hoya, he missed it all after having to check himself into rehab.

A red carpet wound through the MGM Grand lobby as the fighters made their grand arrivals on the Tuesday in front of about 3,000 fans.

Showtime boss Stephen Espinoza admitted trepidation in the months and weeks beforehand, but it was not long before he could see the numbers would make everything okay.

'There was a perception that Mayweather's last fight [with Robert Guerrero in May] was a [financial] disappointment, a perception that I did not agree with but it's certainly out there and on the strength of my vision for the event our company had literally put tens of millions of dollars at stake. By the time we got to fight night we were probably fifty or sixty million dollars at risk. On a basic level, three months prior I had represented to everyone within the company that this event would be worth that amount of financial risk. The company had a lot to lose. I had a lot to lose had the event not performed, but sometimes that kind of pressure is the greatest motivator.'

Golden Boy Promotions also stuck their head on the economic chopping block.

'We had to guarantee Mayweather $41.5 million dollars,' remembered Richard Schaefer. 'And Canelo's money [$12 million] and all the other fighters, with Danny Garcia and Lucas Matthysse on the card, so by Monday of fight week I was going to be well out over $60 million. So even though it was tracking well, it was still a nervous time. Even though you can order pay-per-view weeks before the fight about ninety-eight per cent are coming the day of the fight.'

The final fight press conference was held in the KA theatre of the MGM, home to its Cirque du Soleil show, and while the fighters had one last chance to hype the contest, it did not need it and little was said.

'He's strictly professional,' said publicist Kelly Swanson, who'd been with Floyd since the Arturo Gatti fight. 'Fight week is actually so predictable because he's been doing it so long so he knows what's expected of him and he does it perfectly. I don't have to anticipate any "I'm not doing this". The schedule is comfortable, and we make sure we go over it with him so he knows it but it's pretty much the same now as it has been for all of his pay-per-view fights. With Floyd, people don't understand how professional he is when it comes to the responsibilities of promoting a fight.'

Everyone wanted to be there. A-list celebrities could not even get ringside tickets. Some had to sit in other areas of the crowd. The market for second-hand tickets shrunk because no one was selling. There was talk of the ringside seats, priced at $2,000, going for more than ten times that amount. One media member was offered $4,000 for his credential on the day.

The weigh-in was enormous. It was unprecedented. The ball might have started rolling for these showpiece build-up events with Mayweather's fights against De La Hoya and Hatton, but this was on another level altogether – and it was beyond dispute that he was the A-side.

The whole arena was opened up and more than 12,000 fans (the doors had to be closed an hour before anything started and according to an MGM source a further 2-3,000 were turned away) were treated to a host of boxing's top talent being walked out onto the stage and to deafening live music.

Lil Wayne again did the honours for Mayweather, who was flanked by Bieber for his ringwalk.

He was guaranteed $41.5 million, but if the bout was commercially successful – and it hit a financial home run – then he would make the highest purse of his career.

He was outweighed by fifteen pounds on the night. He'd stayed at the agreed poundage of 152lbs, while Álvarez had regenerated to 167lbs. He looked far bigger than Mayweather in the ring.

'Mon-ey, Mon-ey' chants mixed with 'Ca-ne-lo, Ca-ne-lo' cries as the fans, seemingly mostly Mexican, created a volcanic atmosphere.

In the opener, Álvarez tried to fathom Mayweather's customary movement. A counter-right the young man landed caused the crowd to roar and rise expectantly.

The ear-splitting 'Me-hi-co' chorus caused the arena to shake in the second. Álvarez was looking for openings but Mayweather was finding them, his right hand motoring. He even stood 'in the pocket' and worked in close in round four and Álvarez was starting to swell beneath his left eye. Mayweather looked razor sharp boxing at range, too. On the other hand, Álvarez seemed to be flagging. The 'Ca-ne-lo' chants were becoming more urgent and hopeful than excited or optimistic. Mayweather was on fire. He moved fluidly and picked a delectable right uppercut, even moving the bigger man back in round five.

Unlike many who had tried and failed against Mayweather before, Álvarez started swinging more wildly, trying to turn the tide. But the audience could only gasp in appreciation when a Mayweather left-right jarred Álvarez's head back and sent sweat flying into the ringside area.

Álvarez made another concerted attacking effort in round eight, but the more aggressive he was the more he got hurt.

In appreciation of what they were watching, the crowd heartily started cries of 'T-M-T.'

Álvarez was running out of steam and ideas. He was bamboozled. Not one Mexican punch could rally the Hispanic crowd. In the eleventh, Floyd stopped to pose for photographers at ringside. This was supposed to be the future of boxing, and he was humiliating him.

Mayweather coasted the last session and Álvarez could not get near him. While the connoisseurs savoured Mayweather's excellence, others headed to the exits knowing there was nothing dramatic left to miss.

In fact, the drama was saved for the scorecards.

It was a landslide to Mayweather, surely. Some scored a

whitewash for the American, others charitably gave Álvarez a round or two. Certainly more than three rounds in his favour was stretching it.

Mayweather was all smiles as he accepted the congratulations of his team. Then announcer Jimmy Lennon said, 'Ladies and gentlemen, after twelve rounds of action, we have a majority decision.'

'What?' shouted Mayweather in disbelief, screwing up his face.

He looked puzzled as C.J. Ross's 114-114 scorecard was read out. Media members felt a vile churning in their stomach as one of boxing's worst robberies suddenly seemed stupidly possible.

The tension was palpable, until the two other scoring judges overruled the terrible Ross scorecard.

Even so, the marks of 117-111 (Craig Metcalfe) and 116-112 (Dave Moretti) still failed to reflect the overwhelming opinion that Canelo had been trounced in front of a sell-out crowd of 16,746.

Incidentally, with an average ticket price of $1,240, the gross gate of $20,003,150 smashed the previous largest in Nevada combat sports history of $18,419,200, for Mayweather's split decision over De La Hoya.

Golden Boy Promotions CEO Richard Schaefer branded Ross's scorecard a 'disgrace.'

She said she stood by her verdict and Nevada State Athletic Commission boss Keith Kizer backed her.

Mayweather was full of praise for his beaten opponent. 'I've only got twenty-four months left,' he said. 'And this is the man.'

He predicted Álvarez would be the next big thing, it just wasn't his time yet. 'He will carry the torch,' Mayweather continued. 'Tonight, experience was a major key. He still has what it takes. Tonight was just my night.'

'He's a great fighter,' acknowledged Álvarez. 'I just couldn't catch him. He's very intelligent and very elusive. Frustration was getting in there; we were trying to catch him. I didn't want to lose but it happens and it hurts. He's very fast and accurate. His punches weren't as strong but he was getting points.'

'What else can I say?' said Mayweather. 'We did it again.'

Some could have been excused for saying he did not lose a round against either Guerrero or Álvarez. It was another dominant year.

Based on the success of the promotion, his $41.5-million purse was likely to finish up over nine figures.

With around 2.48 million pay-per-view buys, it was a box office monster.

It generated $150 million from TV alone, surpassing the $136 million from De La Hoya-Mayweather.

'This fight will gross over $200 million when you take into account all of the revenues,' said Richard Schaefer. He said that more than 5,000 official fight T-shirts had been sold. It was a financial snowball that turned into an economic avalanche. 'Any and all revenue sources, whether it was foreign television rights, the closed-circuit rights, the pay-per-view, bars and restaurant sales, movie theatres, not just established records but they shattered old records,' said Schaefer. 'As such, it was the most profitable and most successful boxing promotion of all time. In small events you might sell $10,000 worth of hats, T-shirts and things like that. In big events you maybe sell $100,000 worth. In this fight, it established a new record with almost $2 million sold in merchandise. So again, a record not just gone by a little but by a lot.'

The one downside was Ross, who incidentally had also strangely scored Timothy Bradley a highly controversial winner over Manny Pacquiao a year earlier.

Later that week, the sixty-four year old wrote to the Nevada State Athletic Commission to say she was stepping down as a judge after twenty years of officiating.

With Pacquiao in a rebuilding process, reinventing himself

in Macau, China, Mayweather was struggling for top-tier opponents. He said he would again look to fight twice in 2014, on the Mexican holiday weekends in May and September.

As ever, the world kept spinning and, bar his boxing brilliance, things kept changing. His four-year engagement to Shantel Jackson had ended. He said she was focusing on her acting career in LA and that they were still friends, though their split became increasingly bitter through the year. Mayweather ended up posting an image on Instagram of a sonogram.

He wrote, 'The real reason me and Shantel Christine Jackson @missjackson broke up was because she got a abortion, and I'm totally against killing babies. She killed our twin babies.'

She filed explosive court documents, claiming he had kept her a prisoner in his Las Vegas home, that he threatened to publish naked photos of her and during one confrontation he allegedly pointed a gun at her and threatened to shoot her.

She was seeking unspecified damages, partly for posting the sonogram picture on social media, which she said she had not told her family about. 'Both parties are public figures. Abortion is a public issue,' Mayweather responded.

As he prepared to turn thirty-seven, in February 2014, he hosted a poll on his website asking fans to select his next opponent, hard-hitting Argentine Marcos 'Chino' Maidana or quick-fisted Englishman Amir Khan.

Khan had defeated Maidana in a cracking fight at the end of 2010.

Maidana was running ahead in the poll, but Khan's legion of fans, including his Twitter following of more than a million, rallied and eventually saw off Maidana's challenge. However, Khan seemed to jump the gun on announcing the fight via the *Daily Mail* and no one steals Mayweather's thunder. Maidana had won several independent polls, including one on ESPN by a two-to-one ratio.

'Bottom line,' said Ellerbe, 'we took a look at everything that was coming through on the various outlets and we're fighting the very best guy out there.'

Despite the fans choosing Khan, Mayweather announced he would fight Maidana.

'Marcos Maidana's last performance immediately brought him to my attention,' read an official statement from Mayweather. 'He is an extremely skilled fighter who brings knockout danger to the ring. I think this is a great fight for me and he deserves the opportunity to see if he can do what forty-five others have tried to do before him: Beat me.'

Maidana's stock had never been higher. He'd outscored Cincinnati braggart Adrien Broner, a Mayweather protégé and wannabe, of sorts, in a big upset at the end of 2013.

Many had wanted Broner's mouth shut, and Maidana's reward was the man Broner called his 'Big Bro', Floyd.

As far as the neutral boxing observer was concerned, Maidana was a one-dimensional puncher and the fight did not set the pulses racing. Maidana was not as good as Cotto, not as slick as Guerrero, not as big as Álvarez and not as fast as Khan.

He was solid. Mayweather was sublime. The Argentine had also lost to a couple of the better boxers he faced. If he couldn't defeat smooth southpaw Devon Alexander and technically sound Andreas Kotelnik – both decent fighters – what kind of chance did he have against Floyd?

It turns out he didn't care.

Neither did his trainer, Robert Garcia, who held the IBF super-featherweight title in 1999, when Mayweather held the WBC version of the championship in the same weight class.

'The fighters that give Floyd trouble are those that are aggressive, that keep coming forward and don't respect him,' said Garcia, 'If "Chino" lands and "Chino" hurts Mayweather, then it's over.'

'When I hit Mayweather, it will hurt,' promised the challenger.

At the rules meeting the day before the fight, Mayweather's team rejected the gloves Maidana was going to use. Was it mind games? Brinkmanship? Or did they want the heavy hitter to have more padding? Regardless, the situation was ironed out just hours before the fight, allowing many to claim for the best part of twenty-four hours that the fight might not actually go ahead. Ultimately, the challenger had to change the gloves he had wanted to wear.

He weighed in at 146lbs, half a pound heavier than Floyd, but he was 165lbs a day later when they stepped into the ring, nearly twenty pounds heavier than Mayweather at 148.

Maidana tried to crack the 'May-vinci Code' the only way he knew. He came out slugging.

'Olé, olé, olé. Chi-no, Chi-no,' sang the crowd as Maidana rumbled in.

He crowded Mayweather to the ropes and bowled in huge right hands to the head and body, lashing away with left hooks.

Mayweather was popping in body shots, trying to slow the Argentine's charge but Floyd was cut by the right eye in round four from a headbutt.

The contest was wild and dramatic. Mayweather, who complained about the Argentine's roughhouse tactics, could not stop Maidana's assault but he had given as good as he got over twelve unexpectedly fast and furious rounds.

It was another majority decision, 114-114 from Michael Pernick with the two other judges scoring for Floyd by 116-111 and 117-111. It was another win for the now 46-0 Mayweather but he had been physically pushed like never before.

'It's fine, I know I won,' Maidana said. 'Let's go party.'

'He's a helluva competitor,' responded Floyd. 'You have a beautiful family, but next time don't hit me in the dick so much.'

Robert Garcia translated Maidana's response. 'Okay, next time let me use my gloves.'

They did a rematch in September. The fight did not have a big lead up and a twelve-round commercial for an action fight had already been filmed in May. Maidana's effort, and the dent he had been able to put in Mayweather, meant he was as good as anyone to get the shot.

Again he was aggressive, again he did well, rattling Floyd with a bone-crunching right hand at the end of round three. The margins of victory were greater for Floyd, 116-111 (twice) and 115-111 but Maidana became the second fighter to have a second shot at Mayweather and not do as well as he had the first time.

Mayweather was now 47-0, closing on heavyweight legend Rocky Marciano's final career tally of 49-0. He had two fights left on his Showtime deal.

His rivalry with Marcos Maidana was entertaining, even if it was not one for the ages. But there was another feud that had simmered for five years and was ready to explode to the surface. Finally.

FOURTEEN

PACQUIAO

IT WAS HALF TIME in the basketball game between the Miami Heat and Milwaukee Bucks at the American Airlines Arena in Miami, Florida, on a Tuesday night in January 2015.

The whistle blew and the floor cleared. Mayweather rose and strode over to a fellow basketball fan and fellow professional prizefighter named Manny Pacquiao.

It was the first occasion that they had been in the same building at the same time since 10 November 2001, when they fought on a card at the Bill Graham Civic Auditorium in San Francisco. That night, Mayweather had looked good stopping Jesús Chávez; Pacquiao had taken part in a technical draw after six rounds when he was cut badly against Agapito Sánchez. Pacquiao had been ahead on points but the second-round wound deteriorated, causing the bout to be halted. Bob Arum promoted the show. Pacquiao was fighting at super-bantamweight; Mayweather was almost ten pounds heavier (two weight classes higher) at super-featherweight.

Fourteen years later in Miami – and with both bound for boxing's Hall of Fame courtesy of their wondrous subsequent achievements – the two spoke briefly. Phone numbers were exchanged. Camera bulbs flashed. Smart phones and tablets went into overdrive. Social media lit up. Later that evening, they met in the Filipino's hotel suite.

Mayweather arrived with a woman, a videographer and a member of his security team, who waited outside.

By midnight, he had sent Showtime's Stephen Espinoza a text, asking him to FaceTime him. He did as instructed and saw Mayweather and Pacquiao sat together on the sofa.

'That's probably the moment I realised this negotiation isn't like any other I've been in,' Espinoza told Chris Mannix, for *Sports Illustrated*.

It seemed like everyone was on the same page and both sides wanted the match.

'That's the reason the fight happened,' Mayweather later said of his decision to go to the game.

Members of his team insist it was a direct way for Mayweather to finally address the Filipino. Others have it pegged as a chance encounter. Mayweather has been a regular courtside at Heat games, while Pacquiao was in town to judge the Miss Universe pageant.

Whatever, without that meeting on 27 January, the largest money-making fight in the history of this sometimes violent sport of hyperbole and big cash would never have happened.

*

After Floyd Mayweather widely outscored Juan Manuel Márquez in 2009 he announced his return to boxing at the highest level following a two-year 'retirement'. Two months later, Manny Pacquiao destroyed Miguel Cotto in the twelfth round of a Las Vegas war.

Mayweather-Pacquiao was the fight the sport buzzed about. They had cleared out the majority of the better HBO fighters in and around the welterweight limit.

HBO was the common bond, then, with both fighters contracted to the network.

As they attempted negotiations, striking while the iron was hot, the respective teams signed off on a 50-50 share. Even smaller details were agreed, such as Pacquiao walking out first and Mayweather being introduced first. Mayweather would choose the corner; Pacquiao would select locker rooms, that sort of stuff.

Arum flirted with the idea of holding it in the huge Cowboys Stadium [now known as the AT&T Stadium] in Texas, but when Mayweather rejected it that was no big deal and negotiations continued.

'It took like ten days,' Top Rank's Todd duBoef told *Sports Illustrated* about getting the deal done.

Then came the issue of blood and urine testing. One side, Top Rank said the topic had not been part of discussions. Mayweather's team maintained it was there, it just kept getting deleted from the draft contracts.

Regardless of how and when it entered discussions, Pacquiao would not do it because he said he was afraid of needles.

Yes, he was plastered in tattoos but trainer Freddie Roach said it was a psychological issue because he'd suffered a bad reaction to blood testing a couple of days before his 2005 loss to Érik Morales.

Boom, negotiations – so close, yet so far – imploded.

Arum maintained that the demands were a 'sham.' Mayweather's side countered with the obvious, that if there was nothing to hide then take the test.

As 2009 closed Pacquiao filed the defamation suit, against Mayweather, his father, Golden Boy Promotions and others. It was settled in 2012, although terms have to remain confidential.

Regardless of that, and despite mediation between the two factions, Arum announced the deal had died on 6 January 2010.

Mayweather went the Mosley route in May while Pacquiao travelled to Arlington in Texas, where he took on tough Joshua Clottey in March – outpointing him over twelve rounds.

Talks were then picked back up, financial terms remained the same and Pacquiao agreed to the blood and urine tests. It was not a point of contention any longer.

Then, on 30 June, Arum went public saying a deal had been reached, all that was left was for Mayweather to formally agree. He said Floyd had until 16 July to confirm.

This time, the other side said not only that no deal had been reached, but that talks had not even taken place.

A statement from HBO's Ross Greenburg confirmed they had but, on behalf of Mayweather, Schaefer and Ellerbe denied that was the case. Boxing fans were again left tearing their hair out.

Arum rocked the boat by switching Pacquiao to Showtime for one fight, his win over Mosley, but in 2012, and with the Filipino back on HBO, Mayweather made the $40 million offer. Pacquiao rejected it and a year later the fight seemed to have evaporated when Floyd signed that record-breaking six-bout agreement with Showtime.

Greenburg was left lamenting that he had never been able to get arch-rivals Haymon – who'd actually helped Floyd do the deal to buy himself out of his Top Rank contract years earlier – and Arum together in the same room.

The Mayweather-Pacquiao rollercoaster rolled on, with their tracks sometimes seemingly heading for a collision though more often, heading in different directions.

Golden Boy had enough fighters at the weight to serve up for Floyd, and likewise Top Rank were not short of men for Pacquiao. But when the Filipino whirlwind lost to Bradley and then so devastatingly to Márquez, his value and foothold in any negotiations plummeted.

Sure, he rebuilt with wins over Brandon Ríos, a revenge victory over Timothy Bradley and Chris Algieri, but his performances were merely convincing, no longer scintillating.

By the time he and Floyd met at the basketball game at the start of 2015, he had not stopped or knocked out anyone in six years and had lost two of his last five fights.

The American, on the other hand, had posted imperious

displays against Guerrero and Álvarez, although he had looked enticingly vulnerable against Maidana.

Then, following the Heat-Bucks game, talks were back on and Mayweather signed his contract less than a month later, on 20 February.

Another key figure who had been involved in the discussions this time was Leslie Moonves, the president and executive of CBS, the parent company of Showtime.

Moonves said that the pay-per-view numbers for Mayweather against Maidana and Pacquiao-Bradley were underwhelming and recognised that only one fight really mattered commercially.

Ironically, Moonves was a regular at a Los Angeles diner that was also frequented by Pacquiao's trainer Freddie Roach. One of the waiters told Moonves he should talk to the Wild Card Gym boss. Roach insisted that Pacquiao wanted the fight, while Moonves knew Mayweather had just two bouts left on the Showtime/CBS deal.

'It was the persistence of Les Moonves that got everyone talking rationally,' Arum told the *LA Times*. 'With Les pushing it, people around this started acting like adults. Myself included.'

It was Moonves who, finally, got Arum and Al Haymon in the same room – in the executive's house, no less – where the majority of the deal was thrashed out in a couple of hours.

The fight was on, and set for 2 May 2015.

Mayweather confirmed it on Instagram, posting a picture of the document with his signature on it.

'So this is it!' said Pacquiao the next day. 'The fight is on fans, you deserve it, thank you. To God be all the Glory.'

On 11 March, Mayweather and Pacquiao came face to face in Los Angeles for the only press conference to formally announce 'The Super Bowl of Boxing' and the latest 'Fight of the Century'. No extensive tour was needed.

'It's been a long road. But we are here now,' said Mayweather, who spent a lot of time thanking people who had supported him over the years.

Freddie Roach, never shy of dropping a sound bite for the media, said, 'We are in the toughest fight of our lives. But we are going to kick Floyd's ass. Sorry, Floyd.'

Relations between Floyd and his old Top Rank team had thawed. For a while, one of the main hold-ups for Mayweather-Pacquiao taking place was Mayweather not wanting to work with Arum again.

But bridges had been built. In LA, Arum even joked, 'You missed me, right Floyd?'

Mayweather laughed.

But while he and Arum had infamously bumped heads down the years, Mayweather and Todd duBoef – Arum's stepson – had remained friendly since he parted ways from Top Rank.

Mayweather was at duBoef's wedding, he'd hug him when they saw one another and they would text each other, too. That never stopped.

Mayweather also had not forgotten the work Bruce Trampler, Top Rank's matchmaker, had put into the early part of his career.

'If he's making a speech and he sees me there, he always acknowledges me,' said Trampler. 'Even as recently as the Pacquiao fight we were in the studios filming commercials for it and I walked in and he stopped the shoot, he walked over and hugged me, which I was surprised about because he knew I was on the Pacquiao side of it. But he was very gracious. I don't see him often even though we live in the same town, but he's never failed to be friendly and gracious.'

Pacquiao was still with HBO but they were going to work with Showtime and produce the event together, collaborating as they had done to eventually get the Lennox Lewis-Mike Tyson heavyweight fight on in 2002.

Lewis and Tyson were considered past their prime, certainly

Tyson was. Mayweather-Pacquiao, in boxing terms, was a far hotter match in 2010 than it was in 2015, but the five-year 'will they-won't they' saga had caused it to become the most talked-about event that could be made in all of sports.

Some said it was too late, that they no longer had interest in it because the acceptable time frame for it to be made had slammed shut.

Of course, the final numbers would be the judge of that.

Mayweather's WBC and WBA welterweight titles and Pacquiao's WBO crown were on the line.

Their respective training camps started in early March. Pacquiao and Roach worked together in the Wild Card Gym in LA, the Mayweathers trained at their Mayweather Boxing Club in Vegas.

Mayweather, who posted videos of himself chopping wood in training on social media, was able to call on former opponents and ex-world champions Zab Judah and DeMarcus Corley for left-handed work.

He'd used Corley for southpaw opponents before, bringing him in when he was preparing to face Judah and Sharmba Mitchell.

'It's always about work and business when we are around each other,' said Corley of Mayweather's focus in the gym. 'It's never no one-on-one time with me and him.'

Demand for tickets was unprecedented. Of the 16,800 in the MGM Grand, barely 1,000 were made available for the public and they vanished in seconds. According to one radio presenter, the MGM would not consider selling ringside seats to guests who did not have a $250,000 credit line with them. Some ringside seats changed hands for as much as $150,000.

Because of a row between Mayweather Promotions, Top Rank and the MGM over distribution of the tickets, they were not made available until 23 April, just nine days before the fight.

Again, Moonves had to intervene to get it done.

Officially, tickets were priced at $7,500, $5,000, $3,500, $2,500 and $1,500. There were also some $10,000 tickets, though they were not made public.

On the secondary market, some agencies started by offering floor seats (not ringside) for $45,000. The cheapest seats were attainable at between $5,000 and $7,500, a huge increase from their $1,500 face value.

Mayweather opened a 3-1 favourite, though Pacquiao started to close the gap as the fight approached. According to one journalist, Mayweather's former friend and rapper 50 Cent bet $1.6 million on his old pal winning.

Sean 'Diddy' Combs and actor Mark Wahlberg, who told the scripted story of the rivalry on the big screens before the fight, had a charity side bet of $250,000, with Wahlberg backing his friend Pacquiao.

The MGM Grand Resorts sportsbook anticipated seeing between $60 million and $80 million of action.

Fight week in Vegas was unlike any other. It was like The One for Álvarez, but on steroids. Gone was the usual media centre in the bowels of the MGM Grand, replaced by a sprawling tent just outside, catering for hundreds of journalists from around the world.

'The build-up to the Pacquiao fight was, of course, one of, if not the most incredible,' remembered Sky Sports' Adam Smith. 'There were 700-plus media and cameras at the initial press conference, plus fifteen-odd thousand at the weigh-in, which goes to show Floyd's astonishing magnetism.'

Pacquiao made his fight-week arrival over at the Mandalay Bay, where they'd set up a vast hangar-like structure to accommodate him, his fans and a few entertainers who kept the crowd fired up before he appeared.

'Don't get nervous,' Manny smiled, addressing the thousands

who'd shown up to see him oh so briefly. 'I'm the one who'll win the fight in the ring on Saturday. So relax.'

Meanwhile, hours before Mayweather's official arrival at the MGM Grand, throngs of fans had started to gather to catch a glimpse of him making his way through the hordes of visitors to Sin City.

Mayweather arrived in a TMT van and thanked the fans for turning out. 'Everybody that's in this arena is the Money Team,' he said. 'Of course I make a lot of money but I also like to give back.'

He didn't mention Pacquiao by name, and no one seemed to care. The time for talking was almost over.

The next day the fighters met at the final press conference and despite years of bickering between the two camps, there was no sign of a grudge.

'Pacquiao is a solid competitor,' Floyd said. 'He's a great fighter. He'll go down in the Hall of Fame. It'll be an intriguing matchup come Saturday. I've worked extremely hard during camp. I believe I'll be victorious.'

'My focus is the fight,' stated Pacquiao. 'I don't want to make a prediction but I'm excited, I'm confident. I'm ready for the fight. I'm thankful for all the support.

'My life before, I was sleeping in the street with nothing. I'm so blessed because I came from nothing to something. The most important thing for me is to let the people [know], to inspire them.'

Vegas buzzed like it had never buzzed before. They even charged admission to the weigh-in. It cost $10 per person to get into the MGM Grand Garden Arena with proceeds going to Pacquiao's charity of choice, the Cleveland Clinic Lou Ruvo Center for Brain Health, and to Mayweather's choice, the Susan G. Komen for the Cure Foundation.

Those weigh-in tickets were changing hands in secondary and tertiary markets for up to $600 as desperate fans scrambled to absorb any part of the week's festivities that they could.

The Pacquiao supporters, unsurprisingly, made the most raucous noise. Their man weighed in at 145lbs. Mayweather was 146lbs, one pound under the welterweight limit.

The next day, fight day, some media members queued for more than an hour in the blistering Las Vegas heat to collect their credentials. Some journalists, however, had been denied access.

There was no accreditation for Martin Rogers, who had filed an in-depth follow-up piece with Josie Harris for *USA Today*.

Rachel Nichols of CNN and Michelle Beadle of ESPN/HBO tweeted that the Mayweather camp had blocked them from going in, too.

Kelly Swanson, Mayweather's media relations guru, took to Twitter to say Nichols had a credential and that while Beadle was not on the press list, she had been credentialed through HBO.

Nichols had filmed a difficult interview with Mayweather on CNN the previous September, while Beadle had voiced disapproving opinions of the fighter in the past.

Not only did Rogers revisit the Harris incident and interview her once more, but a few months earlier, after US football player Ray Rice knocked his wife out cold in an elevator in Atlantic City, Mayweather offered a controversial opinion on the attack.

'I think there's a lot worse things that go on in other people's households, also,' he said to the Associated Press. 'It's just not caught on video, if that's safe to say.'

He also believed that Rice's initial two-game suspension by the NFL should have stood, rather than their decision to suspend him indefinitely.

Floyd later backtracked under heavy fire.

'If I offended anyone, I apologise,' he said. 'I didn't mean to offend anyone and I apologise to the NFL and anyone else that got offended. I'm not perfect. I make mistakes and I don't condone that at all.'

Nichols, on CNN, directly questioned Mayweather about his own past.

'You are someone with a history of domestic violence yourself, you've even been to jail for it, why should fans root for you with this kind of history?' she asked, bluntly.

'Everything has been allegations, nothing has been proven,' he replied.

'The incident you went to jail for, the mother of your three children did show some bruising, had a concussion when she went to hospital, it was your own kids who called the police and gave them a detailed description of the abuse. There's been documentation,' she went on.

'Once again, no pictures, just hearsay and allegations and I signed a plea bargain, so once again, not true.'

'But the website Deadspin recently detailed seven separate physical assaults on women that resulted in five arrests or citation, are we really supposed to believe all these women are lying – including the incidents when there are witnesses like your own kids?'

'Everybody is entitled to their own opinion. When it's all said and done, only God can judge me.'

Nichols then said the USA needed the big issue of domestic violence addressed, and asked whether he would consider donating any of his pay-per-view bonanza from the Maidana rematch to organisations that educate against and prevents abuse.

'What I will do is make sure millions and millions of dollars are saved for my children, because my children are who I love and that's who I care about,' he replied.

Rogers ended up watching Mayweather-Pacquiao on a closed-circuit screen inside the Excalibur Hotel and Casino on the other side of the Strip.

'A lot of people said the atmosphere was actually better in the closed circuits than in the arena because in the arena you had mainly wealthy people and celebrities who don't really stand up and cheer and scream,' he explained, 'whereas in the other venues you get a few more drunk people who get into it.

'It [the ban] didn't really interfere with my coverage of the fight. I got into the weigh-in, the press conference on the Wednesday was screened live on TV and nobody said anything at that anyway. I was able to get full access to the Pacquiao camp so it didn't bother me that much.

'My big thing is, and I think I would have taken a different tack, is except for the fact that he continues to deny it. That was the big thing for me. I feel that if someone serves their time and they show a degree of remorse then it doesn't mean you shouldn't mention it but it gives them a little bit more of a free path. The American public has this incredible capacity to forgive, look at Michael Vick, the American Football player who was done for dog fighting. No one thought he would play again and he's had a long career since he came out of prison. People can and do forgive but they do want to see remorse and Mayweather's never shown it. Not only has he not shown remorse but he's lied, and he's called his son a liar, and he's called his ex-wife a liar. He's called police liars. And he's basically said that something he's admitted guilt for and went to prison for didn't really happen. Well, if it didn't really happen why did you plead guilty and take prison time?

'To me, there is zero doubt that it happened. There is zero doubt. And whatever sparked it off, whatever went down, it doesn't actually matter. The point is he was physically violent and aggressive to a woman and that's unacceptable. So put your hands up – and he could spin it. It would be easy for him to say, "I've made mistakes in my past, but I've learned from them and I'm a changed man." He would come out of that looking better. But no, he digs his heels in. I'll be honest, I don't like the way it's been written about in the American press, about how it's been described as "an altercation involving a former girlfriend."

'I mean, sure, it's not false but she wasn't really a former girlfriend, she's the mother of three of his four children. She was a significant person in his life and an altercation is if you and I shove each other outside the pub, not bursting into someone's house and punching and kicking them in the head. There's a difference. That was why I wrote about it and continue to, and the fact that there was still no admission or remorse.

'Mayweather has permanent access to the American media. Anything he says is reported, so all it would have taken is one time for him to say, "I did this, I'm sorry. I'll always regret it. I hope to be forgiven for it." And instantly, within minutes, people would be saying, "Oh, wonderful, Floyd. Well done, Floyd. Good for you for standing up," and honestly, from that point on, there isn't much more you can write about it, because everyone knows it happened and the only thing that's kept it in the media is the fact that he denied it.'

Rogers has been at roundtable interviews with Mayweather since his first story came out, but Floyd has not said anything to him directly.

'His tack on something like that,' Rogers asserted, 'is that if there's anything critical, it's generally to pretend that it doesn't exist. And sometimes, maybe to him it doesn't. I don't know how much he reads of the press, I don't how much of the supposed backlash is him or some of the people around him and honestly I don't care. When I did a positive story about his friend John Shahidi, who is an entrepreneur and lives in Silicon Valley and who started up the Shots app [which Mayweather constantly endorses on social media], he's a big friend of Floyd's and Justin Bieber's, and I did a piece on Shahidi and their relationship and so forth and Floyd's account retweeted it. Now I don't know if that's Floyd being on Twitter or if someone manages his social media but it doesn't bother me either way. I'm not a boxing-beat guy so I'm not at every fight. It doesn't mean the end of my job or it doesn't make my job that much more difficult if a famous boxer, famous footballer or famous NBA player is pissed off at me about something.

'I like Josie. I feel sorry for what's happened to her and I admire her in a way because it would have been very easy for her to really portray Floyd in a different way.

'She still defends him to a certain extent and I believe she's a good mother and she's done a good job of protecting her kids from what happened with the incident and to a certain extent the crazy life of Mayweather.

'Obviously he sees the kids, but from what I can see – and it's a limited snapshot – she's done a good job of helping them grow up to be normal kids, albeit with a famous last name. The first time I spoke with her, when I was at Yahoo, I was with her a long time – four or five hours around the time of the Guerrero fight. I went to her house and she told that story and by the time this one came around it was at a new publication and Floyd continued to deny it and there was the fact that domestic violence in sports was very much the hot topic of the time because Ray Rice, the American football player, had attacked his wife. It was on video, and the way the NFL handled that situation was very much a topic that was not just in sports, even President Obama spoke about it, it was a hugely sensitive topic and I thought it was time to revisit it.

'But they [Mayweather and Harris] see each other. 'Sometimes it's not just the kids flying out to see Mayweather, sometimes Josie will be there as well and I see clips on YouTube of events they've been at and Josie is there and then Melissa Brim, the mother of his other kid is there, and his current girlfriend is there, and a bunch of other women are there. Who knows what really goes on? And it's not something I can pretend to fully understand.'

Of course, the good guy-bad guy dynamic for Mayweather-Pacquiao was in play.

Pacquiao had worked his way up from poverty to become a national icon, an international star and a congressman in the Philippines who always gave back to his people. One athlete inspired a nation, the other – at times – had been loathed by one.

Mayweather, or his alter-ego at least, was the villain. He felt it would be his defining night. 'I worked my whole life to get to this point,' he said. 'I was destined to be where I'm at. My life was supposed to play out like this. I was born to be a winner. I'm happy with my life. I don't hate on people. Some people say I'm an asshole, but I don't hurt nobody. I got a heart. God must love me, because look where I'm at.'

While journalists and fans jockeyed for access to the fight, plenty of well-known people were allowed in.

Beyoncé was there with Jay-Z, so were Ben Affleck, Mark Wahlberg, Don Cheadle, Sugar Ray Leonard, Mike Tyson, Michael Jordan and Yvette Prieto, Tom Brady, Donald Trump, Sean Combs, Jon Voight, Nicole Scherzinger, Drew Barrymore, Nicki Minaj, Andre Agassi and Steffi Graf, Christina Milian and dozens of others from the A and B lists.

There were so many celebrities and high-rollers in town for the event that McCarran International closed its clogged runways to private planes later in the day after the rich and famous parked up and headed for the Strip.

A hoarse Michael Buffer introduced Pacquiao; Jimmy Lennon announced Mayweather's arrival.

Pacquiao and Roach took a selfie together before starting the ringwalk to history's richest fight. Talkshow host Jimmy Kimmel walked by Pacquiao's side. A shattering roar from the crowd greeted him as he stepped between the ropes and waited for Mayweather, who was flanked by Justin Bieber and was booed the instant his image showed on the big screens in the venue. A Burger King mascot also found his way into the Mayweather entourage, with the fast food chain paying a reported $1 million for the privilege.

Jamie Foxx sang the 'Star-Spangled Banner'.

Mayweather was a couple of years older and, after rehydrating, Pacquiao was 152lbs the next day. He'd put on 7lbs. Interestingly, Mayweather had refused to get on the scales again although he was not required to having made the agreed poundage.

HBO's Jim Lampley and Showtime's Al Bernstein called the action in the US, accompanied by former pound-for-pound general Roy Jones.

In the opening round, Mayweather twice hit the incoming Filipino with stern right hands on his way to securing the initial session.

The 'Man-ny, Man-ny' roars encouraged him to be more bold in the second but Mayweather's speed made the difference in a tight round.

'Don't walk into him,' instructed Freddie Roach. 'Forward, then combinations.'

The crowd remained on edge in the third. Mayweather held Pacquiao tight when he came in to let his hands fly, and then Pacquiao ducked too low beneath a right hand and stood up under Floyd as it started to get scrappy.

Referee Kenny Bayless (who was paid a record $25,000 for the night) had to separate them a couple of times but Mayweather, moving on the back foot, caused Pacquiao to swing and miss multiple attempts as the session closed.

'You're doing the right thing, hitting him with the right hand,' said Floyd Sr. 'Come back with the hook.'

Pacquiao's approach to the fourth was more composed and measured. He let his punches go when in range and, because of his patience, he was able to slot a straight left hand speedily over a Mayweather jab. Floyd jolted backwards, towards the ropes. The crowd rose as one and as Pacquiao bombed forwards behind both hands it confirmed what many of them had hoped. Mayweather had been shaken. Mayweather cupped his gloves together in front of his face and brought his elbows into his sides, shutting up shop and closing down potential targets.

The crowd went crazy when Pacquiao flew in behind a right hook and as the round closed there was a buzz that the fight might just live up to the hype, if that was at all possible.

But Mayweather seized the upper hand again in the fifth, scoring with right leads that initially slowed Pacquiao's charge, and then backed him up.

Mayweather's right to the body, a factor from the start, was unfurled with class in the sixth. The Mayweather jab broke up Pacquaiao's rhythm and the right hand picked up points for Floyd.

'I'm telling you right now, they're going to take this fight from you,' said Floyd Sr urgently in the corner.

After six, HBO's Harold Lederman had it all square. Showtime's Steve Farhood had Floyd two rounds up, scoring 4-2.

The pace slowed through the seventh and eighth sessions and even though Floyd earned them, his father was still not content.

'You ain't even threw a hook yet,' he shouted. 'Hit him with a right hand then throw a hook, man. Back him up.'

Pacquiao only enjoyed spots of success, a jab or body shot here and there, as Mayweather began to waltz away with it. The excitement and vigour was exiting the atmosphere by the round as Pacquiao, an attacking force who always used angles to work his way in, chugged forwards in bleak straight lines.

The 'Man-ny' chants were now hopeful and forlorn as the championship rounds went by.

Roach urged Pacquiao to throw combinations in round twelve. With ten seconds left, Mayweather punched his glove into the air to celebrate his victory and the final bell was greeted by boos.

It was one of the biggest fights of all time, but it fell a long way short of being one of the best.

'I know I won,' shouted Mayweather, marching around the ring and beating his chest. Pacquiao, on a team aide's shoulders, received a warming ovation based on a lifetime of achievement if not the night alone.

The scores of 118-110 and two lots of 116-112 saw Mayweather extend his unbeaten streak to forty-eight. More than that, he'd put the Pacquiao argument to bed. Finally.

'I take my hat off to Manny Pacquiao,' he said. 'Now I see why he's one of the guys who's at the pinnacle of the sport of boxing.'

'I knew he was going to push it and win some rounds. He had moments in the fight but I kept him on the outside, I was a smart fighter and I outboxed him. I wasn't getting hit with a lot of shots until I sat right there in the pocket, that's when he would land a lot of shots. My last fight is in September, then it's time for me to hang it up. I'm almost forty years old, I've been in the sport nineteen years and I've been a champion for eighteen years.'

Pacquiao said it was a good fight and he thought he won. 'He didn't do nothing, he was always running,' he said. Even from a pro-Pacquiao crowd, that response provoked a mixture of groans and laughs. He said he would have a vacation and Bob Arum would take care of the rest of his future in the ring.

It was not a wonderful spectacle, even if the occasion was grandiose. Some experts had anticipated as much, predicting that if Pacquiao was unable to drag Mayweather into the trenches then fans would be left watching just another high-class boxing display.

'It always perplexed me,' said ESPN's Dan Rafael, when asked why so many expected fireworks. 'When the Pacquiao fight was finally made and people were so excited, I was happy because I wanted to see it like everybody else, but I wasn't a guy who said this was going to be one of the greatest fights of all time. To be honest, the fight went exactly how I thought it would go. If you're buying a Mayweather fight because you think it's going to be Ali-Frazier or Gatti-Ward, Morales-Barrera or some other epic fight it's your fault because you don't know what you're getting. If you have an understanding of the type of boxer that he is, you need to have an appreciation for a guy who can move and box and mix it up here and there but it's not going to be a knockdown, drag-out kind of fight. So I wasn't disappointed with the Pacquiao fight, or any other Mayweather fight, because they basically go how you think they're going to go. You have to have an appreciation for, as he likes to talk about, the ability to hit and not get hit. Mayweather, I've never thought of as a guy who runs from his opponents, he's just got great movement. It's the same for people who liked to watch Pernell Whitaker also. But he has this certain popularity in the mainstream and people buy his fights even though it's rarely satisfying from an action standpoint. There's been a few, more recently, let's say the Maidana or Cotto fights, but they've largely been exercise in seeing Mayweather totally shut down his opponent.'

Regardless of action, or lack thereof, the fight was a box office and pay-per-view monster. Everyone knew it would be big, but even the most ballsy estimations fell well short of how well it would do.

Those astronomical ticket prices created a live gate of $72,198,500 (the previous record was just over $20 million for Mayweather-Álvarez) from the sale of 16,219 seats.

The pay-per-view record of 2.4 million (from De La Hoya-Mayweather) was annihilated with Mayweather-Pacquiao coming in at 4.4 million buys, generating more than $400 million. In the US, to watch at home, fans were charged a record $89.95 in standard definition, $99.95 if they wanted the high-definition alternative.

Other approximates included a $40 million income in international rights from 175 countries. There was $13.2 million in sponsorship, including the beer Tecate paying $5.6 million, setting a new record as chief sponsor.

Closed circuit revenue from bars and theatres came in just shy of $20 million and there was a further $6.9 million from a staggering 46,000 people in Las Vegas who paid $150 each to watch it on screens in other MGM Resorts properties in Sin City. The sale of merchandise was several million more.

The cash registers 'ca-chinged' for months afterwards as both fighters waited to find out what their final earnings would be.

In the meantime, however, Pacquiao used the post-fight press conference to say he had been concealing a shoulder injury, which he had suffered a few weeks before the fight and that had hampered his performance.

According to CompuBox, the Filipino both threw and landed fewer punches in the fight than in any of his previous bouts that went to the scorecards. In total, he landed eighty-one of just 429 punches. When he had obliterated Antonio Margarito four years earlier, he hurled more than 1,000 punches, and landed 474.

Mayweather had shut down that usually dependable and violent attacking style, though Pacquiao blamed the injury rather than the opponent.

Roach said the injury had happened in sparring. 'They were both throwing hooks and they caught arms and clashed,' Roach said. Pacquiao was assessed at the Kerlan Jobe Orthopaedic Clinic in Los Angeles, and told to rest his shoulder for between thirty and forty days. It was mid-April; the fight was on 2 May.

Rather than postpone, he used painkilling, anti-inflammatory and healing drugs that had been approved by the United States Anti-Doping Agency. It also put a stop to sparring for a week.

Pacquiao gambled that it would be okay on the night but in the third round, he said, the pain came back. 'We didn't throw a lot of combinations because it hurt,' he said. 'The thing is, what we wanted to do we could not do because of my shoulder.'

On 1 May, when the Nevada State Athletic Commission had Pacquiao complete a medical questionnaire, he failed to check the box that asked whether he'd had any injuries to his shoulders, though lidocaine, bupivacaine, Celestone, PRP and Toradol were listed as medications he was taking.

Pacquiao's manager, Michael Koncz, said he filled out the form on Manny's behalf.

Before the fight, in the dressing room, Pacquiao's team asked the physician if they could inject the Filipino with Toradol, a legal non-steroidal, painkilling, anti-inflammatory drug. The commission denied it because they had not been made aware of the injury.

A post-fight MRI revealed a rotator cuff tear, a 'significant one'.

It required surgery four days after the bout and it would be six months before he could train and around nine to twelve months before he would be able to compete again.

Mayweather felt the excuse was hollow.

'I'm not going to buy into the bullshit,' he said. 'And I don't want the public to buy into the bullshit. He lost. He knows he lost. I lost a lot of respect for him after all of this.'

Plenty of fight fans agreed. More than forty lawsuits were filed against Pacquiao by aggrieved customers for failing to declare his injury.

Roach reckoned the outcome would have been different had Pacquiao and Floyd met when Manny was smoking hot, in around 2010.

'Four, five years ago? Yes, of course,' he said. 'But fighters fight and injuries happen. I don't know if I ever went into a fight one hundred per cent when I was a fighter but people have injuries and boxing is a combat sport and sometimes fights go for you and sometimes they don't. We thought we had it under control, enough to win the fight and obviously we didn't. We'd love a rematch and obviously what Manny needs to do to get a rematch is fight a good fight with somebody and show everybody he is healthy, and with Manny healthy I think we do win that fight.'

Pacquiao's delayed disclosure saw him manage to steal Mayweather's bad-guy role. But regardless of the injury, and whether you thought the fight featured high-class skill or not, it had left an unhappily sour taste.

'A bore,' *The Ring* magazine called it. 'From a sporting perspective,' wrote *Boxing News*, 'a sense of disappointment pervaded the atmosphere in the arena following the fight, and no doubt the feeling was the same for the millions watching in bars and households across the globe.'

Forbes website felt it was 'arguably, the least entertaining "mega fight" in memory' while Bill Dwyre, in the *Los Angeles Times*, thought the contest had been 'as compelling as the 405 freeway at 8 a.m.'

The fighters needn't have worried about that. Even before final calculations were made Mayweather's purse was heading towards $230 million for the night; Pacquiao's recuperation could take place with upwards of $150 million to soften the blow. It turned out he'd been right to snub the $40 million offer. Financially, it worked for them that they fought when they did, though from a sporting perspective, it would have been best served at the end of 2009. Pacquiao's short-lived fourth-round success against Mayweather indicated the type of fight it might have been had he still been able to box at his offensive best.

But five years earlier it might not have reeled in more than $600 million.

Mayweather believed the outcome rubber-stamped his greatness.

'Everybody that said throughout the years that I was a coward,

I was scared, he couldn't beat Pacquiao,' he said. 'They gave him this. They gave him so many accolades and he's an all-time great.

'But all these people had to eat their words. So if he's an all-time great, then what does that make me? If they're saying he's the fighter of the century, what does that make me?

'So when they do rate me and when my fight is over, the only thing I can do is believe in myself and believe in my skills. I'm going to be "The Best Ever" till the day I die.'

It was not the Fight of the Century. The most disappointed fans wished that chance encounter at the Heat-Bucks game had never even happened. It was a heist, of sorts. Or, as they'd say in the Mayweather camp, the bank dropped.

FIFTEEN

FOR THE RECORD

THE DAY BEFORE Floyd Mayweather decisively outscored Manny Pacquiqo in the richest fight in history, collection agents from the United States Anti-Doping Agency (USADA) attended Mayweather's Las Vegas mansion, unannounced, to test him.

They found evidence that an IV had been used.

Investigative boxing journalist Thomas Hauser, who also wrote the brilliant authorised Muhammad Ali biography, *His Life and Times*, penned a detailed look into the USADA findings the Wednesday before Mayweather went 49-0 against an overmatched Andre Berto. His absorbing feature was published on the SB Nation website.

USADA agents, Hauser said, discovered that the IV had been used to help Floyd rehydrate. USADA was informed that it included two mixes, one was 250 ml of saline and multi-vitamins, the other was a 500 ml mix of saline and vitamin C.

The World Anti-Doping Agency (WADA), which sets the standards for USADA to follow, does not ban either mix, although it is prohibited for them to be used intravenously.

It is prohibited to put different substances into an athlete's body without a therapeutic use exemption (TUE), and it is also prohibited because IV infusions can dilute and even mask the presence of other substances that are already in one's system.

A therapeutic use exemption can be granted only by the local authority, in this instance, the Nevada State Athletic Commission (NSAC).

One was given to Mayweather, eighteen days after the fight, and by USADA, not the NSAC.

Victor Conte spent four months in jail as the founder and president of BALCO (Bay Area Laboratory Co-operative), which was the hub of several huge performance-enhancing drugs scandals. He pleaded guilty to distributing steroids and to tax fraud in 2005 but on his release became a force for good and started to make amends with an attempt to clean up sport. He has also worked with several fighters.

He said that USADA usually charges around $25,000 to carry out their testing for each fight. According to Hauser, it cost $36,000 to test for the Andy Lee-Peter Quillin WBO middleweight title contest in April 2015, a month before Mayweather-Pacquiao.

However, USADA's contract for Mayweather-Pacquiao testing indicates they were paid $150,000 up front.

Conte finds that troubling and admits Hauser's article overshadowed a fight week he was part of as a training advisor to Berto.

'It became the story of the event,' said Conte.

'The people with Mayweather were not happy,' he went on, about how he was quoted extensively in Hauser's article. 'I can tell you, he [Mayweather] refused to do interviews. I did an interview with ESPN, thereafter they refused to do an interview with ESPN. I talked to Comcast and gave them questions and when the Mayweather PR team learned that I had prepped them, they refused to do the interview. There was a lot of dissension. A lot of people asked me what I thought and I said, "Thomas Hauser is a truth speaker. There's a lot of suspicious questions that need answers." Like why does every other fighter that does testing pay in the neighbourhood – and I've got multiple contracts – of $24,000 and Mayweather pays $150,000. What's he getting for this extra $125,000?'

Conte is also extremely knowledgeable about testing protocols, and contends that there are many drugs that athletes could use that USADA does not test for, including IGF-1 LR3 (insulin-like growth factor-1), liothyronine (T3 or Cytomel brand), thyroid medication, Humalog insulin (fast acting) for recovery, synthetic testosterone (micro-dosing or fast-acting orals, gels and creams) and adrenaline.

They also don't employ carbon isotope ratio (CIR) testing for every sample, and that detects synthetic testosterone, which is one of the more commonly used substances by cheats.

'The whole approach they have, in my opinion, is more about propaganda than it is about catching athletes,' he said.

Mayweather announced the Berto fight on 4 August; thirty-nine days before their 12 September meeting.

'The period of time,' Conte added, 'I know because I was working with Berto, there was only five weeks of testing. The very first week he [Berto] was tested twice by USADA and once by the state athletic commission, and they were testing him a couple of times a week. There was extensive testing, but it's no different to anybody else, so I just don't understand why [it would cost so much more].

'He [Mayweather] turns the testing on and off. So in other words he finishes a fight, it is very gruelling, very strenuous and then what happens? What happened from May the second after Pacquiao until five weeks before the fight with Berto on September twelfth? So May, June, July? What was going on in those three months? Probably no testing. And once the opponent is selected, and we don't know if that's going to be eight weeks, six weeks, Floyd determines that, then it's, "By the way, you're my opponent and testing starts now." That, to me, is not what WADA [World Anti-Doping Agency] code is all about. They call it Olympic-style testing. Mayweather has said this for years. He's never, ever, done Olympic-style testing because at the very core of that definition is

24/7/365 and that is not what Floyd Mawyeather has been doing. We now know that you can use the drugs in conjunction with intense weight training and develop an extensive strength and speed base that serves you months and months later [after you stop taking PEDs]. Do I believe USADA knows this? Yes, I do. Do I believe WADA knows this? Yes, I do. Why do I believe it? Because I told them face to face, "This is what they [athletes] are doing, here's where they're circumventing. You need to reverse this."'

Conte also cannot understand how a TUE was granted – after the testing, eighteen days post fight – retrospectively.

'A retroactive therapeutic use exemption?' he pondered. 'That's not WADA code. They don't say stuff like, "Oh, we found you used prohibited, so let's go back and give you a doctor's note." I mean, god. The Nevada State Athletic Commission has the ultimate jurisdiction and they are the ones that would issue any sort of consequence or suspension. They did not approve it and there was a lack of communication, with USADA thinking that they are the ultimate authority when they're not.

'Someone needs to ask Travis Tygart [CEO of USADA] that question, "Was it medically indicated, and if not why did you grant it? And when you did grant it, why was it eighteen days after the fight?"'

Conte is not a fan of using IV for rehydration anyway, believing something like Celtic sea salt, taken orally, is just as adequate.

'There's lots of things that create suspicion,' Conte concluded. 'So am I suspicious of Floyd Mayweather and the use of PEDs? Yes, I'm suspicious. Do I know with absolute certainty that he has used PEDs? I do not.'

WADA code says that samples should be saved for up to ten years.

Conte would like federal law enforcement to dig deeper and he thinks boxing has a problem with PEDs.

'Thirteen years ago, when the BALCO raid happened, I went on television and I said, "There is no Santa Claus, Easter Bunny or Tooth Fairy at the elite level sport." There's rampant use of PEDs, and I guesstimated that as much as eighty per cent of people at the very top of sport are using PEDs. Not many people wanted to listen to me. Years later, and much more has been revealed, and now we know there's been a rampant use of PEDs, and I believe that to be the case in boxing as well.'

A USADA statement, which failed to address many points – including why Mayweather's costs are far higher than others – stated that there were 'numerous unfounded and false accusations . . . in recent online articles,' referring to Hauser's piece and the fall-out on the web.

They said that 'Subject to the rules of the WADA Code, he [Mayweather] took the additional step of applying for a TUE after the IV infusion was administered in order remain in compliance with the USADA programme. Although Mr Mayweather's application was not approved until after his fight with Mr Pacquiao and all tests results were reported, Mr Mayweather did disclose the infusion to USADA in advance of the IV being administered to him. Furthermore, once the TUE was granted, the NSAC and Mr Pacquiao were immediately notified even though the practice is not prohibited under NSAC rules.'

Mayweather denied that he had committed any violations. 'I follow and have always followed the rules of Nevada and USADA, the gold standard of drug testing,' he said in a statement. 'Let's not forget that I was the one six years ago who insisted on elevating the level of drug testing for all my fights. As a result, there is more drug testing and awareness of its importance in the sport of boxing today than ever before. I am very proud to be a clean athlete and will continue to champion the cause.'

In another exploratory feature years earlier, in May 2012,

Hauser had picked up on the rumour in 'the drug-testing community' that Mayweather had posted positive results on three occasions for an illegal performance-enhancing drug.

The specifics, Hauser heard, were that Mayweather's 'A' sample was three times tested as positive but on each occasion USADA had found 'exceptional circumstances' – via inadvertent use – to grant Mayweather a waiver, thus meaning he did not have to provide a 'B' test.

According to Hauser, 'a loophole in USADA's contract with Mayweather and Golden Boy allowed the testing to proceed without the positive "A" sample results being reported to Mayweather's opponent or the Nevada State Athletic Commission [which had jurisdiction over the fights].'

This information became relevant during the 'peace' talks with Team Pacquiao after the Filipino's lawyers filed the defamation suit against the Mayweathers, and others.

Pacquiao's name was slurred by numerous allegations.

Floyd Mayweather Sr said, '[Pacquiao] can't beat Clottey without that shit in him. He couldn't beat De La Hoya without that shit. He couldn't beat Ricky Hatton without that shit. And he couldn't beat Cotto without that shit. I don't even think he could beat that kid from Chicago [David Díaz] without that shit. He wouldn't be able to beat any of those guys without enhancement drugs.'

Roger was of the same opinion. 'This motherfucker don't want to take the test. That's why the fight [Mayweather-Pacquiao] didn't happen. He got that shit in him. That's why he didn't want to take the test.'

At the end of May, and with Pacquiao's lawyers armed with the rumour, they served papers – demands and subpoenas – to Mayweather, Mayweather Promotions, Golden Boy and USADA calling for them to produce all documents relating to Floyd's fights with Shane Mosley, Victor Ortiz and Miguel Cotto.

Some alleged a cover-up by USADA and Golden Boy. Regardless of that, soon after Mayweather was released from prison, a settlement was swiftly agreed. Its contents had to remain confidential but Mayweather's first offer in talks was 'substantially more' than Pacquiao's advisors had expected.

Around the time of the Berto fight, some wondered whether the noble art had its own Lance Armstrong.

'I've long felt it and said it, that he's the Lance Armstrong of boxing,' opined fight writer Gabriel Montoya, who has spent more than five years investigating the use of performance-enhancing drugs in the sport.

Some felt Colombian-born strength and conditioning coach Alex Ariza had been the smoking gun in the Pacquiao camp. He now operates out of the Mayweather Boxing Club, but Pacquiao – or other athletes Ariza trained – had never tested positive. That was until he started working with rugged lightweight brawler Brandon Ríos, who posted a positive test when, ironically, he fought Pacquiao in Macau at the end of 2013. Ariza contends that the sample was contaminated when Ríos had to urinate into a glass rather than a container that was used specifically for collections. He also said the supplement, dimethylamylamine, was one that could be in anything Ríos had bought over the counter and was not a PED.

Another face at the Mayweather Boxing Club is strength and conditioning coach Bob Ware, a hand-wrapping specialist who Mayweather Promotions fighter J'Leon Love testified had given him an illegal weight-loss supplement.

Then there is Mexican coach Angel 'Memo' Heredia, a former discus thrower who was doping as an athlete and, as a chemist, supplied dozens of athletes with illegal, undetectable substances to boost their performance.

Ariza, Ware and Heredia have all become regulars at the Mayweather Boxing Club.

'I do not know whether or not Floyd Mayweather is using illegal PEDs,' said Hauser. 'If I had to guess, I would guess that he is. Again, I don't know that he is. We all understand, he can talk all he wants about doing Olympic-style testing but Olympic testing is 365 days a year, twenty-four hours a day, this is the antithesis of that. Floyd dictates when the testing starts. What Floyd does is they sign a contract for the fight, they sign a contract for USADA testing and then the testing starts. They have something like six weeks of testing for the Pacquiao fight and anybody who knows anything about PEDs will tell you that if you're a fighter you get the most benefit from them not when you're actually on them but after you're off them. Again, do I know Floyd Mayweather is using PEDs? No. Do I suspect that he is? Yes.'

Montoya speculates it could go back further.

Mayweather's old guardian, Don Hale, opened a number of anti-ageing clinics in Tennessee, Florida and Grand Rapids, Michigan, offering 'bioidentical hormone replacement therapy', also known as hormone replacement therapy. But after a two-year court battle in Tennessee, Hale's clinics were shut down in the state because of 'patient safety and possible overdoses'.

Regulators closed the company, freezing Hale's assets.

According to News Channel 5, 'The state attorney general's office has now asked the judge to hold the Hales in contempt for failing to disclose monthly expenses and income, including tens of thousands of dollars that Hale received from Mayweather.'

'They got shut down for illegal prescriptions, selling testosterone and HGH [Human Growth Hormone],' said Montoya.

With all the talk of PEDs, the Berto fight did not turn into the record-breaking victory lap Mayweather would have been hoping for. Rather than celebrate how he managed to match Rocky Marciano's unblemished 49-0 statistics, fingers of suspicion were pointed. Of course, there were some voices who continued to praise Mayweather for his drive to clean up the sport.

But there was criticism from other quarters, too, concerning the choice of Berto as an opponent to sign off against. Of course, no one was going to match the wild hedonism of the Pacquiao fight week but the Haitian made for an anticlimactic and uninspired choice.

He had lost three of his previous five fights and two of the boxers to defeat him in Mayweather auditions, Guerrero and Ortiz, had subsequently been handled easily by Floyd. He had also been stopped by the game but limited underdog Jesús Soto Karass, after boxing most of the fight with an injured right shoulder.

There was a greater clamour for Mayweather to fight someone like Englishman Amir Khan, a boxer who might at least be able to challenge Mayweather in the speed department, or an undefeated young gun like Sheffield's IBF champion Kell Brook, Philadelphia's Danny García or the big-punching, big-talking Floridian Keith Thurman.

But increasingly shop-worn Berto got the call.

Floyd even seemed unmoved to promote the fight with his usual gusto.

'Talking trash is part of boxing,' he said. 'I'm at the level now that I don't have to do it. I did it, for years, and I had a brilliant game plan, be flashy, be flamboyant, talk trash and back it up. And that's what I did.'

He said over and over that the Berto contest, the sixth and final one in his Showtime deal, would be the last of his career. He said he would leave the sport, tied with Marciano, at 49-0. The 50-0 record was of no interest.

He'd achieved all he wanted to. 'I know that the end is coming,' he said. 'It's something that I can accept.'

Historians pointed out that Mexico's wondrous little man, Ricardo López, had bowed out undefeated after fifty-two fights, though a draw (even though it was 'avenged') blotted that 51-0-1 record, and that the great Julio César Chávez made it all the way to 87-0 before taking a controversial draw to fellow all-time great Pernell Whitaker.

Mayweather did not care about that.

'When I say [I'm] TBE [The Best Ever], it's no disrespect to no legendary champion,' he said at a gathering for the Nevada Boxing Hall of Fame before the Berto fight. 'Every fighter in this room has to feel that he's the best. If not, you're in the wrong sport. I had a great career. No fighter in history has done what Floyd Mayweather has done. And we're just speaking facts.'

There had been little to write about in fight week before the PED story broke. Until then, the biggest news in the build-up had been that Mayweather sparred in public during his media workout – something he did not normally do – and that he attended that training session driving a Koenigsegg CCXR Trevita hyper-car, one of only two in existence.

'This is his biggest payday, what's he getting, $4 million?' said Mayweather of his opponent. 'I got a car out there for $4.8 million, round it up to $5 million. Be appreciative, kiddo. Don't be picky.'

The wealth and pomposity stayed through another *All Access* series – albeit one that showed him forming tight relationships with his four children – with Floyd saying to a crowd of impressed onlookers that he had to hold a wad of money in one hand to keep him motivated while he used the other mitt on the heavybag.

Yes, history of sorts was going to be made, but ultimately, only in front of a smaller crowd of 13,395, with fans able to buy tickets all the way through a quiet and more subdued fight week until the day of the contest.

The bout itself went as advertised. Some felt Mayweather might be able to stop his challenger, such was the gap in class. He spent vast amounts of time picking Berto off with lead rights, countering with left hooks, and scoring points with his right into the pit of Berto's torso.

Before the final session of Floyd's career, the Showtime cameras visited his corner.

'Everything is done already,' said his father, knowing it was in the bag.

'I've been looking back on my career,' his son started. 'Everything you taught me from day one, I'll always remember.'

'Everything's good,' said his dad.

Floyd thanked his corner team, stood and hugged Floyd Sr.

'I love you,' his father beamed.

'I love you, my father,' Floyd replied, on his way back out to battle.

Berto, the challenger and former two-time world champion was in there pitching until the final bell, even though by then it was a lost cause.

When it was finished, Mayweather sank to his knees in the middle of the ring and looked skywards.

'It was finally over,' he said.

Two of the judges sympathised with Berto's efforts, one did not, as they handed down scores of 120-108, 118-110 and 117-111.

The punchstats indicated what Floyd had done throughout his career; he made his opponents miss and made them pay.

According to CompuBox, he landed 232 of 410 punches at a rate of fifty-seven per cent. Berto managed to score with just eighty-three of 495 shots (for seventeen per cent). Mayweather was accurate going forwards and defensively adept. He did what he does, no more and no less.

Floyd took plenty of time to speak to the media at the post-fight press conference. He encouraged them to fire their questions at him because it would be the last chance they would have to see him there. Not many felt that would be the case. The majority assumed there would be an assault on Marciano's record, the chance to go 50-0, in May 2016, perhaps even in the new MGM Arena on the Strip that will accommodate 20,000 fans. Mayweather said he had already received nine-figure offers to fight on.

'You got to know when to hang it up, and it's time for me to hang it up,' Floyd maintained. 'I'm not going to be doing this when I'm forty years old.

'There's nothing else for me to do in the sport of boxing. I made great investments. I'm financially stable, well off. I had a great career. My record speaks for itself.'

The fight toiled at the box office to the extent that it was Mayweather's worst performance on pay-per-view – something he had long since started calling May-per-view – dating all the way back to the Baldomir fight in 2006. Some estimates had the Berto fight doing less than 500,000 buys, though Showtime was not releasing the official figures.

Regardless, Mayeather was guaranteed a minimum $32 million. Profit margins would be far tighter for everybody else. Yet he did not mind that he was leaving on a box-office downer. There were more important things to consider. He was five months shy of his thirty-ninth birthday.

'My career is over,' he repeated. 'I'm leaving with all my faculties; I'm still sharp and smart. I've accomplished everything. There's nothing left to accomplish.'

Floyd was not a young man anymore. Lines jotted up and down his face. His body had worked hard for him for more than twenty years. He knew, too, that not all fighters come out of the fight game unscathed.

During the Nevada Boxing Hall of Fame evening a few days before the fight, Roger Mayweather, now fifty-four, was presented with an award. Floyd spoke on his behalf. He had to. The signs of a hard career in boxing were eminently visible.

Dementia pugilistica had struck.

'Roger is not a hundred per cent,' Floyd said softly. 'The only thing my uncle cares about is coming to the gym and training but I feel like his memory has went away a lot, from getting hit with a lot of big shots in fights, from taking a lot of punishment in fights. The only thing we can do is continue to help Roger get better.'

'Boxing is wear and tear on the body,' he told Fight Hype, a website he's always given exclusives to. 'My uncle Roger, I love him dearly and it hurts me extremely bad that he don't even know who I am no more. Today he was not at the gym, he wandered off and got lost and went somewhere so we have to have different people from our team and our staff out looking for Roger because they don't know where he went. A day before we fought Pacquiao, Roger walked from the MGM Grand to his house. That's twenty miles. Probably more. We are working on getting Roger some help. We have to get him a caretaker, we're working on getting him the best health and that's what's really important right now . . . There are days when I think, "Hopefully my uncle doesn't pass away", and he's only in his fifties.'

Roger still wanted to be in the gym, but he was no longer the same trainer with the same sharp, analytical mind. Punch routines he'd spent a lifetime rehearsing had deserted him.

'He has forgot a lot of the combinations,' Floyd continued. 'And it's getting worse and worse. It hurts. And that's a loss.'

Roger's diabetes was a separate issue, but his health had been assaulted by a hard career inside the ropes.

Floyd's father, Floyd Sr was nearly sixty-three when the Berto fight came round.

He was still coughing a lot from sarcoidosis, the disease from which complications caused the death of entertainer Bernie

Mac when he was just fifty. And Jeff Mayweather, the quiet one, who works with boxers and MMA fighters in the Mayweather Boxing Club, suffered a suspected heart attack the night his nephew defeated Saúl Álvarez. It turned out to be a seizure, of sorts, but now fifty-one – and after that severe health scare – it was a reminder that no one is bulletproof, no matter what their last name is.

Floyd Mayweather knows boxing. He knows it better than he knows anything else. He's seen the destitute champions of yesteryear, the broke ones, the ones who walk with a stumble in their step and who talk with dribble slipping from the sides of their mouths.

Maybe that is why he says he wants out. Maybe, just maybe, he does actually mean it.

Few choose their time to walk away from this addictive curse; that decision is too often made for them by violent losses, old age or poor health. If Floyd goes now, his health, following a twenty-year career, intact, then the gift his father and uncle gave him at the start, the ability to defend himself with such virtuosity, could be the greatest single asset he ever had.

'I came into the sport to be smart,' he said. 'And to leave with a sharp mind.'

If he does not turn back, then it's mission accomplished.

SIXTEEN

THE BEST EVER?

FLOYD MAYWEATHER HAS spent two decades in the public eye, from his arrival in Atlanta to the crossover icon everybody has an opinion about today. He is different things to different people. The meaning of Mayweather, and indeed the meaning of 'Money' can depend upon your age, gender, race, cultural background and your likes and dislikes. Some will be unable to look beyond the dapper suits, the cash, cars, jewellery, the $25,000 mouthpiece he wore against Pacquiao and the private jets. Others will appreciate a boxing scientist, an outstanding defensive wizard who in more than twenty years of boxing has scarcely been nudged outside his comfort zone. They see a boy who was bred to be the best, trained for perfection from childhood and who, at an early age, was so focused on being an elite fighter he could cast aside people that he knew and concentrate on what he needed to do. Some might choose to look at where he lies in history, to assess his greatness, where he stands in that rich tapestry of boxing legends having won world titles from super-featherweight up to light-middleweight and how, five years after his final fight, he will be inducted into the International Boxing Hall of Fame in his first year of eligibility.

Plenty will choose to remember the braggart, the trash-talker who offended countless opponents and their teams as he seemingly allowed his ego to run wild. The prison sentence and domestic violence conviction will resonate far stronger with others, as might the slave contract remark about that infamous

$12-million deal. Even when he has not done anything, he's made headlines. In December 2014, his friend, rapper Earl Hayes FaceTimed him and, while they were connected, Hayes shot his wife dead and then turned the gun on himself, taking his own life. Mayweather pleaded with his friend not to do it, but was powerless to prevent the murder-suicide, and he was later interviewed by the LAPD as a witness.

Then there is the gambler, one who seems to have picked up the money-draining habit in his amateur days, making far smaller wagers with his old Olympic teammates back in Atlanta.

There's also the A-lister, the celebrity who can be seen courtside at basketball games, who has friends in Hollywood, music, in the NBA, NFL and the WWE.

Don't forget he's part businessman, too. He picked his team, surrounded himself with the people who helped him get where he is and he has earned, he reckons, more than a billion dollars and is most likely the first sportsman to make that amount.

But what is real, and what is not? What's his truth and what's his fiction? Where does Floyd's personality end and the 'Money' persona begin?

Wherever it is, he remains one of the sport's hardest workers and is one of the most energetic trainers boxing has seen. Mayweather's acolytes, instead of searching for controversy, maintain it has only been through 'hard work and dedication' that he has been so successful in the ring. 'He trains while everybody's sleeping,' said one of his Money Team protégés, Badou Jack. 'He's a workaholic. He works like he's broke. He trains like he's broke.'

Mayweather reckons training through the night gives him a psychological edge over his opponents. 'I truly believe in busting my ass and dedicating myself to my craft,' he said.

It is not lost on others that his career has been able to continue until into his forties. That can also be seen as testament to years of staying in shape. Regular days have included two gym sessions, totalling six hours, seven miles of roadwork, 700 sit-ups and more than 10,000 punches. He's been known to do as much as forty-minute rounds on the pads.

Before he fought De La Hoya in 2007, he said he was almost immune to exhaustion.

Former WBA light-heavyweight champion Eddie Mustafa Muhammad, who coaches fighters out of the Mayweather Boxing Club, stated, 'I've never seen anyone train like Floyd trains – actually I've never seen anyone close to it,' while Sky Sports' Adam Smith said his favourite memories of Floyd have been from seeing him work in training. 'The stand-out has been the privilege of watching him in the gym – especially over the early years with hardly any media presence,' he remembered. 'His skipping is the most dazzling I have ever seen, his work ethic, his defence, his dedication – the whole package puts him above Roy Jones, Joe Calzaghe, Oscar De La Hoya, even Bernard Hopkins as the best gym trainer I have ever witnessed live.'

Even the most diligent pros give Mayweather props for his work ethic. Micky Ward, the crashing-bashing light-welterweight, said, 'People don't understand how, later in his career, he can do what he does. I respect him so much because he works as hard as he did when he was nineteen, and with all that money it hasn't made him soft. He works harder now than he probably ever did. That's incredible.'

Marvin Hagler once quipped that it's hard to go running when you wake up in silk pyjamas, and obviously Floyd's own analogies almost always involve money.

'They say I train like I'm poor, like I haven't made one dime,' he explained.

'I'll say this,' Top Rank's Todd duBoef once told an interviewer. 'I've been around a lot of fighters. If you want to see someone happier than anybody in their life, put a boxing ring up and put

Floyd inside it. He is at home there more than anybody. It's safe. It's where he feels comfortable. When he gets in the ring it's just incredible. He's a different person.'

Perhaps he finds a safe haven inside the ropes, where he only has one person taking shots at him. But even the 'doghouse', as the sparring rings of the Mayweather Boxing Club are known, have seen their share of controversy. Floyd has traditionally sparred long rounds, but before his rematch with Marcos Maidana, Showtime's *All Access* showed a thirty-one-minute sparring session between two young fighters.

An English amateur, Donovan Cameron, was filmed boxing with Sharif Rahman – easily handling the eighteen-year-old son of former heavyweight champion Hasim Rahman. When Sharif's brother, Hasim Jr, arrived, he challenged Cameron and the long round was filmed, with segments shown on *All Access*. Cameron could not go on beyond that time but during the session Mayweather and others were shown cheering wildly and even betting on the outcome. The Rahmans ended up suing Mayweather, Mayweather Promotions and Showtime, alleging 'battery, tortious assault, false imprisonment, negligence, defamation, unjust enrichment' and for having their names and likeness used without permission. Mayweather told the commission in a hearing – not under oath – that the thirty-one-minute sparring session did not happen as Showtime showed it, that the boxers had been allowed to take breaks. He also said the gambling was fake.

'If you believe in Floyd's testimony then you believe in Santa Claus,' said Thomas Hauser.

'I'm not surprised Floyd threw Showtime under a bus,' he continued. 'I am embarrassed for Showtime that it did not stand up for itself and the people who were working on that show.'

'The secret to that is when you look at the title credits and it says "Executive Producer – Floyd Mayweather",' points out Martin Rogers.

But it is shows like *All Access* and *24/7* that have undisputedly promoted the Mayweather brand to record-breaking heights. The crossover into the mainstream with the WWE and *Dancing with the Stars* introduced him to new audiences and marketplaces and also generated massive interest that helped create the iconic image that can be seen today.

He has won world titles in five weight classes and it is thought the $200 million Showtime contract wound up earning him around $450 million, including that whopping $250 million-plus for the fight with Pacquiao.

Berto was the sixteenth consecutive current or former world champion he faced, the twenty-fourth overall. It was his twenty-sixth world title fight.

Before the Berto bout, Showtime's Stephen Espinoza reckoned the five previous fights in the six-bout Showtime deal had done 10 million buys, generating $750 million.

In his last fifteen pay-per-view fights, Mayweather created more than $1.5 billion in total.

Of course, for every yin there is a yang. Mayweather has done a lot of charity work over the years. He has donated hundreds of thousands of dollars to help families build homes in the Decatur district of Las Vegas and the Floyd Mayweather Jr Foundation was set up to aid people less fortunate.

According to the website, it 'strives to empower community alliances, impact youth leadership, promote health and wellness, and strengthen family foundations through community development, entrepreneurialism, and education resulting in a wholesome community'.

There are many who feel Mayweather should have given large sums to charities that work with domestic abuse, but it was not until Martin Rogers and only a handful of others started to write about it that the magnitude of Mayweather's history has been thoroughly documented.

'Until very recently the lack of media attention to Floyd's abusive behaviour towards women has been shocking,' said Hauser. 'If this were LeBron James, or Peyton Manning, or Alex Rodriguez, or Mike Tyson for that matter, it would have been on the front page of virtually every newspaper in America. And Floyd got a free pass pretty much until the days immediately before the Pacquiao fight, when ESPN had that *Outside the Line* programme, Rachel Nichols visited the issue and more people began to write about it. But even then HBO and Showtime continued to enable that behaviour. I respect the quality of his craftsmanship and his dedication to boxing but I'm disappointed by the manner in which the media, and particularly HBO and Showtime, have enabled him over the years. And in the lead-up to Mayweather-Pacquiao there was a moratorium at both HBO and Showtime on discussing Floyd's problems with women. Not one word about it on either network. That, to me, is inappropriate. You had two networks that are part of great media conglomerates and Showtime was part of the empire that has CBS, [that has] *60 Minutes* and all these wonderful shows, and HBO has CNN and *Time* magazine and each network themselves, especially HBO, has a history of journalistic integrity. So my sense is they both could have done better in dealing with Floyd.'

Rogers does not think the domestic violence black mark will count against Mayweather, or alter his legacy too significantly, particularly because he has plied his trade in what has long since been called 'the red light district of sports'.

'Boxing's history is littered with people who have done bad things,' he said. 'It is, by nature, a violent sport, and that's not an excuse at all. Should it affect how he's remembered as a boxer? Probably not. Should it affect how he is remembered as an athlete in the larger social sense? Look at Muhammad Ali, a significant figure in the twentieth century. His legacy is about much more than what he did in the ring. Now, that kind of legacy, it definitely should be a part of it. Ali wasn't perfect but he is remembered for what is seen as a brave ideological stance against the Vietnam War and that's part of his legacy, and Mayweather's actions towards women and treatment of people and whatever he did outside the ring in general deserves to be remembered in that part of it. I don't think he will be remembered as a great ambassador for sport, and I don't think he cares. I think he made his decision a long time ago that he would judge his career and the scorecard he would keep would be by dollars and, to a slightly lesser extent, victories – but mainly dollars. And in that sense he's been very successful.'

The bank balance does not lie. But when you try to find the real Mayweather with the information that is in the public domain, you are almost as conflicted as the individual himself. It's clear he has a generous and kind side.

'He absolutely has a dark side,' wrote David Mayo, the journalist who arguably knows him better than any other, in *The Ring* in January 2008. 'Which in recent years he has harnessed into his boxing, and into building a cosmetic bad boy image.'

Promoter Lou DiBella has seen the Mayweather brand explode. At Floyd fights in Las Vegas the casino shops sell TMT clothing and fans in their hundreds, if not thousands, can be seen wearing his TMT T-shirts or snapback hats.

'He's created a real marketing hysteria [around TMT merchandise] and he's become a star and the other thing is he understands something that not every fighter has understood, but the smart ones understand: you don't have to be loved by everybody,' said DiBella. 'People have to want to see you fight, even if it's because they hate you and they want to see you lose. Mayweather has lovers and Mayweather has haters in abundance. He has a lot of people that want to see his fights. Some of them want to see him fight because they think he's great and they like The Money Team and are fans of his image. Other people think he's a creep and don't like him. But they pay because they hope a Pacquiao or a Maidana or somebody else can beat him. He comprehends the fact it's not all about being loved, it's about people wanting to see you, whether it be to see you win, lose or simply because you're good. And whatever people think of him, and again I understand the criticisms made of him, I understand a lot of things that go on with regards to people's personal feelings, but you can't take away from the fact that he's a brilliant athlete and he's a brilliant fighter. Period. That's not debatable.'

It is open to interpretation as to whether the world of excess he so often advertises and the persona he portrays is the real Mayweather. Nigel Collins, former editor of *The Ring*, wonders whether it is not as straightforward as the fighter having just one personality trait, good or bad.

'It's been said many times that "Money" Mayweather is just an exaggerated version of Floyd Mayweather, and I think that's probably true,' he said. 'Some of [his] behaviour that is exhibited, from being a real prick to being an overly nice person within a short space of time, is extreme. He had won the welterweight belt outright before he fought De La Hoya and they went on a big media tour all round the country. I had made arrangements to give him his [*The Ring* magazine] belt at the press conference in Philadelphia and I went up there, gave it to him and made a brief presentation and he acted like he couldn't give a shit. He didn't even say thank you. He pretty much ignored me. At one point he held it up with two fingers, pretty much like it was a dead fish, and said, "They gave me this," or something like that and I thought, "What a fucking prick. Couldn't he at least say thank you?" When he left the stage, after it was all over and about ten or fifteen minutes after I'd given him the belt, I was standing along the route that he would take back out of the arena and he was going along like it was a receiving line, shaking hands and talking, and he came over to me and I thought, "This is going to be interesting." And he said, "You're doing a great job, it's a marvellous magazine. God bless you, why don't you come out to training camp and see me?" And I'm thinking, "Is this the same guy?" That was just one of several occasions when he changed so rapidly. Another example, we arranged to have a photo shoot in New York and he was so uncooperative we almost gave up. We finally got some stuff but he was very uncooperative. Later that day, we were at his fight and he came up and apologised.'

Al Bernstein, who, after covering Mayweather's early fights on ESPN was reunited with Floyd when he inked the Showtime deal, reckons the real Mayweather is shielded by the public image. 'It's a fascinating endeavour by him because if you think about it he's one of the great marketers of all time,' Bernstein reckoned. 'Here's somebody who people have continuously gone to see and yet people complain because his fights have a certain sameness to them. He takes a couple of rounds to figure out his opponent, he builds a lead heading into round nine or ten, he's able to tread water and get the win and he doesn't take any extra chances.

'People complain about his style and yet they continue to buy tickets, they continue to buy pay-per-views and it's fascinating. Some may be buying to see him lose and he's played that card very well also. But not everybody is.'

Hauser feels like the 'Money' persona took on a life of its own after the De La Hoya fight.

'He was within the bounds of propriety until after he beat Oscar,' Hauser believed. 'That raised him to a whole new level and I feel that, from my point of view, it's been a steady progression downhill ever since – in terms of acceptability of his behaviour in some respects.

'Is he playing the bad guy? That would have built into it the assumption that this is an act, a choice. And I don't agree with that. I think Floyd is being Floyd. I think this is who he is. There are a lot of things that I admire about him; he's not as good a fighter as he says he is, but he's certainly a very, very good fighter. I respect that. I respect his dedication to his craft and, in some ways, he's a very likeable person. He can be very ingratiating and charming, when he wants to be. But the other side of the coin is the way he treats people, not just women.

'The analogy I would use, and I would even say it to Floyd, Floyd has children and I'm sure he loves them but there are times he doesn't like what they do. My inclination was to like Floyd but I didn't like some of the things he did.'

Some feel the sinister side of Floyd Mayweather comes from his uncle, Roger, and the influence he had over him during some impressionable years when Floyd Sr was locked up.

'Floyd Sr, and some of the wacky stuff Floyd has said, I've always taken it with a twinkle in his eye, I've never taken him too seriously,' said Dan Rafael. 'I've always actually enjoyed my interactions with Mayweather Sr. I find he has a good sense of humour and from a media standpoint he's usually willing to talk and do interviews and never really held back. Roger Mayweather, I can't say the same about and I don't really deal with him very much because he was just always snarly and mean and nasty, you know. I don't take away his experience as a professional trainer and the fact that he was an outstanding world champion for a long time during his professional career – but I never really had too much positive interaction with him. I've had Roger say to my face, "You don't know shit about boxing." I didn't even take it as an insult because that's just his MO.'

Freddie Roach agrees that Floyd Sr is the more convivial of the two.

'Floyd Sr is a little noisy, he's not dangerous,' said the Wild Card Gym boss. 'Roger is a bad guy.'

Roach and Roger sparred together many, many years ago. Their accounts of what happened differ, as you might imagine.

'He ran so much I couldn't catch him,' Roach said. 'He hit me a couple of times, I'm sure. The next day he asked me to spar I said, "No, I already did my roadwork this morning." He never spoke to me since.'

Bernstein sees both sides of the Floyd Mayweather Jr spectrum.

'He's a polarising figure,' he agreed. 'It depends on your outlook, but he is polarising. You find very strong opinions both pro and con. You know, there are a couple of things you can't deny. One is, he's a brilliant boxer and a brilliant tactician in the ring. That part goes without saying. But the rest is all up for debate. His personal life, he's had issues, there's no question about it. Some take issue with the whole money thing and that the message he's sending to youths is skewed and not appropriate – and there's a smugness to the rest of the world about the whole idea of him flaunting his wealth. And inside the ring there are people who are distressed that he takes the air out of every fight he's in. The only common denominator and given for Floyd Mayweather that everyone is going to agree on is his boxing skills are consummate, and that is just a fact.'

Bernstein is correct. Mayweather is wonderfully skilled but behind the glossy record and imperious displays against good fighters lie further grounds for critique.

While his victories over the likes of Genaro Hernández, Angel Manfredy and Diego Corrales are revered in boxing circles, the bouts from De La Hoya onwards will likely be the ones remembered more prominently because of the magnitude of the events. And there is not an opponent since the 'Golden Boy' who, if a critic looks hard enough, could be seen as the perfect foil for Floyd at the perfect time.

De La Hoya was older and had been inactive. Hatton was not a welterweight. Neither was Márquez, and Floyd didn't make the weight himself either. The Mosley fight would have been brilliant ten years earlier, when it was first mooted. Victor

Ortiz was never in Mayweather's league. Cotto, who admittedly reinvented himself afterwards, had endured a long, torrid career and had been brutalised by Pacquiao and Antonio Margarito. Robert Guerrero? See Ortiz. Saúl Álvarez was inexperienced and nowhere near ready for a fight of that magnitude. Marcos Maidana didn't even win Floyd's own poll, and he pushed Mayweather hard. The Pacquiao fight was five years too late, with the Filipino losing two of his five previous contests. When Mayweather took a break in 2007, he walked away from a younger Mosley, a formidable Paul Williams and an on-fire Antonio Margarito. You can shoot holes in any names on his record if you are that way inclined.

Go further back and you could say Hernández, who never fought again, was over the hill, Corrales was weight-drained and distracted by his upcoming prison sentence, Gatti had been battered in countless battles over the years and was running on fumes . . .

Or you could just marvel at how, more often than not, Mayweather has sparkled against some of the best he has fought, even though there are not many who abide by his own notion, that he is TBE.

DiBella, who worked with Mayweather through those early years on HBO, has been able to appreciate Floyd's fighting gifts.

'He's always had tremendous speed,' he said. 'He's the best counterpuncher of his generation and of his time. There are some people that don't like his style because they consider it cautious, or not explosive enough, but his skillset is so remarkable that I don't really understand if you love boxing how you don't love watching Mayweather. And I'm not getting into his personal life, his problems or whatever. I'm talking about Mayweather the athlete, because Mayweather the boxer is sort of like Pernell Whitaker the boxer, or Willie Pep. He's a scientist. He's an artist. And what he's able to do in the ring is technically so superb that

I've been in this business for most of my adult life and certainly in the last twenty-five or twenty-six years he's in the top handful of fighters in that time period.'

'I think Floyd is an exceptionally good fighter,' agreed Hauser. 'I think he would have been competitive with any fighter in his weight class in any era but he has consistently ducked the best available opposition. My sense is Roy Jones, in his prime, was better pound for pound than Floyd. Roy was technically not as good a boxer. Roy had better physical gifts and once he lost that just incredible speed and those extraordinary reflexes he was no longer the same fighter. Someone like Floyd, who is technically so proficient, can fight much longer than someone like Jones. If you took Roy Jones at 154lbs at his best and Floyd went up to 154 – that to me is a knockout to Roy. That's a little unfair to make Floyd go up to 154, but if you're playing the pound-for-pound game my sense is Roy was better. I think that Pacquiao in his prime was as good, and we could throw out other names, like I think Miguel Cotto, in his prime, was probably as good as Floyd. Guys who could hit hard and apply pressure it seems to me would give Floyd trouble. He's a very, very good fighter, but he's not the best ever.'

'Is he TBE?' asks ESPN's boxing man, Dan Rafael. 'I think that he's the only one that actually thinks he's TBE, except perhaps some of the most ardent Mayweather supporters and maybe his own family. But that doesn't mean he's not a great fighter. From a boxing point of view he is a great fighter, there's no question about that. Is he one of the all-time greats? Absolutely. Is he a first-ballot Hall of Famer? No doubt about it. He's certainly been carrying the sport for the last few years. In the post-De La Hoya era, he and Pacquiao have been the two stars of the sport, opposite personalities and so forth, which is one of the reasons people wanted to see those two fight for so long. But he ranks up there.

'There's a lot of all-time greats that he would beat. I'm not sure he would beat a Sugar Ray Leonard, or a [Sugar Ray] Robinson, and he may have trouble with Tommy Hearns and [Roberto] Durán and people like that. But even if you're eighth, that's pretty darn good in the rich history of boxing. It's not a negative to not be TBE when you're still one of the all-time greats. There's no question he's one of the all-time greats.'

Rafael, however, also concurs that it is easy to pick apart Floyd's competition.

'We can sit here and have that debate whether he's TBE in terms of being a boxer, or we can have that same debate in terms of him being a matchmaker,' he went on. 'He has been extremely smart and intelligent in the way that he's picked his opponents. Years and years after he's retired you will take a look down that ledger and say, "Boy he fought everybody. Mayweather fought Pacquiao, he fought De La Hoya, Ricky Hatton, he fought Márquez. You name it. He fought all kinds of guys. He fought all the stars of the sport. Miguel Cotto, Shane Mosley." But you can nit-pick every single one of those opponents and say he did not fight one of those opponents at the proper time. Not a single one of them. Oscar was faded. Shane? He had a victory over Margarito but it became very clear he was not what he once was. Pacquiao, although still a great fighter, clearly having been knocked out by Márquez he was not what he was during the monster years of '08 and '09. Ricky Hatton may have been undefeated but he was coming up in weight. You can go through all of them. He went to Cotto after he had been crushed by a couple of guys in Margarito and Pacquiao. I mean, every one of those big names. If you really want to be negative you can find a reason why he shouldn't get the kind of credit he thinks he should get for those victories, even though those guys are all basically Hall of Fame names. It was the same with Márquez, smaller guy coming up and he didn't make the weight for that fight, either. The names are there but some could say the names are there with a little bit of smoke and mirrors.'

Bernstein might have been an advocate for Floyd over the years and they certainly have always rubbed along well. But he, too, feels Mayweather falls well short of being TBE.

'I think he's a terrific fighter and I think he's in the top twenty fighters of all time,' said Bernstein. 'The reason I have a hard time putting him as the best ever, or putting him in the top five, six or seven, is I believe there are a number of 147 and '54 pounders that would beat him in history. He can't go too high because whether it's Hearns, Leonard, Ray Robinson, probably Durán, possibly [Pernell] Whitaker, Aaron Pryor possibly at 140 that honestly, if they went into the ring with Floyd Mayweather, I think they would start as a slight favourite. And many of them would win. More importantly, if you put them in rematches of three or five I think they would come out with the majority of wins. And in many cases he hasn't fought the same competition. I know he's fought a ton of former champions and if you look at his résumé he's fought many big names; some would argue he fought them at the wrong time but you can't say he fought awful competition. He didn't. But the other guys had better fights so I just don't put him that high. Having said all that, he's the best fighter of this generation, and certainly one of the all-time greats and he is somewhere on the list.'

'I've always said, to me, the best fighter I covered was Roy Jones,' said Rafael. 'But Mayweather has to be considered a close second or tied. Maybe because I was just starting out so I was a little bit more impressionable but some of the stuff Roy did in the fights I covered would just leave your mouth hanging open, with the crazy angles, knockouts he had and the spectacle of the whole thing. There's no doubt that in my fifteen, sixteen years it has to be Mayweather and Roy Jones as one and two; or one and one A. They are extraordinarily talented guys, no doubt.'

Years ago, when discussing Mayweather, Collins once wrote, 'In order to become a legend, a fighter must overcome a perilous brush with disaster or do something no one else has ever done.'

But in the ring, it is not his fault he has not had to overcome the adversity many great champions have. He's simply been too good for almost everyone he's faced, often by a mile. He's never been dropped, albeit he's fought through a fog a few times. Those damaged hands have hindered him too, and he's shown heart boxing with them. But they have never nearly cost him a fight, not even when the pain in them was so great that he had to touch down against Carlos Hernández.

Of course, Floyd's old rival Larry Merchant chronicled many, many fighters during his long career with HBO and before that, in his time as a newspaperman in Philadelphia.

'I go back a long way,' he said. 'I know a lot but not as much as a lot of other people do. The first big fight I covered was Robinson and [Carmen] Basilio. That was 1957. And when people ask me about this I say I think he [Mayweather] was the best pure boxer of his time. I think Manny Pacquiao is the best fighter of his time. That's a distinction that incidentally goes back to [heavyweights Gene] Tunney and [Jack] Dempsey. Tunney himself said, "I'm a boxer, he's a fighter." Tunney beat him twice. Does anyone talk about Tunney? Dempsey represented a particular time, age, culture and had a tremendous impact – just as Joe Louis did, just as Ali did, and Robinson in his own way – and a few others. I would say he [Floyd] was one of the best lightweights of modern times and to me, if you're one of the best of your time that's all you can really be. Do I think he belongs with the greats? I really don't. I know what Emanuel Steward thought, and with the last decade he's been compared to the best welterweights and that's a little unfair to him because I think he was at his best at lightweight. But I don't think he was as good as the guys in the Leonard-Hearns era. He wasn't interested in fighting some of the better welterweights. I never heard him challenge Vernon Forrest. I never heard him challenge Mosley when Mosley was closer to his peak. A person in his camp once told me, "Don't even bring up the name Margarito." And there was Paul Williams. You could say he was smart. And he was. So that's why I have a hard time. And listen, he's not the first one in boxing who manoeuvred through to get there. There's always a question at the time that is consigned to ancient history of who would or wouldn't fight whoever so I'm not sitting here and saying he's unique in that regard. But I think the comparison to those two welterweights . . . I shrug, kind of in a way that Evander Holyfield is one of my favourite fighters of modern times, but I don't make him one of the great heavyweights. I think he was a great fighter. Nobody remembers that Mosley was 32-0 with thirty knockouts as a lightweight, except maybe guys like you and me. I think, from my point of view, high praise is to say he's one of the best lightweights, one of the best of his time, and one of the best that I saw. And I look at him and other fighters and I think Leonard was the best of the modern era and Robinson and Ali I think were just extraordinary athletes and people who in some way represented or transcended their time.'

But has Mayweather not represented his? Does the gaudy excess, the celebrity culture, the in-family *Jerry Springer* fighting, the reality TV element of *24/7* and *All Access* and the breakout into other markets not represent a man who has used the many platforms available today to reach into areas athletes have not been able to before?

That includes social media, with Mayweather's millions of followers on Twitter and Instagram tracking his many moves.

'I think Floyd has been crafty in his own way, manipulating the platforms, the ones he can control,' said online boxing scribe Steve Kim. 'I think that goes for sports in general. A lot of athletes are now taking control of their own message with Twitter and Instagram and stuff like that. I think athletes themselves can control what they say, when they say it and how they say it. I don't think it's necessarily unique to Floyd or to boxing but I do think boxing probably needs platforms like the internet because, quite frankly, it's not being covered by the general media like other sports.

'For Floyd, I think by sheer nature of what he means to the sport he's going to be covered. But I do think he does not want to be asked tough questions so he only speaks to certain people that'll play the game. I think that's what it is. I don't know if he's the king of all media as it relates to boxing. I think by virtue of his stature in the sport that's natural but did he create that? I think that's debatable.'

Creator or not, he's utilised it to help build his brand and convey the character he has launched. Nearly twenty million followers on Instagram and almost eight million on Twitter shows his relevance and that people want to know what he thinks and what he does.

Hauser certainly does not believe the Mayweather persona has been to the betterment of the sport. 'Overall I think that Floyd has had a negative effect on boxing,' he said. 'He is turning off mainstream sports fans and people in general who might be attracted to boxing to the extent that they are aware of him, but they don't like his shtick. Obviously he has his constituency and that constituency shows a certain loyalty to him, but my sense is that the positive feelings that his constituents have for him has not translated into any great benefit for boxing.'

Bernstein, however, believes that in time Mayweather will be appreciated more.

'It's possible,' he said. 'I think that's true with most things, isn't it? It's true with politics, civil servants, it's true of entertainment sometimes. It's true of athletes on both sides of the pond. There have been prime ministers in England who have benefited in time, just like presidents do when you look back on them. He is appreciated in that people do understand his greatness. Ironically, for all the big numbers Floyd's done with pay-per-view, and that he is number one in the sport and he makes more than any other athlete in the United States – and in the world for that matter – the one thing you can say about him is that, in a way, he's not a showman, because creating entertainment is not his goal. Winning is his goal. I don't know if we can fault him for that. It's no different to whether a football, basketball or hockey team does it, you figure out the best way for you to win and you do it. And how many times have you seen a team that maybe is not thrilling a fan base but they're winning?'

'He will be remembered as a great fighter, as an extremely skilled technician, a polarising force,' surmises Rafael. 'He was, or is, the kind of guy that either has that hardcore fan base that loves him and follows him and hangs on everything he says or then there's a very large segment of the boxing population that despises him and they watch him with the hope and prayer that he gets knocked out. So he will be remembered for the ability he has, the titles he won and all the money he made, but I don't think they're going to remember him as a revered fighter from an entertainment standpoint, because Floyd's fights are often boring because he's so good.

'There's certainly a lot of younger fighters that Mayweather's had an influence on, that do want to be like him, act like him and certainly [want to] make the kind of money he's made. But there is only one Mayweather. I don't know if anyone can duplicate that. [Adrien] Broner tried and has failed absolutely miserably to the point where he has almost become a caricature and a joke. But Floyd has a lot of the kind of charisma that young fighters look up to, like Roy Jones did, and they wanted to be like Roy, because Roy had the flashy moves, he was pound for pound and he had broken through into the mainstream with the rap music and the notion that when you went to a Roy Jones fight it almost didn't matter who was on the other side of the ring because Roy was going to give you a show anyway – with his crazy moves, flashy ring entrances and so forth. Floyd has taken that mantle and ratcheted it up a huge notch since Roy exited his prime.'

Speaking to Steve Kim after Mayweather hung 'em up, post-Berto, Merchant said, 'I'm as happy about his retirement as I'm sure he was for mine.'

Of course, while Merchant had his conflicts with Mayweather – particularly after the Baldomir and Ortiz fights – other media members have more pleasant memories of working with him.

'I did have him call my house one morning while I was eating breakfast,' recalled former *Boxing News* editor Claude Abrams, of a conversation he had with Floyd in the early part of the fighter's championship career. 'Two of my mates were in Vegas at the airport and he was there. They got chatting. He then called me. I guess he was more approachable in those days. I remember the discussion. He told me he was retiring because his hands were giving him so much trouble. He kept telling me he was being serious and, for a short time, I think he did say he had quit the sport.'

Bernstein, however, has still been able to call on Mayweather – even with his incredible levels of fame.

'Actually,' added Bernstein, 'because he lives in Las Vegas and I live in Las Vegas and early on in his career – there's many Floyds, as you well know – I did a radio show in Vegas and I was doing an anniversary show. I just called him up and said, "Hey, can you come over?" No big deal, he came over and did an interview. My wife and I have a charity called The Caring Place here in Las Vegas that was founded for cancer patients and he twice came to these radiothons we did. He was extraordinarily gracious in doing it. So that's one side of Floyd that I've witnessed. Obviously that's not in his demeanour all the time but especially early on, for me personally and our relationship, I've never had an issue with him. Never in terms of interacting with him.'

Bernstein's broadcast colleague from 'across the street' at HBO, Merchant, has a slightly different outlook. Despite doing many fights together, he cannot recall any fond memories they shared.

'You know,' Merchant considered, 'he made it difficult to like him personally and that was okay with him. He was trying to impress people and obviously did. But in a personal way he was in a defensive position versus the media with his pronouncements. He didn't seem to have a joy in it, not that he conveyed. There was no twinkle, as there was, for example, with Ali who was just having fun. He conveyed more rage against the system than he did joy with what he was accomplishing in the ring. And he had such big ambitions. Remember, he was a lightweight talking about fighting De La Hoya years before he fought De La Hoya. It seemed nonsensical at the time but that was the beginning of the bigger plan and he's made it work. He's a really complex character and an extraordinary presence in his time as a fighter. I don't know if you'd call it popularity but his appeal, in some way, is maybe a smaller and certainly different version of [Mike] Tyson. There was a time when I heard he [Mayweather] was called a "studio gangsta" – gangster spelled g.a.n.g.s.t.a – which meant, from the point of view of the hip-hop culture, a guy that was not really a bad guy out on the street, but that he was acting like a bad guy. But it helped him. I'm sure it showed a side of him that was real but in terms of the public image of him, it got him a lot of supporters – just as we've seen other fighters have strong ethnic support, he had strong ethnic or racial support. When he once said to me, and this was before our famous – or infamous – on-camera incident, "You don't understand boxing," what I, in my mind was thinking, was he was not just talking about the technical side of boxing, he was talking about that sales side of boxing and the matchmaking side, where you can create illusions and advance yourself in some ways through matchmaking and other things. So if I challenged him about why he didn't fight so-and-so or wouldn't fight so-and-so, he basically understood what was best for himself, even while the media – and there were a number of people in the media who were asking these questions as he moved into the welterweight division – wanted to see the best fights; maybe he had, certainly in the modern day, a clearer vision as to how you advance your personal interests over the interests of the boxing world.'

Hauser recalled one of his meetings with 'Money'.

'We started talking and we talked for about an hour, and Kelly Swanson was there and she kept saying, "Floyd we have to go, we have to get to the gym." Every now and then, Floyd would just give her a look that said, "I decide when we go." I wasn't trying to keep him from doing what he had to do, he was enjoying the conversation and wanted to talk. And then he turned and said to whoever it might have been to get the gym ready and he was gone. We covered a lot of territory there, about boxing and his craftsmanship and what it meant to him and I respect that part of Floyd, that he is a craftsman and he has, when he wants to, an inherent likeable quality about him. I wish he'd show the world more of that and less of the negative side.'

'We're not bosom buddies,' Bernstein said, 'but he's respectful of me and it's a funny thing, in the fights we've done I've had occasion to say things he might take umbrage with. Here's the thing. He does have a long-standing relationship with me. I also have covered him but not called his fights for a long time. However, the last few fights I have called them and there have probably been some things where he's thought, "Um, I'd probably prefer him not to say" even though you have to say certain things, whether I thought he was holding too much against Maidana or wasn't getting penalised for it but I've always given him his due as a fighter and I think he's respected that approach. We don't have that type of personal relationship. I've been closer to other fighters, I try not to be, but I know other fighters better. What there has always been with Mayweather and myself is there's this feeling that I'm not going to bash him for the sake of bashing him. And I'm not going to unfairly criticise his style in a way that is guided by other considerations, like about fights being more exciting . . . I'm going to judge him based on what he's doing in the ring. I believe that's so. He's never articulated that but that's my general impression and it probably does help a little that I knew him at the beginning of his career. That's probably a helpful thing.'

Dan Rafael has also never felt reason to butt heads with Mayweather. 'I think that my business relationship with us and our interactions have always been fine,' he said. 'I've never had any particular issue with Mayweather. We've had some laughs, he's been a cool guy and I've interviewed him many times. The people who sometimes take exception are the people around him. There have been some issues over the years with some of the handlers and people who are part of that team, but when I'm in front of Floyd Mayweather and I'm talking to him or it's on a teleconference or in one of the media scrums before fights or when I've done some interviews with him on ESPN television I've never had a cross word with him. There are people who perceive me to be very anti-Mayweather, which has never been the case. I was anti some of the nonsense that went on as far as trying to get the Manny Pacquiao fight made. I have disagreed with Floyd's selection of opponents here or there. I'm certainly no fan of domestic violence and the way he's treated some people, but on a personal basis and covering his fights, I've never had a problem with him. I can't say he's a good guy, I can't say he's a bad guy. He's a guy. No one is ever as bad as their worst day and no one is ever as good as their best day. That's how I look at it. Floyd's a flawed individual. He has a very high opinion of himself. He's not perfect, as he likes to say. I think he knows he's done wrong things. I don't think he's a bad guy, but I would say he maybe has a problem when it comes to dealing with women. As many times as I've tried, it's hard to get him to go beyond the surface of any particular issue – whatever it may be. Whether you're talking about boxing or his career or even if you're talking about another issue. You don't find him getting involved with his own personal story very much. It's hard to draw that out of him. I've tried; it's not easy. But I get it because he's a famous person, he gets asked this stuff all the time, he tries to maintain a bit of a shell around himself so he doesn't have to open up.'

Former opponents generally have a healthy dose of respect for Mayweather, certainly as a fighter. They have all enjoyed a brush with greatness and have a tale to tell, whether it was Reggie Sanders feeling like he earned a draw, Sammy Girard dining out on rocking him, Angel Manfredy still feeling like he got screwed, Ricky Hatton lamenting the presence of Joe Cortez, José Luis Castillo shaking his head at the judges or Victor Ortiz wishing he'd never dropped his hands. They and Mayweather have their own experiences to share.

And while their paths crossed, sometimes just for a matter of minutes or seconds, the roads they have since taken have differed greatly.

The last man to beat Mayweather, Bulgaria's Serafim Todorov in the Atlanta Olympics, is living on a $500-a-month pension, meaning he would have to work for 35,000 years to make the sum Floyd made for fighting Pacquiao.

'I've suffered from depression countless times in my life and even now I'm depressed,' he said in a 2014 interview with CNN. 'I just live a mundane life with my family.'

He does, however, remain grateful for his win over Floyd.

'The whole world knows about me now,' he added. 'I feared they might have forgotten me. Before, when I was still boxing, people talked about me because of my titles, and now I'm famous because of Floyd.'

Todorov, after retiring in 2003, made a comeback two months after Mayweather fought Pacquiao, winning a four-round bout on points in the Boxing Hall in Pernik, Bulgaria.

Remember Justin Juuko, who in 1999 was a short-notice opponent for Mayweather but who boxed on for a further fourteen years? He fought over in the UK, in Uganda, continued crossing the USA and retired in 2013 after a loss to Mayweather's 1996 Olympic teammate Zahir Raheem.

Then there is Emanuel Augustus, who was previously known as Emanuel Burton when he fought Floyd. The old 'Drunken Master' had been involved in many thrilling televised scraps, and dragged a young Mayweather into the trenches. He remained an erratic entertainer, but lost his last five fights. Living rough in Louisiana, he was caught by a stray bullet in the crossfire of a shootout in Baton Rouge in October 2014. It entered the back of his head and split in two. One part cracked his vertebrae in his neck; another cut an artery. He was in a coma for two weeks and his few friends did not think his brain would function again, if he survived. He recovered slowly, with double vision in one eye and the effects of a hard career hastened. He was confused and destitute, forgotten on boxing's scrapheap.

Diego Corrales only lived for six more years after losing to Mayweather in their grudge blockbuster. He lost four of his last seven, was in one of the greatest fights of all time when he stopped José Luis Castillo and passed away in a motorcycle crash in 2007, exactly two years after that epic clash with the Mexican.

Castillo boxed on until 2014, a shell of his former self. After getting wiped out by Ricky Hatton, obliterated by that textbook body shot, he won more than he lost, but was defeated by some who would not have held a candle to the lightweight version who pushed Mayweather and warred with Corrales.

Phillip N'dou called it a day a fight after losing to Mayweather, but returned in 2009 at a lower level in South Africa. DeMarcus Corley boxed on, too. He helps the best as a sparring partner and is often used as a measuring stick by promoters wanting to test their up-and-coming prospects. He also has his own brand of shoes, 'Chop Chop', and sells boxing boots.

Arturo Gatti, Floyd's first pay-per-view opponent, died in suspicious circumstances in Brazil in 2009. He was found with bloodstains on the back of his head and neck. He was on his second honeymoon, with Brazilian wife Amanda Rodrigues, and she was initially charged with his murder but later released. Some reports suggested he had been strangled but authorities in South America finally ruled suicide, much to the disappointment of Gatti's family and friends who felt the proud warrior would never have ended his own life.

Controversial Zab Judah fought on. Boxing back at light-welterweight in 2015, he was involved in an altercation at the weigh-in with Hevinson Herrera that ended up with his Colombian-born opponent getting injured and the bout being scrapped before they could even get into the ring.

Tough Argentine Baldomir went on too long, losing three of his last four before retiring in 2014. But his Cinderella years would live long in the memory of boxing folklore.

De La Hoya, Floyd's great rival, had an unspectacular homecoming bout at the then Home Depot Center in Carson on the LA outskirts. He defeated Stevie Forbes but the Mayweather return match did not happen and he was then blitzed, made to look hapless by Manny Pacquiao. In retirement, and as a promoter, his relationship with Mayweather remained tense until Floyd called it a day after Berto. 'I'm going to miss Floyd's action-packed fights with prime fighters,' De La Hoya tweeted sarcastically. 'Now that the worst boxing era is over let's look forward to the next ten years.'

Hatton, almost the moment he was announced a loser to Mayweather in their Las Vegas showdown, spiralled into a pit of depression and despair. When he split with long-term trainer Billy Graham, it seemed he had reinvented himself under Floyd Sr, with a convincing win over Paulie Malignaggi, but it was a false dawn. Pacquiao obliterated him in two rounds and he retired. But, tormented by that loss and with his out-of-the-ring battles raging, he came back, only to be stopped by Vyacheslav Senchenko on a sobering night in front of his Manchester faithful.

Then there was Márquez, who had seemed so small against Mayweather, almost helpless in his first fight north of lightweight. He began training with notorious strength and conditioning coach 'Memo' Heredia, filled out massively into the weight and wiped out Pacquiao with one punch in their fourth fight. Although he later lost to Timothy Bradley, he became a fully-fledged welterweight, not the blown-up 135-pounder who boxed Floyd.

Shane Mosley, past his best when he fought Floyd in 2010, continued to box into his forties. That he won only two of his next six bouts indicates his career decline had been initiated. A stoppage defeat to Anthony Mundine in Australia in 2013 should have been the full stop for his Hall of Fame career, but he fought again, and boxed in a circus-like rematch with Ricardo Mayorga, a pointless contest that had not meant much seven years earlier when they first met.

Things went from bad to worse in the boxing career of Victor Ortiz. He suffered a broken-jaw ninth-round stoppage loss to Josesito Lopez and then a second-round defeat to former WBA champion Luis Collazo. But from being a Mayweather opponent, he managed to get onto *Dancing with the Stars* and then had a small role in the second *Expendables* film.

Miguel Cotto's career had a second wind after he pushed Mayweather so hard. He lost his next fight, anticlimactically, when he was upset by Austin Trout in New York, but a move to LA trainer Freddie Roach sparked a career renaissance that saw him win the world title at middleweight, defeating old Argentine Sergio Martinez and then defending against decent Australian Daniel Geale before he lost a superb battle to Saúl Álvarez.

Robert Guerrero's career instantly slowed, too. When he was matched with up-and-coming Keith Thurman, losing on points, it seemed that he was about to begin a run as an 'opponent'.

Álvarez, who was in the blockbuster that was 'The One' with Mayweather, became a bigger star after going twelve rounds with the American. A trio of wins over rough Alfredo Angulo, stylish Erislandy Lara and heavy-hitting James Kirkland saw him rebuild as a fighter, and enhance his reputation.

For a while, fight fans wanted Mayweather to meet Gennady Golovkin, up at middleweight. Mayweather Sr was never keen. The father, who had warned his son against fighting on following Berto, certainly saw no point in facing Golovkin, the big-punching Kazakh terror.

'No, we not fixin' to fight no damn giant,' he said. 'I'm gonna tell you like this right here. He [Golovkin] comes down, he be at 154, by the time he eats and fights that night, maybe 180, you just don't know, man. People can eat up stuff, man, and hey. He don't need to fight nobody like that, man.'

Among the more unusual mooted rivalries, Mayweather had an ongoing social media feud with UFC women's bantamweight champion Ronda Rousey, who in July 2015 pipped Mayweather for the Best Fighter gong in the annual ESPY Awards.

'I wonder how Floyd feels being beat by a woman for once,' she said. 'When he learns to read and write, he can text me.'

She was referring to a story that did the rounds during the ALS ice bucket challenges that went viral in 2014. Mayweather was challenged by 50 Cent, his former friend, but instead of pouring a bucket of iced water over his head, the rapper told Floyd to read a page of a Harry Potter book out loud without making a mistake.

Speculation followed that Floyd was illiterate, which he denied. 'Reading will not define my place in boxing history,' he said. 'Will God not let me in heaven because I didn't read like a news anchor? Look, I would be perfect at reading if it was how I made my living and fed my family. I'm not a news anchor, never claimed to be.'

*

The Mayweather Boxing Club is not a lavish place, but it's real. As well as its main attraction, a number of top fighters and prospects from around the world call it their home. Some of them can name Mayweather as a friend. Ishe Smith, an ageing fighter who never got the breaks and who, for a while, lived on the edge of suicide, credits Mayweather with turning his life around. His pal and promoter lined up a shot at IBF light-middleweight champion Cornelius Bundrage, which Smith won, becoming Las Vegas's first ever born-and-bred world champion.

'Floyd Mayweather is the only promoter that can relate to the fighters and our struggles,' said Smith. 'Even though he's the highest-paid boxer and the highest-paid athlete in the world.'

Another thankful to him is Londoner Ashley Theophane, whom Mayweather has used for sparring a few times and has also promoted for a couple of years. Ahead of a fight on the Mayweather-Berto card in September 2015, he gave Theophane a brand new Chrysler 300 to thank him for his hard work and loyalty.

Floyd stands by his guys. After lightweight Mickey Bey lost a big fight to John Molina Jr, Mayweather put him on two shows to build him back up and then got him an IBF lightweight title contest against Miguel Vázquez, which he won.

What stands out in the Mayweather gym, though, is not the seasoned old pros, the A-list observers or the family drama that has run there for more than a decade, but the youths who train there. Children as young as five can make the speedball sing and they can hit the mitts faster than the eye can see. They can put dents in the heavybag that would make a heavyweight blush and they train incessantly, with hardly any need to stop between stations.

They want to be the next Floyd Mayweather.

But who is that? Is it the multi-millionaire, the boxing maestro, the braggart, the showman, the entrepreneur, the gambler, the opportunist, the criminal or, dare one say it, the mastermind? He maintains he's had a plan from the start, that he always ran his own race throughout his career. 'It was just a smart business move by a young kid from Grand Rapids,' he said. 'I'd rather be hated for being real and who I am than be loved for someone that I'm not. Money doesn't define who I am. I make money; money doesn't make me.'

'I always remember this one quote, I guess it was a few years back when he and his father were having their difficulties,' remembered Nigel Collins. 'Floyd had boasted that he was going to be the first billionaire boxer and Floyd Sr said something like, "Billionaire? In a few years he will be running around Grand Rapids naked with no money." He could probably just sell a few cars and be okay for the rest of his life now.'

Yes, the chances are now minute that Floyd Mayweather will lose everything that he has. And while we will remember the celebrity, the wealth and excess, the showpiece events, the boxing clinics and the damp squibs, one thing will never be disputed: that he is one of the very best fighters of all time. Maybe not the greatest, maybe not The Best Ever, but technically one of the most proficient fighters to lace on gloves.

Strip away the controversy, the jail time, the family feuds, the made-to-order TV personality and you will find a brilliant, masterful boxer.

Of course, no one needs to tell him that. He knows it better than anyone else. Ahead of the Berto fight, he summed up what he is and what he does.

'I'm Floyd Mayweather,' he said. 'And I can fucking fight.'

There was, however, someone else who could fight. A man had emerged in the Ultimate Fighting Championship (UFC) as a mixed martial arts superstar, who had crossed into the mainstream and who had picked up championships in two weight classes. He had been in dramatic bouts with some of his biggest rivals. He had a global fanbase. He was known as a striker, a puncher who had turned out the lights of some elite level MMA stars. He wanted Floyd Mayweather. And Mayweather was listening to the loud, brash Irishman who answered to the name Conor McGregor.

SEVENTEEN

THE MONEY FIGHT

IT WAS A Wednesday. 14 June, 2017.

Boxing aficionados read the headlines through their fingers while casual sports fans salivated at two separate sporting worlds fusing to create a weird, money-spinning extravaganza.

Floyd Mayweather, 49-0 and a sure-fire future boxing Hall of Famer, was staking that undefeated record and making an attempt to surpass the 49-0 unbeaten mark of heavyweight legend Rocky Marciano.

Mixed martial arts star Conor McGregor, making his debut as a boxer, would stand in the opposite corner. The bout would take place at the T-Mobile Arena in Las Vegas on 26 August.

For months, if not the best part of a couple of years, Floyd and UFC icon McGregor had traded public barbs, comparing fighting skills, levels of celebrity, pay cheques and even their position on sporting rich-lists. At the start, it seemed like a joke and something to giggle at. Then rumours of a fight began to circulate. It then started to become strangely real. Slowly, it became inevitable. It was the biggest fight money could buy.

They had flaunted their wealth and fame and in doing so created a whole lot of hoopla about them settling their high-roller beef in the ring.

The thought of an elite boxer, even one who'd been retired for two years but who had kept his tools sharp in the gym, facing UFC's controversial wild man on a global platform made hardcore fight fans squeamish. Even by boxing's mucky standards it was a cynical money grab.

Nothing had been done like it before. Some pointed to Muhammad Ali's bizarre wrestle with Antonio Inoki in Tokyo in 1976, others looked at when boxers tried their hands at MMA, but no mixed martial artist had come into boxing at this level, let alone for a debut. McGregor would have done countless rounds of stand-up prep in his MMA training camps, but this was boxing. Elite boxing.

In defence of Floyd – and he needed it given the admonishments he was receiving for making the oddity an actuality – the options for him left in boxing were few and far between, certainly if you consider the $200-300 million he made for the Pacquiao fight. No one could help him make close to that again while McGregor, strangely, stupidly, ridiculously, might be able to help him exceed that.

By the time the final Mayweather-McGregor calculations had been completed, even 0-fight novice McGregor stood to make more in one night than any boxer in history had for a single contest. Not just any debutant, but any fighter . . . Ali, Tyson, Leonard, De La Hoya, Pacquiao . . . He would earn more for one boxing fight than any of them had for one night's work.

Meanwhile, Mayweather was getting into position to become sport's first billion-dollar earner. It was bonkers. It was boxing, the red light district of sports, where anything goes.

For Floyd, the two most real challenges left in the Noble Art were Gennady Golovkin, the long-reigning middleweight champion, and old foe Saúl Álvarez, who had matured, improved and not lost since Mayweather had schooled him in 2013.

Álvarez, well, Floyd had been there and done that, beaten the young Mexican redhead so convincingly the queue for a rematch was non-existent. The history boys in boxing would have loved to have seen Floyd dare to be great against the Kazakh machine they called 'GGG', but after two years out, and having turned 40, even his staunchest critics could have cautioned Mayweather for making a daring leap to 160lbs, well over his best 2017 weight, which was probably still 147lbs. Besides, 'GGG' and Álvarez had already signed to fight in boxing's mega-fight of the year, something Mayweather was likely to be only too happy to torpedo by announcing he would see action just three weeks before that bout, raiding customers' pay-per-view coffers in advance of the real boxing fans' fight on 16 September, also at the T-Mobile Arena.

There were other possibilities for Mayweather, but they just did not add up.

The likes of Keith Thurman and Errol Spence had emerged since Mayweather's routine victory over Berto but they were not box office, just titleholders who had stayed unbeaten. They had not crossed into the mainstream. They had not taken boxing by storm in Floyd's absence. Long story short, they would not help make Mayweather the Mayweather-type money he had been earning. Yes, Floyd was going to be the A-side whomever he faced, but the B-side would dramatically dictate his top and bottom lines.

Since Berto, he had always been able to draw a crowd. People followed his every move on social media. Retirement was just a word; Mayweather remained relevant.

He was promoting his boxers. One of his young fighters, Gervonta Davis, a precocious super-featherweight from the mean streets of Baltimore, rose to the IBF throne with a dazzling display against capable Puerto Rican veteran José Pedraza. Mayweather was ringside for his coronation in Brooklyn, and again when Davis made his first defence with a win over his mandatory challenger, Liam Walsh, in England. Floyd was an active part of the BoxNation and BT Sport promotion, visiting the UK in the build-up and on fight night. While in Britain, he shared a lucrative autograph signing engagement with Anthony Joshua, whose stock was high following a dramatic heavyweight championship win over Wladimir Klitschko in front of 90,000 fans inside Wembley Stadium.

Floyd had kept busy. He opened a strip club, called Girl Collection, in Vegas, and in his two years off travelled extensively. He took in Stonehenge, the pyramids, Red Square, Brussels, Dubai and Amsterdam.

But it seemed like it was building towards a crescendo, one last big night, a well-paid exit.

Then the McGregor match was finally announced. Casual sport fans were going dizzy, talking about McGregor's youth, hunger, southpaw stance and power. They contended Floyd was too old and had been inactive.

Yet the harsh realities of what McGregor was attempting to do were highlighted just a week after the event was signed. A former UFC fighter, named Tim Hague, who had been active between 2009 and 2011 in the MMA big league, tried his hand at boxing. On a small show in Edmonton, Canada, he was stopped and knocked out by Adam Braidwood. Hague walked from the ring but was taken to hospital, fell into a coma and died.

Meanwhile, boxing rounded on Mayweather-McGregor. There was barely seventy days from the announcement to the bout.

Former Mayweather opponents Ricky Hatton and Oscar De La Hoya condemned the attraction, as did ex-heavyweight kings Lennox Lewis and Mike Tyson. Lewis was quoted as saying it was 'not a serious fight', adding, 'He's [Mayweather's] basically boxing a guy that is a UFC fighter and not a boxer. No other boxers from 49 fights have figured out how to beat Mayweather – now a UFC fighter that doesn't even have a boxing career is trying to beat him at boxing – I think it's a farce to a certain degree.'

Tyson reckoned the fight was 'ridiculous' and added, in typical Tyson fashion, that McGregor 'would get killed' while Hatton said, 'I can't get excited about this.'

De La Hoya, who had a conflict of interest because he was staging Golovkin-Álvarez with Golden Boy Promotions, added to the previous animosity with Mayweather, saying: 'First of all, how did the commission ever sanction such a fight? And how can a fighter who has zero experience in boxing go against the very best, and pretend that maybe he can win? It's almost unheard of.

'Look, Floyd Mayweather is one of the best boxers in our generation, and for McGregor to think that he can outbox Mayweather is a little delusional. It's speaking the truth, but hey, may they have a good fight, and then we can move on to focus on our real fight on September 16th.'

Everyone had an opinion on Mayweather-McGregor. Everyone was talking about it. Positive or negative, it was big news on a worldwide scale.

Sponsorship packages for the event were priced as high as $10million, according to ESPN, which was far higher than the $5.6million Tecate paid to have its branding across Mayweather-Pacquiao. That deal allowed the beer to have its logo in the centre of the ring, on the non-fighter cornerposts, sponsorship on display for the first minute of each round in the broadcast and half-a-million dollars of tickets.

In one fell swoop Mayweather-McGregor and its announcement immediately hurt three of boxing's biggest events of the year. When it was made public it cast a long, dark shadow over the impending light-heavyweight showdown between Andre Ward and Sergey Kovalev. As a consequence, Kathy Duva – Kovalev's promoter – branded Mayweather-McGregor 'a circus'.

The bout was also sharing the date with Miguel Cotto's return to action. The Puerto Rican was facing Japan's Yoshihiro

Kamegai in California, and then, just three weeks later, came Golovkin-Álvarez.

Boxing fans chose to focus on what that event's promoter De La Hoya, and hardcore fight fans, consistently referred to as 'the real fight'. But the headlines were being made elsewhere and some wondered if boxing supporters would put hands in their pockets twice in quick succession for pay-per-views, or if they would have to make a choice.

There was a fight boxing fans wanted to see and another many would not admit to wanting to see.

Dan Rafael tweeted that Canelo-GGG vs Mayweather-McGregor was 'real fight vs freak show', to which Leonard Ellerbe replied online, 'I'll assume there is no need to accommodate you for our event.'

Not many held contrarian views, but one who did was promoter Lou DiBella.

'I'm sick of the whining, "It's bad for boxing,"' DiBella charged. 'No, it's not bad for boxing, you stupid motherfuckers. Anything that's making people watch your sport or bringing attention to it is good for boxing. If Floyd Mayweather does what I sort of anticipate he's going to do, which is slap [McGregor] around like he's his daddy, I don't think that's bad for boxing.'

It was not a contest for the purists. *Boxing News* opined, 'it absolutely stinks'. Bernard Hopkins reckoned it demonstrated Mayweather's 'lack of respect for boxing'.

'This is all fake news,' he continued in an interview with *Boxing Scene*. 'First of all, [McGregor] hasn't fought an amateur [boxing] fight to my knowledge. I've checked around and I've been around the game for a long time. He hasn't had any experience as an amateur or a professional. How does any commission, in Vegas or anywhere, give him a licence to fight a guy like Mayweather, who is one of the icon guys of our era?'

Showtime had unsurprisingly secured the television rights in the US. Stephen Espinoza discussed the bout's appeal.

'In a sport that's often filled with hyperbole there really is no exaggeration to say that this event is truly unprecedented – it's unprecedented in the nature of the competition, it's unprecedented in its magnitude and the attention that it is receiving and will receive and it's unprecedented in the types of personalities that we have participating,' he said. 'Floyd Mayweather and Conor McGregor have taken the art of self-promotion and backed it up with excellence in the ring and elevated it into an art form. We've certainly had colourful characters in boxing and in MMA before, but to get arguably the two most talked about athletes in each sport taking aim against each other in the same competition adds exponentially to the appeal of the event.'

It was the curiosity value that magnetised general fight and sports fans. They felt Mayweather, older and rusty, might have slipped sufficiently enough to walk on to one southpaw left hand that would ring out through the annals of sport. McGregor was hungrier, younger and more unpredictable. That was the basis of their argument.

Four press conferences were arranged for the fighters to meet, square up and engage. The competitors and their teams started in Los Angeles on Tuesday, 11 July, the next day they were in Toronto, by Thursday they were in New York and on Friday, the day McGregor turned twenty-nine, they were in London.

Just a week earlier, unsung Australian Jeff Horn had brought Manny Pacquiao's career at the highest level – or even the next tier down – to an end. Horn won a controversial decision over the Filipino in Brisbane, Pacquiao's fourth loss in nine fights. There was certainly now no money in the idea of a Mayweather-Pacquiao rematch.

On the first day of the press tour, a story broke that

Mayweather owed $22 million in back taxes from 2015. A tax lien had been filed in March, and the *Las Vegas Review Journal* claimed Mayweather had wanted to settle the bill with money from the McGregor fight. He had also requested a short-term payment plan.

'Although the taxpayer has substantial assets, those assets are restricted and primarily illiquid,' said Mayweather's petition. 'The taxpayer has a significant liquidity event scheduled in about 60 days from which he intends to pay the balance of the 2015 tax liability due and outstanding.'

'He does not say he does not owe or can't pay, he says he has insufficient liquidity to pay now,' Vegas tax attorney Bob Grossman told the newspaper.

'Just because he can't pay $22 million doesn't mean he can't pay $2 million,' Grossman added.

Mayweather hit back almost immediately on social media. 'Believe half of what you see and none of what you hear,' he wrote, 'especially when it comes to media in this country. While everyone is counting my money and assuming the worst, these are the facts. Uncle Sam received $26,000,000.00 from me in 2015! What else could they possibly want? I'm sure I would have been notified much sooner if there were any real discrepancies right? Bottom line, everybody just wants to be a part of the "Money May" show, including the IRS! That's fine, you can crunch numbers all day but in the end, my empire is rock solid and intact! Now Calculate That!'

He cited his business empire, his property portfolio and assets as signs of his exorbitant wealth, but regardless of the calculations, the story would give McGregor, and Floyd's detractors, ammunition for the upcoming tour.

So the stage was set for the two to initially face off inside the STAPLES Center in Los Angeles.

Mayweather wore a TMT hoodie, with the logo in red, white

and blue. McGregor donned a bespoke dark pinstripe suit, but if you looked closer the stripes said 'Fuck you' repeatedly up and down the seams.

There was live music, a wild crowd, cheers for the Irishman, boos for Floyd – though Mayweather's reception could be described as mixed – and after the usual suspects spoke, it was down to the combatants.

McGregor opened, joking about how many concessions he had made to get the fight.

'I'm just enjoying it,' chuckled the Irishman. 'All these rules, all these restrictions, it doesn't faze me. It amuses me.'

Then, with a nod to the tax story, he continued: 'He's in a fucking tracksuit. He can't even afford a suit any more. The Rolls is a 2012 outside. He is fucked. There's no other way about it.'

Then it was Floyd's turn.

'I'm the IRS, and I'm gonna tax your ass,' Mayweather replied. He then added: 'God don't make mistakes. And God only made one thing perfect, and that's my boxing record.'

He said he did not mind which gloves were used. Ten ounce gloves had already been agreed but he would drop to eight or four ounces, he suggested. Conor nodded.

McGregor would intermittently attempt to interject as Mayweather spoke, but his mic had been cut off. He felt the deck was being stacked against him and the following day, before the crazy tour stopped in Canada, Showtime issued a full statement by way of an apology.

There was certainly nothing wrong with McGregor's microphone in Toronto. From the moment he arrived on stage he ran the show. He grabbed the mic and started working the crowd.

'On the count of three I want everyone in this arena to scream at the top of your lungs, "Fuck the Mayweathers!" One, two, three!'

Thousands upon thousands yelled as he requested.

He then went on, trying to push Floyd's buttons.

'There is nothing these [guys] can do to faze me. Twenty-eight years of age. I'm getting fight cheques and promoter cheques. When Floyd was twenty-eight he was on Oscar De La Hoya's undercard. And that's just facts.'

McGregor was going into overdrive. 'I'm not getting off this mic. I want him to come and take this mic off me, otherwise I'm taking over this whole shit. It's right here, it's right here; stop me. You won't do shit.'

Then, as he had a day earlier, he focused on Floyd's dressed down approach. Again Mayweather wore a TMT tracksuit. And he had a bag in tow.

'Dress your fucking age,' McGregor went on. 'Carrying a school bag on stage. What are you doing with a school bag on stage? You can't even read! Forty years old, carrying a school bag. The man doesn't even fucking read.'

By the time Mayweather came to the dais the crowd had been whipped into a frenzy. 'Pay your taxes. Pay your taxes,' they chanted.

Floyd said he was now forty but he looked twenty. 'And you act ten,' interrupted McGregor.

However, things went downhill for Floyd when he reached into the crowd for an Irish flag. It wound up McGregor. The only problem was Mayweather had left his man bag at the lectern and McGregor nabbed it.

The MMA star rummaged through it, removing wads of cash.

'That's it?' He sounded astonished. 'That's it? There's about five grand in here! There's about five grand in here! Fuck me. Just know, you do something with that flag you ain't getting this bag or this money back and I'm going to fuck you up on this stage.'

There were more expletives, more back and forths. Some felt Mayweather had the psychological upper hand in LA while

McGregor had dominated in Toronto. Of course, it meant nothing. Not in the ring, at least. But the smack talk did account for something. Mayweather-McGregor was going viral every day and while their media engagements in New York and London became hard to hear, with many of the foul-mouthed lines from earlier in the weak trotted out and repurposed, media outlets and general sports fans ate it up. They talked about it. They speculated over who would win. They wondered what would happen. It was on everybody's lips. Whether you were on board with the fight or not, it did not matter. It was a financial juggernaut that was not going to be stopped. Only now it did not seem to have any brakes.

Of course, the build-up was catered for with an *All Access* series on Showtime. The larger-than-life caricatures were on show, as expected.

There was not a good guy/bad guy dynamic. It looked like they were both just hard-working, extravagant multi-millionaires which, in essence, is exactly what they were. Of course, the millions they had made before would pale into insignificance to the millions they would have after 26 August.

There was little debate over what was coming, certainly in boxing circles. Time and again, those who needed to be reminded were being told it was a spectacle, not a fight. Some said it was detrimental to boxing, some reckoned it was bringing the sport to a wider audience. Really, it felt like a stand-alone production, just with a cast of boxing administrators, reporters and media men and women with a UFC guy in a starring role. Even though the backdrop was boxing and the fight was under the Queensberry Rules it was not boxing. It was entertainment.

The training camps were comparatively low key. After the press conferences, there was little left to say that had not been said.

We were reminded of Mayweather's age. He tried hot yoga, taking himself away from the impact of other conditioning methods he may have been able to endure fifteen years earlier. Meanwhile, McGregor was learning the nuances of the sport.

He hired referee Joe Cortez to supervise sparring while he familiarised himself with the new rules he would be competing under. He drafted in Paulie Malignaggi, former two-weight world champion, for sparring. Malignaggi was on Showtime's broadcast team and he and the Irishman traded punches a couple of times. Then a photo was leaked of Malignaggi on the deck with the implication that he had been put on the canvas. The American left camp, irate, and asked for McGregor's side to release footage if they were so keen to show how their man was coming along. Said footage was released, mere seconds with McGregor in the ascendancy. Malignaggi asked for the full tape to be made public, but it was not.

Rumours in the fight game have always circulated, particularly from training camps. A few weeks earlier, former lightweight champion Brandon Ríos denied speculation that he had knocked out McGregor in sparring, saying he had never even met the Irishman and that he did not know who he was.

It did not take much to get a headline here or there, even if much of it was 'fake news'.

With around a month to go, Sky Box Office won the UK rights to show the event and ticket prices were unveiled for those with pockets deep enough to attend.

The cheapest seats were $500 with ringside going for $10,000. Others in the 20,000-seater arena came in at $1,500, $2,500, $3,500, $5,000 and $7,500 though numerous reports documented slow sales, and some vendors had increased the amount of tickets they would let go to individual buyers from two to six.

Of course, the fight – or the event – was still being pilloried.

'I think, you know, PT Barnum said a sucker is born every minute,' said Bob Arum. 'And people who pay good money to see Mayweather and McGregor, they're going to watch a spectacle and it's not worthwhile, in my opinion, as a boxing match. You want to spend money on a boxing match, buying a pay-per-view, three weeks later Canelo and Golovkin are fighting each other, and that's a terrific match. And I'm saying that as an impartial observer because I'm not promoting either of those shows.'

While the attention of the staunch boxing fan was focused on 16 September, it was hard to look beyond 26 August because it was everywhere.

The media centre in Las Vegas was huge, jammed with an unprecedented number of journalists and reporters pumping out coverage on radio, TV, print and online around the clock.

Referee Kenny Bayless was ruled out from the high profile assignment. He had officiated Mayweather's previous three bouts but had gone on record in an online interview saying, 'I wouldn't want to see it, because it is two different sports. UFC and boxing are two different sports. So what's the point?'

McGregor's camp would have protested if Bayless was given the gig, but the Nevada State Athletic Commission selected 74-year-old Robert Byrd, a former California patrolman, to handle the action while judges Dave Moretti, Guido Cavalleri and Burt Clements would score.

McGregor did not think they would be needed, consistently stating he would beat Mayweather in four rounds. The Irishman would charge, 'I run boxing.'

Not many felt the judges would be required, because Floyd was a clear favourite, certainly with the boxing experts.

Elsewhere, however, money started to come in on McGregor. In Las Vegas, at the MGM Grand, the vice-president of sports and races Jay Rood reported with several days to go that the largest bet they had taken on McGregor was $75,000 but that 6,300 bets had been placed on the Irishman with just 278 for Floyd.

He said that if McGregor did knock Mayweather out in a round, they would be liable to pay out $3 million.

The money coming in for the underdog caused the odds to fall. As did a surprise ruling by the Nevada State Athletic Commission to allow the athletes to wear eight-ounce gloves. It was an outrageous alteration to their own rules, which normally would enforce boxers at junior-middleweight (154lbs) and above to wear ten-ounce gloves. It was a safety measure, waived as a one-off. They were fighting at 154lbs.

The Association of Ringside Physicians quickly moved to condemn the decision, saying in a statement, 'This is a bout that has already been set at a specified weight class. Unless there is scientific evidence to support the view that such a change might improve the safety of this bout, we would strongly caution against allowing current regulations to be overruled. To do so would also set a precedent for future bouts.'

'I do not like the Nevada State Athletic Commission being used as a pawn in a social media bout,' NSAC chairman Anthony Marnell stated. 'Between these two, that part of this request pisses me off.'

The new glove sizes again caused the odds on McGregor to close. Then the usual pre-fight patter began to predictably circulate. Had Mayweather been dropped by Zab Judah in sparring? Was he carrying a hand injury?

The odds narrowed further still, to the point where McGregor, who had never boxed before – let's remind ourselves – was less of an underdog than Maidana, Cotto, Judah, Berto and Ortiz were against Mayweather.

For his part, Floyd kept talking up his opponent's chances. 'When a fighter has been dominating for twenty-something years and never lost, everything is on the line,' he said. 'My legacy. My boxing record. Everything is on the line.'

Then came Floyd's party lines. 'I don't think that I'm the same

Floyd Mayweather that I was twenty-one years ago. Of course not. I don't think that I'm the same Floyd Mayweather that I was ten years ago. I'm not even the same Floyd Mayweather that I was five or two years ago. But I still have a high IQ in that ring.'

The fighters had both prepared in Vegas but made their formal grand arrivals on the Tuesday of fight week. Almost predictably their paths crossed and barriers of security men and camp aides divided them while hostilities were exchanged. There was a brief skirmish between Malignaggi and McGregor, too, as money came in on the former sparmates settling their beef in the ring.

It was typical last-minute stuff, drumming up further interest, whether it had been composed or not.

The intrigue remained, but so did the tickets. Stories circulated a day later that 7,000 were unsold, priced on secondary markets from $500-$107,000. They were just so expensive. Boxing promoters have been known to 'paper the house', which means to give away tickets so the venue appears full. Speculation intensified that would be the case for the event, though no one was ever likely to admit it.

But there was still time.

McGregor reportedly put a million Euros on himself to win at 4/1. Mayweather told journalists he was tempted to back himself to the tune of $5million.

Of course, amongst the excess and the money stood Mayweather's place in boxing history. Victory over McGregor would lift him to an unprecedented final record of 50-0, ahead of Marciano's 49-0 mark. Even superb Mexican flyweight Ricardo López, had a blemish on his unbeaten 52-fight record, with a draw before retiring at 51-0-1.

Some historians said, vehemently, that they would not count the McGregor fight on Mayweather's boxing slate – but it *would* count, no matter how little credence you gave the event and the fact that Mayweather was facing just the third debutant of his long career. Of course, McGregor's MMA record was 21-3, but as a boxer he was 0-0. That was undeniable. Mayweather had boxed 387 professional rounds. McGregor had boxed zero.

That did not stop the smack talk, of course. 'My whole career, I am always told – I can't do this – I can't do that,' McGregor said. 'I feel when someone tells you you can't do something that's when you must do something. He's sparring 135-pound kids. You think I'm a 135-pound kid? I'm a 170lbs Irish gorilla and I am going to rip his head off and play football with it.'

Some felt fight week was surprisingly subdued after the lively grand arrivals. The media press conference was met with nonchalance by the more experienced journalists who had now done this – a Mayweather fight in Vegas – countless times. They had expected fireworks, but there was no fizzle, and although the Friday weigh-in was lively and the Irish fans were out in force, it did not catch fire. McGregor weighed a light 153lbs, Mayweather a svelte 149lbs. McGregor took one last chance to get into Floyd's head and in his face, screaming at him, but the American was not rattled in the least. Just another day in the office, he smiled knowingly.

The bout was obviously not a championship contest but that did not stop the WBC wanting to capitalise on the event. They merrily announced during fight week that the winner would take home a garment called The Money Belt. It was a gaudy version of their famed green and gold straps. It was made from crocodile skin, featured one-and-a-half kilos of twenty-four carat gold, housed 3,360 diamonds, 600 sapphires and 160 emeralds.

It suited the occasion. A star-studded audience included Jennifer Lopez, P Diddy, Mike Tyson, Piers Morgan, Ice Cube, Bruce Willis, Jeremy Piven, LeBron James, Jamie Foxx and Angelina Jolie while dozens of others from the worlds of sport, business and entertainment took their ringside seats.

Referee Robert Byrd's extended instructions drew boos from the crowd who just wanted to see a fight.

Mayweather opened proceedings as Mayweather does. For two rounds, he did very little. In fact, punchstats showed he threw just six punches in round one and ten in round two.

Yes, you could chalk them up to the bold Irishman but Mayweather had not yet started to fight. He had deployed only on a reconnaissance, surveying what was coming back, sizing McGregor up.

He took a good look at McGregor's highly unorthodox style, would have noticed him dropping his hands when he punched, how and which way he moved around the ring, assessed his speed and noted how his chin was often high.

As if the man he was standing opposite were a book, ironically given McGregor's 'You can't even read' taunt, he began to read his opponent.

McGregor looked huge. It seemed as though he had gained at least twenty pounds from the weigh-in. The way he held his hands away from his body made him appear even larger. Floyd, compact and composed – as always – held his gloves up mostly to fence away McGregor's punches.

Conor switched stances, showing off unconventional footwork and shots as he bowled in a left uppercut. Mayweather feinted. Watching. Analysing. Plotting.

McGregor did not box like the madman some predicted, he looked steady and moved sparingly. He appeared alert but tense. It was the kind of tension that can fatigue inexperienced boxers, making their arms and shoulders surprisingly heavy as a fight wears on.

He may have been bringing something different to the table, commercially and stylistically, but of course he was no better than the dozen or so Hall of Fame boxers Mayweather had already hung losses on.

The Irishman picked up his first verbal warning from Mr Byrd for rabbit punching behind the head in round three and it looked like he was beginning to gulp in air. Mayweather was smirking, as if he was trying not to laugh. Behind on points he was in control of the bout and could tell what was going to happen. Perhaps he could already feel the strong UFC star's punches losing their zip.

McGregor came out quickly for the fourth, swiping away as Floyd covered and unfurled his own shots. Mayweather was comfortable enough to wink at former super-middleweight world champion Carl Froch, who was ringside commentating for Sky Sports Box Office.

For the first time in the fight, Floyd ventured out of first gear. CompuBox worked out that he threw thirty-two punches, one more than he had attempted in the previous three rounds combined. The studying was over, now it was time to go to work. The lead overhand right, so successful against fighters over the years, started to flick McGregor's head back and Floyd planted right hands into the body. McGregor was reversing. His hands were dropping. Floyd grinned.

The fifth followed suit. McGregor backed up while Floyd pressed right hands into his face. When McGregor tried to land, there was little or no malice in his gloves. He was becoming increasingly arm-weary. He could not find a way through Mayweather's defensive shell and was getting picked off by stinging counters. It was a familiar pattern. It had happened to better boxers than McGregor and there was no shame in it; certainly he had not disgraced himself and by now had exceeded the meagre expectations many had, even if his own success early on was down to Mayweather choosing to do so little.

McGregor had to hold more and at the end of the fifth, Mayweather shoved his challenger away with one glove.

Round six and McGregor was warned for some rough stuff

when Floyd turned his back but he was walking the 29-year-old down. Mayweather, forty years old and without a fight in two years, was not feeling the pace. McGregor was boxing in quicksand. His hands and feet were slowing. In the seventh, his head was thumped back by right hands with some regularity as Mayweather increased his volume. The gap in class was becoming as apparent as the boxing crowd had suspected it would.

Mayweather permitted McGregor to punch in spurts but he was only allowing him to punch himself out. Volleys in the eighth failed to make Floyd flinch but they drained Conor's dwindling reserves as the odd sickening right hand or body shot continued to deplete him.

The plucky, bombastic and at times outrageous Irishman stood from his stool with gritted teeth for round nine but was soon looking forlorn. Floyd dropped his hands, safe in the knowledge that the hurtful power had left the eight-ounce gloves of his rival while allowing him to toss his punches from a variety of confusing angles. McGregor had no answer. Mayweather stepped on the gas. Rights and lefts forced McGregor to claim him. He was drowning in the deeper waters of a championship fight. Again McGregor held. Referee Byrd intervened but Mayweather was not providing him with any respite. It was looking like just a matter of time.

Yes, it was down to fatigue, but fatigue from Mayweather fighting the way that he did, allowing McGregor success and hope. Floyd remained unfazed but a bedraggled McGregor rose for round ten and continued to bravely unravel. His diminished power was hopelessly ineffective. A right hand sent him reeling around the ring. A copycat shot did exactly the same. He could not lift his arms to defend himself and he wearily cannoned into the ropes. Floyd followed and referee Byrd jumped in, separated the fighters and cradled McGregor against the strands. It was over. Floyd Mayweather was 50-0. Conor McGregor was 0-1.

'This was my last fight, ladies and gentlemen,' announced Mayweather.

'I thought it was a bit early on the stoppage,' McGregor rallied. 'I'd have liked to hit the floor. I'd have liked the ref to, you know what I mean? There's a lot on the line here. He should've let me keep going, I thought . . . I was just a little fatigued.'

'I hear him talking about, "Oh, you should have let me go out on my back or go out on my face,"' Mayweather responded. 'No, the referee saved you because the referee is thinking about your future. Because you're still young and we want you to be able to fight again someday. So the referee is saving you.'

'I think we gave the fans what they wanted to see,' added Floyd, who had officially brought the curtain down after one minute and five seconds of round ten. 'In twenty-one years in the sport of boxing I had some great fights and some boring fights, but I will always go down as a winner and someone who could dissect fighters and follow the game plan.

'This is my last fight for sure. 50-0 sounds good, I'm looking forward to going into the Hall of Fame. I picked the best dance partner to do it with.'

'This was some buzz,' McGregor said cheerfully enough. 'To come here and fight Floyd Mayweather.'

It had been bizarre and unique, but had ultimately played out as many felt it would. Neither sport, boxing nor MMA, had been dragged through the mud on the night; it just proved that the ring was Mayweather's domain the same way the Octagon would have been McGregor's. But that was a redundant point. This was a boxing match and the master boxer won handsomely. He lost only rounds he gave away, allowing McGregor to burn himself out before setting fire to what was left.

It was later revealed that the veteran had not sparred for as much as a month before the fight as he wanted to save his battle-ravaged hands from damage.

'It was an injury, of course,' Mayweather said when asked for more details. 'Not an injury like that, but I wanted my hands to be a hundred per cent for the fight. You know, my hands are real brittle; everybody knows that. I wanted my hands to be solid when I come out here, so when I'm shooting hard shots I'm able to break the guy down. What if I were to box and I have a serious hand injury, I wouldn't be able to punch as hard.'

The circus could leave town. It had been eventful, but it was not anything Mayweather had not seen before. It was the size of the Pacquiao fight with fewer fans than the Hatton night and the grandeur of the Canelo bout. It undoubtedly proved less than those three contests, though there were plenty who said even in a commanding victory, Mayweather had begun to show signs of slippage, something he had gone at length to acknowledge.

And while the 50-0 fight record rung hollow to the aficionados, it was indisputable.

Former heavyweight champion Rocky Marciano had retired in 1956 following forty-nine consecutive wins. His younger brother Peter, aged seventy-six when Mayweather defeated McGregor, believed the fight between boxer and MMA star should have been recorded as an exhibition.

'But it just seemed like everyone was trying to make a fast buck and to hell with the sport's history,' he told *Boxing News*. 'I'm surprised boxing historians weren't up in arms saying, "Is this a circus? What the hell is going on?" I'm sure in his mind, Mayweather thinks he has broken my brother's record by beating McGregor, but in my heart and mind his record is still intact. You can't take anything away from Mayweather. He's a great defensive fighter, but every time Rocky got in the ring, people got their money's worth and can you really say that about Mayweather?'

Indeed, Mayweather felt the need to atone for the drab Pacquiao bore.

'I think we gave the fans what they wanted to see,' Mayweather concluded of his farewell event. 'I owed them for the Pacquiao fight. Our game plan was to take our time, go to him and take him out in the end. I guaranteed everybody this fight wouldn't go the distance.'

You might knock Mayweather-McGregor for setting the record-breaking mark, you could say Marciano had been in against a far higher calibre of opponent in Archie Moore, which he was when he moved to 49-0, but you could not argue that it was now 2017 and Mayweather had boxed his first world champion, Genaro Hernández, back in 1998. He had fought and beaten more than twenty titleholders since. Some boxers have more fights to establish themselves as a pro, so the front half of their stats may be more cushioned than the end of Mayweather's. And regardless of opinion, history is there. It is black and white. Fifty and zero. Fifty and out.

Detractors claimed that he had lost the first Castillo fight. People would place an imaginary asterisk next to it but that did not matter. There are no grey areas when it comes to simple statistics, no matter how hard one may try to incorporate them.

And the cash registers were tallying up the Mayweather-McGregor numbers as this book went to press. Sky Sports disclosed that it had been their highest rated pay-per-view of all-time although the Nevada State Athletic Commission said it failed to generate as much as the Pacquiao fight at the gate. The long-awaited bout with the Filipino had drawn seventy-three million dollars in ticket sales, but Mayweather-McGregor totalled $55.4 million. There had been around five thousand empty seats. The official attendance in the 20,500 T-Mobile Arena was 14,623 meaning that several sections in the upper reaches of the arena were empty. As things stood, the all-time gate-receipts for boxing events saw Mayweather-Pacquiao at number one, Mayweather-McGregor at number two with Mayweather-Álvarez in third.

However, the pay-per-view had been tracking above the four-point-six million set by Mayweather-Pacquiao. UFC president Dana White was recorded saying it had hit a staggering six-point-five million, a truly astonishing figure that had still to be substantiated but was not beyond the realms of possibility. That would likely more than treble Mayweather's basic $100 million purse and McGregor's $30 million.

Afterwards, McGregor kept his options open. The man from Crumlin, Dublin, spoke of a return to UFC or the possibility of trying his hand at boxing again. Mayweather confirmed that would be it and not many felt, this time, there was an alternative. He had done it his way, as he always had.

*

From the sense of occasion and excess of fight night to Monday morning in the Mayweather Boxing Club, a ten-minute drive from the T-Mobile Arena in Chinatown in Vegas, and it was business as usual.

The old hands would have been coaching the hard-working pros. Tourists would have been visiting the home of a legend. Young amateurs would be hoping to catch a glimpse of the main man. The kids would have been standing on platforms pinging the speedbag and putting surprisingly significant impressions in the heavybag. They would skip with enthusiasm, coveting a long future in the fight game. They would repeat their training rituals hour after hour, session after session, week after week, month after month and year after year. They hoped to follow in the footsteps of the 50-0 giant who paved the way for them to be in his gym, who had inspired them with his skills and dazzled them with his wealth and lifestyle.

'I just want to help young fighters,' Mayweather once said. 'My dad is a trainer, he taught me the sport. Everything he taught me from day one is still with me. Trainers help make fighters better and teach fighters about becoming a superstar, not just in the ring but outside. Hopefully I can find the next Floyd Mayweather.'

Some of the kids at the Mayweather Boxing Club may make it to championship level, although most will not. But none of them will achieve what they want the most, because – love him, admire him, despise him, revile him or respect him – there will never be another like Floyd Mayweather.

APPENDIX

FIGHT RECORD

2017

Aug 26, 149lbs, Conor McGregor, 0-0, 153lbs, w rsf 10, Las Vegas, Nevada
Referee: Robert Byrd

2016

Inactive

2015

Sep 12, 146lbs, Andre Berto, 30-3, 145lbs, w pts 12, Las Vegas, Nevada
Referee: Kenny Bayless. Judges: Adalaide Byrd 120-108, Dave Moretti 117-111, Steve Weisfeld 118-110
WBC World welterweight title
WBA Super World welterweight title

May 2, 146lbs, Manny Pacquiao, 57-5-2, 145lbs, w pts 12, Las Vegas, Nevada
Referee: Kenny Bayless. Judges: Burt A Clements 118-110, Glenn Feldman 116-112, Dave Moretti 118-110
WBC World welterweight title
WBA Super World welterweight title
WBO World welterweight title

2014

Sep 13, 146.5lbs, Marcos Maidana, 35-4, 146lbs, w pts 12, Las Vegas, Nevada
Referee: Kenny Bayless. Judges: John McKaie 116-111, Dave Moretti 116-111, Guido Cavalleri 115-112
WBC World welterweight title
WBA Super World welterweight title
WBC World super-welterweight title
May 3, 146lbs, Marcos Maidana, 35-3, 146.5lbs, w md 12, Las Vegas, Nevada
Referee: Tony Weeks. Judges: Dave Moretti 116-112, Burt A Clements 117-111, Michael Pernick 114-114
WBC World welterweight title
WBA Super World welterweight title

2013

Sep 14, 150.5lbs, Saúl Álvarez, 42-0-1, 152lbs, w pts 12, Las Vegas, Nevada
Referee: Kenny Bayless. Judges: Dave Moretti 116-112, Craig Metcalfe 117-111, CJ Ross 114-114
WBC World super-welterweight title
WBA Super World super-welterweight title

May 4, 146lbs, Robert Guerrero, 31-1-1, 147lbs, w pts 12, Las Vegas, Nevada
Referee: Robert Byrd. Judges: Jerry Roth 117-111, Duane Ford 117-111, Julie Lederman 117-111
WBC World welterweight title

2012

May 5, 151lbs, Miguel Cotto, 37-2, 154lbs, w pts 12, Las Vegas, Nevada

Referee: Tony Weeks. Judges: Robert Hoyle 118-110, Patricia Morse Jarman 117-111, Dave Moretti 117-111
WBA Super World super-welterweight title

2011

Sep 17, 146.5lbs, Victor Ortiz, 29-2-2, 147lbs, w ko 4, Las Vegas, Nevada
Time: 2:59. Referee: Joe Cortez.
WBC World welterweight title

2010

May 1, 146lbs, Shane Mosley, 46-5, 147lbs, w pts 12, Las Vegas, Nevada
Referee: Kenny Bayless. Judges: Dave Moretti 119-109, Robert Hoyle 118-110, Adalaide Byrd 119-109

2009

Sep 19, 146lbs, Juan Manuel Márquez, 50-4-1, 142lbs, w pts 12, Las Vegas, Nevada
Referee: Tony Weeks. Judges: Burt A Clements 120-107, Dave Moretti, 119-108, Bill Lerch 118-109

2008

Inactive

2007

Dec 8, 147lbs, Ricky Hatton, 43-0, 145lbs, w rsf 10, Las Vegas Nevada
Time: 1:35. Referee: Joe Cortez.
WBC World welterweight title

May 5, 150lbs, Oscar De La Hoya, 38-4, 154lbs, w sd 12, Las Vegas, Nevada
Referee: Kenny Bayless. Judges: Chuck Giampa 116-112, Jerry Roth 115-113, Tom Kaczmarek 113-115
WBC World super-welterweight title

2006

Nov 4, 146lbs, Carlos Baldomir, 43-9-6, 147lbs, w pts 12, Las Vegas, Nevada
Referee: Jay Nady. Judges: John Keane 120-108, Paul Smith 118-110, Chuck Giampa 120-108
WBC World welterweight title
International Boxing Organisation World welterweight title
International Boxing Association welterweight title

Apr 8, 146lbs, Zab Judah, 34-3, 145.5lbs, w pts 12, Las Vegas, Nevada
Referee: Richard Steele. Judges: Glen Hamada 119-109, Dave Moretti 116-112, Jerry Roth 117-111
IBF World welterweight title
vacant International Boxing Organization World welterweight title

2005

Nov 19, 147lbs, Sharmba Mitchell, 56-4, 145.25lbs, w rsf 6, Portland, Oregon
Time: 2:06. Referee: Richard Steele.

Jun 25, 139lbs, Arturo Gatti, 39-6, 140lbs, w rtd 6, Atlantic City, New Jersey
Time: 3:00. Referee: Earl Morton.
WBC World super-lightweight title

Jan 22, 139lbs, Henry Bruseles, 21-2-1, 138.75lbs, w rsf 8, Miami, Florida
Tine: 2:55. Referee: Jorge Alonso.

2004

May 22, 140lbs, DeMarcus Corley, 28-2-1, 140lbs, Atlantic City, New Jersey
Referee: Benjy Esteves Jr. Judges: Melvina Lathan 119-107, Gale E Van Hoy 118-108, William Boodhoo 119-108

2003

Nov 1, 135lbs, Phillip N'dou, 31-1, 134.5lbs, w ko 7, Grand Rapids, Michigan
Referee: Frank Garza. Time: 1:08
WBC World lightweight title

Apr 19, 134lbs, Victoriano Sosa, 35-2-2, 134lbs, w pts 12, Fresno, California
Referee: Raul Caiz Sr. Judges: Chuck Hassett 118-110, Lou Filippo 119-109, Jack Woodburn 118-110
WBC World lightweight title

2002

Dec 7, 134lbs, Jose Luis Castillo, 46-5-1, 135lbs, w pts 12, Las Vegas, Nevada
Referee: Joe Cortez. Judges: Ken Morita 115-113, Larry O'Connell 116-113, Daniel Van de Wiele 115-113
WBC World lightweight title

Apr 20 134lbs Jose Luis Castillo, 45-4-1, 134.5lbs, w pts 12, Las Vegas, Nevada
Referee: Vic Drakulich. Judges: Anek Hongtongkam 116-111, John Keane 115-111, Jerry Roth 115-111
WBC World lightweight title

2001

Nov 10 129.5lbs Jesús Chávez, 35-1, 129.5lbs, w rtd 9, San Francisco, California
Time: 3:00. Referee: Jon Schorle.
WBC World super-featherweight title
May 26 130lbs Carlos Hernández, 33-2-1, 128.5lbs, w pts 12, Grand Rapids, Michigan
Referee: Dale Grable. Judges: Peter Trematerra 119-109, Bob Watson 117-109, Marty Sammon 116-111
WBC World super-featherweight title

Jan 20 130lbs Diego Corrales, 33-0, 130lbs, w rsf 10, Las Vegas, Nevada
Time: 2:19. Referee: Richard Steele.
WBC World super-featherweight title

2000

Oct 21 134lbs Emanuel Augustus, 22-16-4, 134lbs, w rsf 6, Detroit, Michigan
Time: 1:06. Referee: Dale Grable.

Mar 18 130lbs Gregorio Vargas, 40-6-1, 130lbs, w pts 12, Las Vegas, Nevada
Referee: Richard Steele. Judges Chuck Giampa 118-109, Daniel Van de Wiele 119-108, John Keane 119-108
WBC World super-featherweight title

1999

Sep 11 130lbs Carlos Gerena, 34-2, 130lbs, w rtd 7, Las Vegas, Nevada
Time: 3:00. Referee: Richard Steele.
WBC World super-featherweight title

May 22 130lbs Justin Juuko, 33-2-1, 130lbs, w ko 9, Las Vegas, Nevada
Time: 1:20. Referee: Mitch Halpern
WBC World super-featherweight title

Feb 17 130lbs Carlos Alberto Ramon Rios, 44-2-1, 129lbs, w pts 12, Grand Rapids, Michigan.
Referee: Dale Grable. Judges Jose Juan Guerra 120-110, Gueremo Perez 119-108, Bob Watson 120-109
WBC World super-featherweight title

1998

Dec 19 130lbs Angel Manfredy, 25-2-1 130lbs, w rsf 2, Miami, Florida
Time 2:47 Referee: Frank Santore Jr.
WBC World super-featherweight title

Oct 3 130lbs Genaro Hernández, 38-1-1 130lbs, w rtd 8, Las Vegas Nevada
Time: 3:00. Referee: Jay Nady.
WBC World super-featherweight title

Jun 14 130lbs Tony Pep, 39-6 132lbs, w pts 10, Atlantic City, New Jersey
Referee: Earl Brown. Judges George Hill 99-91, Kason Cheeks 100-90, Calvin Claxton 100-90

Apr 18 130.25lbs Gustavo Fabian Cuello, 20-7, 130.25lbs, w pts 10, Los Angeles, California
Referee: John Schorle. Judges Marty Denkin 99-90, Dick Young 99-90, Lou Filippo 99-90

Mar 23 133lbs Miguel Melo, 8-1, 133lbs w rsf 3, Mashantucket, Connecticut
Referee: Steve Smoger. Time 2:30

Feb 28 130lbs Sam Girard, 17-4-1, 132lbs w ko 2, Atlantic City, New

Jersey
Referee: Earl Morton. Time 2:47

Jan 9 132lbs Hector Arroyo, 16-4-2, 133lbs w rsf 5, Biloxi, Mississippi
Referee: Fred Steinwinder III. Time 1:21

1997

Nov 20 130lbs Angelo Nunez, 14-11-3, 133lbs, rsf 3 Los Angeles,
California
Referee: Lou Moret. Time 2:42

Oct 14 133.5lbs Felipe Garcia, 14-18-1, 130lbs, w rsf 6 Boise, Idaho
Referee: Jerry Armstrong. Time 2:56

Sep 6 131lbs Louie Leija, 132lbs, 18-3-1 w rsf 2, El Paso, Texas
Referee: Jerry McKenzie. Time 2:33

Jul 12 130.5lbs Jesús Chávez, 1-13-1 w rsf 5 Biloxi, Mississippi
Referee: Paul Sita. Time: 2:00

Jun 14 132lbs Larry O'Shields, 12-3-1, 131.75lbs w pts 6 San Antonio,
Texas

May 9 128.5lbs Tony Duran, 12-15-1, 133lbs w rsf 1, Las Vegas,
Nevada
Referee: Tony Gibson. Time 1:12

Apr 12 132lbs Bobby Giepert, 19-8, 133lbs, w ko 1 Las Vegas, Nevada
Referee: Joe Cortez. Time 1:30

Mar 12 132lbs Kino Rodriguez, 9-9-2, 130lbs w rsf 1 Grand Rapids,
Michigan
Referee: Frank Garza. Time 1:44

Feb 1 133lbs Edgar Ayala, debut, 131lbs w rsf 2 Chula Vista, California
Referee: Chuck Hassett. Time 1:39.

Jan 18 130lbs Jerry Cooper, 6-3, 128.5lbs w rsf 1 Las Vegas, Nevada
Referee: Mitch Halpern. Time 1:39

1996

Nov 30 131lbs Reggie Sanders, 1-1, 132.5lbs w pts 4 Albuquerque, New Mexico
Referee: Larry Chavez. Judges Levi Martinez 40-36, William Gantt 40-36, Sandy Pino 39-37

Oct 11 131lbs Roberto Apodaca, debut, 130lbs w rsf 2 Las Vegas, Nevada
Referee: Kenny Bayless. Time: 0:37

Key

Rsf – Referee stopped the fight
SD – Split decision
MD – Majority decision
KO – Knockout
Pts – Points
Rtd – Retired